JEAN-JACQUES
ROUSSEAU

JEAN-JACQUES ROUSSEAU

A STUDY IN SELF-AWARENESS

BY

RONALD GRIMSLEY
M.A., D.Phil., L. ès. L.

CARDIFF
UNIVERSITY OF WALES PRESS
1969

First Edition 1961
Second Edition 1969

PRINTED IN GREAT BRITAIN

FOREWORD TO SECOND EDITION

THE publication of a second edition has given me the opportunity of correcting some minor inaccuracies and misprints, but this has not involved any change in the main argument of the book.

In the course of his review in the *Revue d'histoire littéraire de la France* (vol. lxiv, 1964, pp. 485–90), Professor Jacques Voisine rightly called attention to the importance of '*Émile*' for the development of Rousseau's self-awareness; his involvement with Émile and Sophie in the last part has a psychological as well as a pedagogic significance—a point also made by Dr. Peter D. Jimack in a valuable chapter (chapter 8) of *La Genèse et la rédaction de l'Émile de Jean-Jacques Rousseau* (Geneva, 1960), which appeared after my own had gone to press.

The religious implications of Rousseau's personal attitude have been treated more fully in my *Rousseau and the Religious Quest* (Clarendon Press, Oxford, 1968); I have there tried to show the influence of Rousseau's imagination upon the development of his religious 'mythology'.

FOREWORD

In a few sections I have drawn upon material that has already appeared in articles: the substance of Chapter 4, on *La Nouvelle Héloïse*, was published in *The Modern Language Review*, while Chapter 8, on the *Rêveries*, makes use of an article in *French Studies*. I am obliged to the editors of these journals for permission to use these earlier writings.

I should like to record my gratitude to Professor P. Mansell Jones who read the original typescript with his usual kindly patience and thoroughness and made a number of very helpful comments. I am also indebted to the University of Wales Press's reader for some very useful suggestions which have been incorporated into this final revision.

Finally many thanks are due to Miss J. B. Marston and Miss Sheila Jones for having so efficiently typed and retyped large sections of the book.

R. G.

CONTENTS

ABBREVIATIONS

Annales   *Annales de la société Jean-Jacques Rousseau*, Geneva.

CG   *Correspondance générale*, ed. T. Dufour and P. P. Plan, 20 vols., Paris, 1924–34.

Letters   *The Letters of David Hume*, ed. J. Y. T. Greig, 2 vols., Oxford, 1932.

OC i.   *Œuvres complètes de Jean-Jacques Rousseau*, i, *Les Confessions, autres textes autobiographiques*, ed. B. Gagnebin and M. Raymond, Bibliothèque de la Pléiade, Paris, 1959.

The different sections of this volume are indicated as follows:

Conf.: *Confessions.*
Dial.: *Rousseau juge de Jean-Jacques. Dialogues.*
FA: *Fragments autobiographiques.*
LM: *Quatre Lettres à M. de Malesherbes.*
Rêv.: *Les Rêveries du promeneur solitaire.*

As this volume contains the main texts used in the present study, it will often be quoted by page-number only.

Œuvres   *Œuvres complètes de J.-J. Rousseau*, 13 vols., Hachette, Paris, 1865–70, &c.

INTRODUCTION

UNLIKE many previous studies of Rousseau, this book is not intended primarily as a discussion of his 'psychology' or 'philosophy', for its main object is to trace the development of his self-awareness as it gradually emerges from the correspondence and personal writings. What is kept constantly in view is Rousseau's effort to treat his personality as a subject of conscious and deliberate reflection, and I have tried to follow his at first hesitant and uncertain, and then his more confident and explicit desire to see himself as a certain kind of person, and ultimately as one who was prepared to relate this knowledge to the specific task of self-realization. That this approach to Rousseau is permissible will already be apparent from the personal writings themselves, although these are merely the culmination of a long process of psychological development. At first, the lure of ambition had inspired him with more worldly feelings, while the subsequent sense of literary vocation had caused him to devote his energies to didactic ends, but as he grew older, he became increasingly aware of himself as a man who was confronted by the need to resolve certain enigmatic and contradictory traits in his own character. It is with this specific problem of Rousseau's personal existence—and especially with his determined efforts to clarify its meaning through the medium of writing—that the present study is mainly concerned.

Although this brief introduction cannot hope to deal adequately with all the complex problems involved in such an undertaking—for an adequate discussion of methodological principles would require a volume at least as large as the one now devoted to Rousseau himself—a few preliminary indications may help to eliminate possible doubts and misunderstandings about the nature of the present inquiry. In the first place, I should like to emphasize that its principal concern is with the implications of the literary evidence itself rather than with any attempt to apply to Rousseau's case some preconceived notion of personality and consciousness; the initial task has been to describe as accurately as possible the course of his personal development and to make a careful examination of the various writings which still allow us to follow the main stages of that evolution. At the same time, it has to be recognized at the very outset that we shall be obliged to have recourse to some measure of interpretation. However earnestly we may wish to eschew the use of abstract *a priori* categories, it is obvious that the purely descriptive task cannot be undertaken without certain presuppositions, the documents examined being merely the end-product of a complex inner process, the outward expression of a deeper personal intention which must be made explicit. But, as far as possible, the interpretative principles will be confined to the requirements of the literary data. The sole purpose of the following remarks, therefore, is to forewarn the reader of the writer's own approach to the methodological aspects of this inquiry in so far as they may be said to involve some wider conception of human existence.

While our treatment cannot be strictly limited to the domains of psychology and philosophy, it will not be able to remain completely indifferent to these two disciplines. First of all, we are not dealing with a purely general problem, but with the movement of one man's life as it was lived out in the circumstances of his everyday existence. However idealistic the principles on which he eventually sought to base his life, Rousseau was to some extent the product of a particular psychological history, his character being fashioned not only by his own mental and emotional endowment, but also by the relationship of these factors to the various environments in which he lived. His individual personality being moulded by the dynamic interplay of character and environment, some effort must be made to indicate the internal and external pressures to which he was subjected at different stages of his career, and this in turn means giving some account of his early history—a task to which the first chapters of this book are devoted. Nor can philosophical considerations be completely excluded because the mere fact of his striving to make his individual case the object of explicit meditation was enough to transform and modify the psychological data in the light of certain criteria of value which, he hoped, would provide his personal existence with a basis firmer than the vagaries of individual impulse. In view of this he could not remain unresponsive to the challenge of contemporary ideas or of the more ancient culture transmitted to him through his own reading. Therefore, when considering Rousseau's personality, we have to take into account the formative psychological and environmental influences of his early years and those fundamental cultural ideas through which he sought to transcend the limitations of his own particular position.

This does not mean that we shall be prepared to 'explain' Rousseau psychologically as the result of a rigid process of psychic determinism or philosophically as the more or less faithful (or unfaithful) representative of a certain cultural tradition. The main object has been to trace the course of a self-consciousness which, though undoubtedly influenced by psychological and cultural factors, always related them to its own particular needs and so remained obstinately individual to the very end. One of our chief preoccupations will be to safeguard the uniqueness of a personality for whom the most objective factors were always charged with a profoundly personal meaning.

As, however, this work does make some use of psychological and psychiatric concepts—and especially of the notion of the 'unconscious' —whilst refusing to reject the idea of man's 'free' nature, it is necessary to indicate briefly the way in which the two principles are reconciled. A good deal of confusion has been created by the tendency to treat the 'unconscious' and the 'conscious' as two simple, if opposite, characteristics of the human psyche. The 'unconscious' is clearly, by definition, a hypothetical concept which tries to account for the presence of psychic factors apparently lying beyond the range of rational, conscious behaviour, even though evidence of their existence is supposed to be provided by certain observable effects. But the elements thus excluded from consciousness may be extremely varied, so that the term 'unconscious' can cover a considerable range of psychic experiences. On the other hand, though consciousness itself may seem to be simple, it by no means follows that its *quality* is fixed and unchanging, for not only may it be related to many different aspects of external reality in a variety of ways (as when we 'see', 'imagine', 'remember', &c., real or imaginary 'objects'), but it can express various levels of personal experience in which rational, psychical and emotional constituents have varying degrees of importance and intensity. Clearly the consciousness of being hungry, of looking at the Mona Lisa or of pondering the meaning of 'justice' differ in complexity and quality. Then again, consciousness may bear a changing relationship to 'action', moving from some form of contemplative detachment to an overriding concern with practical affairs. Undoubtedly no behaviour can be described as genuinely 'human' unless it is 'conscious', but consciousness may be merely one element in a complex pattern of personal response which also involves the existence of non-rational elements. It is not enough, therefore, to consider human freedom in terms of a simple and misleading opposition of 'conscious' and 'unconscious' impulses.

Because of its laudable desire to safeguard human freedom, existentialism—especially in its Sartrean form—tends to make it a quality that is quite distinct from the rest of the personality—a kind of consciousness which is 'absurd', 'irrational', and apparently *sui generis*. While recognizing the ultimately unique and undefinable nature of freedom, I should be inclined to assign to it different degrees of intensity and validity, believing that it tends to become deeper and richer the more fully and adequately it involves the complete personality. Perhaps it cannot be identified with any specific element of the self (such as 'reason', 'emotion', &c.), for it is not a special kind of faculty or some higher 'power', but the whole personality expressing itself in the mode of personal choice and decision. This certainly presupposes some capacity for insight and lucidity—and consequently the presence of consciousness—but this does not mean that freedom *is* consciousness, which simply reflects different levels of personal experience.

A further source of confusion may be due to the tendency to equate freedom with the quality of a single act. It is certainly meaningful to ask whether any particular action is 'freely' intended or not, but we can judge the extent of a man's freedom only if we review the whole pattern of his behaviour. Specific actions may be accompanied by varying degrees of explicit awareness, their precise significance depending to a large extent upon their relation to other aspects of conduct. Freedom is a quality of lived personal being—expressing itself through individual actions, but demanding for its complete comprehension the total life span of the man concerned. Some forms of behaviour may be unthinking and habitual without in any way impairing the 'free' and conscious character of other more fundamental decisions upon which a man deliberately brings all his psychic and moral energy to bear. Preoccupied by the thought of having to make some ultimate decision of vital importance, I may accept a temporary limitation of my freedom in a minor matter in order to express it more completely and emphatically later on. Even conscious choices, which I know or feel to be deliberate, may vary in quality. When I decide to visit a certain cinema, to adopt a certain career or to get married, I am in one sense equally 'free', but it cannot be reasonably maintained that the quality of the personal act is in each case the same, for 'equally' free does not mean qualitatively similar, since we are not only dealing with different goals but also calling into play different levels of personal experience.

If freedom involves something more fundamental than consciousness and if consciousness is by itself insufficient to account for freedom, an act may be conscious and yet unfree. I may, for example, be acutely aware of my fear of spiders without realizing the reasons for my fear. The motive remains unknown even though I am vividly conscious of my emotional reaction. Because in such cases I cannot help experiencing these feelings, I am 'unfree' and psychically determined by my past. But, except in acute pathological cases, such 'determined' actions do not cover the whole field of personal decision, since they merely affect my reactions to certain objects. The ultimate meaning of these 'unfree' acts depends largely on the reactions of my personality as a whole. What matters is the way in which they are able to affect the course of my general behaviour and to become integrated into my 'style of life'. Even if such individually unfree acts remain like isolated islands in my personality—irrational phenomena which refuse to allow themselves to be absorbed into the general pattern—I am rarely justified in trying to explain my whole self by means of these particular abnormal features.

Because the motives of an unfree action remain 'unconscious' it does not follow that its existential significance is thereby exhausted, for an irrational and uncomprehended phobia may still be made the basis of a personal decision and become the occasion of a genuinely human choice. I may be unable to overcome my fear at the sight of spiders but I am not obliged to endure it passively; I am still free to adopt a particular attitude of acceptance or rejection. Or again, aware of my fear of this kind of object, I may desire to show greater resolution in other circumstances in order to repudiate any suggestion that I am a 'coward'. Indeed, it may often happen that persons who are the victims of specific phobias react to more normal and natural dangers with great steadfastness and courage. It is, therefore, unwise to take our assessment of isolated acts as a criterion for judging more fundamental and far-reaching personal decisions; it may well be more prudent to relate these abnormalities to the wider context of a man's whole conduct.

The idea of unconscious motivation cannot of course be restricted to such simple instances, for, in the case of phobias and similar aberrations, the subject is usually aware of his irrational feelings even though he feels powerless to overcome them. There still remains the more fundamental type of personal response in which the conscious thought or feeling is but the distorted expression of a completely 'unconscious' desire. A man may be quite convinced that his action is inspired by a disinterested motive when it is really the 'rationalized' expression of some unconscious wish. Such also is the case of the truly psychotic condition where, for example, delusions are accepted by the individual as providing genuinely reliable information about his environment. Rousseau's own paranoid delusions of persecution would come under this latter category and obviously constitute a more radical problem than the fairly limited difficulties created by the presence of specific phobias. Some psychiatrically minded commentators have even sought to attribute the basic ideas of his whole work, as well as the moral foundations of his personal existence, to such disturbingly irrational sources.

The present study does not wish to minimize the serious problems created by this kind of explanation, but it also takes into account two important considerations which, to some extent, limit the validity of this purely psychiatric mode of interpretation. The first is this: that even when the range of mental abnormality is very wide, it rarely includes—except in extreme cases such as those involving a large degree of organic deterioration—the *whole* personality; and this is especially true of the condition known as 'paranoia'. However deeply affected Rousseau may have been by his delusions, they never completely overwhelmed him, for he continued to display remarkable lucidity in matters not appertaining to the machinations of his 'enemies'. Indeed, we shall have occasion to see that his mental aberrations may be more accurately described as a 'disorder of temperament' than as an indication of genuine 'insanity': they are the hypertrophied expression of impulses which form part of the daily life of 'normal' people. It is probably wise to consider each case of abnormal behaviour in the light of its own particular characteristics and to treat it as an individual problem; in this way we avoid the danger of setting fixed theoretical limits to the effects of mental abnormality. In the second place, the striking evidence of irrational delusions in works like the *Dialogues* and the *Rêveries* is apt to create a misleading impression that they suddenly sprang into being at a given moment of his life, whereas they were—as I hope to show—the cumulative effect of a number of separate decisions, going far back into his past and involving different degrees of conscious insight. If it be argued that he never attained complete insight into the meaning of his emotional and mental condition, this is merely a limitation to which many apparently 'free' people are exposed. The habit of seeing a man's life as the inevitable product of fixed conditions is apt to impose upon it a pattern of meaning which appears far less obviously valid when that life is examined in the course of its actual development. Although Rousseau may be held to have become obsessed with certain irrational beliefs which he was not free to overcome, this condition was preceded by a number of personal decisions over which his power of choice was much greater. It is not inapposite to recall that he himself was at first quite ready to recognize the unjustifiable character of his belief in certain forms of hostility—for example, his accusations against his publishers during the printing of *Émile*, and his early suspicions of d'Alembert. It was only with the increase of inner tension and the worsening of material conditions that his mental difficulties became more acute; and even then we find him tormented by a genuine perplexity of attitude which contrasts very markedly with the apparently intractable nature of his later delusions. At this period he gives the impression of a man uncertainly poised between reason and unreason, desperately trying to see more deeply into his own irrational convictions, the monstrous aspect of which he himself was the first to admit. During his stay in England Rousseau's behaviour suggests that, had he been more fortunate in his choice of a friend with whom he could have unburdened himself, he might have escaped the extreme consequences of his quarrel with Hume. (This is not intended as a criticism of Hume, but simply as a reminder of the far-reaching consequences of an apparently fortuitous clash of temperament.) Indeed, the wild and fantastic charges against Hume can be seen upon closer inspection to have had an intelligible if indirect psychic function, of which Rousseau was at least partly aware: the desperate effort of a sensitive and unhappy man to win reassurance and security in the midst of tormenting solitude. However strange and distorted such behaviour might seem to an outside observer, it had for Rousseau a definite existential purpose so that the final plunge into fixed delusions in a sense constitutes his attempt to escape from a state of intolerable tension. Without going so far as to say that Rousseau deliberately willed his delusional abnormality upon himself, we can reasonably maintain that the delusions were not the irrational, chaotic reactions of a properly demented person, but a desperate, albeit tortuous effort to make a *kind* of personal choice which in some respects brings him closer to the attitude of many other people.

What is yet more significant is that, after the delusions had become firmly implanted in his mind, Rousseau was still confronted by the necessity of making a certain basic choice of himself—a choice that transcended the purely psychological limitations of his position. Precisely because his whole personality was not determined by his delusions, the possibility of a deeper form of self-realization still lay open to him. Mistaken though he may have been concerning the true meaning of his beliefs about persecution, he was quite aware that they

B

had to be made the basis of an important personal act and that they formed a challenge that had to be met. The particular idiosyncrasies of his behaviour are not isolated phenomena to be examined for their own sake, but elements in a more fundamental intention which inspires his personality as a whole. He was always free to incorporate even his psychological anomalies into the wider pattern of his existence. It may of course be objected that the delusions were sufficiently strong to impel him to some pre-determined choice and that the conscious moral decision was nothing but the outward expression of some unconscious motive. This is of course a possible explanation that will have to be taken into account, but we can say at this stage that such *need* not be the case—that intense moral and spiritual efforts at self-fulfilment *can* overcome apparently enormous psychological difficulties and that Rousseau's particular case should be judged in the light of its own specific data. The mere fact that human freedom can—at least to some extent—surmount formidable psychic barriers is enough to make us cautious in assigning preconceived limits to its effective operation. In any case, whatever may be our view of the principles animating Rousseau's activities in his last years, and however obvious the effects of his delusions may become, he never ceased to see himself as a man who was striving to attain a certain kind of personal ideal: he continued to seek a form of personal fulfilment which could not be explained solely in terms of individual psychological impulses because it was constantly orientated towards values which were held to be applicable to cases other than his own. This personal ideal, therefore, must be judged in terms of its own intrinsic merits or defects and apart from any question of psychological genesis.

While insisting upon the wider implications of this conception of personal value, we must remember that the impossibility of understanding the individual case in the light of purely general categories means that freedom itself can never be an abstract quality, divorced from the concrete circumstances of personal life; its necessary relationship to the total personality also suggests that, though it goes beyond purely psychological considerations, it can in some measure be influenced by them. Even when finite circumstances are treated as a reality that has to be transcended, that transcendence can never be complete; the loftiest and most spiritual conception of human destiny cannot ignore with impunity the limiting conditions of finite experience. The co-existence within a single individual of a number of different and often conflicting impulses suggests that we are ultimately dealing with a unity of *structure* rather than of *essence*; it is not a question of some simple identity of personal substance, but a dynamic unity which involves the interconnexion and interdependence of physical, psychical, and spiritual factors. Individual capacity to attain an adequate integration of these different levels of experience will no doubt vary. With the development of maturity, impulses which may at first have flourished in isolation or else have been responsive to only limited objects and situations, come to form part of some higher personal synthesis; for example, hitherto unco-ordinated erotic impulses of a physical and emotional kind may become organized into a more complex 'sentiment' such as love, so that a man will not be considered capable of truly adult love until he has reached a certain integration of emotional and physical experience. The apparent simplicity of some adult 'emotion' may thus conceal a complex pattern of personal response.

If this is so, it seems reasonable to suppose that the growth of the human psyche—like that of the physical organism—can be blocked or distorted by unfavourable environmental pressures. Inhibited before the personality has been able to attain full maturity, particular emotions may become dissociated from the rest, although they will perhaps exert pressure upon the self in some indirect or symbolic way. Such dissociated elements may be of varying significance, ranging from minor aberrations to a far-reaching disintegration of personal life.

This disruption or distortion of the self can already occur at the psychological level—for example, in the domain of our emotional relations with other people—and it can subsequently affect the relationship of these psychological impulses to the moral and spiritual life, although it does not follow that a psychological abnormality will *of necessity* affect the quality of a man's religious experience in its most fundamental aspects. On the other hand, a high degree of purely psychological integration may also have its dangers if it is accompanied by a lack of spiritual sensitivity: it may indicate a serious personal inadequacy inasmuch as certain basic moral and religious possibilities of the self still remain undeveloped. The history of Christian thought shows us men like Pascal and Kierkegaard who, though obviously afflicted by psychological difficulties, revealed such authentic spiritual insight that their influence has far outgrown that of other lesser men who were psychologically more 'normal' and better balanced.

In view of the close dependence of any human choice upon the complex pattern of psychic life, freedom will appear to assume the character of a 'more or less'; it will be related to the ability to integrate conflicting impulses and direct them towards authentic personal ends. As we have already seen, freedom cannot be a purely psychological characteristic because it also involves moral and spiritual factors which are inseparable from the life of the fully developed individual; nor, on the other hand, can it be an absolute and 'ideal' value, because it has to express itself concretely through the real imperfections and limitations of finite existence. Except perhaps in the case of a few spiritually dedicated individuals, self-realization will be something of a compromise between complete 'freedom' and the relativity of everyday life —a compromise involving an interaction between conflicting elements within the self as well as between the self and its environment. Perhaps in a subjective sense a life-choice has some kind of absolute value for the individual himself, but this is scarcely a reality that can be made objective to others. The biographer, therefore, must content himself with an approximate estimate of the different factors involved in his subject's search for personal fulfilment, marking, whenever he can, the enrichment or impoverishment of his moral life.

As far as possible the present work will try to make a realistic appraisal of Rousseau's personal development, recognizing that existential choices can be made at different levels of psychic, moral and spiritual experience and with varying degrees of earnestness and intensity. It will acknowledge also that a man's life does not always advance in a simple linear sense, but is often liable to reverse its direction or grope its way along uncertain by-paths. With a writer like Rousseau, who became increasingly conscious of having to solve a problem of personal destiny, we may expect to find a gradual deepening of individual awareness and a progressive clarification of personal values, but this does not exclude the possibility that he too was for certain periods confused and perturbed in his individual choices. Moreover, because the process of self-realization engaged his *whole* personality, it had to reckon with the pressure of psychotic symptoms, especially in his last years, though they may not necessarily have attained permanent ascendancy over his complete self. But the interpenetration of psychic and 'existential' factors will enable us to consider both within a broader context than that of their own respective spheres of immediate influence. Rousseau's delusions of persecution, for example, will not be explained in purely deterministic terms as the inevitable end-product of a previous psychic history (although this is one permissible way of looking at them), they will also be studied for their bearing upon his different choices of himself and for any possible modification they themselves may have suffered through their relationship to his efforts at moral and spiritual fulfilment. Such delusions will thus have a polyvalent meaning dependent upon the psychological, moral or spiritual levels at which they are considered. In other words, we shall not ignore the presence of 'primitive' or 'archaic' affective elements in the total structure of his personality, but our ultimate emphasis will always be placed on the *conscious intention* of which they form part, the explicit goal towards which they deliberately look forward rather than the psychological starting-point to which they ultimately refer back. The present essay, therefore, is not a study in genetic psychology, but the examination of a quest for personal *values*: the psychological material is subordinated to a moral effort which goes beyond the plane of 'scientific' explanation to the domain of active self-realization. No doubt we shall still be justified in asking to what extent these higher values are conditioned by the pressure of abnormal impulses, but this will be only one of a number of issues raised by a study of this new level of experience.

A final factor that seems to have exerted an important influence on Rousseau's later efforts to attain a coherent personal ideal is undoubtedly associated with the need to commit his intimate thoughts to writing. The search for fulfilment was inseparable from a reflection which sought to clarify itself through literary creation. Here again we are dealing with no abstract, impersonal activity but with a genuinely individual response which bears directly upon the problem of Rousseau's personal existence. Of its ultimate effect we shall be able to judge only when we have examined the personal writings themselves, but it will already be clear that, by bringing conflicting and apparently inconsistent impulses within the focus of consciousness, he became increasingly aware of his need to resolve them in terms of some fundamental personal value. His writing thus contributed directly to his search for a more stable and authentic mode of personal existence through its indissoluble link with his persistent efforts at self-analysis. Moreover, as he came to study his inner life more closely and see it in its essential truth, he could not remain satisfied with some purely escapist or solipsist attitude: he was led to believe that his life was in some way exemplary, and that his own particular existence—for all its strangeness and suffering—was inseparable from the life of 'humanity', which, in its turn, was intended by its creator to form part of a divinely harmonious order. Perhaps men had become alienated from their true 'nature', which was fundamentally good because it had been created by one who was himself good, but Rousseau hoped that his own personal example, as well as his teaching, would show them how one day they—like him—could be restored to their true selves.

Towards the end of his life Rousseau was increasingly puzzled and disturbed by the thought that he himself was in some ways an exception, that between his own existence and the universal order there was some kind of inexplicable tension, if not actual contradiction; but he was never led to repudiate his belief in the beneficence of the universal order or the ultimate righteousness of providence. If his own unhappy position was unique in its desperate solitude, this was an enigmatic situation due to the mysterious will of Providence which for reasons of its own 'wanted him to suffer'. Ultimately, however, God would justify Himself to man, and the isolation of Jean-Jacques would itself be triumphantly vindicated.

The following study, then, seeks to trace the efforts of a human consciousness to become the object of its own serious reflection and to make its hard-won knowledge the basis of a fuller self-realization. As the foregoing observations will have made clear, an enterprise like Rousseau's will not remain free from ambiguities and contradictions because it concerns the existence of a personal consciousness which develops amid the concrete circumstances of everyday existence, containing until the very end a strange mingling of idealistic and realistic elements.

The plan of this book will obviously differ in many ways from that of the conventional biography, although it will be frequently indebted to the detailed and painstaking researches of earlier students of Rousseau's life, and especially to the important biographies of F. C. Green and Jean Guéhenno. I have, however, dealt only with those aspects of his biography which seem to throw light on the problem of his personal development, and especially on its emergence in the autobiographical writings of the last phase. The first two chapters attempt to outline the main traits of Rousseau's character as it is revealed in his early years, due weight being given to any important external and internal influences which may have helped to give his life its particular impetus and direction. Then his personality is studied in its efforts to attain happiness through the pursuit of two intimate ideals which played a considerable role in his early years—love and friendship. The frustration of all his efforts to translate his ideals into the reality of lived experience drove him to seek vicarious satisfaction in the creation of a literary fantasy—*La Nouvelle Héloïse*. I am aware that this novel cannot be treated simply as a 'personal' work like the *Confessions*, but, in spite of its imaginative and symbolic form, it constitutes in my view a turning-point in the development of his personal existence, and a study of its contents will throw valuable light on aspects of his personality which could not be expressed directly through his active relationships with real people. From this stage onwards our main emphasis will be upon an examination of Rousseau's more deliberate and self-conscious efforts to grapple with the problem of his personal existence through the writing of autobiographical works, beginning with the *Lettres à M. de Malesherbes* and ending with the *Rêveries*. It is with this fundamental human—and individual—question that the present study is concerned, but it will be constantly borne in mind that Rousseau himself is not only a man grappling with the complexities of his personal existence, but also a writer who seeks to make this problem the object of serious and sometimes anguished reflection.

1

ROUSSEAU'S EARLY PSYCHOLOGICAL DEVELOPMENT: I

Although the primary object of this study is to trace the conscious efforts of an individual personality to attain an authentic form of self-awareness, the evolution of its striving for personal value obviously cannot be separated from the early influences which helped it to develop in a specific direction. This consideration is made especially important by the fact that Rousseau's search for self-understanding, however remarkable and perspicacious at times, was never quite free from ambiguity and contradiction: in particular, the appearance of mental aberration in later life makes it imperative to examine any early factors which may clarify the meaning of adult reactions so apparently irrational as to be at complete variance with his previous behaviour. While, therefore, constantly keeping in mind the uniqueness of Rousseau's personality and concentrating mainly on the conscious intention inspiring his freely chosen attitude, we cannot ignore any elements which help to set the personal pattern in a clearer light, especially as it is a question of a single pattern whose warp and woof represent the movement of one man's life from birth to death.

A particular psychosis is probably not transmitted as a well-defined 'disease',[1] but the role of temperament as an essential factor *predisposing* a person towards a specific form of mental abnormality cannot be discounted: this view will be made all the more plausible in Rousseau's case by our later observation that the form of psychosis from which he suffered was really a 'disorder of temperament' rather than a definite 'disease'. Whatever may be the truth of this, there seems little doubt that he came from a family with a record of emotional instability. A first cousin appears to have shown marked symptoms of 'persecution mania', for while on a journey through the forest of Fontainebleau he is alleged

---

[1] The question is admittedly a difficult one. See David Henderson and R. D. Gillespie, *A Text-book of Psychiatry* (7th ed., Oxford University Press, 1950), pp. 34 ff., and A. H. Maslow and Bela Mittelmann, *Principles of Abnormal Psychology* (New York, 1951), esp. pp. 113 ff.

to have jumped out of his carriage obsessed by an irrational belief that his life was being threatened.[1] What is more relevant still, Isaac Rousseau, Jean-Jacques's father, was a man of an irascible, unstable temperament who was frequently involved in trouble with the Genevan authorities. In 1701 he was prosecuted for having picked a quarrel with an Englishman who was on a visit to Geneva; in 1722 he had a fight with a Captain Gautier and, in order to avoid imprisonment, fled to Nyon. He was also given to unexpected and apparently inexplicable decisions: at the age of twenty-one he suddenly gave up clock-making to teach dancing, whilst in 1705 he left his wife to seek his fortune in Constantinople.[2] In spite of his son's idealistic portrait of him in the *Confessions*, Isaac Rousseau appears to have been, as Eugène Ritter concludes, a difficult, violent, and irresponsible man who may have transmitted to his son something of his own emotional instability as well as certain of his physical features.[3]

Of Jean-Jacques's natural instability there can be no doubt, for it is a characteristic that has been fully acknowledged both by himself and his critics.[4] He recognized that he was given to abrupt and apparently irrational changes of mood. Nowhere did he make this clearer than in the curious self-portrait published in the one and only number of *Le Persifleur*, the review he intended to create in conjunction with Diderot.[5] He there speaks humorously of his 'two weekly souls' which struggle for the control of his personality.

When Boileau says of man in general that he went from one extreme to the other, he has sketched in a couple of words my portrait as an individual. . . .

[1] Cf. V. D. Musset-Pathay, *Histoire de la vie et des ouvrages de J.-J. Rousseau* (2 vols. 1822), i. 263 and ii. 284. This cousin, probably Jean-François Rousseau, the son of his father's brother, was considerably younger than Jean-Jacques, being born in Oct. 1738. Perhaps the significance of the persecution symptoms should not be unduly emphasized in his case since he went on to complete a very successful career in the diplomatic service: at the time of his death in 1808 he was Consul General at Baghdad. However, Corancez, who knew him, was struck by the physical resemblance to Jean-Jacques.

[2] Cf. for these and other details the study by Eugène Ritter, 'La Famille et la jeunesse de J.-J. Rousseau', in *Annales de la société Jean-Jacques Rousseau*, xvi, 1924-5. See also for this and later aspects of Rousseau's biography F. C. Green, *Jean-Jacques Rousseau* (Cambridge, 1956); A. L. Sells, *The Early Life and Adventures of Jean-Jacques Rousseau* (Cambridge, 1929); D. Mornet, *Rousseau, l'homme et l'œuvre* (Paris, 1950); Jean Guéhenno, *Jean-Jacques*, 3 vols. (Paris, 1948-52).

[3] The physical likeness was noted by a contemporary, Marcet de Mézières (cf. Ritter, op. cit., p. 158).

[4] Cf. V. Demole, 'Analyse psychiatrique des *Confessions* de J.-J. Rousseau', in *Schweizer Archiv für Neurologie und Psychiatrie*, ii, 1918, 270-304.

[5] Cf. *Confessions*, Book VII (*OC* i. 347).

Sometimes I am a hard and fierce misanthropist; at other moments I am enraptured by the charms of society and the delights of love. Sometimes I am austere and pious, but I soon become a downright *libertin*. . . . In a word, a Proteus, a chameleon and a woman are less variable creatures than I. . . . It is this very irregularity which forms the basis of my character. . . . I am liable to two main moods which change fairly constantly from week to week and which I call my weekly souls; through the one I am wisely mad, and through the other madly wise.[1]

A friend of his old age, Dusaulx, also observed the same characteristic: 'I was tempted to believe that this extraordinary man's body concealed two rival souls, which got the better of each other in turn.'[2] Another friend, Mercier, made the same point: 'We have seen him pass suddenly from a burst of gaiety to the gloomiest sadness, be happy and unhappy within the space of three minutes without anything appearing to have changed around him. His frightened imagination had done it all.'[3] This persistent tendency to sudden and irrational changes of temper made it impossible for him to form durable attachments; after an initial phase of intense emotional dependence, his friendships usually ended in painful quarrelling and separation. Other aspects of his life show the same instability: yearning for peace and security, he was unable to settle for long in one place; he is said to have taken up no less than twelve professions; he was given to sudden crazes which vanished as abruptly as they appeared—chess, print-collecting, botany. At no point in his life was he able effectively to overcome these restless, changeable moods.

Rousseau's extraordinary mobility was tied to an acute *sensibilité*. In later years he said that 'a sensitive heart' was the only legacy left to him by his parents, and he always insisted that the needs of his heart were greater than those of his mind. He also recognized that his *sensibilité* was rarely simple since it involved a complex intermingling of physical and emotional factors. He readily admitted his extraordinary dependence on his senses and his life-long susceptibility to physical environment, but he also maintained that the physical sensation could never bring him complete satisfaction unless it contained a 'moral' element, and by 'moral' he meant an emotion of the 'heart'. Bernardin de Saint-Pierre, who knew Rousseau in his old age, describes him as a man who 'applied

---

[1] Cf. *FA* 1108. No doubt this passage contains an element of humorous exaggeration which is due to the desire for literary effect, but its psychological basis represents Rousseau's real character.

[2] J. Dusaulx, *De mes rapports avec J.-J. Rousseau* (Paris, 1798), p. 109.

[3] L. S. Mercier, *De J.-J. Rousseau* (1791), i. 240. Quoted by L. Proal, *La Psychologie de Jean-Jacques Rousseau* (Paris, 1923), p. 262.

the affections of his soul to the enjoyments of his senses'.[1] In a passage in the *Dialogues* Rousseau makes the same point:

Jean-Jacques seemed to me to be endowed with a fairly high degree of physical sensibility. He depends very much on his senses, and would depend on them still more if moral sensibility did not often move him in another direction; and, indeed, it is often through the latter form of sensibility that he is so keenly affected by the former. Beautiful sounds, a fine sky, landscape and lake, flowers, perfumes, beautiful eyes, a gentle look, all these things react so powerfully on his senses only after they have somehow managed to reach his heart. I have seen him travel a couple of leagues every day for almost a whole springtime in order to go to Bercy to listen to the nightingale at his ease; water, greenery, solitude and the woods were necessary to make this bird's song affect his ears, and the countryside itself would be less charming in his eyes if he did not see in it the solicitude of the common mother who delights in decking out her children's dwelling-place (*Dial.* 807).[2]

This close interdependence of physical and moral factors did not exclude a varying relationship between the two kinds of sensibility. Although Rousseau was wont to stress the superiority of the inner life, he was so deeply convinced, at one stage of his career, of the influence of physical environment on a man's emotional and moral existence that he proposed to write a book called *La Morale sensitive ou le matérialisme du sage* with the object of teaching men how to acquire 'an external régime which, changing according to circumstances, could put or keep the soul in the condition most favourable to virtue' (*Conf.* 409). If we

---

[1] Bernardin de Saint-Pierre, *La Vie et les ouvrages de J.-J. Rousseau* (ed. Souriau, Paris, 1907), p. 58.

[2] In a previous passage in the *Dialogues* Rousseau analyses sensibility in a rather different way, distinguishing between 'physical sensibility', which is purely organic and passive, operating through response to pleasure and pain, and a more active 'moral sensibility', which affects our relations with other beings: this latter form works rather like magnetic attraction and repulsion, for we seem to be drawn towards certain beings, whilst experiencing a natural aversion to others. Positive sensibility extends and expands our being, and gives us a fuller sense of our own existence. There would also seem to be a case for accepting two kinds of active sensibility—that which involves relations with other people and what M. Basil Munteano in an interesting article ('La Solitude de Rousseau', in *Annales de la société Jean-Jacques Rousseau*, xxxi, 1946-9, 79-168) calls 'sensorial feeling'—a mixed psycho-physical faculty which is orientated towards physical objects though it lacks the simplicity of purely physical sensibility. In the *Dialogues* also Rousseau stresses the great importance of sensibility as a basic aspect of existence. 'Sensibility is the principle of all action. A being who felt nothing, even though he were animate, would not act, for where would be his motive for acting? God himself is sensitive since he acts.' Ultimately the supreme importance of sensibility for human beings lies in its close connexion with *amour de soi* (*Dial.* 805). For a discussion of some other aspects of this question see Pierre Trahard, *Les Maîtres de la sensibilité française au XVIIIᵉ siècle*, iii (Paris, 1932).

knew 'how to force the animal economy to favour the moral order it so often disturbs', we might learn the secret of happiness since we should be able to 'control at their origin the feelings by which we allow ourselves to be dominated'. This is all the more important because in sensitive natures like Jean-Jacques's the slightest variation in external conditions is liable to have far-reaching results on the inner life. He is almost certainly thinking of himself when he makes Saint-Preux say: 'What a fatal gift from heaven is a sensitive soul! He who has received it must expect only pain and grief on this earth. Wretched plaything of the air and seasons, his fate will be controlled by sun or fog, by a clear or clouded sky, and he will be happy or sad at the whim of the winds.'[1]

In favourable circumstances the physical and emotional sides of his sensibility reinforced each other in such a way as to endow his existence with an expansive quality which made him feel that he was enjoying the complete realization of his deepest potentialities: at such times he seemed to have attained a perfect mode of experience compared with which all other forms of enjoyment were quite insipid. In these privileged moments when he rose above the relative, hesitant conclusions of mere reflection, he felt 'a kind of pure and delightful enjoyment independent of fortune and the universe'. Looking back upon these experiences in later life, he was forced to conclude that 'true enjoyment cannot be described' (*Conf.* 354).[2] In one sense this conviction was to create difficulties for him since it strengthened his imperious demand for absolute happiness and his obstinate refusal to make any compromise between 'all or nothing'. 'As far as happiness and enjoyment were concerned, it had to be all or nothing' (ibid. 422). It is evident, therefore, that, though his sensibility gave a very powerful stimulus to his idealistic aspirations, it also threatened to place serious obstacles in the way of their practical fulfilment.

The most important consequence of this mixed sensibility was to inhibit his capacity for making a direct confrontation with physical objects, external reality being tested by its ability to satisfy the requirements of his inner life. This is especially clear in his attitude towards nature. 'I can see only when I am moved', he told the Maréchal de Luxembourg, to whom he had promised to send a description of the countryside around Môtiers-Travers. The interaction of emotions and physical environment means that the enjoyment of nature 'owes more to ourselves than to objects' and 'we describe much more what we feel

---

[1] *La Nouvelle Héloïse* (ed. Mornet), i. 26.
[2] Cf. also 'True happiness is not described, it is felt' (*Conf.* 236).

than what actually exists' (*CG* ix. 6). In *Émile* he had already insisted on the same idea when he affirmed that 'the life contained in the sight of nature lies in man's heart; to see it he must feel it' (*Œuvres*, ii. 139). He was rarely interested in reproducing a purely objective picture of what he saw. Sometimes the emotions aroused by a landscape were only remotely connected with its natural beauty, the physical scene serving as a mere background for indulgence in purely human feelings. Generally speaking, however, he did try to establish some kind of accord between the physical world and his own emotions; at times he felt nature and his own soul to be so akin that the same image sufficed to account for them both. Describing an idyllic walk with Mme de Warens he relates that 'a fresh breeze stirred the leaves, the air was pure, the horizon cloudless, and serenity reigned in the sky *as it did in our hearts*' (*Conf.* 244). He always liked to make comparisons between his own state of mind and the countryside around him. Towards the end of his life we find him observing that the melancholy atmosphere of an autumnal landscape corresponds too closely to his own condition for him not to note the analogy (*Rêv.* 1004).

The power of this mixed sensibility was such that physical objects did not become real to him until they had penetrated the depths of his inner life.[1] His apprehension of the external world was so dependent on the activity of memory that he 'could see nothing of what he saw' and 'that he saw clearly only what he remembered' (*Conf.* 114–15). Memory seemed able to confer on objects a vividness that was lacking in immediate perception. 'As objects generally make less impression upon me than their memories and as all my ideas are in images, the first features which are engraved on my brain have remained there and those which are subsequently imprinted on it rather combine with than efface them' (174). But the intensity of this experience suggests also that it

---

[1] P. Trahard points out (op. cit., iii. 187) that Rousseau's view of music was also influenced by moral considerations. 'The best music', writes Rousseau, 'is that which combines physical and moral pleasure, that is, aural charm and the interest of feeling, for the true interest is that of the soul.' It also helps to explain why he prefers melody to harmony. 'The *pleasure of harmony* is only a pleasure of pure sensation, and the enjoyment of the senses is always short, being closely followed by satiety and ennui; but the pleasure of *melody* and song is a pleasure of interest and feeling which speaks to the heart' (article 'Unité de mélodie', in the *Dictionnaire de musique* (*Œuvres*, vii. 339)). 'It is melody alone which produces this invincible power of passionate accents, the whole influence of music upon the soul' (*La Nouvelle Héloïse*, ii. 163). (Both quoted by Jean Starobinski, *Jean-Jacques Rousseau, La transparence et l'obstacle* (Paris, 1957), p. 110.) The same emphasis appears in Rousseau's attitude towards other forms of beauty. 'Facial attraction (in women)', says Bernardin de Saint-Pierre (op. cit., p. 57), 'had to combine with moral qualities in order to make him sensitive to it.'

sometimes resembles the famous 'involuntary' memory of Proust since the past is not always recalled by a deliberate effort of reflection but irrupts spontaneously and inexplicably into immediate consciousness. Such, for example, was the case with his first sight of a periwinkle at which he 'merely cast a passing glance' during one of his delightful walks with Mme de Warens; it was only some thirty years afterwards that the sight of a similar flower was able to fill him with sudden joy (*Conf.* 226). At other times memory would work in a more normal way, as is shown by the many fresh and picturesque descriptions of his childhood in the *Confessions*. He insists too that his memory of certain early events was infallible.

> I love the slightest details of that period for the very reason that they belong to it. I recall every circumstance of time, place and person. I see the maid or the man-servant busy in the room, a swallow flying in through the window, a fly settling on my hand while I recited my lesson; I see the whole arrangement of the room we were in; M. Lamberciers's study on the right, an engraving of all the popes, a barometer, a large calendar, raspberry-bushes which, from a very high garden into which the house penetrated from the back, shaded the window, and sometimes went right inside (21).

In general Rousseau's tendency to perceive objects through the medium of memory suggests the presence of a powerful emotional factor in these experiences. He himself often insisted that in times of anxiety and stress he would turn back to earlier periods of happiness, his recollection of the past being inspired by his need to re-experience previous emotions or else create, through the medium of memory, a state of feeling which would compensate him for present misfortune. This process was not always comforting because certain kinds of sensations might lead to the involuntary revival of unpleasant as well as pleasant emotions. He always professed a profound dislike of the colour scarlet because it was connected in his mind with the memory of a coat worn by M. Basile whose sudden return to Turin had given him some uncomfortable moments (*Conf.* 79). At one time an ardent devotee of Montaigne, he suddenly formed an aversion for this writer merely 'because he had dipped into him during an attack of stone' (*FA* 1128). 'I have an unpleasant local memory', he explains, 'which reproduces for me along with the book's ideas all the evils I have endured while reading them.'[1] He also confessed to his friend Eymar: 'I can no longer

---

[1] Cf. G. Streckeisen-Moultou, *Œuvres et correspondances inédites de J.-J. Rousseau* (Paris, 1861), p. 28.

look at any book without being distressed by the memory of the misfortunes mine have brought me.'[1] This type of memory can be particularly painful when it is associated with wrongs done to other people.
'It is not when a mean action has just been committed that it torments
us, it is when we remember it a long time afterwards; for the memory
of it does not die' (*Conf.* 132–3).

From a very early age the influence of Rousseau's sensibility was not
confined to a simple revival of sensuous and emotional memories, for
it also involved a modification and re-creation of the past through the
activity of his imagination. He would escape from immediate unhappiness by taking refuge in a 'land of chimeras', in 'an ideal world
which his creative imagination soon filled with beings after his own
heart' (*Conf.* 427). Ultimately he came to feel that the delights of reverie
and fantasy were preferable to those of ordinary life, and it was this
belief which led him to explore hitherto neglected aspects of inner
experience and to make those fascinating discoveries which were to
exercise such a profound influence on later Romantic generations. But
his imagination, being inseparable from his emotional life, could also
have more disturbing effects since it was not related solely to memories
of a happy past but to thoughts of an anxious future. 'My cruel imagination always anticipates my misfortunes' (219). It tormented him
especially through its tendency to 'carry everything to extremes'. He
was constantly complaining of the misery brought upon him by his
'affrighted imagination'. His sensibility, therefore, through its close
connexion with his memory and imagination, could fill him with unbearable anguish as well as indescribable joy.[2]

The effect of Rousseau's sensibility was not merely to weaken his
capacity to make a realistic assessment of objective reality, but to
persuade him that there was an actual contradiction between the
demands of his inner life and those of outward circumstance.

It is a very odd thing [he comments] that my imagination never attains
pleasanter heights than when my condition is most unpleasant and that, on
the contrary, it is less cheerful when all is cheerful around me. My poor head
cannot subject itself to objects. It cannot embellish, it seeks to create. At

---

[1] Quoted in Musset-Pathay, op. cit., ii. 40.

[2] His contemporary, the Marquis de Mirabeau, not inappropriately described Rousseau
as *une âme écorchée*. Hume also said of him: 'Surely Rousseau is one of the most singular
of human beings, and one of the most unhappy. His extreme sensibility of temper is his
torment: as he is much more susceptible of pain than pleasure.' He summed up his
protégé's character as that of a man who had 'only felt throughout his whole life'. See
The Letters of David Hume (ed. J. Y. T. Greig), 2 vols. (Oxford, 1932), ii. 26.

most real objects are depicted as they are; it can adorn only imaginary objects. If I wish to depict springtime, I must be in winter; if I wish to describe a fine landscape, I must be enclosed within four walls; and I have said a hundred times that if I were put in the Bastille, I should paint a picture of freedom (*Conf.* 171–2).

It was probably Rousseau's highly developed sensibility which led the older schools of psychiatry to interpret his character almost exclusively in the light of his temperament. He is classed by Louis Proal as *un dégénéré supérieur* or the type of personality suffering from an acute lack of emotional balance; and various critics have noted how his sensibility could be stirred by the most trivial incidents.[1] All his life he was apt to indulge in bouts of weeping: he shed tears when he received the gift of Mme d'Épinay's petticoat; a similar emotion overwhelmed him at the time of his communion at Môtiers; he wept at the thought of his lost youth; he broke down in the presence of the prostitute Zulietta, whilst the outburst provoked by the famous 'illumination' on the Vincennes road shows that important personal crises were accompanied by the same reactions.

Rousseau always insisted that his extreme sensibility was increased by his physical affliction—a painful bladder complaint marked by an acute retention of urine and (as he grew older) by increasing loss of control. Later medical opinion has differed widely on the subject, some doctors seeing in his stricture the probable source of all Rousseau's later illnesses, both physical and mental, whilst others have affirmed its purely psychic origin, attributing the urinary troubles to some form of neurosis; the negative results of the autopsy carried out after Rousseau's death have also led many to conclude that he was completely mistaken in his belief that he suffered from a congenital malformation of the urethra. In her detailed discussion of this whole question Dr. Suzanne Elosu[2] points out that the post-mortem examination was not carried out in conditions which would satisfy the more rigorous requirements of a modern medical inquiry, significant symptoms having possibly been overlooked; she has no hesitation in affirming that Jean-Jacques did suffer from a congenital malformation of the prostatic region of the urethra. Whatever its precise origin, there can be no doubt that Rousseau was afflicted with a very serious stricture which caused him

---

[1] L. Proal, op. cit., p. 254, where Rousseau is described as 'un déséquilibré de la sensibilité avec tendances paranoïaques, caractérisées par l'orgueil et la défiance'. The same writer refers to J. Capgras and P. Sérieux, *Les Folies raisonnantes, le délire d'interprétation* (Paris, 1909).

[2] *La Maladie de Jean-Jacques Rousseau* (Paris, 1928), pp. 39–40.

acute pain as well as embarrassment. The insidious progress of this malady was probably at the root of his physical ailments, for the distension and infection of the prostatic gland, bladder, urethra, and kidneys, must have produced serious organic deterioration during his last years, which were marked by the onset of a chronic nephritis. It was the toxic effects of this disease which led to uraemia and, finally, to his death from a cerebral oedema.[1]

Rousseau's first reference to his complaint is in 1748, when he was thirty-six years old.[2] Until then he did not have 'the slightest suspicion' of any abnormality. As his condition worsened, he was forced to have recourse to probes and catheters, and the feeling of embarrassment and humiliation associated with his malady eventually led him to shun social gatherings and seek solitude and rural seclusion. The failure of many contemporaries to understand the true nature of his illness probably caused them to suspect mental peculiarities where they did not exist. Thus Rousseau seems to have had frequent recourse to violent exercise, such as vigorous walking and wood-sawing, in order to obtain some relief from his retention by means of abundant sweating, sometimes giving in this way the impression that he was *un malade imaginaire*.[3]

As far as his mental condition was concerned, his physical disorder appears to have been an aggravating element rather than the principal cause of later aberrations. Certainly the fact that his retention was always worse in winter than in summer—cold weather making urination more difficult for him—helps to explain his greater liability to melancholy and mental unbalance at certain periods of the year. Moreover, the general organic deterioration produced during his last years by chronic nephritis may also have increased still further his long-established tendency to fits of depression and moodiness. Nevertheless, the psychosis of the last phase cannot be understood solely—or even mainly—in terms of the particular somatic condition produced by his retention, for it is tied, as I hope to show, to other constitutional and psychological factors.

It would be quite wrong to infer from these indications or from Rousseau's frequent references to his various ailments that he was—in his early years at least—a man of weak or sickly physique. It is highly

---

[1] Dr. Suzanne Elosu, op. cit., pp. 39-40. According to Dr. Elosu, the sudden attacks from which Rousseau suffered—for example, after he had finished the *Dialogues*—were a form of epileptic fit also brought on by his nephritic condition.

[2] See the letter to Mme de Warens of 26 Aug. 1748 (*CG* i. 285).

[3] Cf. *CG* x. 268, 336.

likely that at least some of his physical symptoms were due as much to neurosis as to organic defect.[1] In spite of the pain and discomfort accompanying his retention, he probably exaggerated the extent of his physical disability under the pressure of emotional stress, seeking in this way to obtain sympathy and reassurance at moments of depression and insecurity. Consequently, when due allowance is made for the later physical effects of his retention, there is no reason to doubt his own statement concerning the 'good constitution which nature had established in him' (*Conf.* 109). He was always a sturdy walker and, on his botanizing expeditions, easily tired out his companions. Bernardin de Saint-Pierre, who knew him in his old age, says that he was 'very vigorous' and 'at seventy he would get round the *Bois de Boulogne* without appearing to be tired at the end of his walk'.[2] Hume's impression was the same.

He imagines himself very infirm: he is one of the most robust men I have ever known. He passed ten hours in the night time above deck during the most severe weather, when all the seamen were almost frozen to death, and he caught no harm. . . . I must, however, confess, that I think that he has an inclination to complain of his health, more than I imagine he has reason for: he is not insincere, but fanciful, in that particular.[3]

So far we have been considering Rousseau's personality mainly in terms of its inherited endowment, but, important though these temperamental and constitutional factors are, they are probably less significant in the long run than the developmental influences of childhood. His mother's premature death from purpuric fever when he was only a few days old may well have laid the foundations of a radical anxiety at the very beginning of infancy. Some psycho-analysts, following Freud's suggestions, insist that the act of birth—and especially of a difficult

---

[1] He himself speaks of 'imaginary ills, more cruel for me than real ills' (*Conf.* 572).

[2] Op. cit., p. 47.

[3] *Letters*, ii. 2 and 16. It seems probable that Rousseau was also in the habit of exaggerating his insomnia, of which he so often complains. His contemporary, d'Escherny, relates the following amusing incident which occurred after one of Jean-Jacques's botanizing expeditions with his friends. 'The next morning they asked one another, as is usual: "Have you slept well?" "As for me," says Rousseau, "I never sleep." Colonel Pury stops him in a brisk, military tone. "By Heaven! Mr. Rousseau, you astonish me. I heard you snoring all night; it was I who did not close my eyes. That wretched hay sweats." Thus Rousseau, through a human and very innocent weakness, lay claim to a permanent insomnia as well as to a chronic state of infirmity and ill-health.' According to the same witness, 'it was at this very time that Rousseau was telling Europe about his sufferings and infirmities. I never saw him put out, for he enjoyed the best of health: he tramped, frolicked, as we have just seen, and ate with a very good appetite' (quoted in F. Berthoud, *J.-J. Rousseau au Val de Travers, 1762–65*, Paris, 1881, pp. 183–4).

birth—may be enough to provide the baby with its first real experience of anxiety, and it has even been maintained that this initial emotional impact may evoke anxiety of a 'persecutory' kind. Whilst there must obviously be considerable doubt about the precise nature of the new-born baby's reactions, it seems quite plausible to suppose that the shock of a difficult birth has a disturbing effect upon the child's subsequent emotional life. In Jean-Jacques's case there is the additional probability that his mother's early death deprived him from his very first days of an important source of emotional security and comfort.[1] That he was acutely conscious in his later years of this lack of early maternal love seems to be proved by his filial attachment to a woman like Mme de Warens; all his life he was to be intermittently haunted by the desire for an 'ideal mother' who, by protecting him from external danger, would rescue him from the torment of a divided and incomplete existence. In a more general way, the figure of the 'ideal mother' may well have become the symbol of his search for lost innocence and security, thereby inducing him to seek a state of 'natural goodness' and primordial unity from which all tension and discord are eliminated. Whether this yearning for a primitive unity—which does not exist in isolation in Rousseau (as some critics seem to imply) but forms part of a more complex pattern of emotional reactions and conscious ideas—is to be explained by so precise a cause depends very much on one's acceptance or rejection of the particular psychological theory giving rise to it. Fortunately the aim of the present study does not make it necessary to base our interpretation of the later texts on the uncertain foundations of a limited psychological view-point, but I am inclined to think that these natal and post-natal influences, when taken in con-junction with the hereditary and constitutional features already described, may have helped to create in the young Jean-Jacques a ten-dency towards anxiety, against which in later life he strove desperately to protect himself in various ways.

What does not seem to be in doubt is that his mother's early death was followed by a close emotional dependence on his father, which probably served to increase Rousseau's basic feeling of anxiety. As we have seen, the *Confessions* contain a somewhat idealized portrait of Isaac Rousseau, which suggests an almost fraternal familiarity between father and son. Although we have no cause to doubt the famous account of their odd reading-sessions, the father's affection, if sometimes intense, was also sporadic and liable to give way to fits of extreme irascibility.

[1] 'I cost my mother her life and my birth was the first of my misfortunes' (*Conf.* 7).

On one occasion, young Jean-Jacques was apparently shut up in an attic for several days and subjected to 'a daily chastisement' and 'severe penance' for having torn a Latin vocabulary—an incident not reported in the *Confessions.*[1] Then, later on, Jean-Jacques fails to record his father's displeasure at his conversion to Romanism. In spite of his son's efforts to be conciliatory, Isaac insisted on one occasion that 'he no longer regarded him as his son' (*CG* i. 11). On Jean-Jacques's side there was perhaps a certain humility and timidity, about which nothing is said in the *Confessions* but which suggest that his father's early influence helped to increase his sense of emotional insecurity.

Moreover, when we recall that a child is influenced not only by his emotional ties with his parents, but by the whole family group into which he is born—and indeed by any 'significant person' with whom he later comes into contact[2]—we cannot discount the effect of the unashamed 'spoiling' of Jean-Jacques by his aunt Suzanne and her servant, *ma mie Jacqueline.* The general effect of these early relationships was not merely to create a sense of insecurity and anxiety, but also to develop a characteristic way of dealing with emotional difficulties: in particular, I would suggest that there was formed in this childhood period a tendency to overcome anxiety through an attitude of retreat and submissiveness. In a very revealing remark in the first version of the *Confessions*—later omitted—he says that 'already fearful through the danger of displeasing, I became very prone to acts of submission',[3] while the final text states that 'I was sorrier to displease than to be punished' (14). 'To be loved by all who approached me was the liveliest of my desires. . . . I know nothing so charming as to see everybody pleased with me and all things' (ibid.). Elsewhere he speaks of a 'loving nature' which was also marked by a 'fear of displeasing'. The ultimate effect of this attitude was to weaken his capacity for normal self-assertion at critical moments in later life.[4]

[1] Cf. E. Ritter, op. cit. A. François (*Annales*, xxxi, 1946–9, 250 n.) points out that Ritter's quotation is incomplete for it omits to mention the beatings. Cf. also Musset–Pathay, op. cit., ii. 286, for a reference to the same incident.

[2] Cf. H. S. Sullivan, *The Interpersonal Theory of Psychiatry* (Tavistock Publications, London, 1955).

[3] *La Première Rédaction des Confessions* (*Livres I–IV*), ed. T. Dufour (Geneva, 1909), p. 25.

[4] In addition to the broad emotional pattern created by temperament and parental influence, it is usual to look for the explanation of adult abnormalities in terms of specific phobias produced by some traumatic shock experienced in childhood. Rousseau admitted the existence of adult phobias, especially his fear of the dark and his aversion to crowds. In his correspondence he mentions an occasion when he was thrown into convulsions by the sight of a white sheet dressed up as a ghost (*CG* xix. 291; cf. *Conf.* 566). In order to

In Jean-Jacques's relations with his father critics of the psycho-analytical school find a specific influence of a rather different kind, although it is one that can easily be attached to the attitude just described. Dr. R. Laforgue[1] insists that, during these first years, a particularly powerful emotional pressure helped to build up within Rousseau a kind of tyrannical self or 'super-ego' which caused him to associate his reactions towards his father with acute feelings of guilt and unworthiness. More especially, the father is alleged to have instilled into his son the conviction that he was, by his birth, responsible for his mother's death. In support of this view attention is called to the passage in the *Confessions* where Rousseau states that

never did he [my father] embrace me without my feeling by his sighs, his convulsive hugs, that a bitter regret was mingled with his affectionate gestures; they were only the more tender on that account. When he said to me, 'Jean-Jacques, let us speak of your mother', I would say to him: 'Well, father, we are going to weep', and this remark would already draw tears from him. 'Ah!' he would say with a groan, 'give her back to me, console me for her, fill the emptiness she has left in my soul. Would I love you thus if you were only my son?' (*Conf.* 11–12).

Jean-Jacques admits too that in his father's eyes he stood for 'a beloved wife',[2] while the incident just related clearly left a very strong impression on the child's mind.[3] As a result of this early parental influence Jean-Jacques, suggest the psycho-analysts, may have come to believe—unconsciously and irrationally—that it was wrong for him to enjoy life, and especially everything connected with sex.

understand the full significance of such an event it is not enough (as psychiatrists admit) to recover the actual memory itself, for it is also necessary to restore the concomitant emotional state; in this case, it is impossible to do so since the incident was probably bound up with complex emotional reactions of which the adult Rousseau was no longer aware.

[1] René Laforgue, *La Psychopathologie de l'échec* (Paris, revised ed., 1950).

[2] Cf. *Conf.* 55 (*b*) and variant p. 1260. The first version also has a further variant, 'the most beloved of wives' (*Première rédaction*, p. 77).

[3] Perhaps some significance ought also to be attached to the fact that the novels read by father and son formed part of the mother's library. The theme of the dead mother appears in *La Nouvelle Héloïse* where Julie rejects Saint-Preux because she believes—quite unjustifiably—that she has been responsible for her mother's death; at the end of the story she herself dies as a result of rescuing her son from drowning. It is of course impossible to say whether these themes were due to Rousseau's personal feelings or merely constitute conventional literary devices for eliciting pathos. I should also like to call attention to the curious passage in the *Confessions* where he describes how the 'inquisitor' who instructed him in the Roman faith asked him 'whether his mother was damned'. Although it is impossible to prove the suggestion, I wonder whether it was Jean-Jacques himself who asked the priest this question, the painful memory being later repressed and transformed into the incident related (cf. *Conf.* 94).

A more recent psycho-analytical view has connected this feeling of irrational guilt with the idea already mentioned of the 'ideal mother': he seeks to escape from the inner conflict originating in the pressure of a despotic 'super-ego' by means of a desire to return to the 'maternal breast'; the function of the ideal mother would, on this view, be to protect him against his own weakness and unhappiness and to assuage the guilt associated with the thought that he had been responsible for his real mother's death. Henceforth, it is suggested, he experienced a need 'to make reparation and to suffer' and this conviction, in its turn, influenced his attitude towards sex; he felt that it was wrong to enjoy erotic experience and that to have normal relations with a woman was equivalent to murdering her. As M. Jury puts it:

He had killed a woman by his birth; he did not want to kill a second time. Having killed once, he had to expiate his crime. He had to get himself beaten by women who, avenging his mother, would alleviate the terrible pressure of the feeling of guilt. Moreover, he could not accept punishment from his father, because the latter—through the fact of having fertilized his mother—was as guilty as he.[1]

Without insisting on the validity of this specific point I think that the fundamental experience of anxiety in these early years, as well as the initial efforts to overcome it through submissiveness and withdrawal—in short, through the belief that affection could only be obtained by showing obedience—helped to prepare the way for his later conviction that he was destined to be constantly exposed to the hostility of the external world in so far as it was embodied in the activities of other people. It is worth emphasizing that, although the *Confessions* contain many idyllic childhood scenes, they also show how tenaciously Rousseau clung to memories of early acts of injustice; he depicts himself with a certain complacency as the helpless victim of human folly. It is enough, for example, to recall the episode of Mlle Lambercier's comb, which marked his soul with the indelible feeling of 'violence and injustice' (*Conf.* 20). Moreover, from an early age, he was very much inclined to identify himself vicariously with the sufferings of other beings who were also—in his eyes—the objects of unjust actions; he relates how the ill-treatment meted out by other children to his inoffensive cousin Bernard (as well as to himself) soon made him a 'redresser of wrongs'

[1] Cf. Paul Jury, 'La Fessée de Jean-Jacques Rousseau', in *Psyché*, fasc. 4 (Feb. 1947), pp. 159 ff. See, in addition to the work of Dr. R. Laforgue quoted above, the paper by Ernest Fraenkel, 'La Psychanalyse au service de la science de la littérature', in the *Cahiers de l'Association Internationale des Études françaises*, No. 7 (June 1955), esp. pp. 42–45.

(ibid. 26). The need and desire to share in the punishment of those with whom he felt some emotional tie is also revealed by the impulsive gesture with which he flung himself between his brother, Francois, and his angry father. 'I thus covered him [François] with my body, receiving the blow meant for him, and I so persisted in this attitude that my father had in the end to pardon him, either because he was disarmed by my cries and tears, or because he did not want to ill-treat me more than him' (ibid. 10). The brutal treatment of the adolescent Jean-Jacques by his master, the engraver Ducommun, to whom he was apprenticed, only served to aggravate this feeling that he was the unfortunate victim of injustice. The lack of early discipline and the absence of any adequate sense of social obligation made him only too ready to consider any punishment (even when it was well deserved!) as unmerited.[1] Further unhappy experiences such as the set-back involved in his unlucky secretaryship to the French ambassador at Venice—which others might have taken in their stride—also strengthened his early belief that he was always liable to be unjustly treated by stronger men. By a not unnatural transition Rousseau later became apt to interpret an attitude of mere reserve or discretion as a sign of definite hostility; then, by yet another subtle emotional development, he came to believe that this hostility was actually inspired by his own superiority. Rousseau's account of his treatment in the household of Mme de Vercellis suggests that he was made the victim of a sinister conspiracy on the part of the unscrupulous stewards who were only too anxious to exclude 'this disturbing character' from the presence of his dying mistress. According to Commandant E. Gaillard, these so-called villains were very faithful servants anxious to protect their mistress from the prying eyes of an inquisitive lackey as she made her last will and testament.[2] If this is so, then Rousseau interpreted understandable precautions as a mark of hostile intent.

The cumulative effect of all these early influences was to make him

---

[1] Cf. F. C. Green, op. cit., pp. 9 ff.

[2] See E. Gaillard, 'Jean-Jacques Rousseau à Turin', *Annales*, xxxii, 1950-2, 55-120. Of course we cannot be sure that Rousseau is not reading into this early episode certain of his later paranoid reactions, but his account does suggest that he felt this hostility at the actual time of the events related. His description of himself as a 'disturbing character' reveals in an interesting way how the perception of hostility on the part of others may stand in a kind of dialectical relationship to the process of self-evaluation. The others fear him because he is in some mysterious way an important, unusual man, already marked out by his mistress as the object of special attention. Whatever its objective truth, the episode shows how subtly a sense of hostility may be bound up with 'ideas of reference'.

feel a sense of irremediable solitude; he became increasingly conscious of himself as a man destined to be separated from his fellow men. He was 'a being apart', 'isolated from men and holding on to nothing in society' (*CG* ii. 132). Although he did enjoy periods of more harmonious relationship with his surroundings, this feeling of loneliness permeated all his attachments from the time when he was first protected by Mme de Warens to the last days of his life when he was 'alone on the earth, without any brother, neighbour or companion other than himself' (*Rêv.* 995).

Rousseau's insistence on his loneliness has given rise to two possible misinterpretations of his attitude, one of which was due to his detractors and the other to himself. Although people often tended to see him, in his own words, as a 'sad and misanthropic character', he affirms that those who accuse him of 'misanthropy and taciturnity' have not taken the trouble to examine his character with any care (*CG* i. 378). Far from being those of a 'hard, unsociable man', his reactions represent the outlook of a lonely man who, 'left to himself', has 'learned to be alone when necessary' (ibid. 370, 378). Later on he went beyond these reasonable observations to make the further and more doubtful suggestion that he was born 'with a natural love of solitude'. Although many biographers have accepted this explanation, it seems unlikely that his 'love of solitude' was as innate as he says. Indeed Rousseau himself was at times quite prepared to admit as much. In *Mon Portrait* he writes: 'I am lonely only because I am ill and lazy. It is almost certain that if I were healthy and active, I should behave like other people' (1125). As will become clearer later on, Rousseau's loneliness was not a merely passive acceptance of some inescapable peculiarity of temperament, but a dynamic response and an active choice aimed at relieving the acute anxiety generated by his relationship with his environment. More fundamentally still, his love of solitude represents the frustration of an intense need for affection. Far from being a merely misanthropic character, he was—as he acknowledged—a man with a desperate need for others' love and at times he could be (as his contemporaries insisted) an extremely agreeable companion. His predilection for solitude, therefore, was not absolute, but an attempt to compensate for life's disappointments and frustrations; when the occasion seemed propitious, he was very willing to abandon himself to an intense, if short-lived, affection for others. Even though his growing belief that he could find no happiness in the world itself led him to 'withdraw into himself', the imaginary world thus evoked was often filled with 'beings after his own heart', so that his need for companionship remained none the less persistent for being purely ideal. As he himself explained, 'this apparently so misanthropic and gloomy disposition' really 'comes from a too affectionate, loving and tender heart which, because of its failure to find others like its own, is forced to feed upon fictions' (*Conf.* 41).

Because the world of social and personal relationships seemed fraught with danger, Rousseau had to look for happiness within the resources of his own inner being. As the difficulties of life increased, he sought compensation in subjective, autistic escape-mechanisms such as reverie and imaginative fantasy[1]—an attitude towards which his sensibility and early psychological development had already predisposed him without of course making its explicit acceptance inevitable. In particular, we here encounter that very fundamental aspect of Rousseau's personality which has been variously described as 'primitive', 'romantic', and 'childlike'. Often his indulgence in imaginative flights and 'romantic visions' has the emotional quality of primitive infantile 'phantasies'; he seeks an immediate, uninhibited gratification of his desires, which recalls in many ways the child's 'magical', almost 'hallucinatory' view of the world.[2] He always showed a remarkable capacity for a direct imaginative identification with the object of his desire. His real enjoyments too had to be total, completely untrammelled by the presence of any 'intermediary'.

Jean-Jacques himself was often wont to speak of his childlike nature. 'Although born a man in certain respects, for a long time I was a child, and still am in many others' (*Conf.* 235). His adult fears often retained, as he admitted, a childlike character. After referring to his early terror at the sight of a white sheet he adds: 'On this point, as on many others, I shall remain a child until my death.' Towards the end of his life he declared in his *Dialogues* that he was 'an old child' (800), thereby repeating an expression already used nearly twenty years before.[3]

---

[1] Psychiatrists have of course laid particular stress on this point. See, for example, Dr. Adolf Heidenhaim, *J. J. Rousseau, Persönlichkeit, Philosophie und Psychose* (Munich, 1924); Victor Demole, 'Rôle du tempérament et des idées délirantes de Rousseau dans la genèse de ses principales théories', in *Annales médico-psychologiques*, 1922, pp. 13–34, and 'Analyse psychiatrique des *Confessions* de J.-J. Rousseau', in *Schweizer Archiv für Neurologie und Psychiatrie*, ii, 1918, 270–304. Dr. Demole sees Rousseau's autism in 'cet abandon à la rêverie, cet éloignement de l'action, ce recueillement en soi-même, cette faculté de se complaire dans un monde factice' (p. 278).

[2] See Susan Isaacs, 'The Nature and Function of Phantasy', in *New Developments in Psycho-Analysis* (ed. M. Klein and others, London, 1952), pp. 67–121.

[3] Cf. *CG* ix. 6, where he describes himself as 'an old child who still regrets his early games'.

Several of his contemporaries confirm this impression. 'When he was himself', says Corancez who knew him in his old age, 'he was of a rare simplicity which still retained something of the character of childhood; he had its ingenuousness, gaiety, goodness and especially its shyness.'[1]

In one respect, the 'pure happiness' which Rousseau associated with the 'earthly paradise' of childhood remains a kind of criterion by which all subsequent forms of happiness are to be judged.[2] Not until a man has attained the absolute immediacy of childhood experience can he be said to have truly realized his essential nature. Genuine happiness has to be as direct, intuitive, and all-absorbing as that of the child. The simple sincerity of this ideal represents both the strength and weakness of Rousseau's position as a man and writer, for if it sometimes enabled him to attain that higher form of childlike saintliness which is the prerequisite for entering the kingdom of heaven, it also betrayed, in less propitious circumstances, those infantile reactions which are merely the sign of emotional immaturity. If he revealed a remarkable capacity for spontaneous feeling and a gift of intuitive apprehension of which the majority of his contemporaries were quite incapable, he was at times unable to face the hard, compelling reality of the world around him. Without insisting on the moral aspect of this question we may say in a general way that Rousseau always retained something of the simplicity characteristic of the child who is unable to distinguish between dreams and reality. He yearned nostalgically for a paradisaical state of innocence and unity which would enable him to lead a life without pain or conflict. This desire for a kind of primordial unity— already revealed at a lower psychological level by his yearning for an 'ideal mother'—remained an inspiration which, if often cruelly frustrated by the harshness of real life, formed a persistent and ineradicable aspect of his personality. The 'primitive' implications of this childlike quality in Rousseau have already been noted by other critics. Professor

---

[1] Quoted in H. Buffenoir, *Le Prestige de Jean-Jacques Rousseau* (Paris, 1909), p. 228.
[2] Cf. *Conf.* 220. The significance of the 'paradise' of childhood for Rousseau's whole outlook has been emphasized by M. Jean Starobinski in his extremely interesting book, *Jean-Jacques Rousseau, La transparence et l'obstacle* (Plon, Paris, 1957). M. Starobinski stresses that the attraction of childhood for Rousseau lay in its ability to effect a perfect coincidence of 'being' and 'appearance'. 'Le paradis, c'est la transparence réciproque des consciences, la communication totale et confiante' (p. 8). The evil of civilization is precisely to have destroyed this primordial unity. I should like to add that, in spite of its much later publication, my own book was virtually complete before I was able to read M. Starobinski's. However, I have taken the opportunity of a final revision to indicate a number of points of contact between the two interpretations and to benefit from his perspicacious observations.

Trahard sees a link between his primitivism and the 'primitive mentality' described by Lévy-Brühl and asks whether Jean-Jacques did not always show 'the power to make a future event real and immediate, to confound the visible and invisible worlds . . . and to establish a constant communication between sensuous reality and mystical powers'. A. Schinz also sees Rousseau's 'romanticism' in the same blurring of reality and dream—a type of reaction which enabled him, in moments of acute tension, to escape from everyday life into a world of chimera and reverie.[1] The result of this attitude always remained ambiguous: although his inability to accept the unpleasantness of ordinary life often led to unhealthy escapism, it also acted as a spur towards a fundamental idealism and a deepening of personal consciousness which induced him to see everyday existence transfigured by the possibilities of feeling and imagination and so laid the foundations of a kind of spiritual faith. By sharpening his perception and intuition, this mood often led him to challenge with fervour and sincerity the artificial values of French civilization. It seems clear, therefore, that the interest and complexity of the Rousseau 'case' involve the curious mingling of valid insights into the spiritual and moral malady of his generation and a frequent incapacity to see the real implications of his own personal position and attitude.

This 'primitivist' and childlike element also helps to explain Rousseau's subsequent attitude towards time. He never envisaged this as an abstract, philosophical question that ought to be treated objectively, since it was an issue which formed part of his own personal existence. Haunted at different stages of his life by anxiety for the future and nostalgia for the past, he also dreamed of finding fulfilment in a present that overcame all the limited discreteness of the passing moment: the present would attain an immediate intensity capable of lifting it up on to another plane and of transforming it into a kind of eternity, a 'prolonged present' which would also constitute a form of personal fulfilment. This aspiration is reinforced by his growing belief that existence in the realm of ordinary clock-time involves a separation from complete selfhood since society constantly exposes man to a fragmentation or corruption of his authentic personality. Later on this awareness of an insufficiency that can be overcome in an eternal present is reinforced by his tendency to associate feelings of guilt with the sense of inner division. Those deep-seated emotions which prevented him from experiencing

---

[1] P. Trahard, op. cit., iii. 213–4; A. Schinz, *La Pensée de Jean-Jacques Rousseau* (Paris, 1929), p. 114.

enjoyment in ordinary life would, he imagined, be eliminated in this new 'magical' state of existence. His primitivism thus strengthened his preoccupation with a 'moment' which would mean not only personal fulfilment but the re-establishment of a lost innocence. In an interesting passage of the *Confessions* he admits that such an experience attracts him because 'it has no interval and acts continuously' (187). In this way he hopes to enjoy the best of both worlds—the temporal and the infinite, since the intense movement of the immediate present is joined to the permanence of an unchanging eternity.

As certain developments in modern psycho-analysis have suggested, an exclusive emphasis on the child-parent relationship is apt to produce a distortion of perspective if it fails to take into account the cultural influences exerted by the social group into which the child is born,[1] while comparative anthropological studies also seem to show that the specific kind of child-rearing practised in any given community can be an important factor in determining definite aspects of the adult mentality. As far as Rousseau is concerned, critics, interested primarily in the impact of religious, social, and political ideas of Geneva upon his mind,[2] have neglected the remoter, more emotional pressure exerted by his native city. In this respect it is not inapposite to recall the statement of an early-nineteenth-century observer that there was apparently a high incidence of mental unbalance in Geneva.[3] Such a purely impressionistic account falls short of a properly documented statistical survey of the question, but even an observation of this kind may have value in so far as it indicates the extent to which the cultural pattern of the time was liable to set in motion certain psychological reactions which would now be termed 'abnormal'. In Rousseau's case, the impact of Calvinistic puritanism may have become involved with certain irrational guilt-feelings created by his early relations with his father, for the 'moral' self is by no means a simple entity, as recent psycho-analytical investiga-

[1] Cf. Clara Thompson, *Psychoanalysis, Evolution and Development* (London, 1952).

[2] Particularly important are: Gaspard Vallette, *J.-J. Rousseau genevois* (Geneva, 1908) (later criticism has modified certain of this book's conclusions about the specifically 'Genevan' aspect of Rousseau's thought, but it is still indispensable for a study of the Genevan background); J. S. Spink, *J.-J. Rousseau et Genève* (Paris, 1934); P. M. Masson, *La Religion de Jean-Jacques Rousseau*, 3 vols. (Paris, 1916).

[3] See G. Vallette, op. cit., p. 339, who refers to a report submitted by the *préfet* of the Léman to the French Minister of the Interior, where it is stated that 'melancholy is much more frequent in Geneva than anywhere else. . . . It is a fact that in this city the tendency to mental disorder, and especially melancholy, is hereditary.' Rousseau himself in the *Lettre à d'Alembert* (ed. Fuchs, p. 158) says: 'Beneath a cold, phlegmatic expression the Genevan hides an ardent, sensitive soul, readier to feel emotion than to hold it back.'

tions seem to have shown, and may be compounded of acquired psychological habits as well as innate moral feelings. There is no reason to deny that from his earliest years both individual and cultural influences predisposed Jean-Jacques to reject the legitimacy of certain desires, especially sexual desires, to which, in his own words, his 'combustible temperament' so readily inclined him. The puritanical atmosphere of Geneva may well have been insufficient to overcome innate impulses—and his moral lapses and weaknesses were frequent—but it was strong enough to prevent him from giving assent to feelings which he might otherwise have been prepared to accept and enjoy. In any case, it seems very possible that the rigid ethical code which the Genevan authorities sought to impose on their citizens and the great importance attached to what other countries might consider to be trivial deviations from moral standards (for example, card-playing and dancing) would help to initiate in a highly emotive personality like Rousseau a conflict between moral principle and the more spontaneous expression of natural feeling. The conflict would be made all the more real by the fact that the 'moral' element, although clashing with the more affective basis of the personality, still remained in him as a real and fundamental aspect of his being. In spite of lapses from the highest standards, his conscience continued to form an integral part of his personality, ever ready to criticize and condemn and to keep alive in his mind a tormenting awareness of guilt and anxiety. This moral influence derived from his Genevan background may also help to explain Rousseau's essential *seriousness*. Conspicuously devoid of any real sense of humour, he clearly had difficulty in seeing the point of much French scepticism (which he was often wont to dismiss as mere immorality). In spite of his early admiration for his eminent contemporary he never really had sympathy for the typical Voltairian irony. As Carlyle aptly says of Rousseau, he was always 'heartily in earnest'[1] and this spirit of seriousness may be due—in part at least—to his early origins.

The effect of this influence is to set limits to a *sensibilité* that was often

---

[1] See Thomas Carlyle, *On Heroes, Hero-Worship, and the Heroic in History* (1841), Lecture V, 'The Hero as Man of Letters: Johnson, Rousseau, Burns'. Here is Carlyle's impression of Rousseau: 'Poor Rousseau's face is to me expressive of him. A high but narrow contracted intensity in it: bony brows; deep, strait-set eyes, in which there is something bewildered-looking,—bewildered, peering with lynx-eagerness. A face full of misery, even ignoble misery, and also of the antagonism against that; something mean, plebeian there, redeemed only by *intensity*: the face of what is called a Fanatic,—a sadly *contracted* Hero!'

too indulgent to the outpouring of emotion and imagination; it served to remind him, for example, that the workings of conscience cannot be limited to the individual himself, since every man has within him 'a divine model' which brings him into relation with his true self and his fellow men.[1] Morality is social as well as personal. In certain moods also Rousseau was apt to invoke the authority of 'reason', 'virtue', and 'duty' as a means of restraining the dangerous effects of abandonment to excessively facile emotion, although conscience must ultimately be understood as a higher 'feeling' or 'instinct', and not as a mere judgement.[2] His puritanism thus carried him far beyond any sense of irrational guilt that might have been derived from early paternal influence since it formed an important part of the cultural inheritance of his Genevan contemporaries. Moreover, it often blended with those very emotions which also led him outside himself towards a more intimate relationship with other people. From the outset important psychological and cultural factors thus checked the growth of an undisciplined self-indulgence.

The contradictory nature of these early influences is already apparent in his account of his reading-sessions with his father, for he precociously imbibed the substance of sentimental novels like *Astrée* as well as the heroic qualities of Plutarch's *Lives*.[3] It is now recognized, as Rousseau himself was already fully aware, that early reading during a child's impressionable years may have a lasting effect upon his personality. Certainly he was never able to forget the impact of these first literary experiences which symbolize in some way the sentimental and heroic— the imaginative and moral—strains which were to play such an important role in his later life and which link up very obviously with some of the influences already described. It will be clear, therefore, that his personality is not to be explained in terms of any single—or simple— principle, for it is constantly torn by tensions resulting from the impact of moral as well as emotional factors.

[1] 'It is in the moral system formed by the double relationship to oneself and one's fellow-men that the natural impulse of conscience originates' (*CG* iii. 367).

[2] For Rousseau's view of conscience see M. B. Ellis, *Julie or La Nouvelle Héloïse, A Synthesis of Rousseau's Thought (1749–1759)*, Toronto, 1949, pp. 99 ff.; F. Bouchardy, 'Une définition de la conscience par J.-J. Rousseau', in *Annales*, xxxii, 1950–2, 167–75; M. Hellweg, 'Der Begriff des Gewissens bei Jean-Jacques Rousseau', in *Marburger Beiträge zur Rom. Phil.* (1936).

[3] The taste for seventeenth-century novels never left him, and he was still reading *Astrée* in his old age (cf. *CG* ii. 17; xvii. 220; *Conf.* 164). He told B. de Saint-Pierre that he had read right through *Astrée* twice and wanted to read it a third time (op. cit., p. 120); the same writer also reports Rousseau's affection for the *Arabian Nights* (p. 122). Of eighteenth-century novels he loved especially *Robinson Crusoe* and Prévost's *Cleveland*.

However powerful the early influences exerted upon the individual, their relevance must always depend to some extent upon the later development of his life. In particular, it is important to remember that Rousseau was destined to spend most of his adult existence in 'foreign' environments; he was never able to feel that he was fully integrated into any of the cultural backgrounds of his later years. Albert Schinz rightly observes that terms like 'Genevan', 'Protestant', and 'foreign' are apt to remain distressingly vague or inconsistent, and a complex personality like Rousseau cannot be clarified by the mere affixing of some convenient label;[1] problems of personality and philosophy are not so easily solved! However, it does seem to be an important and relevant consideration that Rousseau always felt himself to be in some way a 'stranger' living in an alien and often unsympathetic environment which was based on values different from those of his native land. This certainly does not mean that he was consistently opposed to all these foreign cultures: the very reverse is often true. We have only to recall how he was for a long time fascinated by Parisian life, how earnestly he sought to play the role of *philosophe*, and how he repeatedly maintained that it was only in France—and especially in Paris—that a man could acquire good taste. Already in 1740 his *Mémoire* for M. Mably's son praises the merits of social life—and it was probably during the period of his tutorship at Lyons that he was given his first real taste of social life—and when he came to write *La Nouvelle Héloïse*, he was still fascinated by the brilliance of French conversation; in spite of its many evils, French society—as we shall have occasion to see—was able to satisfy certain powerful needs of his character. On the whole, however, the satisfactions were outweighed by the drawbacks, and he never accepted the full implications of Parisian life. As a writer especially, he often dissociated himself from the principles and values of his French environment, looking upon himself as 'a foreigner who upheld in a foreign land the maxims of his own country' (*CG* ii. 168). He agreed that, wherever he might be, it was always his duty 'to respect the prince and obey the law', but he did not feel that he had any further obligation to his adopted country since his heart was always in his own (ii. 214). It was impossible for him to forget 'this free, republican spirit, this indomitable and proud character, impatient of yoke and servitude', which he had inherited from a country and a father 'whose patriotism was his strongest passion' (*Conf.* 9). In short, he tended to see French culture as the embodiment of principles which were incompatible with

[1] A. Schinz, op. cit., p. 17.

those of his early upbringing. The importance of this is apt to be obscured by the insistence of some modern scholars that the Geneva which Rousseau so often extolled as the model of true government did not always resemble the real Geneva of his day and that he appears sometimes to have created a Geneva of his own—for example, in the *Lettre à d'Alembert* where some of his observations about his native city were unacceptable to his fellow countrymen;[1] Rousseau's Geneva was the historical city modified by the subjective needs of his own cultural and philosophical outlook. Yet even when all this is allowed, he was still conscious of being identified with a culture other than that in the midst of which he was actually living, and this sense of not belonging to his environment helped at certain periods to reinforce the feeling of isolation already derived from his sensibility and childhood influences.

At times he would turn to these older cultural values, especially those of Geneva and the Ancients so eagerly read about during his early years, as a means of obtaining moral and emotional security in a hostile society. He would, for example, hold up Geneva as a small state that ought to be admired by the world, because, not having yet suffered the corrupting influence of French life, it still seemed capable of that moral strength which was completely absent from the decadent atmosphere of contemporary Paris. Such an attitude helped Jean-Jacques to gain momentary protection against the dangers of isolation, for, by identifying himself with these older and simpler cultures, he was able to feel independent of and superior to his immediate surroundings; the role of Geneva in the early formation and development of his personality thus remained contradictory, since in one way it helped to provide him with an outlook that protected him against what he considered to be the corrupting influences of his day, and yet, in another, it accentuated his feeling of being isolated in an unfriendly world.

When considering these early cultural influences, we ought not to forget a further important fact: that Rousseau was largely a self-educated man. He always maintained that, apart from certain exceptional cases like the lessons he received from M. Gâtier, 'the little he knew he had learnt alone' (*Conf.* 119). He found it difficult to follow the ideas

---

[1] According to G. Vallette (p. 137) Rousseau's suggestion about the establishment of *cercles* was looked upon with disfavour by the ruling oligarchy since they were considered to be centres of subversive discussion and criticism. This, however, does not prevent the *Lettre* from being a vigorous defence of old Genevan values against the corrupting influence of French taste and particularly the dangerous *sensibilité* stimulated by the theatre.

of others in an objective, impersonal way. 'My mind desires to work in its own time, it cannot submit itself to another's.' It may reasonably be maintained that much of Rousseau's originality was due to the fortunate chance of his having escaped the conventional academic discipline of his time; but his autodidacticism was not all gain, for he was never able to overcome a certain diffidence in the presence of thinkers brought up in the recognized educational institutions of their country. No doubt his innate genius made it quite unnecessary for him to feel any kind of intellectual inferiority, the more so as he had acquired by his own efforts a culture that compared very favourably with the learning of the *philosophes*. What is here in question, however, is the subjective aspect of the question, what Rousseau himself actually felt and not what he *ought* to have felt had he been capable of a genuinely objective review of the situation. In spite of his earnest endeavours at self-education, he may have continued to feel that he could never bridge the gap between himself and his educated French contemporaries. Whatever their hostility to the existing system, the latter had at least experienced it at first hand. Thus d'Alembert's severe strictures on French education in the *Encyclopédie* article, 'Collège', were those of a writer who had himself been educated by the Jansenists. Even in their hostility to the existing educational order the *philosophes* were bound to show something of its cultural influence; their immediate claim to superior educational insight reflected the attitude of men who had direct knowledge of the system they were attacking. Rousseau's animadversions, on the other hand, contained something of an outsider's resentment against institutions that he did not always understand. In a more general sense his attitude towards French intellectualism was not without a certain ambivalence. In spite of himself, he always revealed a certain emotional dependence on the *philosophes*—a dependence which often alternated with outbursts of violent hostility; at certain moments he was inclined to adopt an attitude of deference towards men whose sole merit was to have had a better formal education than himself, and he could not escape a certain malaise in the presence of the professional intellectual.

In a different way his lack of formal education, by limiting his capacity for seeking purely disinterested knowledge, constantly inclined him to relate intellectual knowledge to personal need: having rarely been forced to study against his will, he selected his subject-matter from fields of knowledge which found some deep inner response within himself. Furthermore, even when he did sometimes manage to struggle with what was for him arid material, he was inclined to put intellectual reflection at the service of a deeply personal, intuitive attitude which was closely related to that 'primitive' outlook we have already seen to be part of his character. His thinking was not aimed primarily at a painstaking examination of empirical data but at the elaboration and clarification of primordial intuitions derived from his own inner life. He did not exclude the use of historical and scientific knowledge, but this was usually adapted to the requirements of his personal 'illumination'.

The consequences of this interpenetration of thought and feeling for the subsequent development of Rousseau's attitude towards his personal existence will be discussed later, but it will already be clear that it was inseparable from his reactions towards his *social* environment. One of the first effects of his introduction into French society was to make him acutely conscious of his own quite different origins. His Genevan social status was respectable, if not exalted; Eugène Ritter describes him as a 'child of the middle classes of Genevan society', who belonged by his antecedents to 'very good old families'.[1] On his mother's side he was linked to the more 'aristocratic' section of the Genevan community, although other ancestors seem to have had an admixture of peasant blood; but his father's immediate social status was never high and was not improved by his personal reputation. It will be recalled that the Geneva of his day tended to remain divided between the more select members of the dominant *bourgeoisie*, who occupied the privileged positions of the higher magistrature, and the humbler representatives of the lower *bourgeoisie* who were excluded from active participation in the city's government. The eighteenth century saw bitter political strife between these two sections of Genevan society, although in Rousseau's early years there was little direct conflict. Both groups, however, being animated by the aristocratic pride of citizenship, were ardent patriots who showed considerable civic devotion to the political institutions of their city.[2] In spite of an oligarchic form of government nobody seriously contested the basic principle of the sovereignty of the people. Isaac Rousseau himself could have had little time or inclination for political activity, and, if he was frequently suspect to the authorities, it was probably for his private misdemeanours rather than for any dubious political connexions.[3] In principle Isaac Rousseau and his family were *Genevois du bas* and so belonged to the more plebeian

[1] See E. Ritter, op. cit., pp. 138–9, and F. C. Green, op. cit., pp. 2–3.

[2] Cf. G. Vallette, op. cit., pp. 4 ff.

[3] As E. Ritter points out, it is unlikely that his sudden departure from Constantinople in 1705 was due to political reasons.

section of the community. Even so, the mere fact of being Genevan at all was enough to fill Jean-Jacques with a certain pride. His social origins were such as to endow him with an outlook that was different from the middle-class mentality of the monarchistically-minded *philosophes*. His actual experience, as well as his early social background, gave him an understanding of the common people that was markedly lacking in the French writers of his day. Generally speaking, the *philosophes* had little sympathy with the lower orders and a long-established tradition tended to make them look upwards towards the king rather than downwards towards the politically ineffective masses for all social reform. At no stage do they seem to have considered the possibility of change through democratic action. As has been frequently observed, their ideal was an enlightened monarchy rather than a republic, and if improvements were to come to the country as a whole and to the lower orders in particular, it would be (they thought) because the monarch had been wise enough to listen to the counsels of his philosophical advisers. It is true that a writer like Voltaire might say some harsh things about the futility of the French aristocracy, but all his life he remained on excellent terms with the higher social classes and had nothing but contempt for the common people whom he did not deem to be worthy of any serious education. During the first half of the eighteenth century the *philosophes* considered that the main enemy to be attacked, and if possible destroyed, was not the aristocracy or the monarchy, but the Roman Catholic Church.[1] At first the middle classes were content to strive for more active participation in the government and had no thought of radical political action. Rousseau, on the other hand, could remain aloof from the movement of internal French politics, and he stressed time and again that, as a 'republican' of Swiss origin, he did not consider himself in any way bound by the political principles of contemporary France. Being free from many French political and social prejudices, he could sympathize with the humbler classes and even represent himself as their spokesman and champion.[2]

Nevertheless, this sympathy for the lower classes did not exclude an early enthusiasm for the French way of life. Having perhaps been given a foretaste of the pleasures of refined society during his stay at Lyons in 1740, he was soon fascinated by his Parisian environment. He seems to have thrown himself with some enthusiasm into the cultural life of

---

[1] Cf. D. Mornet, *Les Origines intellectuelles de la Révolution française* (Paris, 1933).

[2] Cf. *Conf.* 198–9 for the famous account of his meal with the peasants.

the capital: he collaborated with the *Encyclopédie*, was an enthusiastic visitor to the theatre, participated in various philosophical discussions, both in the *cafés* and in the more dignified atmosphere of the *salons* of La Pouplinière and d'Holbach, and eventually acquired among police circles a reputation for being something of a hot-head.[1] In spite of his later animadversions against the philosophers he was probably flattered by the invitation to participate in the *Encyclopédie* and was one of the first contributors to have his articles ready on time. This was the period of his greatest ambition and desire for glory.[2] The ultimate disappointment of his hopes was probably due more to his 'lethargy' and lack of will-power than to the absence of deep desire. Indeed the whole tone of his later reform suggests an awareness of paths imprudently but eagerly followed.

This indulgence in worldly ambition was probably strengthened by his unconscious need to compensate for the attitude of submission and withdrawal inculcated in early childhood; by asserting himself in a society which would (he hoped) give him much needed recognition, he would at last be able to overcome feelings of personal inadequacy. Perhaps this explains why he felt the need to convince himself of his own worth by gestures which struck others as offensively egotistical. Admittedly the Comte de Montaigu, the French ambassador in Venice, is not a very sympathetic witness but there may well be some justification for his complaint that his young secretary showed an 'ill-humour and insolence caused by his good opinion of himself'; Jean-Jacques was even tactless enough to 'take a book and look pityingly' at his master as he struggled to dictate a letter! Rousseau himself later wrote of himself: 'I do not bother about being noticed, but when people do notice me, I am not sorry for it to be in a somewhat distinguished way, and I would rather be forgotten by the whole human race than be taken for an ordinary man.'[3] Bachaumont was thus not entirely unjustified in describing him as a man who 'aspired to singularity'.[4]

That the drive for ambition and glory was an extremely powerful incentive at this Parisian phase is very convincingly shown by the

[1] Cf. Bibliothèque Nationale (A.F.), MS. No. 22158 (an anonymous diary attached to Hémery's *Journal de la Librairie*). D'Alembert, Diderot, and Rousseau are said to be friends. 'All three of them are enthusiastic over Italian music. They are three somewhat hot-headed fellows.'

[2] On Rousseau's striving for glory at this time see Jean Guéhenno, i. 152 ff.

[3] Cf. *FA* (*Mon Portrait*), 1123. For Montaigu see *CG* i. 248–52.

[4] Cf. P. P. Plan, *J.-J. Rousseau raconté par les gazettes de son temps* (Paris, 1916). On Rousseau's need to distinguish himself from others, see B. Munteano, article quoted, pp. 135 ff.

bitter resentment at first aroused by his initial failure to satisfy it. Nowhere are his true feelings more strikingly revealed than in the *Épître à M. de l'Étang* (1749), which contains a searing attack upon the Parisian life of his day. The professional writers, the priests, the aristocrats, the rich and their hangers-on are mercilessly castigated as the enemies of all true probity and virtue. How far removed are such people from the upright simplicity of those truly worthy men who are content with the reward of being their humble but admirable selves! In a letter to Mme de Warens he frankly admits that he may have been carried beyond the limits of seemly behaviour by 'the ardour of his hatred', while the *Confessions* also refer to his bile and ill humour at this time. Moreover, if he takes a certain pleasure in contributing to the *Encyclopédie*, it is because 'I have got where I want them the people who have done me harm; bile gives me strength and even wit and learning.'[1] Clearly his feelings contain a great detail of bitter indignation against an environment which at first threatened to keep him in a desperate state of 'opprobrium and destitution'.[2] Although he intermittently felt aware that, even if he could follow such a way of life, it would not satisfy his real needs, he remained for a long time a prey to worldly ambitions. Ironically enough, when he did at last burst unexpectedly into literary fame, it was thanks largely to an essay inspired by resentment at disappointed hope.

Because the resentment created by frustrated ambition contained a large element of psychological compensation, the sudden advent of success did not bring him real satisfaction. He affirms that, as soon as he was 'sought after by everybody and honoured with more consideration than his ridiculous vanity had ever dared to lay claim to', he was overcome by 'disgust'. He eventually came to believe that in his Parisian years he had been striving to make up for previous poverty and obscurity by means of an ideal that was much less a spontaneous demand of his own true nature than the prompting of a 'social' self largely determined (in his opinion) by the false values of his day. To attain true happiness he had to find a more intimate and personal mode of fulfilment. That is why literary fame, though appearing to satisfy the demands of self-esteem and compensate for a long period of public neglect, was ultimately transformed into a violent rejection of the very society from which he had at first expected so much.

---

[1] See *CG* i. 287. See also the fragment on p. 299 of the same volume.
[2] *CG* i. 286. It will be recalled that it was in Aug. 1748 that he had his first acute attack of retention.

As he himself admitted, his reactions to social life were complicated by far more than a conflict of principle: a great deal of his unhappiness was due to the pressure of an at times almost pathological shyness and timidity. In its most obvious form, his shyness resulted from a lack of upbringing in social matters: his unfamiliarity with the ways and habits of higher French society was a source of acute embarrassment, especially when he was anxiously trying to adapt himself to the life of the *salons*. Later on he was to treat this incapacity as a singular piece of good fortune, for he thought that he had thereby been prevented from becoming permanently seduced by the insidious attractions of French civilization, but his behaviour during this early period of great hopes and ambitions was of a completely different kind. His occasionally rude and boorish manners were largely due to a feeling of inferiority: his most earnest wish was to succeed in society, not reject it. In his first letter to Malesherbes (written in 1762) he admits that a good deal of his former distress arose from the conviction that 'his mind was not alert enough to show in conversation the little wit he had' and that consequently he 'did not occupy in society the position he thought he deserved'. In the *Confessions* he speaks quite frankly of the reasons for his gaucherie. 'My extreme need that people should think of me was what robbed me of the courage to show myself' (287). Elsewhere he says: 'I should like society as much as anybody else, if I were not sure of revealing myself not only to my disadvantage, but quite other than I am' (116). Another passage is equally revealing:

> Cast unwillingly into society without having its tone, without being in a position to assume it and comply with it, I decided to adopt a tone of my own which exempted me from the need of so doing. My unconquerably foolish and sullen shyness being rooted in my fear of falling short of good manners, I resolved to give myself courage by riding rough-shod over them. I became caustic and cynical through shame; I affected to despise the politeness which I could not practise (368).[1]

These psychological difficulties were undoubtedly aggravated by the physical effects of his painful retention. In the rough draft of a letter

---

[1] He was always liable to become tongue-tied and embarrassed at the thought of having to make a public speech. F. Berthoud (op. cit., p. 238) gives a graphic account of Rousseau's anxiety when he had to make a brief speech of thanks to the villagers of Couvet who, in 1756, had offered him the title and rights of member of their commune. In spite of a careful study of his speech, 'as soon as he was in the presence of the august assembly of the commoners of Couvet, the confused orator could scarcely utter a few intelligible words'. Later on he was to remain inarticulate in the presence of the ex-convict Thévenin who had falsely accused him of being his debtor (*CG* xviii. 374).

originally intended for the Marquis de Mirabeau in 1767 he complained bitterly of the suffering caused by social constraints.

I have to speak when I have nothing to say, to remain standing when I want to walk, to sit when I want to stand, to remain shut up in a room when I long for the fresh air. . . . In a word, I must spend the whole day doing what I least know how to do and what I dislike doing in any case; not only must I not do anything that I want, but I cannot even do what nature and the most pressing needs require of me—not least of all the need to urinate, more frequent and painful for me than any other. I still shudder to think of myself in a circle of women, compelled to wait until some fine talker has finished his sentence, not daring to go out lest someone should ask me whether I am leaving; I find in a well-lit staircase other fine ladies who delay me, then a courtyard full of constantly moving carriages ready to crush me, ladies' maids who are looking at me, lackeys who line the walls and laugh at me; I do not find a single wall, vault or wretched little corner that is suitable for my purpose: in short, I can urinate only in full view of everybody and on some noble white-stockinged leg (*CG* xvii. 3–4).

Probably this need of frequent urination, although of physical origin, was increased by psychological causes. It seems to be recognized today that genito-urinary disorders can have important mental repercussions on sensitive characters who already—for other emotional reasons—have difficulty in adapting themselves to social life. In other words, a urinary disorder such as that from which Rousseau suffered might well become a syndrome of acute anxiety, since increase in anxiety (as has been shown experimentally)[1] invariably increases intravesicular tension and so aggravates physical discomfort. The physical and psychological factors thus react upon each other in such a way as to increase the suffering of both aspects of the personality.

Rousseau's 'foolish', 'natural', and 'accursed' shyness was clearly not a simple innate characteristic (though it may have been rooted in some peculiarity of temperament or sensibility and subsequently increased by his physical malady), but a psychological phenomenon of complex origins—the end-product of a number of divergent impulses and the outcome of an inability to cope with unresolved emotional difficulties. This seems to be borne out by his own contradictory attitude towards it: he hesitates between a frank recognition of its painful inhibiting effects and a determination to make it a source of pride and virtue. At first he admits that he looks a 'rather foolish character' and suffers intensely from behaviour which makes him feel abashed, even 'in the

[1] Cf. Maslow and Mittelmann, op. cit., p. 469.

presence of people who are as stupid as himself' (*CG* i. 377). Later on he was to interpret his social inhibitions as a proof of his devotion to a freedom which made it impossible for him to compromise with the false values of his age. However, the immediate social effects of his shyness—such as his fits of tongue-tied embarrassment as well as his impulsive rudeness—were apt to conceal its deep psychological importance: he did not suffer from any deficiency of feeling but from a superabundance of emotion which could not find an adequate outlet in normal life; far from revealing the absence of powerful desires, his shyness denoted a high degree of intense, unexpressed feeling. Jean-Jacques always insisted that he was 'eager to desire but slow to act' and in his old age he told Bernardin de Saint-Pierre that he had 'a bold nature but a shy character'. The impulse to action, though strong, was checked by a contrary feeling which made it seem a hazardous enterprise.

This shyness is only one element in a complex process of withdrawal from others. The social implications are liable to conceal the important fact that Rousseau's inhibition is not derived solely from an immediate awareness of external hostility, but also involves a subtle process of personal reflection through which the self is imaginatively identified with others' critical scrutiny. He flees from others only because of a considerable emotional dependence on them: he feels a strong need for an approbation and affection which he fears will not be forthcoming. His view of his own personality is thus conditioned by what he imagines to be others' attitude towards him. Certainly Rousseau's childhood experiences had made him extremely dependent on the approval of 'significant persons', and his adult shyness seems to have been the maturation of a tendency that originated very early in life. With considerable insight into his own psychological state Jean-Jacques relates a characteristic boyhood reaction:

A thousand times during my apprenticeship and since, I would go out with the purpose of buying some delicacy. I approach a confectioner's shop, notice women at the counter; *I already see them laughing and making fun of the little glutton.* I pass by a fruiterer's, cast a sidelong glance at some fine pears and am tempted by their aroma; near by two or three young men are looking at me; a man who knows me is standing in front of his shop; from afar I see a girl coming: isn't it the servant of the house? My short-sightedness [and my fear][1] constantly deceives me. I take passers-by for acquaintances;

[1] The significant phrase in brackets occurs only in the first draft (cf. *Première rédaction*, p. 52).

everywhere I am intimidated, held back by some obstacle; my desire grows with my shame, and I go home like a fool, consumed by cupidity, having in my pocket the wherewithal to satisfy it, and yet daring to buy nothing (*Conf.* 37).

This plainly shows how Rousseau's typical habit of imaginative anticipation evokes anxiety while increasing his desire: the thought of being the object of another's hostile gaze paralyses the power of action and yet intensifies the emotion which would normally inspire it. This childhood anecdote foreshadows behaviour which was to be very typical of his later life. Whether it was a question of appearing before the king—'I then imagined myself in the King's presence . . .'—or before the Genevan Consistory—'I already believe myself to be in the illustrious assembly . . .'—he became the helpless victim of his 'accursed shyness' and was reduced to ignominious retreat or tortured embarrassment.

Since the desire itself persists, Rousseau will try to satisfy it in devious ways, and this perhaps explains his early inclination to kleptomania. 'I would rather take than ask', he declares defiantly (*Conf.* 38). What the other has must be obtained by ruse because he dare not make a direct request.[1] Since the world becomes a place which malevolently withholds from young Jean-Jacques what he feels to be his due, he must force it to yield what it will not give of its own accord. In this way he maintains his self-esteem, for he has proved to himself that after all he is not afraid to take what he wants. To be caught in his guilty act and punished for it does not cure him of his kleptomania, for, as he shrewdly observes, he merely welcomes punishment as an excuse for continuing his thefts! Moreover, the fact that these petty thefts— whether those of later life (such as his pilfering of wine from M. de Mably's cellar) or of adolescence—lead to solitary enjoyment suggests that this outwitting of others is accompanied by a secretly complacent image of himself as someone who has momentarily triumphed over the world.

The frustrations imposed on Jean-Jacques by these complex forms of withdrawal from others also help to explain his early disposition to attacks of depression and 'melancholy'. He was inclined at times to

---

[1] In his adult life he experienced a similar kind of inhibition at the thought of having to ask strangers his way in an unknown district, 'because that makes me dependent on the person who answers me. I prefer wandering about for two hours looking in vain' (*Mon Portrait*, 1127). He might think that this was a proof of his independence, but it is plainly connected with his timidity and anxiety before the other's critical gaze. To depend on the other, even for a trivial thing, is to feel one's inferiority.

treat his melancholy as if it were a congenital malady, although he later admitted the role of experience. Already in his early years he speaks of 'an invincible inclination to melancholy which, in spite of myself, is the bane of my life'.

> Whether it is due to temperament or to the habit of being unhappy, I bear within me a source of sadness, the origin of which I cannot discern. I have always lived in loneliness, have long been infirm and listless, considering the end of my short life as its immediate goal; in my soul, which has never been exposed to anything but pain, there is a keen desire for sensitivity, and I bear continually in my heart both my own troubles and those of all who are dear to me. That was only too good a reason for increasing my natural sadness (CG i. 377).

This melancholy was a trait noticed by many of his contemporaries, who often urged him to throw it off. In 1757 we find Mme d'Houdetot exhorting 'her dear citizen' not 'to give way to the black melancholy which obsessed him' (CG iii. 130). That sympathetic observer, M. de Malesherbes, was later to attribute Rousseau's unfounded charges against the publisher Duchesne (who had been accused of being in league with the Jesuits in an attempt to mutilate Émile) to 'an extreme sensibility, an underlying melancholy and a great tendency to see objects in the most unfavourable light, but an equal readiness to yield to justice and truth as soon as it is offered to him' (CG vii. 10). However, it would be wrong to infer from these observations that Rousseau had a permanently melancholy temperament, for he was far from being predisposed to a state of continuous gloom. At times he undoubtedly took a secret satisfaction in seeing himself in this unhappy light; but it seems likely that this melancholy was a periodic disturbance that depended on the reactions of his cyclothymic temperament and, later in life, on the effects of his retention;[1] he was easily led—when the physical and psychological pressures making for melancholy were removed—to moods of excitement and elation. In the same way the removal of restraints could produce an extraordinarily fluent and confident eloquence. 'In his moments of unconstraint when nothing disturbed him, words flowed like an impetuous, irresistible torrent.'[2] Rousseau's melancholy—like his shyness—does not represent a simple and durable state of mind, but, being bound up with a complex pattern of emotional

---

[1] As he himself observed, the effects of his malady were also dependent on the seasons, being particularly painful in winter.

[2] Cf. Musset–Pathay, op. cit., i. 184. His source is Dusaulx.

response, is inseparable from an underlying condition of anxiety and inner conflict.

The complex significance of these attacks of depression is revealed by Rousseau's own ambivalent attitude towards them. While lamenting his melancholy and no doubt suffering acutely from his sense of loneliness and unhappiness, he also derives a secret satisfaction from his inner torment; it is almost as if he willed his own unhappiness upon himself. This was a point observed by some of his more intelligent contemporaries. Thus the perspicacious Mme d'Houdetot, after urging him not to abandon himself to his melancholy, did not hesitate to say: 'It seems that your embittered heart *takes pleasure* in feeding and increasing the feeling which torments it' (*CG* iii. 130). It is also worth noting that, when it did not involve direct relations with others, this melancholy could be transmuted into a (for him) more acceptable emotional state— a kind of sentimental sadness vaguely associated with objects (for example, those of nature) which were pleasant in themselves. In the *Confessions* he speaks of the 'gentle melancholy' experienced at such times (152), whilst *Émile* describes melancholy as being 'fond of pleasure'.[1]

In so far as it cannot be explained by purely physical causes, Rousseau's melancholy was a psychological response to the frustration of powerful emotions, and especially to a feeling that his life had failed to fulfil its highest possibilities. He is constantly lamenting—and this sums up his whole attitude on the point—that he will one day be forced to die 'without having lived'. His melancholy thus enables him to obtain a certain amount of relief from emotional strain. Instead of having to face and overcome external obstacles and personal limitations, he takes refuge in a melancholy introspection which serves to allay the anxiety engendered by the thought of having to make an active and practical response to the difficulties confronting him. This mood also serves the subsidiary purpose of transforming him into an object of attention and sympathy and so provides him with some of the emotional support that he is unable to attain by a more direct approach to others. It need scarcely be said that such a solution to his difficulties cannot afford more than a temporary relief, for it is inadequate both in relation to his own character and his actual situation. The need for self-affirmation is too great to be satisfied by this substitute solution which comes to grief on the failure of other people to conform to his own desires.

The same essential attitude of withdrawal from others is probably at work in another reaction of which Rousseau is wont to talk a great deal

---

[1] Cf. *Émile*, Book IV.

—his 'laziness'. Although his vitality may ultimately have been impaired by uraemia, he probably exaggerates, for psychological reasons, the physical effects of his illness in developing a tendency to inactivity and inertia. His 'laziness' expressed his resistance to impulses which he was unwilling or unable to translate into action. At times a reference to his laziness might serve the useful purpose of enabling him to believe that he *could* do a thing if he wanted, while allowing him to escape the anxiety and strain involved in actual effort. More simply still, it often helped him to avoid the performance of distasteful or worrying tasks. Elsewhere he stresses that he was 'eager to desire but lazy to act'. This was not, as he seems to imply, a purely constitutional incapacity, but another example of a defence-mechanism aimed at protecting his self-esteem; 'laziness' is here a form of inhibition, although this may have been aggravated by a constitutional inability to make sustained efforts to satisfy his desires.[1]

The general impression created by these various forms of withdrawal is that they are means of protecting Rousseau against the psychological hazards of self-affirmation. In the end he interprets these different tendencies as essential conditions for the achievement of positive happiness because they are treated as an integral part of his 'nature'. This, however, is a well-known psychological development through which acquired responses that satisfy certain emotional needs become accepted as part of the subject's 'character', and later on we shall find Rousseau speaking of 'the contemplative and lonely life' as the one 'for which he was born'. It will always be possible to detect in his attitude the presence of a compensatory mechanism brought into action by the frustration of impulses which he has been unable to satisfy in his everyday life.

This attitude of withdrawal is certainly reinforced, if not actually caused, by Rousseau's sexual development, about which something must now be said. A preliminary difficulty is that of deciding the extent of his sexual vitality. Medical opinion has differed on this point, ranging from suggestions of complete impotence to affirmations of obsessive preoccupation with sexual questions. As far as his didactic writings are concerned, it may fairly be said that Rousseau treats sexual questions

[1] J. Guéhenno (op. cit., i. 251) says that 'laziness' might become, when Rousseau felt the need to justify himself, 'a taste for independence' or even an 'indubitable spirit of freedom'. Pierre Burgelin, in *La Philosophie de l'existence de J.-J. Rousseau* (Paris, 1952), pp. 130 ff., stresses the philosophical importance attached by Rousseau to *la paresse* as a fundamental constituent of human existence. 'To do nothing is man's first and strongest passion after that of self-preservation.'

with considerable discretion, and if he has occasion to refer to abnormal habits of which he himself is or has been a victim, he often proffers much sound advice to his reader; he indulges in none of the pornography which sometimes mars Diderot's work. As for his own sexual endowment, a study of all the available data suggests that his capacity was not less than normal, although it seems likely that with advancing years his urinary malady made it increasingly difficult for him to complete the physical act. Far from indicating a weak sexuality, his shyness and habit of withdrawing from others may be taken as the distorted expression of a high erotic feeling which was unable—because of inhibition—to find a normal outlet. Since Rousseau's shyness is a psychological as well as a constitutional trait, and really masks a strong desire for self-assertion, the sexual motive ought perhaps to be understood within this wider context. The deviations we are about to examine will appear as symptoms of a deeply rooted anxiety and maladjustment which, far from being limited to his sexual life, affect his whole personality. This view by no means excludes the possibility that, at a given stage of his existence, the onset of his retention may have restricted his physical capacity, although his abandonment of intimate relations with Thérèse by no means proves that the emotional and psychic concomitants of the sexual drive were impaired or weakened.[1] He himself constantly stressed that it was the emotional—rather than the purely physical—aspects of the sexual relationship which brought him greatest satisfaction,[2] or rather would have brought him greater satisfaction had he been able to experience them. His middle-aged infatuation with Mme d'Houdetot suggests that in 1757, at any rate, his erotic feelings were as strong as ever and—according to some critics—may have been accompanied by sexual satisfaction of a perverse kind.[3]

Probably Rousseau's attitude towards sex was greatly influenced by the puritanical outlook of the Geneva of his day. His own account in the *Confessions* certainly suggests an early repugnance. 'Not only did I have until my adolescence no distinct idea of the union of the sexes, but this confused idea never presented itself to me except in an odious and

[1] According to P. Jury (op. cit.) retention would increase sexual excitability but hinder genital activity; it might thus even force a feeling of organic inferiority.

[2] 'My senses were always directed by my heart' (*Première rédaction*, p. 26).

[3] Cf. J. Guéhenno, ii. 114, and H. Guillemin, *Un Homme, deux ombres* (Geneva, 1943), pp. 186 ff. For Dr. Demole the affair with Mme d'Houdetot proves Rousseau's impotence. The suggestion of perversity seems to me to be the more plausible, unless we view 'impotence' in a very special way.

disgusting image.' He associated sexual relations among human beings with the 'sickening' sight of dogs coupling in the street (*Conf.* 16). This initial aversion may have been increased by his unfortunate experience at the Hospice at Turin, for although this incident may not have been without its influence upon his subsequent later practice of self-abuse, it undoubtedly helped to reinforce his *conscious* resistance to sex as something repellent. Such experiences were not enough to stifle the sexual urge itself, but they made its direct, normal satisfaction more difficult.

A survey of all the available evidence suggests that Rousseau's was a case of sexual maladjustment rather than total impotence. He seems to have been able to obtain normal physical satisfaction only with women who did not stir his deeper emotions—towards whom, in a word, he did not feel genuine love. In other cases, it would perhaps be more accurate to speak of a kind of temporary functional impotence (for example, with Zulietta), although this may have had physical causes that are unknown to us; his typical reaction, however, is not an incapacity to complete the physical act, but a failure to establish a mutually satisfactory physical and emotional relationship with a woman. In no case need we suppose that the 'combustible' Rousseau lacked strong desires. More probably, these desires, instead of expressing the emotions usually associated with sexual maturity, were bound up with feelings produced by abnormal developmental influences.

The first deviant phenomenon to which Rousseau calls attention is the well-known episode concerning the beating administered by Mlle Lambercier, for it was this incident which (according to the *Confessions*) first aroused his masochistic reactions. Although the importance of this episode cannot be denied, it may have simply reinforced certain abnormal emotional responses which had already appeared in childhood —especially the tendency to submissiveness—and which, under the impact of this experience, for the first time received a specifically sexual colouring. It is worth recalling that when he was staying at Pastor Lambercier's house Rousseau was already ten or eleven years old (and not younger, as he says in the *Confessions*) and some of the most impressionable years of early childhood were already past. In any case, even if the theories of childhood sexuality were much more certain than they are, it would be very difficult to determine the precise cause of this deviation. In a general way, it seems not unreasonable to suppose that the circumstances of his early childhood, especially the lack of a mother's influence, the unpredictability of his father's moods, the adoring affection of his aunt, and the subsequent loss of all genuine love, as well as his own cyclothymic temperament, predisposed him to masochistic reactions inasmuch as these childhood experiences may have convinced him that he could only escape from anxiety and insecurity by adopting a passive, compliant attitude towards persons on whom he felt emotionally dependent;[1] at certain times it perhaps seemed to him that the affections of which he had such great need could be secured in no other way. At the same time there is no reason to suppose that the adult Rousseau practised masochism as a definite form of sexual perversion: he was more inclined to what may be called a 'moral' masochism, through which he obtained a secret, if sometimes distressing, pleasure in the idea of a self-abasement and humiliation which made him the passive object of other people's feelings.[2]

The masochistic longing to become the object of the other's active desires is clearly linked with another aspect of Rousseau's sexual history—his exhibitionism. Here again there is no evidence that it was more than a merely passing adolescent phase of his life for, as a man, he does not seem to have been given to this particular abnormality. The sexual aspect of the adolescent mood itself was also of limited significance since—according to his own account—he exposed the 'ridiculous' and not the 'obscene' object. It is as though his puritanical self was already strong enough to protect him against a complete indulgence in this aberration. In a more general way, he may be said to have carried over into his adult life the psychological basis of this exhibitionistic attitude in so far as he was frequently obsessed by the need to feel himself the object of another's attention. He finds satisfaction in playing an apparently passive emotional role and in abandoning the aggressive sexual response, through which the male usually pursues

[1] The whole question of masochism is recognized as a difficult one by most psychiatrists. Freud seems to have changed his mind on the subject, first treating it as a secondary phenomenon produced by some deeper frustration, and then considering it as the result of a fusion of the sexual drive with the 'death instinct'. The view of masochism as a hereditary taint—a view put forward by Krafft–Ebing and taken up by some of Rousseau's biographers like Professor Sells (cf. op. cit., pp. 134–7)—seems more like a desperate attempt to find a radical answer to a puzzling problem than a hypothesis capable of explaining all the facts. For a wider philosophical discussion of the question I refer the reader to some curious pages in Jean-Paul Sartre's *L'Être et le néant* (Paris, 1944), pp. 428 ff., which have been analysed and discussed in an article, 'An Aspect of Sartre and the Unconscious', *Philosophy*, vol. xxx, no. 112, Jan. 1955, pp. 33–44.

[2] Dr. A. Heidenhaim (op. cit., p. 26) extends Rousseau's masochism to tears shed before certain landscapes; he also recalls the curious emotions experienced during a performance of *Le Devin du village* (*Conf.* 379), when aesthetic pleasure was coloured by sexual feeling. Cf. also J. Starobinski, op. cit., p. 217.

its object, in favour of an effort to achieve gratification by making himself the object of another's desire. No doubt he himself still desires intensely, but this desire expresses itself in an indirect way. What I wish to stress here is less the purely sexual aspect of the question (for Rousseau's attitude towards women is, as we shall see, far from consistent) than the more fundamental affective structure of his personality which is characterized by an extreme emotional dependence on other people, especially on those for whom he experiences affection or admiration. It is as though he can feel safe only if he is the object of another's undivided and perhaps exclusive affection. Such an attitude, moreover, also helps to allay feelings of inferiority and guilt since to see himself as the object of another's love is to be assured of his own personal worth. Unfortunately for Rousseau, however, the role of the other person is not quite so simple, since the other's look may also be a source of fear and anxiety. The other is the one who can destroy as well as save. Jean-Jacques may want him, but in a way that runs the risk of arousing his hostility as well as his affection. This ambivalent attitude, already apparent in the specifically sexual sphere, tends to dominate the whole of his adult relations with other people.

Because his reactions towards the other are liable to oscillate between love and fear, he tries at times to eliminate him as a significant term in his erotic feelings or else reduce him to the status of a fantasy-object. This is one of the main psychological functions of his persistent habit of self-abuse, of which he himself has spoken quite freely.[1] Particularly important is his admission that he could not give up the practice even in adult life. That modern psychiatrists should stress the damaging psychological effects of this habit for the adult rather than the adolescent is not surprising since for most adolescents self-abuse seems to fulfil a kind of auto-erotic function by means of which the personality releases some of its undischarged developing sexual energy, while the continuance of the practice in adult life suggests serious maladaptation and lack of adequate emotional integration: when feelings become detached from the object on which they would normally be projected in order to turn inwards, the individual may become preoccupied with unhealthy fantasies about himself instead of directing his physical and psychic energy on to a person of the opposite sex. It seems probable, however, that self-abuse is the effect rather than the cause of emotional maladjustment, being a symptomatic attempt to solve emotional difficulties which are to be traced in the first place to other sources;

[1] Cf. *Conf.* 109, 316, and comments in *OC* i. 1282-3.

even so, it is liable to set up a vicious psychological circle from which the victim finds it increasingly difficult to escape. That Rousseau's habit of self-abuse was the effect or symptom of his troubles rather than their cause seems to be confirmed by the presence of the various emotional factors making for withdrawal from others: it is not simply a form of auto-eroticism (although it may have begun as such), but the expression of an incipient narcissism by which he directs his libidinal and emotional energies upon himself. The grave consequence of this attitude is that, as he seeks to escape from emotional stress by turning inwards, the development of strongly autistic reactions makes it increasingly difficult for him to face up to the realities of his situation and to establish satisfactory relations with other people.

It seems to be generally recognized too that self-abuse is liable to increase feelings of guilt and unworthiness. That Rousseau was never able to dissociate his solitary act from such feelings is revealed by his own account of a chance encounter at Lyons in Book IV of the *Confessions*; the sight of another man's addiction to his own secret vice so shocked him that for a time he completely desisted from the practice. Moreover, if there is any truth in the previous suggestion that Rousseau was predisposed from his earliest childhood to secret and perhaps irrational feelings of guilt, adult habits would merely reinforce reactions that were already deeply engrained in his character, self-abuse serving to tie them more closely to the sexual impulse.

A more general consequence may well have been to increase his sensitivity to criticism. It is now widely acknowledged that onanism is likely to have this effect; if he does not think that others actually suspect his shameful secret, such a person may be in constant fear of their doing so, thus strengthening the tendency to see himself as the object of a critical and perhaps hostile attention. Self-abuse was certainly calculated to develop a propensity already encouraged by the important emotional factor already described: his habit of seeing himself as the object of others' contempt. But if it ultimately reinforces his tendency to retreat from others, self-abuse also brings into play the 'primitive', 'romantic' aspect of his personality, for it leads to a gratification of desire which eliminates the necessity of facing the obstacles normally lying in the way of its fulfilment. Momentarily he can move in the realm of illimitable fantasy, for to possess any woman he has only to desire her: to enjoy he merely surrenders himself, Aladdin-like, to the omnipotence of his imagination. His exhibitionism also forms part of the same general mood, for, by exposing himself, he hopes to induce the

E

other to come freely to him: fascinated by Jean-Jacques's gesture, the other becomes the unwitting instrument of his solitary enjoyment.[1]

Nevertheless, an episode like the Lyons encounter which has been referred to above shows very well the complexity of Rousseau's character, which is never completely dominated by his weaknesses: he always remains—perhaps only confusedly and hesitantly at times—the critic of his own faults, and so reveals the persistence of a powerful moral strain which never abandoned him, even in his greatest humiliations. The immoral Jean-Jacques cannot completely forget the moral Rousseau who is his constant companion. At the purely psychological level, the same tendency is also apparent, for the elements making for withdrawal from others are often counterbalanced by an equally powerful, if erratic, need for self-affirmation. It is in fact his own profound awareness of these contradictions which ultimately prompts him to undertake a searching examination of his enigmatic character with a view to discovering its underlying personal unity.

[1] Cf. also J. Starobinski, op. cit., p. 214.

2

ROUSSEAU'S EARLY PSYCHOLOGICAL DEVELOPMENT: II

THE feeling of being inwardly divided is, then, a vital factor in Rousseau's development, since his awareness of puzzling personal contradictions spurs him on towards more adequate self-understanding. If he quails before the other's gaze, it is not simply because he is conscious of an intimidating presence, but also—and especially—because the other has the mysterious power to alienate him from his true self, to make him appear different from what he really is. 'If I had been present, they would never have known my worth, or even have suspected it' (*Conf.* 116). Moreover, if people treat this embarrassed, tormented Jean-Jacques as the real Rousseau, they are merely falling into an error typical of the society which prefers 'opinion' to 'nature', 'appearance' to 'reality'. 'Under the sway of opinion, what precautions must we not take to distinguish appearance from reality in our estimate of things' (*CG* iii. 353). But Rousseau's own problem is not merely that of separating his true self from the false mask seen by the outside world; he is also confronted by inner conflicts which make him an enigma even to himself. No doubt this is also a general problem affecting most men who 'during the course of their lives are often unlike themselves' (*Conf.* 408); it is a consistent feature of modern civilization that man is perpetually 'in conflict with himself', both in his personal and his social life.[1] But if Rousseau is particularly impressed by this feature of the contemporary situation, it is because he has experienced it in his own existence: he has often behaved in a way so out of keeping with his normal character that he seemed to be a totally different person. 'I believe that I have already observed that there are times when I am so unlike myself that I should be taken for a man of a completely opposite character' (*Conf.* 128). This sense of being 'another' is particularly evident in times of crisis, especially when he is carried away

---

[1] This too is to become the test of sound political institutions—that they will help to restore man's unity. 'All institutions which put man in contradiction with himself are worthless' (*Œuvres*, iii. 385).

by the excitement of inspiration. He cannot forget 'those brief moments in his life when he became another and ceased to be himself' (*Conf.* 417). Such, for example, was the occasion of his 'illumination' on the road to Vincennes when he 'saw another universe and became another man' (351). But it is precisely this sense of being other than his everyday self which makes him realize that his character is not fixed and static, that his personal existence has no obvious and simple meaning: for if he is so often 'unlike himself', what is his real self? How can he move beyond these contradictions to a stable, permanent personal unity? His individual problem is thus not so very different from the one which preoccupied him in the philosophical sphere—how to recover or restore the primordial unity of a self that has become divided and fragmented by the factitious multiplicity and incoherence of modern existence?[1]

Although he is especially struck by his contradictory attitudes of affirmation and withdrawal, Rousseau acknowledges the presence of other tensions which expose him to 'constantly renewed oscillations'. He often sees himself alternating between exaltation and depression, 'sublimity' and 'langour' (*Conf.* 14). His emotions are intense, but his capacity for action is weak. On one occasion he speaks of 'this proud and tender, this effeminate and yet indomitable heart, which, constantly hovering between weakness and courage, softness and virtue, has set me at odds with myself and withheld from me both abstinence and enjoyment, pleasure and wisdom' (*Conf.* 12). In 1757 he asks: 'Now in a state of agitation, now in a state of depression, when shall I find the calmness necessary for freedom of mind?' In the second letter to Malesherbes he was to sum up the contradiction as follows: 'A slothful soul that is frightened of every care and an ardent irascible temperament that is easily affected and over-sensitive to all that affects it cannot harmonize in the same character, and yet these two opposites form the basis of mine. Although I cannot resolve this opposition by means of principles, it nevertheless exists: I feel it, nothing is more certain' (*LM* 1134). Aware of himself as a man inwardly divided, he introspects his character with such great interest and tenacity that he will one day be emboldened to affirm that 'nobody knows himself better than I'—even though this 'I' remains curiously puzzling and contradictory in the midst of self-analysis. Self-knowledge and self-realization are thus inseparable from a psychological situation which, at first sight, seems to stand in the way of their adequate expression.

[1] For a detailed discussion of the philosophical aspect of the question, see Pierre Burgelin, *La Philosophie de l'existence de J.-J. Rousseau* (Paris, 1952).

One particular kind of inner contradiction to which he constantly refers and which he deems to be especially significant is that which he supposes to exist between his 'heart' and his 'mind', his 'lively passions' and his 'slow ideas'. 'It is as though my heart and my mind do not belong to the same individual' (*Conf.* 113). In the *Rêveries* he was to write: 'I have sometimes thought fairly deeply, but rarely with pleasure and almost always against my inclination and, as it were, by force; reverie refreshes and amuses me, reflection tires and saddens me' (*Rêv.* vii. 1061–2). He also told his friend Eymar that 'he was not born to think' and that 'his good health dated from the day when he ceased to devote himself to intellectual work'.[1] His later life thus confirms his previously expressed preference for the satisfactions of the 'heart' to those of the 'mind'.[2] In view of what has already been said about his highly developed sensibility and emotivity, it will not be surprising to find him repeatedly describing himself as a 'man of feeling' whose chief quality lies in the sincerity of his heart. Yet his resistance to mental effort is not due solely to natural inaptitude for this kind of work (as he suggests), but at least partly to a difficulty in co-ordinating thought and feeling—a difficulty that may well have been increased by a lack of early mental discipline in dealing with questions to which he was not emotionally attuned. His inability to separate thinking from personal feelings always made him reluctant (as he recognized) to write on topics by which he was not deeply stirred: to be able to think intensely he had to be inwardly persuaded of the value of the subject with which he was dealing, and he was always opposed to an abstract speculation which had little or no reference—however indirect—to his own inner life.

His initial effort, however, to resolve his inner divisions was through personal action rather than intellectual reflection. As we have already seen in the previous chapter, he sometimes sought to obtain relief from tension by an impulsive form of self-affirmation; often shy and self-effacing, he was capable of outbursts of violent emotion. He himself was the first to recognize this, for he speaks of his 'passionate' and 'quick-tempered' character. He was apt to treat people with a brutal frankness and sudden brusqueness which he attributed to his 'sensitivity of soul'. He was particularly prone to explosions of anger,[3] and, even in

---

[1] Quoted in Proal, op. cit., p. 316.

[2] Already in 1744 he had stated: 'I find more satisfaction in my heart than in my mind' (*CG* i. 203).

[3] Two well-known examples are the outbursts at Mlle Quinault's and Baron d'Holbach's, the first involving Jean-Jacques's passionate defence of God against the atheists,

his last days, we find him still wondering how to deal with the onset of these apparently overwhelming fits of exasperation (*Rêv.* viii. 1083–4); he finally decided that the wisest course of action was for him to abandon himself to the first involuntary impetus of his 'ardent nature', for this would soon give way to the 'pacifying' influence of his 'indolent' character. Even at this stage of his life he was compelled to admit his life-long inability to resist the pressure of 'immediate impulse'. He insists, however, that though his anger would sometimes deprive him of all 'presence of mind', its rapid disappearance left him without any feeling of rancour against the person who had first of all provoked the outburst.

Other aspects of his affective life reveal the same impulsive tendency and the same overwhelming preoccupation with immediate feeling. 'Distant prospects are rarely strong enough to make me act. The uncertainty of the future has always made me consider long-term plans as a snare and a delusion. . . . The slightest pleasure within my grasp tempts me more than the joys of paradise' (*Conf.* 146). It was in the intensity of the present experience that he could temporarily forget his inner contradictions, and later on he was to lay great stress on the idea of immediacy as an essential element in all true self-realization. A powerful, if sometimes irrational, feeling might seem a surer basis for self-affirmation that a more hesitant, reflective approach to life; by expressing himself in terms of immediate emotion, he could obtain a considerable diminution of inner conflict. Perhaps this helps to explain why his attitude towards his 'quick-tempered' character is by no means one of unrelieved disapproval, for he tends at times to treat his anger as righteous indignation—as the outburst of a proud, sincere man who cannot accept the unworthy prevarication and cowardice of men of the world: if he is 'true, tactless, proud, impatient, quick-tempered' (*Conf.* 446), he falls an easy prey to egotistic, calculating persons. Thus his psychological development ultimately reinforces the natural inclinations of his innate sensibility.

Such psychological reactions, being too fitful to offer a permanent means of overcoming personal contradictions, and too compensatory in character to satisfy his deepest emotional needs, express only one of Rousseau's attitudes; at times they give way to a genuinely *expansive* type of feeling which reveals a more fundamental aspect of his nature.

the second a violent protest against the coterie's mockery of a naïve *curé* who had submitted his feeble productions to its literary judgement. Cf. for details J. Guéhenno, op. cit., ii. 125–8.

He often speaks of his 'expansive' nature, although he never defines it, largely perhaps because it is bound up with the memory of 'indescribable' happiness. It clearly differs, however, from mere emotionalism because it involves a much deeper and richer level of personal experience than the subjective feelings of resentment created by his frustrating social environment or the escapist, 'autistic' flights of imagination and reverie provoked by his tendency to self-effacement: at the same time, there occurs a movement away from the self towards a reality—whether human or inanimate—other than the self, so that these expansive moods enable him to establish some kind of sympathetic relationship with the profounder aspect of his own personality and the world—the true world—around him. At such times he has the feeling of being in harmony with the physical universe, other people and his own higher self.

This expansive inclination was not limited to a single mood, for it appeared in a wide range of reactions. Already his youthful journey to the Hospice at Turin had provided him with a striking example of his ability to give way to expansive feelings before Nature. 'Young, robust, full of health, security, confidence in myself and others, I was in this brief but precious moment of life when its expansive plenitude extends our being so to speak through all our sensations and in our eyes embellishes the whole of nature with the charm of our existence' (*Conf.* 57–58). This kind of experience obviously represents a compound of sensuous and emotional reactions, in which the external and internal sources of inspiration are intimately blended. The same expansive mingling of human and non-human elements is evoked with great charm and vividness at a number of places in the *Confessions*. It was particularly during his lonely wanderings that he attained this extraordinary sense of emotional fulfilment in the presence of Nature. 'I am complete master of nature: my heart, flitting from one object to another, fuses and identifies itself with those which flatter it, surrounding itself with charming images, growing intoxicated with delicious feelings' (*Conf.* 162). Often such experiences contain a strongly imaginative element which transforms them into a kind of rhapsodical reverie. Of his sojourn at Annecy in 1729 he writes:

That gave my reverie a sadness which, however, was in no way sombre and was tempered by a flattering hope. The sound of bells, which has always moved me strangely, the song of the birds, the beauty of the day, the softness of the landscape, the scattered country-houses in which I imaginatively placed our common abode—all that made such a vivid, tender, sad and touching impression upon me that I saw myself as it were ecstatically transported to that happy time and place when my heart, possessing all the bliss that it could enjoy, relished it in inexpressible delights, without even thinking of sensuous pleasure (*Conf.* 107–8).

As this extract makes clear, Rousseau was apt to let his enjoyment of nature become mingled with the emotions aroused in him by a human being. This is especially true of his feelings for Mme de Warens. 'In my eyes her charms and those of spring were commingled. My heart, constricted till then, had more room to expand in that spacious environment and my sighs found a freer outlet amongst those orchards' (*Conf.* 105). A similar impression of complete contentment emerges from his account of his idyllic excursion with Mme de Warens on 25 August 1736. Looking back upon those days some forty years later, he was to say that only then was he 'what he wanted to be . . . himself, without obstacle or contradiction' (*Rêv.* x. 1098–9). It was 'those peaceful and fleeting moments that gave him the right to say that he had lived' (*Conf.* 224).

His literary and artistic interests are often marked by the same expansive movement. In his youth a visit to the theatre could affect him intensely. In 1737, for example, we find him shedding tears at a performance of Voltaire's *Alzire* 'where I did not fail to be so moved that I lost my breath; my palpitations increased astonishingly, and I am afraid that I shall feel the effect for some time. . . . Why are there hearts sensitive to the great, the sublime and the pathetic, while others seem made to live only in the abject baseness of their feelings?' (*CG* i. 58). His later animadversions against the theatre are perhaps tinged by a certain shame at his own early enthusiasm. In the same way *Le Verger de Madame la Baronne de Warens* (1739) expresses admiration for another emotional work, Prévost's *Cleveland*, in which Jean-Jacques detects a 'nature which, in his eyes, always appears touching and pure', and it is sufficient to recall his life-long attachment to a novel like *Astrée* and to the *Idylls* of Gessner in which he found 'a touching and ancient simplicity that goes to the heart' (*CG* vi. 210–11). Some of his own major writings were the result of a similar expansive tendency since they were inspired by a 'noble enthusiasm'. It is scarcely necessary to insist on the famous 'illumination' on the road to Vincennes, one of literature's most celebrated moments of 'inspiration': the first *Discours* was meditated in a 'state of inexpressible turmoil' and at a time when the author experienced 'a giddiness resembling intoxication'. 'A violent palpitation oppressed me, making my breast heave; no longer able to breathe as I walked, I sank down under one of the trees on the avenue and there I spent half an hour in such agitation that when I got up I saw all the front of my jacket wet with tears, although I had not been conscious of shedding them' (*LM* 1135). The *Confessions* reveal that the second *Discours* was also pondered in a mood of emotional exaltation, for, as he wandered through the forest of Saint-Germain, his soul, 'excited by these sublime contemplations', recaptured the 'image of early times' and 'the true character of natural man' (*Conf.* 388). If the writing of the *Lettre à d'Alembert* was accompanied by less intense feelings, it none the less was full of 'tenderness and gentleness of soul' and contained, insists Rousseau, some of his most intimate and personal emotions (*Conf.* 495). The inception of *La Nouvelle Héloïse* (of which we shall have occasion to speak later) was due to a mood of imaginative personal fantasy in which he sought for a vicarious expression of all those expansive emotions which he had been unable to satisfy in real life; it was written, he tells us, 'in the most burning ecstasies' at a time when 'he no longer belonged for a moment to himself' (434). The fifth book of *Émile* was likewise composed in a 'continual ecstasy'. Indeed, of his creative period as a whole he says: 'From the lively effervescence which then took place in my soul there came forth sparks of genius which have been seen to shine in these writings for ten years of delirium and fever.' It was only in a state of 'fever', as he was later to tell Grétry, that he could write anything worth while.[1] It was because 'he no longer had the courage to give himself fever' that he composed no didactic works in his old age.

In its most intense form this emotionalism emerges as involuntary ecstasies and 'sublime frenzies' which 'raise us above our own being and bear us into the highest heaven to the side of God himself' (*CG* iii. 360); it is a 'consuming ardour' and a 'sacred fire'; Rousseau clearly believes himself to have been endowed with, as he puts it in the *Lettre à d'Alembert*, 'this celestial fire which warms and kindles the soul, this genius which consumes and devours, this burning eloquence, these sublime transports which bear their ecstasies to the depths of our hearts' (ed. Fuchs, pp. 138–9, note 2). If these experiences have a strongly affirmative function and allow him to feel the fundamental nature of his own being, it is largely because of their indissoluble connexion with some kind of ideal object, the truly spiritual character of which is revealed by the intensity and vividness of his vision or intuition. It was

---

[1] Quoted in L. Proal, op. cit., p. 266.

his belief that such inspiration could find no proper outlet in the immediate world of everyday life or at the level of lived relationships which later provided him with an incentive to explore their metaphysical and quasi-mystical potentialities.

This type of expansive self-fulfilment was for the most part experienced in periods of freedom when he did not feel inhibited by the presence of social barriers and irksome discipline. Although spontaneous and intimate, these ecstatic experiences were too rare and fitful in his early years to offer a sound basis for a 'philosophy of life' and they often gave way to quite different reactions which impelled him towards a contraction and withdrawal of his personality. They could become an adequate criterion for living only when they had been transformed into a conscious value. Whatever be the precise meaning of this question-begging term 'value', it does seem to involve at least some subordination of individual feeling to the universal, permanent aspects of human experience, so that the personality is given a coherence and strength which transcend any merely subjective satisfaction it may derive from its emotions; in such cases feeling becomes inseparable from some degree of conscious evaluation and reflection. But at this stage of his life, Rousseau has not yet explored the objective or even the deeper personal implications of these experiences: he feels obscurely that they have value because, involving more than a merely passing emotion, they have an important bearing on the meaning of his own existence and that of other men; but as yet his ecstasies serve less as positive elements in a carefully elaborated philosophy of personal existence than as experiences which, through their very infrequency, help to strengthen his conviction of the inevitable divorce existing between 'natural man' and 'civilization'; they lead him to condemn 'civilization' without at first providing him with a constructive approach towards the reality constituted by this 'man' upon whom society has such disastrous effects. At the personal level they help to confirm his belief that between the world and him there is opening up an unbridgeable chasm and that between Jean-Jacques and the society of his day no compromise is possible. Henceforth he is to feel that he does not really belong to his surroundings and the epigraph from Ovid which he puts at the head of his first *Discours* clearly indicates his sense of isolation—'Barbarus hic ego sum quia non intelligor illis'.

No doubt this feeling of solitude is not without an admixture of suppressed resentment at the thought of frustrated ambition and abandoned hopes—and the emotional intensity of his prize-essay owed a good deal to personal feelings which had the power to imbue a more or less banal theme with particular warmth and colour—but he realized more and more that mere indulgence in personal feeling was not enough, that he had to generalize his ideas and reflect more deeply on some of the wider implications of his attitude. The subsequent adoption of a literary career, inspired by what he felt to be a genuine sense of vocation, led to a diminution of purely egotistical reactions and to a growing awareness that henceforth he must write in the name of 'truth' and 'justice'. His previous efforts to build up a 'storehouse of ideas' and his belated efforts to educate himself for a worthier role than that of Mme de Warens' protégé already revealed the first dim stirring of a nobler ambition, even though his initial efforts to make his way in the world had been largely inspired by a self-centred desire for personal glory. Now that he had at last declared himself as an uncompromising critic of French civilization, he had to prove himself worthy of his new vocation by clarifying the meaning of his intuitions and showing an earnestness of purpose and depth of reflection which lifted both his thinking and his existence above the level of merely subjective emotion. Within and beyond himself he had to seek 'humanity' and the true 'nature of man'. This meant that the relationship between himself and his environment could no longer be reduced to one of mere opposition, but had to express itself in a kind of dynamic interaction: conscious of himself as a man who was against his age and yet concerned to penetrate the meaning of its spiritual malady, he was impelled by his awareness of personal strength and weakness to seek a deeper understanding of his own nature, for it soon became clear that his criticism of contemporary values was inseparable from a careful examination and—ultimately perhaps justification—of his personal existence. At the same time self-understanding would lead to a more perspicacious examination of the needs of his age. The question: What is true? was thus inextricably bound up with the further question: What am I? and the difficulty of Rousseau's position was that it did not imply a mere juxtaposition of the two problems but their complex and intimate interpenetration. Truth could not be limited to the idea of intellectual assent to objectively valid propositions, but was partly dependent on his personality's choice of its own mode of being.

Some of the profounder implications of this effort to set the question of personal existence on a more philosophical plane emerged only in Rousseau's last years, for his first writings were dominated by a didactic purpose. But even in this early period, the personal question was linked up with wider issues: didactic writing and individual reflection already showed a reciprocal influence, so that with the awakening of his sense of literary vocation there occurred a simultaneous development of personal reflection and moral consciousness. The self which is here in question is not the empirical, everyday self of ordinary experience, but a kind of *ideal* ego which, through looking higher than the banalities of social life, provides the source of literary inspiration. 'Whence', he was to ask in the *Dialogues* (936), 'can the painter and apologist of nature, to-day so disfigured and calumnied, have drawn his model save from his own heart? He has described it in accordance with his own feelings.' In its turn the act of writing helped to develop the expression of this ideal self, so that when we describe Rousseau as a 'personal' writer, we ought not to establish—as some psychiatrists like V. Demole do—a simple correlation between his psychological or psychopathological condition (abnormal complexes, psychotic state and so on) and his ideas; for, as has been pointed out in the introduction, this kind of explanation ignores the 'ideal' and 'free' elements which, in spite of considerable psychological difficulties, can animate a genuine moral quest for personal and philosophical truth. Rousseau himself was some-times willing to admit his personal inadequacy while insisting that the full extent of his idealism, which looked towards a domain of being greater than that of his own circumscribed experience, could only be gauged by those who knew his deeper—and this meant in one sense his potential—self. But as a teacher of truth, he could not remain satisfied with merely acknowledging the link between his writings and his ideal self, for he felt that henceforth his personal existence ought to reflect something of the idealism inspiring his literary output: if he was to identify himself personally with the truths he was proclaiming, the gap between lived experience and didactic principle had to be closed.

Having thus discovered both his sense of literary vocation and the meaning of his personal moral destiny, he began to see himself as the representative of a 'heroic', almost austere moral attitude which, while giving him a sense of superiority over his surroundings, also allowed him to make a more dispassionate and rational appraisal of their short-comings. But since French civilization was in his view largely decadent, he had to look elsewhere for sound moral values, and his mind im-mediately began to turn to those cultural principles which, through their connexion with a tradition that was older and firmer than the shifting pattern of individual emotions, could offer a safe refuge from the dangers of his immediate environment. However delightful and, at times, comforting he might find his expansive flights, he realized that they were too subjective to be genuinely paradigmatic: he had to attain a self-awareness based on principles having a much wider validity—in other words, to seek values which belonged to an outlook that transcended his own feelings and yet evoked a genuine response in his own 'ideal' inner self.

It was perhaps quite natural that, in his effort to find a stable attitude for his existence as man and writer, Rousseau should revive memories of his early upbringing, and especially of those moral and religious values which he had inherited from his Genevan background—ideas which were undoubtedly modified in accordance with his own individual needs, but which also allowed him to be identified with a cultural tradition different from that of his French contemporaries. The essential point about the religious outlook of his boyhood Geneva was that it had tended to stress the moral rather than the dogmatic aspects of Christianity;[1] the quasi-theocratic government had been anxious above all to control the moral life of its citizens. Indeed it was for various infringements of this strict ethical code that members of the Rousseau family had been sternly reproved and chastised. In a more general way the emphasis on simple virtue, the dislike of luxurious and easy living and a strong disapproval of the delicate sophistication of 'civilized' France might well seem a natural and inevitable element in every citizen's upbringing. Of course this 'Genevan' influence could not exist in isolation and would either harmonize or clash with other influences to which the individual was exposed by his particular situation: the ethical principles of Geneva were modified by the specific psychological factors to which attention has already been called, and especially by Rousseau's early relationship with his father. If in some respects this relationship provoked deep emotional disturbances which were to make him resist the pressure of Genevan morality, it was also associated with the reading of ancient authors like Plutarch, in whom the heroic moral ideal was very strong. Thus, no matter how powerful and different the later influences to which Rousseau was subjected, the imprint of his early moral upbringing could never be completely eradicated. When

[1] Cf. G. Vallette, op. cit., p. 17. It was especially the influence of J. A. Turrettini (1671–1737) which encouraged this tendency. According to Vallette, his principles were 'liberty of thought, Christian toleration, morality preferred to dogma, Christianity restored to its essence which is charity, the fraternal union of all Protestant of all denominations'.

for particular personal reasons he was led to defy the society of his day in the name of moral principles, he could readily find inner support in the memory of those childhood experiences whose influence had never been completely effaced.

That this ideal of 'heroic' morality may not have corresponded to the actual situation in Geneva is irrelevant for our immediate purpose, for we can readily admit its modification and transformation through the particular influences of temperament and psychological development.[1] It is enough to recognize that Rousseau's early years provided him with an emotional and moral attitude which ran counter to that of his French contemporaries. The exact nature of this fundamental difference was at first obscured, because the Parisian scene provided, as we have already seen, opportunities for the expression of certain emotional impulses—especially those involving the drive towards self-assertion—which his life hitherto had been unable to satisfy. Yet, even before his arrival in Paris, Rousseau recognized the importance of certain beneficent civilizing influences in his life. In particular, Mme de Warens had done much to smooth out the rougher sides of his character; earlier still some of his adolescent experiences in Geneva had already prepared the way for an important change in his personal attitude, while his later sojourn at Lyons in 1740 brought him into active contact with social life. In his *Confessions* he was to stress a different kind of influence—the brutal treatment he received at the hands of the engraver Ducommun to whom he was apprenticed. Not only did Ducommun help 'to brutalize his loving and lively character' but he also effaced the noble ideals imparted to him through his early reading of stories about Greek and Roman heroes. As he goes on to admit with characteristic perspicacity, these ideals were not so deeply grounded in his character as he had supposed, and he is led to observe somewhat disingenuously that 'in spite of a very honest education, I must have had a great propensity for degeneration; for it came about very quickly, without the slightest trouble, and never did a precocious Caesar so promptly become a Laridon' (*Conf.* 30–31). In this respect his father's early influence on his emotions, the spoiling effect of the women who helped to bring him up, the unhealthy stimulation of precocious passions by the reading of sentimental novels, as well as the pressure of his own

[1] Every child, from his earliest years, tends to modify the values 'introjected' by parental influence in accordance with his own psychic needs, so that the first moral notions are not objective factors passively accepted by him, but ideas having a particular affective significance determined by the emotional relationship with the parents as well as with purely endopsychic elements.

unbalanced temperament, must have already helped to undermine his moral stability.

Yet the stern moral ideals of his boyhood were not so easily forgotten and he could not throw off their influence as lightly as he had been able to abandon physical contact with his native city. The presence of a distinctly moral note is very interestingly revealed in the semi-auto-biographical poetic efforts produced during his stay with Mme de Warens—*Le Verger de Mme de Warens* (1739), the *Épître à M. Bordes* (1741), and the *Épître à M. Parisot* (1742). Whilst admitting an element of poetic exaggeration—due to the desire for literary effect and the will perhaps to 'show off'—we may observe how Rousseau sets himself up as a stern and proud Genevan, a young man who is dominated by an inflexible, republican spirit, a devotee of 'fierce maxims' and 'Gothic simplicity'. Self-conscious and ostentatious though much of this verse is, it is an interesting indication of the way in which he wished others to see his earlier life. He perhaps hoped thereby to correct any impression that he had fallen a very easy prey to those who had so swiftly con-verted him to Romanism and to the very unrepublican atmosphere of Chambéry! No doubt too Rousseau presents this portrait with a some-what apologetic air, for he is anxious to give credit to *Maman* who had been able to civilize and humanize him and show him that a too austere morality was as foolish as it was unnecessary; and he is now prepared to admit that stoic virtue and 'ancient simplicity' must sometimes yield to more epicurean enjoyment. Nevertheless, if he is inclined to treat his uncompromising republicanism as a fault, it is obviously treated as a fault which is little more than an excess of virtue. No doubt his picture of himself as an almost ascetic young man dominated by the highest ethical principles scarcely accords with the actual circumstances of his earlier history, but it does give us an interesting insight into the kind of *ideal* portrait he was anxious to draw of his life at Geneva.

Something of this attitude is also revealed in the prayers which were apparently composed at this time.

I shall remember that You witness all my actions. . . . I shall try to do nothing unworthy of your august presence. I shall be indulgent to others, severe to myself. I shall resist temptations, live purely and never allow myself anything but the pleasures authorized by virtue. . . . As far as possible, I shall detach myself from the world's taste, the comforts and conveniences of life, in order to occupy myself solely with You and your infinite perfections.[1]

---

[1] Cf. *Annales*, I, 227–8, and, for other prayers, pp. 221–4. The prayer quoted in the text is partly translated in M. Josephson, op. cit., p. 103. See also A. L. Sells, op. cit., pp. 130–1, for other extracts.

The first *Discours* merely served to reinforce these moral feelings. Its originality, as we have seen, lay more in the intensity of its tone than in its subject-matter, but the element of personal feeling was also subordinated to the formulation of certain ideas, the ultimate purpose of which was to recall his fellow men to the path of 'virtue'. As well as being the crystallization of a deeply felt experience, the essay, with its emphasis on the split between morality and civilization, and its eulogy of simple austerity, also reflected the impact of older cultural values such as those found in the Bible, Plutarch, Montaigne, and others.[1]

The existence of a close link between Rousseau's efforts to establish an ideal relationship with himself and his desire to express certain ideas about 'virtue', which he thought to be beneficial to his fellow men, meant that his moral principles were not always free from a certain ambiguity, the more so because they were not simply abstract, impersonal notions to be accepted or rejected as a whole, but ideas that had to be assimilated to his own personal and, in some ways, conflicting needs. Albert Schinz has already pointed out that Rousseau's praise of 'Roman' courage is not always very explicit in its purpose, being at times associated in his mind with the aggressive, self-assertive striving of a Caesar and at others with the disciplined, ascetic self-restraint of a Cato; heroic morality might well lead to the domination of other people as well as of one's own passions.[2] Rousseau's view of Roman morality could not remain indifferent to those contradictory aspects of his character which often made him seem to behave inconsistently; but, whatever its particular form, this appeal to the cultural values of ancient Rome clearly represents an admiration for the firm, unbending attitude which refuses to make concessions to human weakness and

---

[1] For a full discussion of this point see the excellent introduction to G. R. Havens's edition of the *Discours* (New York, 1946).

[2] Schinz also points out that from the sixteenth century the Romans were held to be models of abnegation and austerity, and even of Christian asceticism: to praise the Romans was to praise Christian morality. The same attitude was found in Calvinistic Geneva, where it lasted longer than in France. Before the Pont du Gard Rousseau exclaims: 'Why was I not born a Roman? I remained for several hours lost in a delightful contemplation' (*Conf.* 256). 'At twelve years of age', he told Tronchin in 1758, 'I was a Roman, at twenty I had run about the world and was nothing but a rascal' (*CG* iv. 143). The connexion in his mind between Genevan and Roman virtue is interestingly revealed in Claire's letter to Julie. 'The more I consider this little state [Geneva], the more magnificent do I find it to have a fatherland, and may God keep from harm all those who think they have one and have only a country. As for me, I feel that *if I had been born in this one, I should have a quite Roman soul.*' Geneva, for her, is 'the land of wisdom and reason' (*La Nouvelle Héloïse*, Part VI, letter 5).

indecision and so—in the last resort—promotes the cause of a quasi-heroic moral integrity.

As far as his personal life was concerned, the integration of individual feelings into a definite cultural tradition helped to transform subjective resentment into moral indignation. Of itself mere emotion would have little power to convince either himself or others of the rightness of his attitude, but, when it was once associated with principles drawn from the Geneva of his youth and the more effulgent glories of ancient Greece and Rome, it appeared to offer a solid support for both his ideas and his existence. Gradually he came to believe that worldly ambition and the pursuit of position and wealth were incompatible with his new role as a preacher of 'virtue'. The transition to this viewpoint was facilitated by the revival of early moral principles, so that in taking his stand on virtue, he was not simply adopting one idea among others but really finding himself in a more intimate sense. If he had been unable to sustain the hard struggle for literary existence and to show the insensitivity and tenacity of purpose necessary for success in this field, this might well be explained (he thought) not as a result of his own inadequacy but as the sign of a moral superiority which would not allow him to sink to this degrading level; if he had in fact once taken part in the general search for worldly favours, was this not due to the corrupting influence of his Parisian environment which had temporarily stifled the promptings of his higher moral nature? Now, thanks to his reaffirmation of ethical truths which belonged to an old cultural tradition, he could bear witness to the emergence of a moral outlook which offered sound protection against outward corruption and inner uncertainty.

The extent to which Rousseau personally identifies himself with the moral viewpoint of his published writings is revealed in a number of public or semi-private declarations. In a statement published in the *Mercure de France* in November 1755 he says: 'I desire no other defence for my writings than reason and truth, and no other defence for my person than my conduct and my morals: if these props are lacking, nothing will support me; if they do support me, what have I to fear?' (*CG* ii. 242). He sees himself as a man whose private life conforms to the principles already laid down in his published writings. The fact that he is already committed to the defence of heroic virtue in ancient Rome, Sparta, and modern Geneva reinforces his determination to maintain an attitude already adopted towards his immediate environment for more personal reasons.

Perhaps this mood of heroic virtue also helps to explain a resurgence

F

of patriotic feeling at this period. Already in the first *Discours* he had invoked the theme of patriotism. Of modern educators he had said that 'the sweet name of fatherland will never strike their ear'; as for professional writers, 'they smile disdainfully at these old words of Fatherland and Religion' (ed. Havens, pp. 132–3). Personally he had always considered himself as a 'true Swiss'—a 'patriot', 'citizen', and 'republican'—whose heart was full of an ardent love of the fatherland. 'It is through living with slaves that I have felt the value of freedom' (*CG* i. 312). In *Le Verger* he affirmed that the thought of Geneva in danger was enough to bring tears to his eyes, while his visit to his native city in 1754 merely served to develop his 'republican enthusiasm'. 'There freedom is well established, government calm, citizens enlightened, firm and modest, knowing their rights and courageously maintaining them, but respecting those of others' (ii. 94). In a later letter he was to say that 'the Genevan is naturally good' (ibid. 225), while *La Nouvelle Héloïse* was also to contain the view that 'the Genevan feels himself to be naturally good'. His renewed sympathy with Geneva was given official form by the renunciation of his allegiance to the Church of Rome and the reassumption of his rights as a Genevan citizen—a gesture that had as much political and civil as religious significance since he had long ceased to be an orthodox Christian. His return to Protestantism was largely determined by 'patriotic zeal', for 'wanting to be a citizen I had to be a Protestant and return to the cult established in my fatherland' (*Conf.* 392). Perhaps we should not be justified in supposing that Rousseau thereby acquired any very accurate knowledge of the Genevan political constitution and his 'Geneva' may well have presented a fusion of idealized memories and immediate impressions, but there seems little doubt that he now proposed to associate himself quite openly with the Genevan tradition, which was, in G. Vallette's words, 'Protestant, popular and republican'. It is about this time too that he assumes the title of 'citizen of Geneva', which figures prominently on the title-page of the *Discours sur l'inégalité*—a work that was publicly dedicated to the Genevan republic.[1] The manner of this dedication (which was made to the republic rather than to its ruling oligarchy) certainly offended some of the more influential citizens by seeming to ignore their privileged position, but Rousseau's invocation of the Genevan tradition was intended to go beyond any purely local question since it was inspired by the 'purest patriotism', Geneva being eulogized

---

[1] The title first appears, says G. Vallette, in his *Lettre sur une nouvelle réfutation de son discours par un açadémicien de Dijon*, 1752.

as the only modern state really worthy of 'an honest and virtuous patriot'.

Interesting though it is as a sign of his 'patriotism', the *Dédicace* is perhaps a less noteworthy statement of his personal attitude than the long letter written to his compatriot, M. Perdriau, on the same subject (*CG* ii. 130–6). In it he explains the reasons for his having dedicated—without official permission—the second *Discours* to the republic of Geneva. In the course of this letter Rousseau gives a clear indication of the moral attitude with which he is now personally associated. He insists that his devotion to the cause of 'justice and reason' makes it impossible for him to compromise with the 'pusillanimous circumspection much relished in this age'; he prefers to show 'a general boldness which—to do good—sometimes shakes the yoke of convention'. If he is not seeking the permission of the Genevan authorities before actually dedicating his work to them, it is 'because, isolated by men, clinging to nothing in society, deprived of any kind of pretension and seeking my happiness only in that of others, I at least believe myself to be exempt from the political prejudices which cause the wisest men to adapt their judgement to the maxims most advantageous to them'. In fact he recognizes only one authority and sanction for his conduct: conscience, 'this inner, incorruptible judge which passes nothing bad and condemns nothing good, and which never deceives us when we consult it in good faith'. He is the more justified in being 'his only Censor' as he is not concerned with personal interest. 'If the detachment of a heart which values neither glory nor fortune, nor even life, can make it worthy of proclaiming the truth, I dare to believe that I have been called to this sublime vocation: it is in order to do good to men according to my capacity that I abstain from receiving any good from them, and that I cherish my poverty and my independence.'

No doubt Rousseau is here indulging in a somewhat idealized view of his role; his actual existence was far from being a perfect example of disinterested devotion to such high ethical ideals, although in this letter he was thinking mainly of his writer's vocation rather than his private life. Yet the predominance of a markedly moral attitude is very noticeable at this time and is further illustrated in a number of specific reactions. Freedom and independence tend to be identified with the maintenance of virtue and, even though his personal existence could not always express this remarkable quality, there seems no reason to doubt that he was, for the time being at least, carried away by a kind of inner exaltation which seemed to raise him above himself. Some of the emotional expansiveness which he had hitherto directed into other less moral channels is now allowed to imbue his attachment to moral principles of the Genevan kind.

It is this moral fervour which helped to give him the courage to break with Parisian society and carry out his famous reform. Of his state of mind at this period, Rousseau himself has spoken in the *Confessions*:

Until then I had been good; henceforth I became virtuous, or at least intoxicated with virtue. This intoxication had begun in my head, but it had passed into my heart. The noblest pride sprang up on the ruins of uprooted vanity. I did not play a part: I became indeed what I seemed, and for the four years at least that this effervescence lasted in all its strength, nothing great and beautiful can enter a man's heart of which I was not capable between heaven and earth. . . . I was truly transformed; my friends and acquaintances no longer recognized me (*Conf.* 416).

I am not here concerned with the well-known distinction between goodness and virtue which plays an important role in more recent discussions of Rousseau's thought;[1] it will be enough to recall that, while goodness tends to be identified with spontaneity and the natural expression of man's essential nature (and not simply of his bodily impulses and his passions), virtue, on the other hand, seems to involve an act of will and reason which causes him to subordinate much of his personality to a higher ideal—and one that may demand some limitation of his spontaneous emotions. Capricious fancies are subjected to moral principles which involve an appeal to man's heroic affirmative nature, as the example of the Ancients clearly shows.

Rousseau readily associates the idea of virtue, as the expression of heroic will, with the notion of reason and truth. In the *Confessions* he insists that the first *Discours* was already inspired by the trinity of truth, freedom, and virtue, the three concepts being understood as reinforcing one another. A letter addressed by Rousseau to the *Mercure* on the subject of his *Discours* concludes with the sentence: ' "Virtue, truth!" I constantly exclaimed, "Virtue, truth!" If anyone notices only those words, I have nothing more to say to him' (*CG* i. 319). Truth and virtue have a universal validity because they express the basic moral nature of every man who has attained authentic self-realization. That is why he can say later (1757) that 'the torch of truth' is carried 'in the depths of the soul' (*CG* iii. 350). From this point of view truth is 'moral' rather than 'metaphysical'; it is to be found in man's inner being rather than in the external reality around him; it expresses a conviction concerning

---

[1] See, for example, P. Burgelin, op. cit., *passim*.

human nature rather than the structure of the universe as a whole.[1] Hence Rousseau can see himself in the 1750's as a man of 'virtue' and at the same time as the guardian of truth who yields only to reason. If he is a 'lover of virtue', he is also 'a friend of truth'.[2]

Translated into the concrete facts of everyday existence, this virtuous independence and devotion to truth would seem to commit any man who professes such principles to a life of poverty, for the refusal of riches is a test of his sincerity. Rousseau's attitude towards money is not free from a certain ambiguity (as he himself admits),[3] but there can be no doubt that he frequently speaks of his poverty as a proof of his contempt for the enslavement involved in the possession of wealth. Perhaps his unhappy experience at Venice did not make it possible for him to say much more than 'I would rather live free and poor to the very end than make my way by such a dangerous path' [as that of soliciting for material rewards] (CG i. 257). In 1751 we find him referring to 'the riches which I despise and the grandeur which I hate' (i. 311). In 1755 he tells his Genevan correspondent, M. Jallabert: 'As I know how to live poor, I shall know now to die independent, and I wish to change neither my maxims nor my trade' (ii. 237). He gives this as a reason for his decision to remain in France instead of settling in Geneva, for near Paris he can lead a 'peaceful, solitary and perfectly free life' which has the added advantage of the charms of intimate friendship. He may be poor, he tells Mme d'Epinay in the following year, but 'he is not for sale' (ii. 263). He will be able to say to Saint-Lambert in 1757: 'I despise money; I cannot put a price on my freedom' (iii. 255).

Indifference to money and material advancement leads to a rejection

---

[1] Clearly the division is not absolute since Rousseau's 'system' stresses the link between man's moral nature and the beneficence of the universal order; it is, however, to the more 'spiritual' aspects of the natural world that man's moral nature can actively respond.

[2] Cf. CG ii. 134 and iv. 248, 249.

[3] While professing contempt for money, he acknowledges 'an inclination to avarice' (Conf. 206). Elsewhere (pp. 36–37) he gives an interesting analysis of his attitude: the chief drawback to money is that it spoils the 'purity' of his pleasures since it introduces— or threatens to introduce—an awkward intermediary between the thing and its enjoyment. That is why 'it is useless in itself; it has to be transformed to be enjoyed'. The general effect of society and its conventions is to place obstacles in the way of immediate enjoyment by making pleasures depend on money. (Primitive man, on the other hand, confronts nature directly and needs only physical effort to enjoy its benefits. Similarly an ideal society, such as the one described in La Nouvelle Héloïse, attaches far more value to the production of goods (not luxuries) for consumption than to the accumulation of wealth and capital.) On the other hand, Rousseau cannot dispense with money since, in modern life, it is an indispensable means—ultimately the only means—of security and independence. For an illuminating discussion of Rousseau's attitude towards this question see Jean Starobinski, op. cit., pp. 131 ff., and some useful comments in OC i. 1250–1.

of those worldly values which cause other men to follow the demands of 'pride' and 'glory'. Refusing to be affected by 'men's opinion', he begins to profess 'a profound indifference to all that is called brilliant' (*CG* i. 377). No doubt it was easy for a man who had failed to make a name for himself to say in 1743 that he was 'without ambition, self-interest and any desire to shine' (i. 188), and for a time he was to forget this noble principle as he suddenly found himself dazzled by fame. But as soon as the first emotional effects of this change of fortune had passed, he reverted to his former attitude, insisting that he would henceforth follow the principle of 'honour', showing himself as a frank, courageous man, 'ignorant of these roundabout ways whose vain subtleties transform our weaknesses into so many virtues' (i. 163). He is an 'upright, frank man' with a heart 'as transparent as crystal', one who 'will speak the truth without bitterness and without flattery'. He is impatient of those polite conventions which merely serve to conceal true character. 'Formulae, compliments and all that appertains to etiquette are unbearable to me' (312). But, as he tells M. Perdriau, a certain boldness is required to break with such well-established habits. In an age like theirs it requires courage to tell the truth because so few people are willing to hear it. Only a man prepared to follow the promptings of 'this inner incorruptible judge'—that conscience of which he had also spoken in his letter to M. Perdriau—was worthy to proclaim the truths that could set humanity once more on the road from which it had so tragically strayed. As he listened to the call of a conscience which brought him back from the deceptions of the world to an awareness of his real nature, Rousseau realized that he must abandon the tumult of life in order to seek that solitude and silence in which the true voice of the inner self could be effectively heard.

This heroic moral attitude owed much of its consistency to the fact that it was developed in opposition to an unsympathetic environment and a social situation which Rousseau considered to be both corrupt and frustrating. Although it provided him with firm support against the false values of his age and allowed him to appeal to the principles of a cultural tradition which he thought his French contemporaries had either forgotten or ignored, this moral outlook could not satisfy the spontaneous needs of a personality so frequently dominated by the quite different demands of a highly emotive sensibility. Sometimes his own professed adherence to moral ideals was to be undermined or perverted by the subtle pressure of selfish emotions, the notion of 'duty' being invoked to defend extremely equivocal behaviour. A typical instance is the reason put forward in the *Confessions* for the desertion of Mme Larnage, sacrificed, he insists, to a high-minded ethical resolve, but in reality to sordid sexual jealousy.[1] His later behaviour towards Saint-Lambert at the time of his infatuation with Mme d'Houdetot was also quite reprehensible. Much of his moral idealism remained merely potential and never went beyond the realm of intention; too often he claimed credit for intentions that were never carried out, thus seeming to suggest that his admiration for virtue was by itself enough to justify him.

Nowhere do the complexity and ambiguity of Rousseau's personal outlook, with its strange and often confused intermingling of psychological and moral factors, become more evident than in his attitude towards his children, abandoned as soon as they were born to a Foundlings' Home.[2] After being off-handedly explained as an irresponsible gesture due to the pernicious example of contemporary society, his conduct became a subject of bitter remorse that tormented him all the more because he could never bring himself to admit the full extent of his wrong-doing. Eventually the actions themselves—for there were, according to his own account, five children shamefully treated in this way—were openly acknowledged, but instead of taking full responsibility upon himself, he at first blamed the society—and especially the aristocracy—of his day for his children's unhappy fate. The famous letter written to Mme de Francueil in 1751 makes this attitude only too tragically plain. If he has not married, he tells his correspondent, 'blame your unjust laws'. But this does prevent nature from wanting even the poverty-stricken Jean-Jacques to have children since 'the earth produces the wherewithal to feed everybody: but it is the condition of the rich, your condition, which steals my children's bread from people like me' (*CG* i. 309). His growing resentment against 'the great' and his animadversions against 'that hardness of heart given by wealth' clearly owe a great deal to his own unacknowledged guilt.

At a rather different psychological level, his moral criticism of his social environment was partly due to a desire to overcome the acute anxiety generated by his earlier efforts to win recognition. Although

[1] Cf. F. C. Green, op. cit., p. 62.

[2] Much has of course been written (often needlessly) on this subject, but in spite of ingenious arguments and impassioned pleas, there seems no adequate reason for doubting the substantial truth of Rousseau's own account. The first child appears to have been born in 1746. Cf. F. C. Green, op. cit., pp. 87–94. See also a useful note in J. S. Spink's edition of the *Rêveries* (Paris, 1948), p. 179, note 1, and the discussion in *OC* i. 1416–22.

the sudden achievement of success did enhance his self-esteem and convince him that he was not a 'fool', it also helped to increase his anxiety by threatening to bring him into still closer contact with society. As long as he could 'write and hide'—an attitude which he felt to accord with his deepest personal needs—he was prepared to adopt an apparently simple and courageous moral viewpoint, but the threat of being forced to accept some kind of social responsibility immediately filled him with alarm, so that even the problem of earning his living seemed fraught with danger. Characteristic of his reactions at this time was his attitude towards the post of cashier offered to him by the wealthy M. de Francueil and considered by his friends to be a lucrative sinecure, or at least a fairly easy way of gaining his livelihood; but Rousseau admitted that the responsibility of looking after somebody else's money worried him so much that he fell ill. 'The cares, the mental anxiety which this charge gave me made me feel that I was not meant to be a cashier, and I do not doubt that my agitation during this [Francueil's] absence contributed to the illness from which I suffered after his return' (*Conf.* 360–1). He found it far more satisfying to adopt a trade which brought him lower financial remuneration but greater personal independence—that of copying music 'at so much a page'. As the son of a Genevan artisan who was proud to live by the work of his hands, he found a means of livelihood which enabled him to bring his desires into harmony with his principles.

A final incentive to make a definite break with Parisian life was provided by his rapidly deteriorating physical condition which suddenly gave his personal decisions a particular urgency. Already subjected to a severe attack of retention in Venice, he now became so ill that he had to take to his bed. On consulting the famous Dr. Morand, he was told that he had only six months to live. Personal decisions thus became a matter of extreme importance and he soon felt that there could be no doubt as to the course of action he must take. 'I gave up for ever all idea of fortune and advancement. Determined to spend the little time that remained to me in independence and poverty, I applied all the strength of my soul to break the fetters of opinion and to do courageously what seemed good to me, without bothering in any way about men's judgement' (*Conf.* 362).

Equally important was the wonderful sense of relief afforded by the thought of an existence henceforth freed from the anxieties of social life: no longer would he have to worry about 'falling short of social conventions', for he would henceforth follow a mode of existence determined by the needs of his own nature rather than the dictates of society. Away from the constricting influence of people who were themselves the slaves of convention, he would be free to indulge in some of those expansive tendencies which he had already enjoyed at privileged moments of his life but which had become increasingly restricted by the restless striving of self-seeking ambition. Long before his actual decision to carry out a personal reform, he had formed the habit of taking lonely walks in the country, and it was in the course of one of them that he had meditated the essentials of his second *Discours*. In 'shunning a too numerous society' he felt that 'he was punishing neither himself nor anyone else' (*CG* ii. 63). Withdrawal from society was not simply a means of retreating from others but also of finding an opportunity for recovering the freedom and independence he deemed necessary for true self-affirmation. This freedom also had a certain ethical value because it did not mean mere abandonment to the 'laziness' of his temperament or the desire to escape from anxiety-provoking situations but expressed a determined effort to proclaim the validity of moral principles; it represented the outlook of a man who defied his corrupt and degraded environment in the name of superior virtue. If he lived 'isolated from men and holding to nothing in society', it was simply because he was now conscious of being destined for a higher role—that of a man responsible for upholding a forgotten ideal. Rousseau did not thereby merely wish to teach a lesson to others; he also affirmed his own real self against the claims of an artificial society which was judged to be incapable of providing an adequate basis for his personal existence. He sought the 'free, virtuous' existence of an independent Rousseau who, no longer a slave to his surroundings, would henceforth be a 'self-sufficient' man content to live in accordance with his own freely chosen moral ideal.

The famous reform of the 1750s, which began with a simplification of his material existence—he sold his expensive clothes and social accoutrements, renounced civilized luxuries and proposed henceforth to earn his daily bread by the work of his hands—and continued with a re-organization of his moral life, was obviously inspired, as Rousseau himself recognized, by a variety of motives. Ostensibly, as the result of 'heroism and virtue', it had a noble moral purpose since it allowed him to bring his desires in accord with his principles, but, by freeing him from the anxiety of social life, it also opened the way to a genuinely spontaneous and free existence which meant that what he *ought* to do corresponded with what he *wanted* to do. In fact, it led ultimately to a modification of the ethical attitude of which it was intended to be a logical culmination. The heroic morality he had professed during this period, though rooted in the Genevan outlook of his early life, represented only one side of his nature and was in many ways opposed to the natural impulse of his sensibility: it was largely sustained by the need to defend himself against the harmful psychological and moral pressures of social life. His retirement into the country having at last enabled him to escape from these pernicious influences, he felt that he was no longer called upon to face the particular problems still confronting those people who had to grapple with the task of adapting themselves to society. No doubt when the occasion arose, he could still adopt a strongly puritanical tone, especially in his published writings: the necessity of attacking some particular evil of civilized life (such as Voltaire's insidious project of trying to establish a theatre in Geneva) could provoke a strong moral protest (as the *Lettre à d'Alembert* shows), but in his personal life the austere character of his moral ideal gradually gave way to a desire to express those expansive needs which had not been satisfied by his reading of the 'heroic' moral writers of antiquity like Plutarch. Rousseau himself well indicates his change of mood when he says that 'until then virtuous indignation had been my substitute for Apollo: it now gave way to gentleness of soul' (*Conf.* 495). At last life at the Hermitage enabled him to satisfy those longings which had been frustrated for so many years.

Perhaps one of the most significant consequences of this reform was the way it freed him from the tyranny of that clock-time to which every social being had to submit. 'The moment when, giving up all ambition in order to live from day to day, he got rid of his watch was one of the pleasantest in his life. "Thank Heaven!" he exclaimed in a transport of joy, "I shall no longer need to know what time it is." '[1] In Rousseau's mind, thought of the future had always been frought with anxiety. If he had always envied the primitive man it was because of his complete indifference to any kind of *prévoyance*: such a being is never 'outside' himself, striving towards some uncertain future, for he is completely identified with what he is in the immediate present. Although Rousseau was perfectly well aware that modern man could never return to this state of primal innocence, the 'primitive' side of his nature caused him to associate happiness with the enjoyment of a 'kind of prolonged present'—a genuinely spontaneous and free existence which permitted him to be truly himself.

[1] *Dial.* 845–6; cf. *Conf.* 363.

Perhaps it is this mood which also helps to explain the change of emphasis in the second *Discours*. Whereas the first had been sustained by a tone of righteous indignation which contrasted the heroic virtue of the ancients with the decadent morality of modern times, the second lays greater stress on the unhappiness of civilized man whose divided, tormented nature contrasts so markedly with the independent, self-sufficient, and unified nature of primitive man. Rousseau was certainly not suggesting that man should return to this primitive condition or even that, in a strictly human sense, it was a desirable form of happiness (since it obviously excluded the development of rational, moral and social potentialities without which, for good or ill, a really mature human being could never lead a full life), but he did look nostalgically towards a state of being so natural and simple as to allow a spontaneous and immediate expression of existence. The savage man and the reformed Jean-Jacques at least had this in common that both were freed from the tyranny of *prévoyance* and all anxious concern with the morrow: their existence—though lived at different levels—was based on the whole-hearted enjoyment of an undivided present.

Because it expressed a movement of liberation and expansion the reform of the 1750s thus led to a significant change in Rousseau's existence. Being in no sense intended as a prelude to a life of ascetic discipline, it induced him to preoccupy himself more and more with the question of personal *enjoyment*. Able at last to indulge in the direct and spontaneous expression of long-pent-up emotions, he now had the satisfaction of feeling that he was himself in all immediacy and completeness. This certainly did not mean that he would cease to be 'virtuous', but that henceforth virtue and happiness would tend to coincide. Hitherto, in the stern struggle for moral survival in a corrupt society, virtue had appeared to involve an act of will, a rational decision to resist the soul-destroying influences of the environment; the desire to denounce all the evils of civilization and to overcome his own inner anxiety had exasperated his need to feel morally secure in the principles of an ideal self. Now that this pressure was removed and he had 'rooted out' social prejudices from his heart, virtue and happiness seemed to be capable of much greater harmony. The mere fact of being able to live in the present, to experience all the fullness of immediate experience and to enjoy 'the charms of complete freedom' was enough to make him forget —for a time at least—the heroic moral ideals of the Parisian years.[1]

Moreover, he had always believed that the true aim of human existence

---

[1] Cf. Rousseau's own account of his reactions in the *Confessions*, Book VIII.

was happiness. Men were born to be happy, he had affirmed in 1740 (*CG* i. 367–8). Now more clearly than ever, he could 'live free and happy in his own way' (*Conf.* 367). Moreover, he had already indicated in his early poems the kind of happiness for which he craved. In 1742 he had been able to express his conviction that happiness could only be found in the quietness of the countryside, far from the noise and bustle of the towns. 'A good book, a friend, freedom, peace'—these had been some of the things he had longed for in those early years. *Le Verger de Mme de Warens* had tended to stress the same idea, for in that 'charming solitude and peaceful refuge' he had been able to say that 'each day he enjoyed himself' to the full; at last he had been able to experience 'man's true happiness'. Here we find little Genevan austerity, even though the poem does end with a reference to 'Stoic pride'. In Paris itself he had been able—thanks to the company of Thérèse—to savour the pleasures of a simple domestic life with all its 'friendship, confidence, intimacy and gentleness of soul' (*Conf.* 354). His ambition too had been largely concerned with creating material conditions which would one day enable him to enjoy 'that blissful rural leisure' for which his heart ever craved, even in the midst of city life. His removal to the Hermitage inevitably reawakened his desire to find again this idyllic happiness which he had so rashly thrown away in the years of social and literary ambition. His first impulse, on arriving at his new home, had been to take 'those lonely walks' which would enable him to abandon himself to 'the impression of rural objects'. Henceforth his aim was to lead 'a peaceful, lonely and perfectly free life' (*CG* ii. 237), and when he came to write the *Confessions*, he was to look back to these days as a time when he could lead 'an independent, even and simple life'. 'I felt that I was made to live in seclusion in the country; it was impossible for me to live happy anywhere else' (*Conf.* 401). Although, therefore, the heroic ideal associated with the principles of poverty, frankness, and the like constituted in some sense the moral basis of his rejection of society, it tended to be restricted to his role as a writer, since the positive aim of his actual existence was towards a life in which the notions of happiness and enjoyment played a preponderant role.

In spite of the deep personal satisfaction derived from the adoption of this new way of life, Jean-Jacques was unwilling to accept its purely subjective implications. Being convinced, as a thinker, that his task was to recover the true 'natural' man so tragically obscured by the present order, he considered that the 'man of nature' was as yet a potential being who would emerge only after a careful diagnosis of existing social evils. The enlightened philosopher's first duty was to withdraw from the stifling influence of town-life and provide men with a concrete example of the type of existence they should henceforth follow. In leaving Paris for the country, therefore, Jean-Jacques believed that he was not merely satisfying a personal need but also providing men with an illustration of the type of life they should follow, far from those cities which were, as he was later to say in *Émile*, 'the abyss of the human race'. Already *Le Verger de Mme de Warens* (1739) and the *Épître à M. de l'Étang* (1749) had compared the delights of the country with the 'sad boredom' and 'din' of Parisian life. The benefits of the country were not merely those of self-indulgent solitude, for 'it is in the country that we learn to love and serve humanity, while people learn only to despise it in the towns' (*CG* iii. 29). This participation in simple rural life, with its unsophisticated pleasures, such as those provided by the feeling for nature and the enjoyment of plain but wholesome food, was particularly suitable to a man who, like himself, had at last discovered 'his true vocation' (ii. 355). (Later on *La Nouvelle Héloïse* was to advocate a return to country life.) For the time being Rousseau had the satisfaction of feeling that he was leading a life that was not merely agreeable, but in some way *exemplary*.

A simple action in itself, the reform of the 1750s was thus inspired by complex motives. Whereas Rousseau saw it basically as a means of setting his own life in harmony with his principles and of finding a mode of existence which freed him from 'personal subjection', his enemies dismissed it as the expression of mere hypocrisy or misanthropy. His eulogists were later to see it as a remarkable example of moral courage. Clearly neither view is true if taken by itself. Both the criticism and the eulogy fail to take into account the close interdependence of the psychological and moral aspects of the action. If Rousseau was fitting practice to precept, he was also seeking escape from a purely psychological conflict occasioned by his inability to adapt himself to the demands of social life as well as from a mode of existence which his physical ailment made almost unbearable. In his franker moments he himself was willing to admit this fact, sometimes with an almost brutal directness. Yet he held at the same time that this personal problem afforded him an opportunity of gaining valuable insights into man's essential moral nature. Only because he himself was to some extent an exception was he able to attain this deeper understanding of the human condition. In seeking to escape from the intolerable anxiety associated with social life and in striving for this 'free and independent existence' he was also putting himself (such was at least his hope) in a better position for fulfilling the role of the 'friend of truth'. Yet it was the actual way of life thus created for himself rather than the secret and intimate feelings evoked by this new-found solitude that was particularly relevant to his function as a writer. As far as his own personal existence was concerned, the strictly ethical aspects of his new situation were for the moment less pressing, for in this retreat he still had work to do and friends to love. The truly moral and universal implications of his new way of life were easily forgotten in his eagerness to savour all the delights of his newly won freedom; at last he could be himself and, above all, he was now free to worship at the shrine of those two 'idols' for which he was willing to sacrifice so much—'love' and 'friendship'. It was not until he had passed through the harrowing experience of perceiving the vanity of all such worship that he would be able to face the full consequences—both moral and personal—of this radical separation from society.

3

'TWO IDOLS': LOVE AND FRIENDSHIP

In spite of its great importance for Rousseau's later development, the reform of the 1750s did not lead to an immediate increase in self-awareness because its primary emphasis was upon action rather than reflection, enjoyment rather than understanding: it was intended as a prelude to a truly expansive mode of personal existence that would find its fullest expression in his relations with others. Separation from the many would lead (he hoped) to closer intimacy with the few; he wanted to lose the crowd only to discover his friends. As far as his intellectual activities were concerned, he hoped to direct his mental energy upon the dissemination of truths deemed beneficial to humanity at large rather than upon a systematic examination of his own inner life. No doubt didactic thought and personal existence would continue to interact as they had done from the beginning (and would not he himself, he implied, be a striking example of the validity of his teaching?), but the personality thus involved was not so much the unique, contradictory being of the individual Rousseau as the ideal ego whose significance depended upon an understanding of 'man' in general. Moreover, introspection was held in check by his confident belief that he was now in a position to develop possibilities that had so far been cruelly frustrated by life in 'society': henceforth he hoped to be able to live out in actual experience the ideal of which he had so far merely dreamed—perfect intimacy with devoted friends. Nor had he abandoned the thought that in love too he might find a new form of happiness. Therefore, before considering his first attempt at rigorous self-analysis, we have to deal briefly with these two forms of personal relationship, for it is in the frustration of these that the impulse to self-examination partly originated.

I. *Friendship*

Rousseau did not realize the full extent of his dependence on his friends until he had withdrawn from immediate contact with them; it was only when he was left to himself in his rural solitude that he began to feel the complete effect of his emotional need. Friendship, it is true, had always been an important ideal, for its delights had already been extolled in the *Épître à M. Parisot*, but his subsequent wandering life had made it difficult for him to give substance to this early dream. Indeed it is one of the many paradoxes of Rousseau's life that, in spite of his constantly professed devotion to the ideal of friendship, he rarely succeeded in establishing a permanent and intimate attachment to particular persons, his closest friendships tending to break up through misunderstandings and quarrels. After he had settled in Paris, and especially after he had begun to experience the irksomeness of social life, he felt a resurgence of his need for friendship. His 'hatred of society' was counterbalanced by his 'liking for his friends' (*CG* ii. 30). As he says in 1754, 'the only fellowship that seems desirable to me is the one that we maintain with our friends, and its enjoyment brings me too much happiness for me to regret my relations with high society' (ii. 63). It will also be recalled that one of his main reasons for refusing to settle in Geneva was his desire to remain with his Parisian friends. Writing from Geneva in 1754 he says: 'Although I am living in a free country, in my own country, although I am entertained and fondly received by my fellow-citizens, it is not without pleasure that I think of the moment when I shall once again be in Paris in the midst of the small number of true friends whom I have left there' (ii. 89–90). In the following year a letter to M. Jallabert emphasizes the same point. 'It seems that, in spite of my most ardent desires, I shall end my days in Paris, for the peaceful, lonely and perfectly free life that I lead there is not without its charms. The only bonds that keep me there are those of friendship: do I not thus have more than freedom itself?' (ii. 237). In 1757 he was to tell Mme d'Houdetot: 'I feel more than ever that sublime virtue and sacred friendship are the sovereign good that men must try to reach if they are to be happy' (iii. 162). Of himself he could say in the *Confessions* that he was 'born for friendship' (362), while in his correspondence he insists that he knew and sought only one kind of happiness—friendship. 'What I hunger for is a friend; I know of no other need in which I am not self-sufficient' (iii. 314). In 1760, when he was to look back upon his search for a true friend as a mere 'castle in the air', he wrote: 'I imagine no other true happiness in life than an unqualified intimacy' (v. 304).

Rousseau's attitude towards friendship was very much influenced by his desire to satisfy the deep expansive needs of his sensibility. What he particularly enjoyed were the wonderful opportunities thus provided for mutual *épanchements*: he loved to 'unburden himself with another' and feel that his friends and he could experience the 'sweetness of weeping together'. 'A continual need to unburden myself at every moment puts my heart on my lips.' 'Never', he told his publisher Rey, 'did a man who unburdened his heart in mine regret his honesty and frankness' (*CG* iv. 3). The value of any particular friendship, therefore, is to be tested by its capacity to satisfy an intense emotional—not a mental—need: Rousseau is not concerned with establishing intellectual communication but with finding an outlet for his feelings; it is his heart, not his mind, that needs the other person. 'Although I find ordinary human intercourse hateful', he was to tell Malesherbes, 'intimate friendship is very precious to me, because it involves no obligations: one follows one's heart and all is done' (*LM* 1132).

For Jean-Jacques, therefore, friendship is not simply one human relationship among others, but an experience which causes two persons to abandon themselves to each other with complete spontaneity, giving everything and holding nothing back. He cannot accept anything less than absolute devotion: 'He who is not passionately for me is not worthy of me', he writes in language reminiscent of Christ's. He admits the impossibility of moderation and in this respect his attitude towards friendship links up with the 'all or nothing' aspect of his sensibility to which attention has already been called. 'I have never been able to steer a middle course in my attachments, and simply fulfil my social obligations. I have always been everything or nothing' (*Conf.* 522). He is incapable of the half-hearted, limited attachment of the man who is merely on good terms with 'acquaintances': he has no time for acquaintances because 'his heart does not know how to give itself by halves' (*Conf.* 616). He felt his personal tragedy to be that of a man who, though born with an 'expansive' soul and 'exquisite faculties' capable of giving such an idealistic expression to his overwhelming need for love, would have to die without ever having realized these possibilities in real life.

How was it possible that with a naturally expansive soul, for which living was the same as loving, I, who was so well fitted to be one myself, should not have found until then a friend who was completely mine, a true friend? How was it possible that with such passionate senses, with a heart so full of love, I should not have been consumed at least once by its fire for a specific object? Devoured by the need to love, without ever having been able to satisfy it, I saw that I was approaching the portals of old age and dying without having lived (*Conf.* 426).

It was the very loftiness of his ideal which doomed him to bitter

G

frustration and disappointment. 'I was happy in my retreat; solitude is not a burden to me; I have little fear of destitution, am indifferent to the world's neglect, bear my ills patiently; but to love and discover only ungrateful hearts, that I find unbearable' (*CG* iii. 21).

Since for Rousseau feelings are the only test by which the quality of friendship can be judged, other factors may be not merely irrelevant but positively harmful. The function of friendship is not the normal one of companionship and personal reciprocity, but the fulfilment of an overriding emotional craving which usually takes the form of heartfelt *épanchements*. This means the elimination of all intermediaries between the impulse and its satisfaction. He shows, for example, an almost obsessive preoccupation with the idea of friendship as a relation which excludes all thought of mutual service and obligation. 'Gratitude and friendship cannot co-exist in my heart' (*CG* ii. 25). 'All your eagerness and zeal to obtain for me things that I don't want move me little. I want only friendship; that is the only thing that I am refused! ... Callous and hard man! two tears shed on my bosom would have been worth more to me than the kingdom of this world' (iii. 51). In more moderate language he writes to Mme d'Houdetot.

Self-love, like the friendship which is but a part of it, has no other law than the feeling which inspires it; we do everything for our friend as for ourselves, not out of duty, but with delight; all the services which we render him are benefits which we give ourselves; all the gratitude inspired by those which we receive from him is a fond token that his heart responds to ours. That is what befits all friendship. As for me, I admit that I am more discriminating. Consumed by the good of loving and being loved, and indifferent to all the rest, I do not want my friends to be more worried about my poverty than I am myself; but let them love me as I am; I do not want them to transform their attachment into officious attentions, but into feelings; I want them to reveal their friendship by signs which are so much a part of it that they can have no other motive. That is why, of all the marks of friendship, services are for me the least valuable, for any honest man gives them to all and sundry, and merit alone is entitled to expect them from humanity. That is why, of all services, I set least store by those which are drawn from the purse, especially when they are public. For of all kinds of sacrifices money is the one that costs least to give and most to receive. Thus, between two friends, the giver is undoubtedly very much beholden to the recipient; without friendship a host of questionable intentions can corrupt the purity of the kindness: vanity, ostentation, the interest of acquiring a slave cheaply and of arousing a great gratitude by means of small kindnesses, can play their part in this sham generosity. Is it then merely a question of pursuing, money in hand, a man who has no care for it and sets more value on an hour of his time and freedom than all the treasures in this world? . . . O my friend, whoever you may be, if there is in the world a heart made to be mine and to feel all that it can inspire in me, abandon all this array of services and love me; do not build me a house in your lands and then visit me no more as you say to yourself 'I have him,[1] and have no further need of cultivating him'. Build me one in the depths of your heart, for it is there that I shall fix my abode, it is there that I wish to dwell my whole life long, and be no more tempted to leave it than you are to drive me out. Let us constantly seek each other; let me read in your eyes the joy which my presence causes you; let us take scores of delightful walks on which the sun goes down all too soon after a day spent in innocence and simplicity.[2] Console me in my troubles, unburden your own in my bosom, in order that our very sorrows may be a source of pleasure, and that our life together may be woven from acts of mutual kindness and true marks of friendship. In all that, what matters difference of fortune and rank save to make two friends still more worthy of each other's esteem by enabling them both to forget their wealth and their poverty? Friendship does not reckon services, but feelings, and the one who has loved the other more is the real benefactor (*CG* iii. 231–2).

This letter has been quoted at some length because it goes to the heart of Rousseau's attitude. Friendship, in its perfect form, expresses a direct and immediate confrontation of two personalities; its spontaneous sincerity immediately vanishes as soon as it becomes involved with material considerations or external principles of any kind.[3]

It may be granted that Rousseau's reactions are at least partly inspired by genuine concern for a disinterested and idealistic conception of friendship as an experience free from all considerations of self-interest. But a closer examination of his attitude reveals that its simple idealism conceals a certain complexity of outlook. Obviously in ordinary life the performance of services may demand the sacrifice of time, pleasure or money, as well as the subordination of one's own desires to a willingness to perform an unpleasant task, which, because it is inspired by affection, is carried out without complaint. This, in its turn, usually implies that the person to whom the service is rendered will, if the need arises, be prepared to make the same sacrifices on his friend's behalf. Rousseau, however, is quite unwilling to admit this

[1] This idea, expressed in the same words, is to play a very important role in his quarrel with Hume. Cf. *infra*, p. 204.

[2] He is here referring to Mme d'Houdetot.

[3] Cf. also *CG* iii. 255, where he says: 'I always separate possessions from the person, I do not see that he who gives money gives anything of his own.' See also *CG* iii. 235, 260, for a development of the same idea.

kind of reciprocity. For him the only test is feeling, and, if the spontaneous inclination is lacking, no action is required. He does not want
services from others because at heart he does not want to be called upon
to perform services for them. The mere knowledge that he is being
placed under an obligation is enough to upset him, especially when it
is for something that he does not want. He admits that for 'services
which are dear to him' he is the 'most grateful of men', but if anyone
seeks to 'bind him with millions', 'his heart is as free as it was before'.
'Why', he goes on to ask with some intensity, 'should I owe return
for something that does not give me the slightest pleasure?' (*CG* iii.
234). The service which the other performs without his consent he
interprets as a demand to be rejected at all costs.

If the bestowing of such services creates nothing but resentment and
suspicion in Rousseau's mind, how willing is he, on the other hand, to
respond to the slightest gesture of affection and emotion! The man who
spends time and energy on Rousseau's behalf will receive few thanks
but he who sheds a tear on his bosom will be greeted with the greatest
effusion. However deeply felt his resentment against a person, it can
always be overcome, he insists, by a 'gentle word'. Never, he says time
and again, was he able to 'resist an affectionate gesture'. 'There was
never a fire in his heart that could not be extinguished by a single tear'
(*CG* iii. 45). He was to make the same point in the *Confessions*, where
he affirms that he was always 'subjugated' by 'the slightest signs of
affection'.

The genuinely idealistic aspect of Rousseau's views was complicated
by the presence of psychological factors of a different kind. His desire
for immediate, complete emotional identification with others was apt to
take the form of a naïve, uncritical infatuation with persons of whose
real character he was quite ignorant; the intensity of his enthusiasm
was often quite disproportionate to the quality of its recipient. He had
only to see Bâcle, Venture de Villeneuve, and Sauttersheim to feel an
overwhelming need to attach himself to them. In his friendships he
was, as Professor Hendel has already insisted, highly suggestible.[1] But
this excessive dependence on friends was often accompanied by an
acute anxiety which made him seek constant reassurance and consolation. To Mme d'Épinay's suggestion that he should be less sensitive to
criticism he replied: 'Your advice is sound and henceforth I shall make
use of it; I shall love my friends without anxiety, but without coldness.
I shall see them with enthusiasm, but I shall know how to do without

[1] *Jean-Jacques Rousseau Moralist* (London, 1934).

them. I feel that they will never cease to be equally dear to me, and that I have lost for them only this excessive delicacy which made me sometimes importunate and always dissatisfied' (*CG* ii. 282). Alas! Jean-Jacques did not live up to these sensible resolutions, for he was unable to shake off an anxiety whose presence he himself was the first to acknowledge: he was tormented by the nagging fear that his friends would not consider him good enough to merit their esteem. In order to quell this anxiety he needed constantly to be reassured of their feelings towards him. It was the very magnitude of his emotional need which made him attach so much importance to relationships which others accept with equanimity.

Rousseau's undue emphasis on the emotional satisfactions of friendship shows that feelings which, when they are actually being experienced, seem self-sufficient, really form part of a deeper and more complex personal intention. We have already noted how his sensibility, with its striving for immediate, total gratification, was complicated by developmental influences which induced him to make himself the object of other people's attention, yet in such a way as to cause him to relate his attitude to others to some form of self-evaluation: if he wants to enjoy close intimacy with the other, it is largely because the latter forms part of Jean-Jacques's own need to establish a certain relationship with himself. The outpouring of emotion always refers—however indirectly—to a certain image of himself which he wishes to develop in his own heart. It is significant, for example, that his seemingly exclusive concern with direct feeling is accompanied by an insistence on the idea that friendship is inseparable from 'the most perfect independence'. 'I want to preserve my freedom in my attachments' (*CG* vi. 29). 'I do not want to alienate the freedom of my person' (iii. 29). His freedom, he insists, is 'not for sale'. This means that the other must always be to some extent subordinate to the demands of Rousseau's own personality. It is because the other is necessary to the preservation or elaboration of this private image of himself that Jean-Jacques clings so desperately to the ideal of friendship.

Rousseau's over-anxious dependence on his friends suggests that the sense of insecurity and unacknowledged guilt which had tormented him periodically during the Parisian phase of his existence could not be overcome by the mere renunciation of society: these deep-seated feelings were no doubt aggravated by the presence of a hostile environment which was sometimes arraigned as the cause of all his misfortunes, but they obviously had personal roots which a mere change of physical conditions could not eradicate. Though at first rejoicing in his rural retreat and savouring to the full the delightful sensations stimulated by country life—and did he not tell his friend Lenieps that a man must indeed be 'sick in mind' who could not enjoy such wonderful solitude? —he was soon to discover that he had carried over into his personal relations with intimate friends some of the psychological problems which he had at first thought to be bound up with social life alone.

The peculiar nature of the feelings still disturbing him is indicated by his reiteration of the great importance of esteem in friendship: he has constantly to be upheld in the idea that he is worthy of esteem. If he attaches so much importance to friendship, it is at least partly because of his need to strengthen his belief in his own worth. His 'just pride', he says, is enough to preserve him against all forms of unkindness save contempt: he cannot bear to feel that he is being despised. 'Let my friends always speak to me freely and frankly. They can say anything: I permit them everything except contempt' (*CG* iii. 44). The mere fact of being tormented by secret feelings of inadequacy and guilt makes it necessary for him to seek explicit reassurance of his true merits. The severest criticism that he will allow is a certain gentle 'scolding' which he interprets as a sign of affection.

The role of the other in Rousseau's conception of friendship is thus plainly ambiguous: he is desired and loved as the one who can bring comfort and reassurance, but he is also feared as a potential threat to personal security. It is the very intensity of Jean-Jacques's need for love which causes him to transform love into potential hatred. This is very apparent in his discussion of esteem which is frequently linked up with the idea of domination and enslavement. His greatest fear is that his friends will want to force him to be 'happy in their way rather than his.' This is what makes him so sensitive to presents and services, which are always liable to become instruments of degradation and humiliation: by doing Jean-Jacques a service the friend runs the risk of making him seem inferior. This was his real grudge against Diderot. The latter's great crime (in Rousseau's eyes) was to have affected 'an air of superiority which displeased him (Rousseau)': Diderot was 'so proud of his behaviour' that Jean-Jacques felt humiliated. His fatal mistake was to have laid down the line of conduct Jean-Jacques should take. 'I want my friends to be my friends and not my masters; let them advise me without seeking to rule me; let them have all kinds of claims upon my heart, but none upon my freedom' (*CG* iii. 44). Anyone who ignores this axiomatic condition of friendship is setting himself up as a master who, by treating Jean-Jacques as a servant or slave, forfeits all right to be considered as a friend.

The effect of this mood was to blur the distinction between deliberate ill will and mere tactlessness. When he insisted that Diderot was an 'aggressor who obstinately sought to oppose him' and 'govern him like a child', Rousseau was probably misinterpreting the actions of an officious friend as those of a spiteful enemy. Moreover, it is the misfortune of highly sensitive characters like Rousseau that they are often susceptible to a certain hostility which is merely latent in those with whom they come into contact since it is for the most part subordinated to more positive and friendly feelings. Diderot's officiousness did perhaps contain more resentment than *le bon Denis* was willing to admit, for he may have been somewhat envious of the solitary and free Rousseau who had dared to throw off the restraints of a society to which he himself was too completely and tiresomely chained, but this was probably only one element—and not the most important—in his feelings for Rousseau, and it is doubtful whether his reference to the 'wickedness' of the 'solitary' man was intended to have the insidious personal implications which Jean-Jacques attributed to it.

This growing preoccupation with the idea of 'enslavement' and 'degradation' rapidly diminishes the already limited satisfactions which Rousseau obtains from friendship: he begins to lose his capacity for enjoying moments of unrestricted expansiveness, and since this, in its turn, helps to thrust him back into himself, there is an increase in inner tension. Characteristically he tends to solve the problem of mounting anxiety by attributing its origin to others. Probably his inability to 'resist affectionate gestures' helps to prepare the way for his later belief in the hostility of others. If the latter show 'gentleness', then Rousseau is at once ready to forget his earlier resentment and he allows himself to be 'subjugated with his usual weakness'. Yet this subjugation is not the result of mature reflection, but a direct consequence of his inability 'to say a disobliging word to anyone' (*Conf.* 369). But to give way in this manner cannot bring him any permanent satisfaction, for it does not remove the real cause of his original resentment and, in the end, serves only to remind him of the very weakness it at first seemed to conceal. It, therefore, remains necessary for him to make yet another effort to calm his anxiety and, since he cannot do this by acknowledging his own inadequacy (for such an admission might well lead to a catastrophic breakdown of his whole personality), he attributes the source of his unhappiness to other people. The effect of all this is to transform the affectionate gestures of others, as well as his own, into a means of building up resentment against his former friends. It is surely no accident that the former loved persons become the objects of suspicion; the earlier recipients of all Rousseau's emotional outpourings are now held responsible for his present unhappiness; erstwhile friends are treated as 'barbarous tyrants' whose sole intention is to bend their pliant victim to their own implacable will.[1] As soon as his mind begins to dwell on this idea, Rousseau transforms it into a firmly held conviction which has the insidious effect of making him seem justified in all his fears and suspicions.

The ambiguous role of the other person as the one who is now feared as well as loved produces an important modification in Rousseau's developing self-awareness. Conscious of himself as the object of the other's attention, he yet feels that this aggressive, hostile appraisal is based on a misunderstanding of his true character. The man seen by others is different from the being as he exists in himself. There thus occurs a split between the public and private image of Rousseau's personality and, in order to resist the critical scrutiny of the outside world, he is led to place increasing emphasis upon the idea of his own worth. At the same time, this process of self-evaluation reacts strongly on his attitude towards others, who become the object of more systematic suspicion than hitherto. It is not simply a question of isolated individuals and friends who occasionally thrust their irksome counsels upon him, but of the concerted effort of deceitful friends to play the part of tyrants and enemies who are banding together in a kind of 'league' or 'plot', the precise purpose of which is to bring about his enslavement and humiliation. The idea of tyranny is gradually transformed into that of active hostility and evil intent. 'All those whom I loved now hate me' (*CG* iii. 171). As yet such notions do not become permanently systematized, for they tend to emerge only in moments of acute tension, when he feels a particularly strong need to fight anxiety, but the onset of paranoid symptoms at this stage of his life seems unmistakable; they are apt to be concealed by the fact that he was by no means completely in the wrong.[2]

Although the cause of this projection is essentially subjective in the

---

[1] Cf. *CG* iii. 140, 158, 171, &c.

[2] That Mme d'Épinay's circle were far from guiltless is sufficiently proved by their latter efforts to 'doctor' the evidence in their favour. Cf. the story of the so-called *Memoirs* of Mme d'Épinay, first exposed by Frederika Macdonald and subsequently re-examined by George Roth in his edition of *Les Pseudo-mémoires de Mme d'Épinay. Histoire de Madame de Montbrillant*, 3 vols. (Paris, 1951).

sense that Rousseau is plainly externalizing personal conflicts which his own conscious mind cannot face, we should not too readily assume that there is a perfect correspondence between the beliefs derived from the projected feelings and their unconscious cause. In other words, we must not oversimplify a complex pattern of reaction by saying that Rousseau's attitude is *simply* the projection of a hostility unconsciously experienced towards himself in relation to some forbidden wish. Specific reactions, however abnormal, are related to more general and normal emotions, such as the need for affection, intimacy, and understanding. Nevertheless, the relation between projection and the effort to escape from inner conflict seems very significant, and it is the continued pressure of this basic anxiety which helps to strengthen his belief in his former friends' hostility.

It is equally certain that he is also prone to attribute to others at least some of his own feelings. The notion of tyranny and enslavement, of which he is so ready to speak, is a very convenient means of concealing his own tyrannical attitude towards his friends. That Jean-Jacques was a very exacting person is evident from his correspondence, and is no doubt partially explained by a loneliness which made him still more dependent on the few real friends who were left to him. As I have already insisted, his feelings were partly determined by his need to protect— through his relations with his friends—a certain image of himself: it was essential for him to feel that others could give firm emotional support to his own conception of his personality. When he says that 'he demands as much as he gives', he is understating the case. This tyranny exercised by Rousseau over his friends did not, of course, take the form of material requests, but it reveals itself in other small ways, all of which tend to make him the object of constant attention and solicitude on the part of others. He insists, for example, on his own right to be lazy in matters of correspondence, but refuses to accord to his friends the same privilege. A similar attitude applies to the question of visits. His friends must constantly visit him—or at least visit him when he is disposed to receive them—but he must be dispensed from the obligation to do likewise. His friends must also give frequent signs of their affection for him, but he must be excused from showing the same concern for them. In the same way they must allow for his excessive sensitivity and touchiness on certain matters, for this is the result of his loneliness and ill-health. Others must show a tolerance and forbearance of which he himself is incapable.

The insecurity of Rousseau's attitude is very obvious in the reactions provoked by the failure to achieve his ideal of friendship. At times he takes refuge, as we have seen, in a quasi-heroic moral ideal which, he feels, becomes a man of integrity and high ethical principle; he defiantly proclaims his faith in his value and insists on the real respect that is his due. At other times this heroic affirmation collapses and gives way to a totally different mood which is dominated more by lachrymose self-pity than heroic resolve. If he cannot obtain the respect of others, he is apt to fall back upon pathetic appeals for their sympathy. In this way he hopes to obtain the emotional satisfaction which he had previously sought to achieve through emphasis on his worth. When he feels incapable of stressing the meritorious aspects of his character, he calls attention to the fact that he is 'a wretched man tormented by a painful and incurable illness' (*CG* iii. 48). If he henceforth refers more frequently to his miserable physical condition, it is not simply because the effects of his retention are more acute (although this is certainly one of the reasons) but also because he hopes to make his misfortune an opportunity for obtaining the indulgence and affection of his friends.[1] Unfortunately the abnormal psychological basis of this attitude tends to make him incapable of showing the self-restraint and moderation which are usually a necessary prerequisite for achieving such an aim; his impatience and his hypersensitivity serve to make him still more wretched by alienating the very sympathy of which he has such desperate need. Hence he is apt to plunge into a kind of introspective melancholy, which frequently seems very close to hypochondria.

A favourite reaction is for him to see himself as a man destined to bring together friends who subsequently become so attached to each other that they are estranged from him. Already in 1756 there is a slight preliminary indication of the storm that is to come when he wonders (not too seriously) whether Grimm will obtain for him a visit from the friend (Diderot) 'whom I acquired for him' (*CG* ii. 279). Later on one of Rousseau's main charges against Grimm was that the latter deliberately tried to deprive him of his friends. The same accusation was made against young Coindet who was accused of having tried to replace Rousseau in the affection of the Luxembourgs. D'Alembert was also to be charged (among other things) with having insinuated himself into the good graces of Mme de Luxembourg at Rousseau's expense. Already in 1751 Rousseau had refused to share with d'Alembert a visit to Mme de Créqui, the presence of a third party being enough to disturb his pleasure in her company.[2] In the *Confessions* Dr. Tronchin is

---

[1] Cf. *supra*, p. 13, for his tendency to exaggerate his ill-health.   [2] Cf. *CG* ii. 13.

held responsible for a similar lack of good faith, for, as soon as Jean-Jacques had introduced the doctor to Mme d'Épinay (who wished to consult him about her health) 'they began under my auspices relations which they then made closer at my expense'. 'Such', Rousseau goes on, 'has always been my fate; as soon as I have brought together two friends whom I formerly had separately, they have never failed to unite against me' (*Conf.* 397). His inner insecurity clearly made him particularly susceptible to this idea of people becoming friendly at his expense, whether or not it was justified in specific cases. His very sensitiveness on this point was partly due to his excessive fear of losing that almost exclusive devotion to which he clung so eagerly.

It would be unjust to place too much emphasis upon the more unusual psychological aspects of Rousseau's attitude towards friendship, for it did contain a genuine element of idealism, which was undoubtedly reinforced by his retreat into rural solitude. Moreover, all his friendships did not end unhappily. In 1759 he was fortunate enough to receive overtures of friendship from the Maréchal and Maréchale de Luxembourg who showed remarkable tact and understanding in their relations with Jean-Jacques. What would have been the ultimate consequences of this intimacy it is impossible to say, for in 1762 Rousseau was forced to flee from France as a result of the publication of *Émile*. Later on, as his mental condition worsened, Mme de Luxembourg became an object of suspicion and was accused of being a member of the 'plot' that sought to hound him to his doom. However, the Luxembourgs showed what sympathy and perspicacity were able to achieve even with a tormented character like Jean-Jacques and their behaviour proves that his earlier friends had often lacked tolerance and forbearance in their dealings with a sick and unhappy man.

Even in the very last years of his life Rousseau was to go on forming new friendships, as we shall see, but, after his departure from France, he seems to have abandoned his idolatrous worship of the intense friendship which had marked his relations with Diderot. He gradually sought to develop a compensatory view of himself as a man who no longer needed friendship in order to live, because deep within himself he had found (he thought) resources which made him independent of the attentions of false and faithless friends.

II. *Love*

That Rousseau's emotions could not be completely satisfied by friendship—however 'ideal'—with a person of his own sex is clearly indicated by the type of escapist feeling that eventually produced *La Nouvelle Héloïse*. He himself admitted that the intimacy for which his heart longed required the presence of a woman rather than a man.

The first of my needs, the greatest, the most powerful and the most inextinguishable, lay completely in my heart; it was the need of an intimate society, a society that was as intimate as possible; it was especially on that account that I needed a woman rather than a man, a woman-friend rather than a man-friend. This strange need was such that the closest bodily union could not be enough: I should have had to possess two souls in the same body; otherwise I always experienced a sense of emptiness (*Conf.* 414).

In particular, he sought to express in love some of those expansive needs he had already associated with friendship. Through a woman he hoped to experience these feelings in a specifically erotic form. But all his life he was tormented by the impossibility of providing them with an adequate outlet. He writes desperately in the *Confessions*. 'To enjoy! Is this fate meant for man? Ah! if I had ever once in my life savoured all the delights of love in their completeness, I do not think that my frail existence would have been able to cope with them; I should have died in the act' (219). It was the frustration of this fundamental need that led him to think more and more of a perfect woman, a fantasy-figure compounded of various idealized memories of the past and the unfulfilled longings of the present.

Before considering the literary elaboration of this personal fantasy in *La Nouvelle Héloïse*, it will be as well to examine Rousseau's love-life in the light of his actual experience. Since he has himself recounted the history of his amours so vividly in the *Confessions*, we shall here consider them in relation to the total structure of his personality rather than as experiences valid in themselves. The previous account of his psychological development will already have suggested that considerable obstacles stood in the way of all Rousseau's efforts to establish genuinely adequate relationships with women. Although at certain times his ideal of love may seem to have arisen from a simple and absolutely spontaneous demand of his inner self, and one that a sensitive man like himself ought to have been able to satisfy without difficulty had he been fortunate enough to find a woman capable of responding to his own feelings, there remained the inescapable fact that this participation of the whole personality in the love-relationship demanded a far-reaching integration of the physical, emotional, and moral aspects of his personal existence; the physical act of sex was but one element in a complex pattern of response, in which—as he acknowledged—the needs of the 'heart' were far more important than those of the body. Now it was precisely this harmony between the different aspects of his personality that Rousseau lacked. He himself admitted that all too often his 'senses' and his 'heart' were never aroused at the same time and that 'the needs of love consumed him in the midst of enjoyment'.

Whatever precise psychological principles are used in the interpretation of Rousseau's attitude towards love, his experience clearly contained serious elements of maladjustment. Some of the disturbing factors have already been indicated in our account of his masochist and exhibitionist aberrations, the effect of which was to produce a withdrawal or suppression of the aggressive psychic function of sex in favour of a passive attitude that inclined him to see himself as the complete and exclusive object of another's affection. Moreover, his psychological difficulties may have been increased by his early disgust at the thought of sex. Basically, however, his reactions to love are not dissimilar from those involved in his search for friendship, for in each case he desires a kind of absolute emotional satisfaction which will relieve the anxieties and conflicts of his inner life, and this mood, in its turn, tends to prevent him from attaining genuine personal reciprocity in his love-relationships.

Although in one way or another this basic attitude affects all Rousseau's love-relationships, its precise form depends on his reactions towards particular women. The masochistic mood was more evident in his early experiences when he felt a need to be dominated and perhaps humiliated by the women to whom he was attracted. As the relevance of this abnormality to his sex-life has already been discussed, it will be enough to recall here that his first conscious memory of his masochistic feelings was the castigation administered by Mlle Lambercier, although this type of response probably originated, as has been suggested, in much earlier childhood experiences. Something of this mood is revealed in his account of his relations with Mme Basile (*Conf.* 73 ff.). Apart from the inhibiting influence of adolescent shyness, there is probably a deeper psychological significance in his admission that 'nothing that I have been led to feel through the possession of women is worth the couple of minutes that I spent at her feet without even daring to touch her dress' (74–75). The original draft of the *Confessions* brings out still more clearly the nature of Rousseau's reactions to this woman. 'On my knees before her', he says, 'I was certainly in the most delightful but also the most constrained situation that I have ever experienced in my life. I dared neither to breathe nor to raise my eyes. . . . We did not make the slightest movement; a profound silence reigned between us, but how many things did our hearts say and feel! . . . I would have passed there my whole life, nay, eternity itself, without desiring anything more' (*OC* i. 1160–1). His comments show that he derived a curiously deep but quiescent emotional satisfaction from an erotic experience which nevertheless lacked active physical content. A similar state of mind is revealed in another early fragment of the *Confessions*, where he says that 'his heart was at peace in her presence and desired nothing'. Although this unnamed woman apparently treated him with some rigour, he comments: 'This severity was a hundred times more delightful to me than her favours would have been.' He adds significantly: 'It seemed to me that she treated me like a thing which belonged to her, that she received me like a chattel, and that she took possession of me' (1161). It is as though he obtained a certain sensual pleasure from the thought of being possessed, even of being created by the women for whom he felt affection. 'To be at the knees of an imperious mistress, obey her orders, ask her pardon, were for me very sweet joys' (17). As soon as he feels 'love' for a woman, his personality seeks to efface itself before her, to become lost and absorbed in her, and to find a peculiar delight in the idea of being plunged in a static ecstasy from which all active, physical desire is momentarily excluded. As other less idealistic episodes also reveal, Jean-Jacques did not always remain at this level of physical detachment, but even the sporadic emergence of these reactions is an important indication of his complex attitude towards love.

It is generally agreed that Rousseau's basic emotional experience, as far as women were concerned, was dominated by his relations with Mme de Warens. Some writers maintain that her memory coloured all his later reactions towards women and that his ideal woman is simply a projection of his feelings for her. Although this view contains an important element of truth, it needs considerable qualification since the specifically *sexual*, as opposed to the more purely *emotional*, aspects of his feelings for her, seem to me to have been much exaggerated. Briefly, it may be said that Rousseau did not really 'love' her in the adult sexual sense, not necessarily because of any inherent incapacity on his part but rather because of the peculiar nature of his emotional attachment. Dazzled though he may have been by the sight of this charming and cultured *grande dame*—and he was always attracted, as he admitted, by women of superior social standing—Jean-Jacques eventually developed for her an affection which was filial rather than erotic, as his use of the famous *Maman* shows.[1] At the time of their first encounter he was little more than a lonely and shy adolescent; never having known a mother's affection, he not unnaturally found in this woman who was some twelve years older than he the kind of emotional support of which he was in such great need. Although sexual desire was not completely lacking, it tended to blend with solitary fantasies which left him 'caressing her image in the depths of his heart' (*Conf.* 109). The real nature of his feelings is more clearly indicated by his statement: 'I always saw in her an affectionate mother, a beloved sister, a delightful friend and nothing more.' He felt himself to be 'her work, her child'. In spite of the sporadic emergence of sexual feelings, his typical emotional reaction was one of untroubled calm: with her he experienced 'peace of heart, calmness, serenity, security, assurance' (52). In her presence he was 'as it were ecstatically transported into this happy time and this happy abode in which my heart, possessing all the bliss that it could wish for, relished it in inexpressible raptures, without even thinking of sensual pleasure'. It was a kind of 'reverie' in which 'the days and the years and the whole of life slipped by in an unchanging tranquillity' (108). He insists particularly on this almost passive enjoyment from which the desire for active possession was absent. 'With her I had neither transports nor desires; I was in a ravishing calm, without knowing what I was enjoying. I should have spent my life and eternity itself without being bored for a single moment.' He was content merely to be in her presence. Even when she was wrapped up in her own thoughts, 'I let her dream, I remained silent, I contemplated her and was the happiest of men.' On the other hand, when she was absent, he felt an anxiety that bordered on pain.

There thus seems to have been a split between his sexual desires and his affectionate feelings for Mme de Warens. The latter were those of a shy, lonely youth who had at last found emotional support in a person for whom he felt both respect and affection. There seems no reason to doubt Jean-Jacques's word that he experienced a kind of repugnance at the thought of sexual relations with her, for this is in complete accordance with reactions described in the *Confessions*. His oft-quoted remark that sexual intercourse with her was like 'incest' does not indicate (as some critics seem to suggest) any psychological abnormality in

[1] E. Ritter insists (op. cit., p. 12, n. 2) that Rousseau's use of *Maman* was not unique, as Voltaire was wont to use the same expression; but it plainly has a special significance in Rousseau's case.

Rousseau but rather testifies to the non-sexual nature of his attachment. The feelings of filial devotion and tenderness inspired in him by his 'mother' and 'benefactress' were genuinely revolted at the thought of physical intimacy. Erotically he was still an adolescent who was not emotionally ready for a completely adult sexual relationship. He himself rightly felt that the establishment of physical relations between them was a violation of his own intimate nature. This conviction is not inconsistent with a later experience of sexual jealousy with regard to Claude Anet and Wintzenried; it is natural that Rousseau, once he was committed to physical relations with Mme de Warens, should have diverted some of his sexual feelings towards her personality. But the subsequent ease with which he was unfaithful to her is explained not only by his own instability and resentment, but also by the fundamentally non-sexual nature of his own reactions.

Although it is no part of the purpose of the present study to apportion degrees of moral praise or blame to any of the persons concerned, it is impossible to escape the conclusion that Mme de Warens' influence on Rousseau's erotic development was a bad one. As his seducer, she forced him to indulge in a physical relationship for which he was not emotionally prepared and so helped to reinforce the abnormal tendencies to which he was already prone. Whether her motive was genuine concern for her young protégé's moral well-being (as Jean-Jacques loyally insists in the *Confessions*) or whether she was a sexually promiscuous and frigid woman who took a certain perverse pleasure in seducing an innocent youth it is now impossible to say.[1] We shall simply record that Rousseau himself, while speaking of her promiscuity, also mentions her 'cold' and 'icy temperament', which he deems to have been consistent with 'a sensitive character' (*Conf.* 195-9). In any case, Jean-Jacques's sexual inexperience at this stage of his life, as well as his highly idealized portrait of Mme de Warens, make it very difficult to form an objective picture of her true character. Certainly her later biographers have not been inclined to treat her with the same affectionate reverence as her protégé. What is important for our immediate purpose is to record the fact that her advances to Jean-Jacques administered a profound emotional shock by arousing erotic sensations in a youth who was prepared—as far as she was concerned—to feel no more than tenderness and gratitude. The deeper satisfaction he obtained from her was—or should have been—a sense of emotional security, a feeling that he was being protected by someone in whose love and

[1] Modern psychiatrists recognize the close link between promiscuity and frigidity.

understanding he could really trust. To disturb this emotional balance by transferring it unwarrantably on to a definitely sexual plane was to degrade the whole relationship without actually destroying its deeper emotional basis. He records that the performance of this act of 'incest' was always followed by a profound feeling of 'sadness', not merely the *tristitia animalis*, we presume, but the melancholy that comes from deep emotions violated or unsatisfied. In any case, his reactions to Mme de Warens were such as to make even more difficult his later efforts to achieve proper sexual relationships with women—relationships that might have matured into real love.

The general nature of Rousseau's feelings for Mme de Warens are clearly brought out in the poetic and rather pathetic *Promenade* written during the last months of his life. He there evokes nostalgic memories of his past happiness, a happiness that now seems all the more perfect for being remote and for ever unattainable. If he might at one stage of his life have been fortunate enough to experience complete fulfilment and happiness, it was (he thinks) assuredly then. 'If only', he writes sadly, 'I had been as sufficient for her heart as she was for mine! What peaceful and delightful days we should have spent together!' (1098). It was during this 'unique and short period of his life' that 'he was himself, in an unalloyed and untrammelled completeness'. Then could he indeed say 'that he had truly lived': he was at peace with himself, enjoying the expansive expression of his most intimate feelings and experiencing 'a pure and full happiness' in perfect rural surroundings and in the company of 'a woman-friend after his own heart'. Even time itself seemed to have been eliminated, so complete and tranquil was his existence in those days. Poetized and idealized though these feelings are under the influence of adult experience, they do help us to understand more fully the exact nature of Rousseau's attachment. With Mme de Warens he had experienced a wonderful sense of security which permitted the fulfilment of emotional needs while eliminating active desire. Together they formed a kind of closed world which demanded the presence of no third party to make it complete:[1] in both the *Rêveries* and the *Confessions* he stresses the idea of a reciprocity of feeling which was 'sufficient' in itself. 'We were not only necessary but sufficient to each other', content with a 'mutual possession' which owed nothing to differences of sex or age but depended solely on 'everything by which one is oneself' (*Conf.* 222). Yet with this reciprocity there was mingled a comforting sense of being dependent upon a superior being

[1] Cf. P. Burgelin, op. cit., p. 380, for an important statement of the same point.

who completed his happiness by conferring on his existence a unity that was so deep and pure as to assume at times an almost religious quality. In a startling phrase Rousseau insists that 'his heart was open before her as before God' (191). It is sentiments such as these which explain the importance of Mme de Warens' influence not only upon his subsequent relations with women but upon his more fundamental search for personal values.

Being much more definitely restricted to the sexual plane, Rousseau's adventure with Mme de Larnage is psychologically less interesting. Having already produced ten children and still prepared for further amorous episodes, this woman had the great merit—in Rousseau's eyes—of being able to put him at his ease and give him the self-confidence he so sorely needed. While his physical relations with Mme de Warens were constantly accompanied by complex emotional over-tones which made a frank acceptance of their full sexual nature impos-sible, with Mme de Larnage he could—for the first and only time in his life—abandon himself to the sensual side of his temperament.

> With Maman my pleasure was always disturbed by a feeling of sadness, by a secret pang which I could not overcome without difficulty; instead of being thankful to possess her, I blamed myself for degrading her. With Mme de Larnage, on the contrary, proud of being a happy man, I abandoned myself joyfully and confidently to my senses: I shared in the effect which I made on hers: I had enough self-control to contemplate my triumph with as much vanity as pleasure and to find therein the means of redoubling it. ... I gorged on the most pleasant sensations and was intoxicated by them. I savoured them in their pure and unalloyed vividness: they are the first and only sensations that I have enjoyed thus, and I can say that I owe it to Mme de Larnage that I shall not die without having known pleasure (*Conf.* 253–4).

Nevertheless, he admits that this combination of 'burning sensuality' and 'sweet intimacy' was not really love; nor was it the more ambigu-ous tenderness he felt for Mme de Warens. It is scarcely surprising that a man as sensitive and complex as Rousseau should have failed to find complete emotional satisfaction in this brief, promiscuous encounter; but it remains—if Jean-Jacques's account is to be trusted—a proof of his sexual vitality and shows that with a woman of tact and experience he could forget some of his inhibitions and, for once in his life, assume a more aggressive sexual role. On the other hand, it was precisely because his deeper feelings were not involved and because he knew that he was not experiencing true love that he was able to identify himself thus freely with this limited sensual aspect of his personality.

In spite of such episodes Rousseau's basic attitude frequently had an entirely different emphasis, for he was wont to speak of his desire for *perfection* as a necessary constituent in both his personal and objective view of love. It was because of this desire that his love-relationships failed to bring him complete satisfaction. 'No, nature did not intend me to enjoy. It has put into my wretched head the insidious desire of this ineffable happiness for which my heart craves' (*Conf.* 320). Already in *Émile* he had written: 'What is true love but chimera, illusion? We have far greater love for the image we create for ourselves than for the object to which it is applied'. 'All is merely illusion in love, I admit, but what is real are the feelings it inspires in us for the true beauty it makes us love. This beauty is not in the loved object, it is the work of our errors.' The second preface to *La Nouvelle Héloïse* has a similar sentiment. 'Love is only illusion; it creates for itself so to speak another universe, surrounds itself with objects which do not exist, and to which it alone gives being' (*NH* iv. 347). The attraction of love lies in the unattainability of its goal and in the subjective feeling of being possessed by illimitable and unrealizable desire. The famous letter to Saint-Germain reiterates the same theme. 'The love which I conceive and have been able to feel, is fired by the illusory image of the loved one's perfection; and it is this very illusion which leads it to enthusiasm for virtue, for this idea always forms part of a perfect woman' (*CG* xix. 243–4).

When considering Rousseau's views and experience, it is probably useful to distinguish between two types of perfection which are frequently bound up with human desire. There is the idealist dream of perfection so eloquently extolled by romantic writers; this is the element of youthful idealism that seems to be present in the first spontaneous manifestations of sensuous love. The tendency to idealize the loved object is a common and far from blameworthy feature of this kind of experience and probably shows how the aspiration towards perfection forms part of all men's deeper emotional experiences; on a much higher plane it reveals itself as the love of God and the desire for sanctity, and as such it has led to some of man's greatest spiritual triumphs. On the other hand, there is the much lower form of 'perfectionism' which is a sign of emotional maladjustment. In this case a man may think that his ideal is so lofty that it is useless for him to attempt to reach it. His dream of love may be so 'perfect' that normal love-life is thereby seriously inhibited as the individual remains imprisoned within the circle of his own unattainable desires. That such an attitude is a sign of neurosis and not of incipient sanctity is shown by the complete failure to translate this dream into concrete personal endeavour. The chief psychological function of this perfectionist aspiration is that it enables a man to escape from the intolerable anxiety associated with the thought of actual physical possession. In this way he comes to interpret personal inadequacy as a mark of superiority; obsessed by this escapist dream, he refuses to treat the erotic object as a real person who may be as incomplete and fallible as himself. The perfectionist mentality thus retreats from life and fails to attain any kind of genuine emotional reciprocity, especially in the realm of love-relationships. Rousseau will probably be found to share in both of these characteristics, for though he was often inspired by a genuine idealism, his behaviour also suggests an unconscious desire to seek situations (for example, in the case of Mme d'Houdetot and Mme de Larnage) in which he did not have to accept full responsibility for the complete erotic relationship.

One of the most curious examples of Rousseau's 'perfectionist' attitude is his brief escapade with the Venetian prostitute Zulietta, for this shows clearly his tendency to embellish the physical reality of women who aroused his sexual interest, and yet in such a way as to preclude the consummation of his desire. During the early days of his stay in Venice he had already been inclined to see the ugly singers, whose performance he attended every Sunday, as 'angels of beauty', until he was one day disillusioned by a closer view. His first reaction to Zulietta was to find the beauty of this 'enchanting girl' unsurpassable. 'The young virgins of the cloisters are less fresh, the beauties of the harem less striking, and the houris of paradise less piquant' (*Conf.* 320). Immediately this courtesan is transformed into a 'divinity' whose room is 'the sanctuary of love and beauty'. Then, when he is about to indulge in a more earthy enjoyment of this epitome of feminine perfection, he breaks down and 'weeps like a child': he is overwhelmed by the thought that 'this masterpiece of nature and love' whose 'mind and body' are equally 'perfect' is nothing but a wretched prostitute who is prepared to sell herself to the first man ready to pay for his pleasure. The idea of her miserable trade and condition induces him to seek for some 'secret defect' which would 'destroy the effect of her charms and make her hateful to those who ought to be fighting for her'. Already it would seem Rousseau is unconsciously seeking for some limitation to his enjoyment, and even for some pretext not to indulge in it. The discovery of *un téton borgne* thus merely reinforced a feeling that he had already experienced in relation to her condition as a prostitute. The existence of this deformity transforms her from a 'divinity' into 'a kind of monster, the reject of nature, men and love'. Finding himself temporarily inhibited, Jean-Jacques is dismissed from her presence with the suggestion that his time would be more profitably spent in the study of mathematics! Although he continued to be disturbed by the difficulty of 'reconciling the perfections of this adorable girl with the indignity of her condition', Jean-Jacques was soon anxious to make up for his earlier short-coming, only to find that she had decided to transfer her activities to another city. The interest of the episode for an understanding of Rousseau's personality lies in the curious way in which his unrealistic dream of perfection caused him to feel such an exaggerated sense of disgust before the living object itself that his sexual capacity was momentarily inhibited. Indeed, as Dr. Demole suggests,[1] Rousseau seems unconsciously to place obstacles in the way of his desire. In any case, this aberration shows that his needs could not be satisfied in the arms of a prostitute and that, to give himself completely, he needed a fuller and more intimate relationship with a woman.

Even in situations involving far deeper feelings than those aroused by Zulietta, Rousseau could not abandon the thought of a perfection which made the fulfilment of love impossible. 'I loved too sincerely, too perfectly', he says of his relations with Mme Basile, 'for me to be able to be happy' (*Conf.* 77). The same preoccupation was to recur in his passion for Mme d'Houdetot. It is particularly significant that this 'love' should have taken possession of him when he was in the act of creating an imaginative fantasy, *La Nouvelle Héloïse*. His feelings, as he admits, were first of all concerned with the evocation of a perfect woman, made up of the idealized memories and frustrations of his real-life experience. If he fell desperately in love with Mme d'Houdetot, it was largely because his ebullient emotions could not remain satisfied with a merely imaginary object, but projected themselves on the first reasonably attractive woman who happened to cross his path. The purely subjective and personal origin of this love is worth emphasizing, for it suggests that it was not in the first place inspired by the woman herself: Jean-Jacques still preserved in middle age something of the adolescent's idealistic attitude towards the loved object. No doubt we must treat with some caution his noble assertion that the perfection of this love was such as to have made it impossible for him ever to have

---

[1] *Analyse psychiatrique*, p. 293. The same author also points out that in this case Rousseau may have indulged in self-abuse before going to Zulietta, for he admits that while in Venice he had not lost the sinister habit of 'forestalling his needs' (*Conf.* 316).

possessed her. 'I loved her too much to want to possess her.' The same idea appears in the draft of a passionate letter intended for Sophie: 'This terrible voice which never deceives us made me shudder at the mere idea of besmirching by perjury and infidelity the one whom I love, the one whom I should like to see as perfect as the image I bear of her in my heart—the one who must remain sacred to me for so many reasons' (*CG* iii. 93). Perhaps too much reliance should not be placed on Rousseau's profession of moral rectitude on this occasion, for his high-minded protests conceal baser motives and probably abnormal erotic reactions. Moreover, subsequently conscious of having played an inglorious role, he not unnaturally had to find some means of saving his pride. In any case, the idea of perfection may here be directly related to a sense of guilt aroused by the whole affair. At the purely psychological level, too, his early interest in Sophie may have been stimulated by the subconscious thought that her steadfast devotion to Saint-Lambert made her unattainable. In his eyes she remained—and perhaps he wanted her to remain (to some extent at least)—a figure of fantasy, about whom he could weave the wildest chimeras with the full knowledge that they would never be tested by the reality of physical possession.

Of his relations with Thérèse Levasseur it is not necessary to speak at length, for he never treated her as an equal or 'loved' her in the fullest sense. If he eventually married her, it was more in recognition of her devotion than because of any genuine emotional dependence on his part. Of his real feelings for her he speaks quite openly in the *Confessions*. The 'gentle character of this good girl' seemed to accord with his own and so became the basis of an attachment which 'was proof against time and error', but 'from the very first moment that I saw her until the present day, I have never felt the slightest spark of love for her, I have no more desired to possess her than I did Mme de Warens, and the sensual needs which I satisfied through her have been solely those of sex, and never contained anything that appertained to the individual' (*Conf.* 414). In so far as his attachment to her was not determined by physical desire, it depended solely on feelings that were largely devoid of genuine amatory content. Particularly noteworthy is his admission that he needed 'a successor to Maman'. His feelings for *Maman* never having been genuinely erotic, he transferred to his new companion the type of emotional need he had satisfied with his former benefactress. In spite of vast differences between the illiterate Thérèse and the enchanting Mme de Warens, he sought to escape through them both from the 'emptiness' and anxiety of solitude. Thérèse, at least, was a simple girl before whom he had to play no part and with whom, as Mr. Josephson says, he could 'feel safe'.[1] Impinging in no way upon his inner life, she allowed him to go on living in a world of private fantasy.[2] With her too he could momentarily forget the unhappy consequences of his 'extinguished ambition' and, by setting up house with her, perhaps show 'society' that happiness was possible without the sophisticated luxury demanded by so many of his contemporaries. In addition to offering him compensation for 'the brilliant destiny he had given up', she also had the more mundane but extremely important qualification of being a good cook, housekeeper, and nurse. Later on, after the abandonment of their children (which, as the *Confessions* indicate, was his wish rather than hers), he may have also clung to her through a vague but persistent sense of guilt which he could not expiate alone. In a different direction, the psychological effect of her presence upon Rousseau seems to have been frequently disastrous. Quarrelsome and discontented as far as others were concerned, she fomented Rousseau's paranoid suspicions and created difficulties around him at times of acute emotional crisis when he needed the tact and sympathy of a truly understanding person. It is tragically ironic that Rousseau should often have placed implicit faith in this mendacious woman at a time when he was devoured by pathological suspicions against innocent persons. Nevertheless, the permanence of this attachment is significant, if only through its exclusion of all real love. In his relations with Thérèse Jean-Jacques was able—as far as his intimate life was concerned—to remain emotionally intact.

We ought not to leave this subject of Rousseau's attitude towards love without referring to the curious mingling of erotic and non-erotic elements involved in yet another attempt to deal with the problem— the idea of triangular friendship and the *ménage à trois*. Permanently unable to realize his ideal of love or friendship as specific objects of his endeavour, he is often fascinated by a type of relationship which seems to combine all the best elements in love and friendship and yet avoids the anxiety and unhappiness involved in pursuing either of them in isolation. In this new relationship he sees himself as the intimate friend of a man and woman who are already on terms of physical intimacy. Although the most interesting example of his adult attempts to live out this idea was his projected friendship with Mme d'Houdetot and

[1] *Jean-Jacques Rousseau* (London, 1932), pp. 135–8.
[2] As Dr. A. Heidenhaim (op. cit., p. 36) also points out.

Saint-Lambert, the preoccupation first emerges in his early experience with Mme de Warens, whom he shared with Claude Anet. (Its final literary expression is to be found in Saint-Preux's friendship with Julie and M. de Wolmar, but we will defer an examination of the literary treatment until the wider implications of *La Nouvelle Héloïse* have been considered.) The two friendships differed in a number of ways. In the first place, the relationship with Mme de Warens was not of Rousseau's own choosing, for it was she who more or less forced him into it against his will; the discovery of her physical intimacy with Anet came some time afterwards. Then, whilst in the adult phase of the *ménage à trois* Rousseau's role was purely platonic, there was, in the case of Claude Anet and Mme de Warens, a sharing of actual physical intimacy. However, we have already seen that Jean-Jacques' attachment to his benefactress was not primarily a sexual one, and, although his first discovery of Mme de Warens' intimacy with Anet caused him a certain misgiving, it was not due mainly to sexual jealousy. 'I had not even thought', he says, 'of desiring this position [of lover] for myself, but it was hard for me to see it filled by another.' His immediate reaction is very noteworthy. 'Instead of feeling aversion for the one who had stolen her from me, I really felt my attachment for her extending to him.' The result was a remarkably pleasant and peaceful triangular friendship. 'We thus lived in a union which made us all happy, and which death alone was able to destroy' (*Conf.* 178). Rousseau attributes the success of this peculiar relationship to the character of 'this lovable woman', since 'all who loved her loved one another'. The integrity and wisdom of 'that rare man', Claude Anet himself, was also an important contributory factor. But Rousseau says least about the most important element of all—his own character which was able to remain satisfied with such a passive role. His account suggests that he found a sense of peace and security in thus living in a state of emotional and physical dependence on two 'superior' and older people towards whom he experienced filial feelings of respect and affection. Through them he was able to lead a life remarkable for its pleasant 'uniformity' and the absence of all strain and anxiety. After Anet's death Jean-Jacques took less kindly to the idea of sharing *Maman* with the vulgar Wintzenried, for the obvious reason that he could not readily transfer to another man, whom he considered to be little more than a coarse-grained adventurer, the tender, respectful feelings he had experienced for his dead friend. Moreover, the advent of Wintzenried seems to have caused some alteration in Mme de Warens' attitude towards Jean-

Jacques with whom she was now prepared to be far less patient. Once the steadying and wise influence of Claude Anet had gone from the household, its economic and financial condition inevitably deteriorated under the auspices of the unpractical and erratic Jean-Jacques. His ultimate response to her less indulgent feelings was to assure her that henceforth he 'honoured her too much to possess her' and would 'sacrifice all his pleasure to the union of their hearts'. Whether this observation was an afterthought aimed at preserving a pride that had been rudely shaken by the intrusion of Wintzenried or whether Jean-Jacques really believed this to be the explanation of their henceforth less intimate relations is unimportant for our present purpose; the essential point is that with the death of Anet and the arrival of Wintzenried the whole idea of a peaceful *ménage à trois* was irrevocably impaired. Nevertheless, the notion continued periodically to haunt his mind and emerged once again at the time of his friendship with Mme d'Houdetot and Saint-Lambert. In this instance he wishes to see himself as the platonic friend who is admitted to the emotional intimacy of the two lovers. Now, however, Jean-Jacques seeks a more benevolent, even paternal role. Looking back on this period of his life a few years later, he recalled that Sophie herself spoke of 'the intimate and sweet society which we might form between the three of us, when I had become reasonable' (*Conf.* 441). That it was also Rousseau's own ardent wish at the time is also clear from the correspondence, for he describes it as 'a charming project'. He wrote to Saint-Lambert in 1757: 'Yes, my children, be for ever united; there is no other soul like yours, and you deserve to love each other until death. It is pleasant for me to be a third member in such a loving friendship' (*CG* iii. 153). Rousseau assured Sophie that their 'three hearts were made to love and honour, not to despise and fear one another' (ibid. 186). In these words he was merely re-echoing an earlier hope that they might form between the three of them 'a charming society' (119). Like so many of Rousseau's dreams, this one did not materialize, no doubt because Mme d'Houdetot and Saint-Lambert had begun to find him a somewhat disturbing friend. Yet Rousseau still continued to cling to the chimera, though in a modified form. In 1760 he realized that the triangular friendship might have to be a purely male one. After telling the importunate Coindet that he 'imagined no other true happiness in life than an unqualified intimacy' he added:

It seems to me that if we could form between dear Carrion, you and me, an exclusive little society to which no other being would be admitted, it would be too delightful. But I cannot cure myself of my castles in the air. Although I am growing old, I am all the more of a child because of it. Oh! when shall I be forgotten by the mob and loved by two friends. . . . But I should be too happy, and I am not made to be happy (*CG* v. 305).

Various explanations have been given of this apparent deviation from normal love relations. One of the most precise is the psycho-analytical interpretation offered by Dr. R. Laforgue.[1] According to this theory Rousseau's preoccupation with the *ménage à trois* repro-duced his unconscious reaction to the mother–father relationship; the third member of the group, the male without whom it remains incom-plete, is the son who is hated by the father, because, through his birth, he has killed the mother; he must expiate his guilt by sacrificing her to the father and by remaining himself a kind of superfluity. Thus he always abandons the woman of the group to the other male, because she is for him a mother-substitute who must be sacrified to the father. On this view Mme de Warens and Mme d'Houdetot become mother-figures who are surrendered to the superior claims of the father-substi-tutes (Anet and Saint-Lambert); the relationship constituted by the *ménage à trois* conceals a secret desire for self-punishment, an immola-tion of his own pleasure under the influence of feelings of guilt; ultimately he extends the attitude to all women, being unable to accept any as his wife. There would thus be a link between his concern for the *ménage à trois* and his fundamental masochism. As Pierre Burgelin puts it, 'perhaps we must see in this relationship his secret masochism, a desire for humiliation which vegetates on the threshold of his conscious-ness and which would explain by its after-effects the extraordinary susceptibility of his pride'.[2]

Whether Rousseau's obsession really did originate in these precise emotional strains and stresses may be left—as far as the present study is concerned—an open question, although the idea of a connexion between these reactions and the masochistic tendencies already examined is certainly plausible. What I should like to stress here, however, is the more fundamental psychological aspect of the experience and the way in which Jean-Jacques tries to invest it with some kind of conscious value. The *ménage à trois* forms part of his desire for security and the alleviation of anxiety through participation in a closed group whose intimacy seems to offer protection against the assaults of the outside world and the conflicts of his own inner life. This narrow society has

[1] Cf. R. Laforgue, *La Psychopathologie de l'échec* (Paris, 1950).
[2] P. Burgelin, op. cit., p. 383.

the great merit of allowing its members to be 'self-sufficient' and in no need of any 'extraneous addition' to complete their happiness (*Conf.* 479). Secure in his dependence on his friends, who are both equals and superiors, he escapes from the torments of desire and the uncertainties of possession, for his personality is merged into a unity greater than that of his own individual self. No longer compelled to face the burden of solitude, he would at last be happy were it not for the short-lived character of relationships which depend on conditions that can never be permanent.

Rousseau's attitude towards love thus remains complex, for even at the purely erotic level he admitted the co-existence of two apparently distinct needs—the sensual (aggressive) and the emotional (passive). He was already conscious of this in his early years, as is evident from the account of his childhood reactions to Mlle de Vulson and Mlle Goton: 'I am acquainted with two kinds of love which are very distinct, very real and yet have almost nothing in common, although they are both very intense and different from affectionate friendships. The whole course of my life has been divided between these two loves of such diverse kinds, and I have even experienced them both at once' (*Conf.* 27). The one is 'sensual', the other 'platonic'.[1] He then goes on to describe his 'calm joy', which 'did not go as far as emotion', in the presence of Mlle de Vulson; he was tormented by her relations with other men and yet 'I loved this torment'; but her caresses did not stimulate him sensually, although they were 'pleasant to his heart'.[2] 'I was charmed without being moved.' 'I loved her as a brother, but I was jealous of her as a lover.' With Mlle Goton, on the other hand, he suffered a violent, erotic passion which made him—in her presence— 'see nothing else': for her he would have acted 'like a Turk' or 'tiger'.[3] In some sense these divergent attitudes dominated the whole of his relations with women. Either he experienced a calm, tender affection from which strong desire was absent, or else he felt a more definitely erotic urge which excluded real affection; either he wanted 'a loving mother, a beloved friend' like Mme de Warens, who left his 'senses calm' and yet made him conscious of the 'needs of love that devoured him even in the midst of pleasure', or else he restricted himself to sensual liaisons with women like Mme de Larnage or Thérèse Levasseur.

[1] Cf. *Première rédaction*, p. 37.
[2] Ibid., p. 38.
[3] The first draft adds: 'If, in my moments of sadness, I thought, in order to console myself, of Mlle de Vulson, I devoted my expansive moments, when my heart was full of life, to Mlle Goton' (pp. 39–40).

Since, at the same time, he continued to be obsessed by the dream of absolute love, he was constantly disturbed by an ideal that he could never fulfil but which, in some obscure way, he felt that he might have fulfilled had fate been kinder to him.

Rousseau's attitude towards love—and especially towards sexual love—thus remains complex. Perhaps its most significant feature is this dream of a perfection which so haunts all his real attachments to women that he is prevented from making a complete and satisfactory identification with any of them. At the end of his life, therefore, he will be reminded of great potentialities that were destined to remain unrealized, wonderful opportunities that seemed fated to go awry. Although Rousseau himself tended to attribute these disappointments to the cruelty of fate or the incapacity of others to share his ideal, it is clear (as he himself was wont to see in his more perspicacious moments) that his failure was largely due to peculiarities in his own nature. In particular, the separation of 'tender' and 'sensual' feelings may be largely explained by an abnormal psychological history that prevented an adequate integration of the various levels of his personality. The normal psychic components of love were either disconnected from the sexual object and displaced to another sphere of activity, or completely eliminated, or, finally, related to the loved object in such an unrealistic way that they could never form the basis of a proper attachment. Jean-Jacques, therefore, lay at the mercy of the irrational and incomplete emotions associated with his erotic impulses.

Although his obsession with the idea of perfection may be a partial expression of his inability and perhaps unconscious refusal to see the loved object as it is in itself (his vision being constantly distorted by the pressure of his own subjective and abnormal longings), we must allow that his sensitivity made him feel more deeply than the average man and that his tormented desires did contain an element of genuine idealism. But he eventually came to realize that the intensity of his aspiration involved a scale of values incomprehensible to most of his contemporaries. Moreover, the growing need to know himself more intimately and to bring his inner conflicts to the level of conscious thought in a way that enabled him to see them against the background of a search for personal values ultimately led him to recognize that there were certain elements in his character which made his continued struggle to realize such aims in real life quite impracticable. He became convinced that all his efforts to establish full and perfect union with a woman would always suffer the fate of his attempts to secure true friends. 'I have spent my days', he wrote to Mme de Luxembourg in 1759, 'in a vain search for firm attachments' (*CG* iv. 297). But the illusion did not die easily, and if he transferred his idealistic strivings to another existential plane, he continued to be haunted by dreams of happiness. If he could not live out his amorous ideal at the level of actual experience, he still found some satisfaction in projecting it on to the realm of imaginative fantasy, obtaining in this way relief for all his suppressed and tormented feelings as well as gaining some insight into their real nature and value. Before the struggle with real existence was renewed, he made a final attempt to create a 'society after his own heart', and so express in the domain of imagination what could not be found in life itself. The result was *La Nouvelle Héloïse* which, as the crystallization of the complex and conflicting emotions of these years, provides a vital clue to our understanding of Rousseau's development because here, for the first time, his emotions led to the elaboration of an ideal which was both literary and personal.

4
LA NOUVELLE HÉLOÏSE

ALTHOUGH Rousseau's complete disillusionment with his two 'idols' was to take place only after the tragi-comic conclusion to the story of his passion for Mme d'Houdetot, the months following his arrival at the Hermitage produced a state of mind which presaged ill for his future efforts to establish affectionate relations with his fellow-men; he began to feel the pressure of feelings and emotions that could never be satisfied at the level of ordinary human experience. Prominent among these impulses was a profound sense of 'emptiness' which could not be overcome by any of the activities available to him. He was more and more convinced that he would never find a heart capable of responding to his own in the way that he wanted. 'Consumed' by an insatiable 'need to love', he feared that he might have to die 'without ever having lived'. Still believing that the possession of 'exquisite faculties' was enough to justify him in indulging in the 'feeling of his inner worth', he was now tormented by the pressure of frustrated erotic emotions. What worried him most was the thought that his past life actually contained situations which, in more propitious circumstances, might have brought him the happiness he so much desired. He began to take refuge in a world of fantasy created from the idealized memories of women he had encountered in his youth and with whom he had occasionally begun amorous adventures that were destined to remain incomplete. 'Meditating in the finest season of the year, in June, beneath fresh groves, to the sound of the nightingale's song and the babbling of the brooks', he recalled 'all the objects which had inspired me with emotion in my youth, Mlle Galley, Mlle de Graffenreid, Mlle de Breil, Mme Basile, Mme de Larnage, my young pupils, and even the piquant Zulietta, whom my heart cannot forget' (*Conf.* 426–7). These memories now served to stimulate an imagination that produced an 'ideal' and 'enchanted' world where all his desires were satisfied with a 'society of perfect creatures . . . after his own heart'. Yet this world of fantasy was clearly dominated by his own personal hopes and desires and had no independent existence outside his own mind: it was a compensation for the disappointment and inadequacy of lived experience.

According to his own account he was driven still further into this imaginative escapism by the tedious limitations of his day-to-day life. He gradually saw that the freedom for which he had struggled so hard was constantly being threatened by the obligations he still owed to his hostess, Mme d'Epinay. Moreover, he was often besieged by strangers who refused to leave him in peace. Other difficulties associated with old Mme Levasseur, the d'Holbach coterie, and his own desire to reply to Voltaire's attack on Providence made his dream of 'pure enjoyment' seem remoter from reality than ever before. Small wonder that he was driven to seek refuge in the realm of fantasy!

His emotions at this period contain an *absolute* element which makes them irreconcilable with the limitations of ordinary life, but, in their inception at any rate, they appear to have very little religious content. What he dreams of is an immediate happiness, a form of earthly enjoyment that can be experienced here and now. This accords with what we have already seen to be the motives of his 'reform'. The expansive impulses of his personality are mainly concerned with the two elements of eroticism and self-assertion. The ideal world which gradually takes shape in his mind contains 'ravishing images' which embody 'love and friendship, the two idols of his heart'. In his mind he sees two women with 'analogous but different characters', having faces which 'are not perfect, but in accordance with my own taste and animated by kindness and sensibility'.

I made one dark and the other fair, one lively and the other gentle, one wise and the other weak, but of such a touching weakness that virtue seemed to gain thereby. I gave to one of the two a lover of whom the other was the affectionate friend, and even something more; but I allowed neither rivalry, quarrelling nor jealousy, because I am reluctant to imagine any painful feeling, and I did not want to dim this bright picture by anything that degraded nature. Enamoured of my two charming models, I identified myself as far as possible with the lover and the friend; but I made him young and likeable, endowing him besides with the virtues and defects which I felt were mine (*Conf.* 430).

Jean-Jacques tried to give substance to this dream by situating it in a real setting. After some hesitation he chose the Lake of Geneva, for this was an environment with which he was intimately connected. Even though this background was subjected to various imaginative modifications, as Daniel Mornet points out, it was real enough to be immediately recognizable.

At first Rousseau's 'enchanted world' remained a merely idyllic dream of happiness without definite shape. If he put on paper a number of letters written by these imaginary beings to one another, it was without any proper connexion or logical sequence. What he sought above all else was to relieve his own pent-up feelings and satisfy through this imaginary correspondence, so charged with intense emotion, all those cravings which he had not been able to express in real life. In its early stages *La Nouvelle Héloïse* was, according to Rousseau, little more than a 'vague plan' involving three characters in a particular setting. It was, in other words, a free fantasy aimed at catharsizing its author's own secret longings. In this sense it is an intensely personal piece of writing, but not personal in the same way as the *Confessions, Dialogues,* and *Rêveries* which attempt a more deliberate probing and analysing of his personality and so constitute a conscious attempt at self-understanding. It is an imaginative projection of the author's idealized longings transformed through the deliberate creation of a seemingly independent world that has an intimate but indirect and symbolic connexion with Jean-Jacques's inner life. Slowly this vague plan began to assume a coherent shape and became 'a kind of novel', so that from the first indefinite musings there emerged a proper literary work. Moreover, after further elaboration, the original erotic ecstasies were subordinated to more moral considerations. After her fall Julie, who has so rashly given way to her lover's demands, marries another and becomes a virtuous wife and mother uplifting all around her by her integrity and steadfastness until she finally moves on to a plane of spiritual consummation.

Upon this later development the events of real life had an important influence. Not least of these was Rousseau's sudden infatuation with Mme d'Houdetot. When her carriage was embogged near Rousseau's house, this lively young woman, the mistress of the distinguished Saint-Lambert, insisted upon completing the journey on foot and eventually arrived at the Hermitage—laughing and muddy. Rousseau was soon to transfer to this real person the emotions which he had directed until then on to his imaginary characters. It seems clear from his account that his subjective feelings—as much as the qualities of the lady herself—were responsible for the sudden frenzy of 'love' with which he was then filled. 'It was love this time, and love in all its energy and fury'; but his own comment is significant: 'I was drunk with love which had no object; this intoxication bewitched my eyes, this object became attached to her; I saw my Julie in Mme d'Houdetot, and soon I saw nobody but Mme d'Houdetot, but clothed in all the perfections with which I had just adorned the idol of my heart' (*Conf.* 440). As we have already pointed out, his subsequent 'sublimity' and high-mindedness in refusing to 'possess' a woman for whom he had so much respect must be seen in the light of more matter-of-fact psychological considerations. Daniel Mornet thinks that the transformation of the 'erotic' theme (which was no more than 'a simple love story about a seduction and a departure') into a 'moral' novel is to be explained by Rousseau's experiences with Mme d'Houdetot. On his view the change of emphasis is due to Rousseau's desire to atone for his guilty passion for another man's mistress; it also constitutes an attempt to satisfy his pride as well as his conscience. The novel would thus be a literary counterpart to his own moral conversion. The idea is attractive, but scarcely seems justified by the chronology of events, as F. C. Green has recently pointed out.[1] A letter from Deleyre on November 23rd 1756 shows that Rousseau was already well advanced with his novel and actually intended to bring it to a close by 'drowning' his main characters. Since Rousseau's passion for Mme d'Houdetot did not really disclose itself until May 1757, it seems likely that the idea of Julie as a wife and mother, as well as that of the recall of Saint-Preux to the Wolmar household, antedate the real-life love affair by some months.[2] It is far more likely that the last two parts of the work were added under the pressure of external events, for Rousseau insists that the introduction of a definite religious theme having a didactic purpose was due to his desire to reconcile the philosophers and the Christians. This is not to deny that the encounter with Mme d'Houdetot had important effects on the final form of the novel—for the parallels between certain passages and the letters written to Mme d'Houdetot are too numerous to be coincidences, but it is not necessary to suppose that his experience with her caused him to introduce any new psychological considerations of a major kind. F. C. Green insists that Julie's death-bed admission of her love for Saint-Preux was Rousseau's way of saving his pride: Julie preferring Saint-Preux to Wolmar would be Sophie really admitting (in Rousseau's imagination) that she preferred Jean-Jacques to Saint-Lambert. In this way she is allowed to remain faithful to her first love and yet not abandon her role as a virtuous woman. This is certainly a plausible interpretation, but, as I shall try to show, such a conclusion could follow quite logically from the human data of the novel itself.

---

[1] Op cit., pp. 189 ff. Mornet's conclusions had already been challenged by Albert Schinz in *La Pensée de Jean-Jacques Rousseau* (Paris, 1929), pp. 245 ff.

[2] This is also M. Robert Osmont's conclusion in an important article, 'Remarques sur la genèse et la composition de "la Nouvelle Héloïse",' in *Annales*, xxxiii, 1953–5, 93–148.

In fact, the fundamental elements in the work reproduce for the most part, though in a more deliberate and specific way, the basic psychological factors we have already seen at work in Rousseau's earlier life. Although their projection on to the realm of imaginative fiction naturally causes them to assume a symbolic and imaginative form that is different from their direct appearance at the level of lived experience, the link between the personality of Rousseau and his literary creation remains very close. Indeed it is largely because of this interconnexion—rather than because of its genuine merits as a piece of imaginative fiction— that *La Nouvelle Héloïse* still remains a fascinating subject for anyone seeking a deeper understanding of Rousseau the man.

Into the novel are also incorporated various didactic elements which are connected only remotely (if at all) with the human situation it attempts to depict. There are long sections in which Rousseau is plainly concerned with expressing his views on various topics ardently discussed by his contemporaries—the nature of music, the problem of duelling, the real nature of Parisian life. These discussions must be related to Rousseau's wider philosophical views and will be largely ignored in our subsequent analysis since they lie outside the scope of the strictly human problem of *La Nouvelle Héloïse*.

Finally, we have to bear in mind that, when once Rousseau had decided to publish his work, he could not be unmindful of the contemporary literary situation, and especially of the growing taste for English novels in the style of Richardson. The desire to modify his own fantasy in accordance with prevailing literary fashion is obviously not without importance as far as its significance for literary history is concerned, the full meaning of *La Nouvelle Héloïse* being incomprehensible without some reference to the work of predecessors like Richardson and Prévost. In isolating for the present discussion what may be called the 'human problem' of the novel I do not wish to underestimate the relevance of these more conventional literary influences, but as they tend to be outside the immediate purpose of the present study, I must refer the reader to the many able investigations already made by scholars into this aspect of the work.[1] What I wish to do here is to relate *La*

---

[1] See especially Daniel Mornet's introduction to his classic edition of *La Nouvelle Héloïse* (Hachette, Paris, 1925, 4 vols.); this is the text used in the present discussion, being quoted simply by volume and page number. Also valuable are the same author's *La Nouvelle Héloïse de J.-J. Rousseau, Étude et analyse* (Paris, 1929), and *Rousseau, l'homme et l'œuvre* (Paris, 1950). See also P. van Tieghem, *La Nouvelle Héloïse de Jean-Jacques Rousseau* (Malfère, Paris, 1929). The works of P. Burgelin, A. Schinz, and F. C. Green already quoted contain important sections on the topic. For a general survey of the

Nouvelle Héloïse to the development of Rousseau's personal life and see how far the deliberate and conscious effort of literary creation has modified the factors so far analysed at the level of lived experience. In this respect we shall constantly bear in mind that the final work is not a simple entity but the result of a considerable process of development and adaptation. It seems to have passed through at least three main stages—the passionate love-story (the personal fantasy already perhaps modified, as Schinz suggests, in the direction of an 'effeminate love-story'), the theme of passion transformed into an account of the happy and virtuous life of the idyllic society of Clarens, and the more specifically philosophical and religious discussions of the last two books. I think that it is possible to relate these three phrases of the novel not simply to the external events of Rousseau's life (although these had some influence on the elaboration of the story) but also to the evolution and tensions of Rousseau's own inner history. From this point of view I shall consider the novel not as the mere sum of various heterogeneous elements, but in terms of an internal dialectic which derives its fundamental unity from the fact that its conflicting elements are ultimately contained within the limits of the author's own personality.

As a free fantasy *La Nouvelle Héloïse* naturally places an early emphasis on the *idealistic* element in the love-story, for it was, as Jean-Jacques insists, the frustration of his intense idealistic desire for absolute and total love that first impelled him to write the letters: literary composition provided him with an outlet for all those dreams of perfection which, though constantly obsessing him, had never been realized in everyday life.[1] This does not mean that Julie and Saint-Preux are 'perfect' characters in a purely human and moral sense, for their perfection lies mainly in the authentic quality of their feelings and the 'goodness' of their sensibility rather than in the virtue of their actual conduct: their love is 'perfect' because it springs from the pure sources of 'nature' and expresses the spontaneous, reciprocal attraction of two

---

work as a whole we refer to Charles Dédéyan, *La Nouvelle Héloïse, Étude d'ensemble* (Centre de documentation universitaire, Paris, 1955), which also contains a full biblio-graphy. An analysis of certain of the novel's basic concepts is given in M. B. Ellis, *Julie or La Nouvelle Héloïse, A Synthesis of Rousseau's Thought (1749–59)* (Toronto, 1949). For the notion of happiness in the work see J. R. Carré, 'Le Secret de J.-J. Rousseau', in *Revue d'histoire littéraire de la France*, xlvi, April–June 1949, 130–41. There is also an important discussion of the novel in Jean Starobinski's *Jean-Jacques Rousseau* (pp. 99 ff.) and in the two articles by R. Osmont and J. L. Bellenot quoted elsewhere in this chapter.

[1] Cf. *Conf.* 426–31. He admits that for a time he was *le berger extravagant*, living in 'an ideal world' and indulging in 'the desire to love which I had never been able to satisfy and by which I felt myself to be consumed' (431).

souls who feel from the very first that they are meant for each other. 'Although we are still so young', says Saint-Preux in his very first letter, 'nothing corrupts in us the tendencies of nature, and all our inclinations seem to harmonize with one another. Before assuming the uniform prejudices of the world, we have uniform ways of feeling and seeing' (ii. 7). They are striking examples of a perfect conformity of personality, of a 'certain unison of soul which is immediately discernible' (ii. 150). This love which, in Claire's words, 'bears a natural character of sympathy' comes from 'nature's purest laws' (ii. 113; iii. 9). In spite of all her fears and hesitations, Julie has ultimately to admit that 'her only regret is to have struggled against such dear and well-founded feelings'. 'Nature! O sweet nature', she is to exclaim, 'resume all your rights! I abjure the barbarous virtues which destroy you. Are the inclinations which you gave me more untrustworthy than a reason which has led me astray so often?' (iii. 37). A telepathic experience makes her ask: 'Cannot two souls which are so closely united have between them an immediate communication which is independent of the body and the senses?' (iii. 31). Heaven is frequently invoked as the power which justifies their acceptance of a perfect love and Saint-Preux well sums up the situation when he says: 'Before your father's tyranny, heaven and nature had united us to each other' (iii. 81).

Another element which shows the presence of imaginative projection in the novel is the author's insistence that, although passion can often assume an idealistic language which is apt to conceal its erotic content, Julie and Saint-Preux love with their entire personalities. It is not a partial, hesitant emotion, but an absolute identification of the whole self with the object of its love. Precisely because Jean-Jacques himself had never been able to experience such completeness of feeling in real life, he dwells with particular pleasure on this aspect of his story. 'Our souls', says Julie in a curious mathematical metaphor, 'have touched each other so to speak at every point, and we have everywhere felt the same coherence' (ii. 38). Her lover speaks of 'this divine harmony of virtue, love and nature' which is expressed through their relationship. The very fullness and spontaneity of their love gives it a certain innocence and child-like naïvety which are never completely destroyed by the turbulence of passion. At the same time their idealism makes them truly 'exceptional' beings who express nature's impulses with a nobility and grandeur which belong only to 'strong' and 'sublime' souls. The very fact that a commoner like Saint-Preux can win the affection and esteem of a nobleman's daughter proves him to be capable of a love which rises above social prejudice and so attains, through its revelation of the highest potentialities of human feeling, a genuinely paradigmatic value.

If this perfect love is not consummated in marriage, it is because 'nature' is frustrated by 'society'—identified here with the irrational tyranny of an 'inflexible father' who is prepared to sacrifice his daughter's happiness to his own 'absurd prejudices'. This general point gives a kind of symbolic significance to the first part of the novel by contrasting an 'ideal' and 'perfect' love with the irrational cruelties of civilized life. In this way the personal imaginative fantasy produced in Rousseau's rural solitude readily harmonizes with his general convictions concerning the relationship of human existence and civilization.[1]

This early idealistic element is already implicit in the expansive erotic desire which Rousseau imaginatively associated with the image of a perfect woman, and so *La Nouvelle Héloïse* bears the marks of a compensatory fantasy imbued with all the emotional fervour of an unhappy man's frustrated day-dreaming. Yet as soon as the love-letters become part of a literary plan and are integrated into a definite plot, they do not remain at such a simple psychological level, for they encounter other psychic elements which at first sight seem to conflict with this naïve idealistic impulse. As we have seen, it is not necessary to suppose that Rousseau had already encountered Mme d'Houdetot before he thought of depicting Julie as a woman who was separated from her lover and married to another man; the truth seems to be that the subsequent relations with Mme d'Houdetot were not unaffected by the earlier mood of escapist fantasy. At the same time the experiences of real life would serve to confirm his first intention of modifying the imaginative fantasy in a more realistic sense. While he was constantly preoccupied with idealistic and often frankly escapist impulses, Rousseau nevertheless always preserved a certain psychological honesty and a determination to probe his own state of mind, and, in spite of the obvious limitations of his self-knowledge (especially during periods of paranoid breakdown), he was haunted by a desire to find out the truth about himself. It seems unlikely that Jean-Jacques would ever have found complete satisfaction in the kind of naïve day-dreaming reflected in the idealistic mood of *La Nouvelle Héloïse*. The process of deliberate literary creation would also serve to bring him back to a more realistic appreciation of his own inner being and, while still remaining on the level of imaginative

---

[1] On the cultural implications and antecedents of this idealism see J. L. Bellenot, 'Les Formes de l'amour dans "La Nouvelle Héloïse"', in *Annales*, xxxiii, 1953–5.

fantasy, he would be impelled to resolve his inner conflicts by means
of a development that was in closer conformity with his complex personal needs. In a word, the frustration of Saint-Preux's love for Julie
was not merely an occasion for evoking a mood of conventional literary
pathos (although Rousseau was certainly not unmindful of this aspect
of the question), but also a means of enabling him to analyse certain
elements of his own personal situation.

Rousseau is quite aware that love, however ideal and perfect it may
be, cannot remain a mere symbol, for it involves two particular human
beings who must adapt themselves with all their idiosyncrasies to the
demands of a specific situation. The most idealistic efforts to achieve a
perfect union have to overcome not only external obstacles but inner
resistances and tensions which originate in the personalities of the
lovers themselves. Moreover, since these lovers are directly related to
their author's own inner life, Rousseau will not hesitate to link their
efforts to overcome the peculiar difficulties of their situation with some
of his own deepest convictions concerning the relations of the two sexes
and the wider problem of erotic love. Thus we shall find re-emerging
in the pages of *La Nouvelle Héloïse* many features that have already
been examined within the context of Rousseau's psychological development, but transformed and modified through a deliberate effort of
conscious literary creation and personal analysis.

One of the main problems of the novel is tied to the lovers' own
awareness that the difficulties of their position are exasperated not
simply by the presence of external obstacles (and particularly by the
prejudices of 'society') but also—and especially—by their awareness
that each is a separate personality embodying the distinctive characteristics of his own sex as well as the more intimate qualities peculiar to
himself. From the outset Rousseau saw in Saint-Preux an image of his
own personality, a being whom he invested with his own virtues and
defects. It is not a case of a simple, direct projection of his immediate
self into a fictitious character who lives out his own immediate situation: it is not a question of a thinly disguised autobiography; Saint-
Preux is a much younger and fresher man than the tired and partially
disillusioned middle-aged author who was the real Jean-Jacques. As the
latter well puts it to Bernardin de Saint-Pierre, 'it is not quite what I
was, but what I should like to have been'.[1] In some ways Saint-Preux
appears as a kind of simplified Rousseau, a personal might-have-been
whom he creates out of his own frustrations and disappointments. More

[1] B. de Saint-Pierre, op. cit., pp. 139–40.

especially the novel's hero is a Rousseau who might have existed had he been able to find an object worthy of his love and (more important still) had he been able to pursue that object with a genuinely single-minded purpose. Saint-Preux is thus a Jean-Jacques reflecting upon the possibilities of his earlier life and imaginatively reliving them in such a way as to reduce the whole meaning of his existence to this single dimension of erotic love. In sacrificing everything to the pursuit of his love for Julie, Saint-Preux is expressing an attitude which his creator was never able to adopt in his own life but with which his imagination now plays as a means of relieving the tensions and frustrations of his immediate existence.

That Saint-Preux is invested with many of the characteristics of the real Jean-Jacques is obvious enough, and Daniel Mornet, in his classic edition of the novel, has noted various interesting parallels. Like Rousseau himself, Saint-Preux is a man who lives on his emotions; he is impulsive and quick-tempered, endowed with a highly sensitive imagination that frequently involves him in a state of tormenting anxiety; he is also revealed as a 'weak' but not a 'wicked' man, and, in the last resort, appears to be almost pathetically dependent on the affection of others. However, the main emphasis of the novel does not ultimately fall on any of these characteristics, for what really distinguishes Saint-Preux is the fact that for him love expresses the *absolute and unique value of his life*, and only in a purely imaginative sense may Rousseau be said to have pursued this ideal. What remained for the real Rousseau a merely entrancing if disquieting possibility becomes in his hero a reality governing the whole course of his life. 'But I, Julie, alas! a wanderer, without family and almost without fatherland, I have only you on earth, and love alone takes the place of everything else' (ii. 70). Nothing in his subsequent behaviour really belies this early statement. He lives and exists only through Julie and his love for her (ii. 301); this love which forms 'his life's destiny' is the source of a pleasure which is independent of fortune 'and the rest of the universe'. He is particularly fond of insisting how the 'whole universe' is circumscribed by this single factor of his love.[1] His complete personality is utterly absorbed by his love for this 'unique', 'incomparable' and 'perfect mortal', who combines within herself all the perfections of which a living woman is capable. Since it is so absolute and exclusive, his love emerges as a dynamic, irresistible force which lies beyond the control of his will. Drawing its strength from the very depths of his being, it is 'a

[1] Cf. iii. 79, 158; iv. 102, 108, 120, for similar expressions.

consuming fire' and 'an intoxicating ecstasy'—a basic impulse which animates the self's other feelings, giving them their 'greatness', 'elevation', and 'sublimity'.

The thwarting of his passion by external obstacles intensifies certain contradictions which had always formed part of Saint-Preux's character, and here again we can detect a close resemblance between him and his creator. Like Jean-Jacques himself, he is a man of a fundamentally unstable temperament; he is impetuous, quick-tempered, and ebullient, and yet shy, fearful, and inhibited; often eager and passionate, he is at other times diffident and insecure. Moments of great joy may give way to moods of despair and melancholy; the supreme felicity of love is followed by deep despondency. The effect of these contradictions is to expose him to a feeling of precariousness which, while not making him doubt his love for Julie, constantly reminds him of the mediocrity of his fortune and the frustrating, hostile nature of the world in which he lives. This insecurity is exacerbated by the very factor which helps to raise his love to such sublime heights: a 'fiery imagination' which 'carries everything to extremes' (ii. 235).[1] Although his imagination is 'fiery', 'ardent', and 'over-heated', it is also 'disordered' and 'anxious' and so increases his torment when he is away from his beloved. He is even led to nurse pathological suspicions of his friend Lord Bomston and in this respect the novel curiously prefigures Rousseau's later relations with Hume. Hence both the idealistic and anxiety-ridden aspects of his love involve him in an unrealistic appreciation of his situation. Ultimately these contradictions will lead him, as we shall see, from an affirmative and aggressive attitude to one of extraordinary emotional dependence on the woman he loves; the violent, passionate lover is really a 'weak' and 'frail' man whose virtue, honesty, and greatness of soul remain possibilities rather than actual attributes of his everyday life. Here again the parallel between Saint-Preux and Rousseau is striking, for, although both are convinced that the thought of doing evil never entered their hearts, their 'weakness' leads them into grievous errors of judgement and conduct.[2] Because he is tormented by anxiety and insecurity, Saint-Preux is 'easy to subjugate', as the perspicacious Wolmar rightly observes (iii. 274). It is typical of such a man that he should be given (again like Jean-Jacques himself) to sudden infatua-

---

[1] Cf. *supra*, p. 21.

[2] Cf. iv. 259. 'If your heart is capable of an unexpected fault, most certainly it never came close to premeditated evil. That is what distinguishes the frail man from the wicked man.'

tions which bring him under the sway of personalities stronger than his own. Lord Bomston is admittedly a noble, high-minded aristocrat who is a worthy mentor, but, as Julie shrewdly remarks, Saint-Preux's sudden affection for him shows 'how liable he is to become prejudiced for or against somebody at first sight' (ii. 153).[1] A powerful and dominant personality while still full of passion, he has only to encounter apparently unsurmountable obstacles in order to become dependent on other people (against whom he may later harbour feelings of hostility and resentment). The way is thus prepared, from the very first, for the 'ascendancy' of a reformed Julie over a lover who—in everything except his passion—is a weak, unstable personality. As Claire puts it, he is 'a simple soul who clings to all that surrounds Julie'.

Particularly remarkable in this respect is the way in which Saint-Preux reflects yet another essential trait of Rousseau's own character: his persistent tendency to see himself through other people's eyes. We have already suggested that, in Jean-Jacques's case, this type of reaction may have its origin in the emotional experiences of his early life. To seek the origin of any characteristic in a fictitious character is, of course, an otiose task, but it is interesting to note how Saint-Preux echoes Rousseau's constant need to feel himself the object of another's *esteem*. This is already discernible in his early reactions to Julie. 'Even though I were to die a hundred times, I must be esteemed by Julie' (ii. 144). 'Let the rest of the world think of me as it will', he tells her, 'all my worth lies in your esteem' (ii. 122). Once the possibility of marriage has disappeared, the emphasis upon esteem becomes even stronger. It is not only Julie but other 'superior' characters like M. de Wolmar and Lord Bomston who must give him their approbation. From Bomston he wants 'an enlightened esteem'; he fears nothing so much as Wolmar's disapproval. In this way he obtains, in spite of his solitude and anxiety, a certain sense of his personal worth: he can esteem himself and be sure of his 'virtue' because he is esteemed by others whose personal value and superiority he readily acknowledges; he is conscious of belonging to the select company of 'privileged souls' (iv. 120).

Rousseau's involvement with his characters also facilitates a development which had already played an important role in his personal existence. Although he was 'consumed' by an all-powerful need for

---

[1] 'In my youth when I thought that I had found in the world the same people as I had known in my books, I abandoned myself unreservedly to anyone who could take me in with a certain jargon by which I have always been duped' (*LM.* 1134). Already in 1740 Jean-Jacques had told Mme de Warens: 'You have taught me not to fly to extremes on first appearances' (*CG* i. 131).

love, his experience convinced him that perfection was never likely to be found in real life. In the same way, the simplified outlook of Saint-Preux, who is tied to an absolute love for a single person, tends to conflict with other elements in his unstable temperament. While not doubting the strength of his feeling for Julie, he has to recognize that even the most intense erotic passion, especially when it is unfulfilled, is fraught with certain dangers. As soon as he is faced by an irrevocable separation from Julie as a potential wife, he readily dwells on the limitations of his earlier outlook. However idealistic its first expression, physical passion is always threatened with satiety and *ennui*. There may come a moment when the two lovers are unable to sustain their erotic ecstasy, and with the diminution of passion there may rise to the surface of the personality those tormenting contradictions which we have already seen to be an integral part of Saint-Preux's character, but which are held in abeyance by the intensity of his love. The dream of ecstasy is often disturbed by the thought that consummation will be followed by despondency and lassitude. This conviction is strengthened by the more general consideration that passion is liable to founder on the reef of *time*. Erotic love owes its ecstasy to the moment, and in the actual experience of love this moment seems like an eternity which has neither past nor future; but this 'eternity' appears retrospectively as a mere isolated moment of life. As Saint-Preux puts it;

Days of pleasure and glory, you were not those of a mortal man; you were too beautiful to be perishable. A gentle ecstasy absorbed your whole duration, and gathered it into a single point like that of eternity. For me there was neither past nor future, and I savoured in a single moment the delights of a thousand ages. Alas! you have vanished like the lightning-flash. This eternity of happiness was only one moment of my life. Time has resumed its slow movement in the moments of my despair, and tedium measures out in long years the unhappy days which remain to me (iii. 13).

Even when circumstances are propitious, the ephemeral character of passion demands a constant renewal of the experience which may finally lose its freshness and vivacity. In the restriction of Saint-Preux's actual existence a depressing awareness of passion's futility is only too likely to take hold of his personality; he may come to see that the reduction of life to a single erotic dimension is incompatible with the complexity and contradictions of complete human experience.

The anxiety and danger associated with the direct expression of erotic passion help to explain Saint-Preux's acceptance of his apparently false position in the Wolmar household, for, as we have seen, the idea of the *ménage à trois* is in conformity with the demands of Rousseau's own temperament. From this point of view, there is no reason to suppose that the theme was due to Jean-Jacques's relations with Mme d'Houdetot, for his dream of a triangular relationship with her and Saint-Lambert merely reflected an already deeply implanted tendency in his character. At first sight this relationship appears as a mere compromise, an inadequate substitute for full erotic love, but it has the great advantage of bringing to Saint-Preux a sense of inner peace by freeing him from the temporal limitations of sexual love. Whereas passion tended to exasperate his anxiety by isolating him and making him conscious of his loneliness, the new triangular relationship allows him to feel that he is at last integrated into an intimate society greater than himself. He is also relieved of sexual anxiety since he can obtain a vicarious satisfaction from an imaginative identification with another's erotic experience. Here again Rousseau's own outlook is reflected in this curious attempt to find a substitute for the complete sexual relationship, from which he had been largely excluded by his own masochism and conviction that the absolute erotic 'enjoyment', which he supposed would follow from the fusion of his personality with the body and soul of a woman, lay for ever beyond his reach. In the *ménage à trois* Rousseau–Saint-Preux can play a passive role which nonetheless brings some positive emotional satisfaction. In this respect the mood of Saint-Preux in the presence of the married Julie is very similar to that of Jean-Jacques with Mme de Warens, although in the novel it is idealized through the elimination of any specifically sexual implications. Here Saint-Preux feels himself to be sustained by the loving presence of a superior human being: the 'ardent' but 'weak' lover alleviates the pain and disappointment of his most cherished ambitions by developing an emotional dependence on persons who are psychologically more secure than himself. Moreover, he no longer feels himself alone in a hostile world since he forms part of an intimate group which seems sufficient in itself.

He is further encouraged to accept this solution to his personal problems through the belief that the act of falling in love is not reversible. So completely is he committed to his love that he would rather remain with Julie as a 'friend' and 'brother' than lose her for ever. As soon as she refuses to continue the old love-relationship, he realizes that through her he has experienced a kind of 'alienation' of himself, which has transformed for all time the essential quality of his existence. 'One night, one single night, has changed my whole soul for ever' (iii. 40). Henceforth he no longer belongs to himself but to Julie. 'I admit that I no longer belong to myself, my alienated soul is completely in you' (ii. 114). 'Yes, my Julie, it is indeed you who form my life and being' (ii. 186). 'Your will is enough for me' (ii. 300). He also feels that he is somehow possessed by the loved object, that a part of her personality has been incorporated into his. During the years of separation he carries within his heart an indestructible 'pure image', 'this faithful reflection of Julie', whose presence testifies to the disappearance of his 'first soul' and the 'animation' of his immediate existence by the soul 'which she has given him' (ii. 304–5). 'No, delightful source of my being, I shall no longer have any soul but your soul. I shall be nothing but a part of you' (iii. 42). No doubt this process was initiated through physical possession, but the 'consuming fire' of passion has now become 'celestial', 'eternal', and 'immortal'—purified and transformed by the spiritual element which was present even in its erotic moments.

What is particularly interesting about Rousseau's treatment of erotic love and what also shows a distinct development in his awareness of the implications of personal existence is his effort to relate the problem to a more conscious and definite conception of human personality. Many of the psychological features analysed in our earlier survey emerged only sporadically at various stages of his life and were not always consciously present to Rousseau's own mind. In his novel he tries to see the issue within the context of a more definite view of human existence. It may be said at once that he does not attempt to solve the problem of frustrated passion through the development of some kind of anarchic individualism. On the contrary, Saint-Preux–Rousseau tends to suggest the spiritualization of his attitude through the elaboration of a Platonic outlook which sets very definite limits to any excessively individualistic attitude. If Saint-Preux can undergo this quasi-spiritual transformation of his personality, it is only because every man has within him a 'divine model' whose actualization in real experience provides the true goal of human endeavour. If the 'pure' and 'immortal image' which inspired Saint-Preux was at first little more than an idealized memory of Julie and, as such, remained unsubstantial and precarious—even though it did form such an intimate part of himself—the re-establishment of communication with the real Julie replaces this idealized memory by a living presence—her 'pure soul'—which henceforth animates his spiritual being and provides the basis of a reciprocal, personal relationship. Such briefly is the solution given to the problem of his thwarted passion.

Yet this solution is not complete, firstly, because it is not yet embodied in a specific, concrete mode of existence, and, secondly, because it has not been properly related to the evolution of Julie's own character. This is all the more important as Julie, like other characters in the novel, is to some extent a composite figure. She is not merely a portrait of the perfect woman as Rousseau imagined her in the light of his idealized memories of his own early experiences with women,[1] for in the later stages of the novel, especially when she turns to religion, she becomes identified with a part of his own personality. In one respect, therefore, she is just as much a dimension of the author's character as Saint-Preux himself. In the passionate phase of the work this element of subjective projection is not so marked, for Julie there emerges as the ideal woman. Yet even this element of idealization will provide us with valuable insights into Rousseau's own attitude towards women and will help to support or modify the attitude already examined in our last chapter. Because she is the spontaneous projection of his own idealized memories, she will enable us to obtain a useful view of Rousseau's basic attitude towards women—a view that will be all the more interesting for being free from the distorting influences of self-conscious auto-biography or personal apologetic.

If we consider her character as it is depicted in the first two parts of the novel, it looks as if she is as sure of her love as Saint-Preux himself, for she too insists on the perfect conformity of their characters, the reciprocity of their feelings and the completeness and permanence of an affection which involves their entire personalities. In short, for Julie as well as for Saint-Preux, their love would be a perfect example of what 'nature' intended men to be, were they able to escape from the corrupting influence of society. Even the inner conflict to which Julie is ultimately subjected does not go beyond the limits of this basic dichotomy. As the daughter of a tyrannical father obsessed by his nobleman's status, she has been brought up to respect the sacredness of family ties and, being naturally affectionate, she feels very strongly the claims of 'blood'. When the baron refuses to allow her to marry Saint-Preux, she is faced with a 'horrible alternative': she has either to bring disgrace and misery on her parents or to reject the 'love' which is a free and spontaneous attachment to the man of her choice. If 'love' is finally sacrificed, it is because natural ties of blood prove ultimately stronger than those of erotic inclination. Yet both feelings are 'natural' in their different ways, for they correspond to fundamental impulses within the

[1] For V. Demole, 'Julie is Mme de Warens, Clarens les Charmettes' (op. cit., p. 32) This is partly true, but too simple as a complete explanation of her character.

personality. Whilst the blood-relationship is primordial and instinctive, love is linked to the development of certain potentialities which involve higher and more complex elements of the personality. Nevertheless, the responsibility for this conflict does not rest upon Julie but upon a society whose harmful prejudices place her in such a cruel dilemma. It is clear that, from this point of view, there is nothing in the order of nature which justifies this conflict. In a properly organized society parental and erotic love would (we may suppose) not be incompatible. On this particular plane, therefore, the interpretation of the novel presents no special difficulties and the pathos generated is quite in accordance with that traditionally associated with the conflict between love and duty.

Thus far Julie's character does not rise above an ideal, symbolic level. To these general features, however, are added a number of specific characteristics which are psychologically more revealing. The early stress upon Julie's *pudeur* and timidity underlines a feature that Rousseau always considered to be essential to every woman.[1] But this modesty is given particular significance in *La Nouvelle Héloïse* since it expresses more than a conventional means of enabling a woman to defend her virtue against masculine aggression. Even when due allowance is made for the fact that Julie is indulging in an erotic union which inevitably conflicts with the values inculcated in her by her upbringing, her *pudeur* seems to reflect a deep emotional resistance to the physical side of love. At times she appears to be convinced that sexual union involves a degradation of love: because it is bound up with a passion that first of all seeks 'pleasure', physical possession corrupts the heart (iii. 47). For her the happiest time of their love was when 'its sacred ardour made modesty all the dearer and honesty all the more lovable', for 'desires seemed to be born only to give us the honour of overcoming them and being on that account all the worthier of each other' (iii. 59–60). Her greatest delight is 'to love purely', for 'paradise on earth' is equated with a life of 'love' and 'innocence' (ii. 33). Julie tends to see love as an essentially peaceful, innocent, and platonic relationship 'which speaks to the heart without stirring the senses'. Already at the beginning of their relationship she had made the striking statement: 'My too affectionate heart needs love, but my senses do not need a lover' (ii. 32). Throughout the novel she is inclined to resist the absolute passion which forms the substance of Saint-Preux's life; she does not deny her love, but she does not wish to see it in a physical light; she seems to recoil before the feeling of being utterly committed to an erotic union.

[1] Cf. also *Émile*, Book V, and the *Lettre à d'Alembert*, for the same idea.

It is not inappropriate that on one occasion she should be addressed as a 'cold and mysterious sweetheart' (ii. 114). Such an attitude is not of course consistently maintained, for it alternates with affirmations of undying love, and Julie in the end gives way to Saint-Preux's physical demands, but this element of reserve and discretion is strong enough for us to treat it as a significant factor that helps to determine her ultimate decision.

A curious, if indirect, confirmation of her resistance to Saint-Preux's attitude is revealed in the statement, made after her marriage, that Wolmar was in fact a more suitable husband for her than Saint-Preux and that, if she had to choose again, it is Wolmar rather than Saint-Preux who would be favoured (ii. 90). The 'cold' Wolmar, with his lack of passion and refusal to make absolute emotional demands, was in the end more congenial to her than the intense and fiery Saint-Preux. Shortly before her death she tells Wolmar that he was 'of all men the one who suited her best' because he helped her to live 'happy and wise' (iv. 306). In Julie's eyes, the danger of passion is that it removes from love that element of 'perfection' and 'uprightness' which forms its greatest charm.

This brings us to the main divergence of attitude between the two lovers. Whilst the frustration of his love casts Saint-Preux into despair and melancholy, he rarely shows any genuine sense of guilt, for, deep within himself, he cannot really believe that what he has felt and done is blameworthy. The evil does not lie in his own soul, but in the cruelty of a society which has prevented the consummation of his love in marriage. If he occasionally speaks of his 'criminal passion', it is simply because the influence of Julie's personality has momentarily induced him to echo her opinion. Julie, on the other hand, constantly treats their passion as a source of shame and guilt. Their relationship was a 'criminal intercourse' which corrupted her whole being. Her sense of guilt is so strong that she sometimes gives way to an almost masochistic desire for self-abasement. Indeed her self-reproaches are such that her friend Claire is induced to observe that 'this affectionate soul always fears that it is not experiencing sufficient grief, and it is a sort of pleasure for her to add to the feeling of her troubles all that can embitter them' (iii. 19). Julie thinks that she has an 'ungrateful' and 'unnatural' heart that has been 'degraded' by this shameful relationship with Saint-Preux. Admittedly, her sense of guilt is exasperated by her (subsequently unjustified) belief that this illicit love has hastened her mother's death, but, even when due allowance is made for the effects of this intense emotional strain, the idea of having been corrupted through physical passion still remains. When, finally, she is about to marry Wolmar, she sees herself as 'an impure victim who defiles the sacrifice at which she is to be offered up' (iii. 62).

Yet this feeling of guilt is clearly distinguished in Julie's mind from a genuine sense of having really sinned through an act of will. Though speaking constantly of shame and guilt, she seeks to minimize the extent of her misdoing by attributing it to 'error' and 'weakness', as though it were something she had done almost in spite of herself. Either she was temporarily carried away by Saint-Preux's passion and imbued with a desire which would not have arisen spontaneously in her own self, or else she yielded through 'pity' for her unhappy lover. If this fall from virtue is described as a 'crime', it was one that was in some sense involuntary and carried out against the prompting of her intimate nature. She is 'weak' and 'guilty', but not 'depraved' and 'sinful'. Such a viewpoint is in complete conformity with her resistance to physical love as such. Moreover, for Julie, erotic passion means first and foremost a loss of innocence and purity, and it is from this awareness of lost innocence that she derives much of her guilt. Whereas Saint-Preux seeks to intensify their relationship by carrying it on to an ecstatic plane, Julie tries to idealize it by limiting it to a 'union of heart and soul'. In this way she hopes to retain or recapture something of her lost innocence. Long before they give way to their physical desires, Julie expresses her true feelings when she speaks of a love in which 'the charms of our hearts' union are joined to those of innocence: no fear, no shame disturbs our bliss; in the midst of love's true pleasures, we can speak of virtue without blushing' (ii. 33). Julie will never abandon this idea of a 'perfect union' with a 'soul that knows how to love purely and innocently'. She is all more inclined to adopt this attitude as, unlike Saint-Preux, she is closely integrated into a fixed social and family pattern that provides her with emotional stability. Whilst Saint-Preux's passion is likely to be intensified by his social isolation, and his sense of being in an environment which is different from that of his *roturier* upbringing, Julie's fear of being uprooted from her settled position makes her cling more tenaciously to the ideal of an innocent happiness. She will look back with increasing regret to the days when she led 'a simple and industrious life', for this was 'the happy time when she lived quietly in the midst of her family', confident that her existence was in conformity with the 'honesty' and 'modesty' she always held so dear. The happiness of that period came from a 'gentle and charming security' associated with the thought of leading a 'uniform' life without conflict. Hence, whilst Saint-Preux's love is essentially a forward-looking, tormenting, and constantly developing aspiration towards the possession of its object, Julie tends to retreat into a retrospective, almost regressive attitude which is haunted by the nostalgic memory of a lost innocence; and this attitude is encouraged, as we have seen, not only by her attachment to her parents but also by her resistance to the erotic aspect of love.

So far, then, Julie shows an attitude towards love which is curiously reminiscent of Rousseau's own views. Love's emotional content reflects a yearning for innocence and peace which not only involves the exclusion of sexual passion, but offers a powerful resistance to the whole idea of physical possession. If Julie and Saint-Preux fail to find happiness, it is not simply because of the evils of 'society', but because woman (in Rousseau's eyes) cannot properly reciprocate the male's desire for complete erotic experience. Woman, he seems to say, is exposed to a fundamental erotic incapacity which must keep the two sexes emotionally apart. Julie thus plays a dual role: she seems to represent two aspects of Rousseau's experiences with women—the influence of his relationship with the promiscuous and 'cold' Mme de Warens who perhaps helped to create the conviction in Rousseau's mind that the 'sensitive' woman separated love from sexual pleasure; more fundamentally still, she may reflect his own inability to integrate the instinctual and emotional elements of erotic experience and so accept the idea of love as a relation embracing both the emotional and sexual aspects of the personality. To this should perhaps be added a feeling of guilt (already observable in his early views) about the whole question of sex. Everything thus impels him to retreat from the full implications of sexual experience and take refuge in a nostalgic desire for a state of primordial emotional innocence. But passion is too vivid to be excluded from his experience and so he embodies it in the character of Saint-Preux, thereby giving it an autonomous idealistic existence which is nevertheless unable to free itself completely from the attraction of non-erotic emotions. Both Julie and Saint-Preux, therefore, represent different aspects of Rousseau's attitude towards love, though simplified and idealized in accordance with the needs of his imagination.

Had the two lovers been free to marry, this conflict might have been resolved, because Julie, for all her fears, does 'love' Saint-Preux as the man for whom 'heaven' intended her, and this love might well have overcome her sense of guilt. But the sacrifice of love to duty helps to

K

increase rather than diminish this guilt, so that her problem will be to find a new 'innocence' and a new 'virtue' that are capable of 'giving her back to herself' and restoring her self-respect. Her task will be to show that this sacrifice, which is ostensibly due to morality and necessity rather than to inclination, can in fact provide the basis of an outlook which is actually preferable to the old relationship in the sense that it will provide a sounder basis for their mutual happiness. It is not simply a question of making the best of an awkward situation but of showing that the new solution is intrinsically more satisfying to the emotions than the old passionate relationship. The subsequent stress on morality, therefore, should not be allowed to conceal the essential truth that in each phase of their relationship the fundamental psychological purpose is the same: the attainment of happiness. This becomes all the more evident when we recall that the earlier relations, for all their ecstatic idealism, were imbued with certain anxiety-provoking elements. However, these elements remain too unobtrusive to be made the occasion for a sudden change of attitude, since they are subordinated to the main idealistic emphasis of the 'love' novel; psychologically too, they correspond to only one part of Julie's personality. The immediate event enabling her to change from an ardent mistress to a virtuous wife is the 'conversion' which transforms her from a weak and fearful girl into a strong, dominant woman.[1] This 'happy revolution' is, in the first place, the apparent result of divine intervention but, very significantly, Julie acknowledges that it is a change which she had already desired on her own account. Painful though it is in many ways, her 'sacrifice' implies a secret complicity on her part inasmuch as it corresponds to the impulse which had already resisted Saint-Preux's absolute erotic demands. Fully alive to the dangers of her former love, she now draws comfort and strength from the 'inner peace' which comes from 'a clear conscience and calm senses' (iii. 64). Moreover, this sense of security is strengthened by a continual condemnation of her past behaviour as a 'blind' and 'disordered aberration'; indeed her present state of mind suggests that she sometimes takes an almost pathological pleasure in vilifying the earlier relationship.

A consequence of her conversion to a 'moral' outlook and a life of virtue in a loveless marriage is the release of emotions which change the fearful, inhibited girl into a mature woman remarkable for her tenderness and sensitivity. She now has an 'expansive soul' that is endowed

---

[1] G. Vallette (op. cit., p. 162) sees in Julie's wedding resolution an expression of the Protestant moral conscience with its horror of lies and equivocation.

with such a 'gift for loving' that her heart 'gives life to all around her' (iii. 139). Julie's personality radiates an irresistible emotional warmth. This expansiveness may take the form of affectionate benevolence to social inferiors or of a more intimate feeling for her children, husband, and friends. All this forms part of an 'invincible ascendancy' which 'subjugated them all', a 'sublime elevation' and influence which, for Saint-Preux at least, is truly 'despotic'. Although this new Julie is obviously drawn after Rousseau's idea of a grown-up woman, it is worth noting that his stress on the expansive side of her nature corresponds to another very powerful need of his own personality. In the section of the *Confessions* which deals with the genesis of *La Nouvelle Héloïse* he stresses how he needed an outlet for the expansive side of his nature, and, in attributing this remarkable capacity to Julie herself, he prepares the way for a closer identification between her character and his own. Already, therefore, she loses the clarity which belongs to a completely independent character existing in its own right, for Rousseau is not simply evoking idealized memories of his own experience but looking more closely into the emotional needs of his own soul.

This movement towards the identification of Rousseau and Julie is clearly indicated, I think, by the introduction of an important new theme in the novel—that of religion. Already at the time of Julie's marriage to Wolmar God makes a brief appearance, but it is only in the last two parts that His role is quite preponderant, so that God-fearing Julie is at the very end little more than a mere mouthpiece for Rousseau's religious ideas and ceases to have a convincingly independent existence of her own. It is this direct projection of the author's own feelings and ideas into his heroine's personality that weakens the psychological credibility of the last stages of the work. What is particularly interesting from our point of view is not so much the didactic aspect of Rousseau's religious teaching as the specific emotional satisfaction which her relationship to God allows her to give to her expansive needs. The God whom she adores is one of peace and love; He satisfies the 'infinite need to love' which she now experiences in a spiritual sense only. The religious attitude tends, however, to become an emotional impulse which leads to a state of reverie and contemplation. It is an occasion for a sort of quietist ecstasy and an expansive identification of the self with the 'vast being' which is the source of ultimate peace. So far from strengthening the self in its relationships with its fellow-men, this attitude threatens to draw it away from the world and absorb it into a self-sufficient solitude. From this point of view the novel's conclusion will in a sense show that Julie, after all, cannot find lasting peace in the strictly 'moral' life of marriage (the qualities of which she is frequently extolling) since her contemplative religious moods—and her ultimate death—give her an emotional peace which is denied to her in her everyday life at Clarens, idyllic though it is supposed to be. In spite of herself she still experiences an absolute emotional need which religion alone is able to satisfy. We are far from suggesting that the novel's religious outlook can be strictly limited to this kind of emotional reaction, for Rousseau (through the person of Saint-Preux) is fully alive to certain spiritual dangers inherent in this contemplative outlook, and he does not hesitate to reproach Julie for her 'quietist' tendencies, but it is certainly an attitude which prolongs one essential aspect of the work's mood.

Although the introduction of the religious element suggests that this was Rousseau's way of resolving the psychological difficulties of the novel's main theme, and so of fundamental emotional conflicts within himself, the adumbration of the religious theme is preceded by an effort to suggest a more definite and stable conception of human existence, even in its psychological and moral aspects. From this point of view Julie's outlook tends to implement certain ideas already outlined in connexion with Saint-Preux's character. Rousseau is here taking the opportunity of defining more explicitly than hitherto his own conception of human personality. Man's essential being cannot be assimilated either to his passionate, instinctive nature (however idealistic it may sometimes appear to be) or to the social self which is but a factitious production of civilization. To find his real being a man must 'retire into himself' (*rentrer en lui-même*) and search his own soul; he will then discover that the source of truth lies in a spiritual element which lifts him above the vagaries and vicissitudes of sensuous existence. As Julie puts it in an eloquent letter to Saint-Preux: 'My friend, withdraw into your own soul; there you will always find the source of this sacred fire which inflamed us so often with the love of sublime virtues; there you will see this eternal image of true beauty, the contemplation of which inspires us with a saintly enthusiasm, and which our passions incessantly disfigure without ever being able to destroy it.' Once he has found this 'divine model' and this 'inner effigy', a man will receive the strength to resist the lure of guilty passion; he will become aware of a 'sublime and pure soul, triumphing over its passions and ruling over itself' (iv. 3). As Julie says, 'withdrawing into myself, I find there the calmness of reason', for she thus escapes from the torments of a divided existence to live henceforth in the 'silence of the passions' and the 'tranquillity of meditation'. Such a person, it seems, must be happy because God has endowed him with 'freedom to do good, conscience to wish for it and reason to choose it' (iii. 106).[1] This spiritual essence is in fact always there and is probably indestructible, although its image may easily be obscured by passion and prejudice. Hence the task of those who have lost their first purity is to recover this pristine innocence by an act of will. In one of Rousseau's favourite phrases a man must be 'given back to himself'. There must be—in an expression later used by Kierkegaard—a kind of 'repetition' by which a man wins back his spiritual nature. This will certainly be Julie's object—to be restored to herself in all her virtue and self-respect.

Although this process of moral and spiritual rehabilitation is to be Julie's and Saint-Preux's primary task in life, it is not easy to 'change a tender love into a friendship which is not less keen'. They hope certainly to create a 'brotherly familiarity' marked by the 'peace of innocence', and to do this they must 'see and love each other', feel each other's presence and win mutual esteem (iv. 219). But this transformation cannot be effected by their own strength and will; they need another person to guide and help them in their struggles and doubts. The presence of a living person is all the more necessary to Julie as she is not freed—in spite of her conversion—from inner conflict; she continues to suffer from feelings of guilt, and, for a long time, her sense of un-worthiness is increased by her inability to confess to her husband the truth about her past wrong-doing. Her impulse towards virtue, though real, is largely the result of an emotional need which of itself is unable to provide the inner discipline necessary to secure victory over tempta-tion; for this purpose she needs the stimulus of reason and will—a semi-heroic morality which cannot be drawn from her own expansive soul. Just as Saint-Preux has to draw strength from an ideal self whose virtue is sustained by an awareness of his beloved's esteem, so must Julie herself find support in the esteem of a morally superior personality. The importance of M. de Wolmar lies in the fact that he is able to perform this precise function.

I do not propose to discuss here the question of Wolmar's atheism, an incidental trait introduced into the final version of the novel for

---

[1] The idea recurs in Part VI, Letter VII (iv. 246), but worded rather differently: 'reason to know what is good, conscience to love it and freedom to choose it'. Mornet also reproduces the version given in Rousseau's draft: 'He has given us freedom to follow our will, conscience to wish for what is good and reason to know it.'

purely didactic purposes. The atheistic Wolmar probably did not form part of Rousseau's original literary intention, and the question scarcely arises in the first parts of the work. A rather clumsy note (iii. 87) shows how the author tried to graft on to his original novel this additional characteristic. As critics have suggested, Wolmar finally emerges as a typical eighteenth-century rationalist, a *philosophe* who incorporates various aspects of real people like Saint-Lambert and d'Holbach. As in Julie's case, he is a composite figure who fulfils a number of literary roles. As far as the fundamental structure of the novel is concerned, Wolmar's significance is (in my view) not to be found in this direction, but in the specifically *moral* element he brings into the situation. This ethical content is what Julie and Saint-Preux are not able to provide from their own inner resources. Saint-Preux's strength lay (as we have seen) in his dynamic conception of erotic love, and the frustration of this side of his personality leaves him utterly disoriented and eventually leads him to complete emotional dependence on Julie. She, in her turn, strives after an ideal of calmness and security which is essentially emotional rather than ethical in origin. Moreover, in spite of all the psychological limitations already noted, they continue to be drawn to each other and their 'love' can be held in check only by a prohibition which seems to come from outside themselves and yet is intimately connected with their personalities. In many respects Wolmar thus seems to symbolize the *moral conscience* which Rousseau, in his more lucid moments, thought to be an integral part of every human being and which at certain times he felt to be very active within himself, even though it was apt to be obscured by other emotions. The introduction of this highly moral element is all the more natural when we recall that, for all his many lapses, Jean-Jacques was never able completely to forget the stern ethical ideals of the Geneva society in which he was brought up and in which he spent his earliest and most impressionable years. We have also seen the influence of this outlook on his earlier sporadic efforts to adopt a 'heroic' attitude towards life and to appear as a man of principle and truth. Wolmar thus represents, like Saint-Preux and Julie in their different ways, an important dimension of Rousseau's own personality—the ideal moral self whose influence cannot ultimately be avoided.

Viewed in this light, the presentation of M. de Wolmar has several interesting features. It will be recalled that he is a rather mysterious and remote figure—a foreign aristocrat with an obscure history. Separated from Julie and Saint-Preux by a great difference in age, he is a man who comes, as it were, from another world. Throughout the novel he rarely forsakes his detachment. He is 'cold'—a man of reason and a stranger to passion, essentially an observer who is not emotionally concerned with the situation in which he finds himself; he has 'a calm soul and a cold heart' (iii. 249). His basic inclination is a 'natural taste for order' which gives his character a certain rigidity and detachment—and it is precisely with this 'love of order' that Rousseau tends to identify 'virtue' and 'morality'. Wolmar's sole emotional indulgence seems to have been his marriage with Julie. Generally speaking, he represents ordered understanding, and his aloofness from life gives him a certain immutability and strength. Yet this austere, rather forbidding figure is benevolent and wise. He is in fact a father-figure—a 'father', 'bene-factor', and 'liberator' to his 'children' who, as they admit, are sorely in need of guidance. Julie and Saint-Preux constantly acknowledge his superior wisdom and treat him with filial deference. Wolmar is also a kind of soul-surgeon, an eighteenth-century psychotherapist who has set himself the task of 'curing' a sick man of his guilty 'love' by putting him through a series of carefully devised 'tests' calculated to purify his personality of its morally dubious content. His method, it will be recalled, rests on the assumption that Saint-Preux loves in Julie only a creature of his imagination, an idealized memory of Julie d'Étange—a girl who no longer exists, for she has become Julie de Wolmar, the virtuous wife and mother. Once he has been confronted by the real Julie, he will be cured of his passion. Such at least is Wolmar's belief and hope.[1] More remarkable even than this aspect of Wolmar's character is the way in which he is occasionally identified with God—not Julie's quietist God but the Supreme Being who is the source of all moral power (iv. 42). Wolmar at times seems to have something of God's omniscience and omnipotence; he is described as a kind of all-seeing eye which has the power of looking into the most secret recesses of the heart (iii. 265–6), and Wolmar himself says that he 'loves to read into men's hearts'. 'If', he adds, 'I could change the nature of my being and become a living eye, I would willingly make this change.' At times the other characters look upon him as a man in whom this transforma-tion has already been effected. 'The discerning Wolmar', says Julie, 'has some supernatural gift for reading into the depths of people's hearts' and of seeing them 'as they are' (iii. 257, 265). 'I do not fear',

---

[1] Cf. É. Gilson, 'La Méthode de M. de Wolmar', in *Les Idées et les lettres* (Paris, 1932). M. Gilson sees Wolmar's 'method' as an application of the principles Rousseau proposed to develop in his treatise on *La Morale sensitive* (cf. *supra*, p. 17).

says Saint-Preux on another occasion when he is feeling particularly confident of his virtue, 'lest his enlightened eye should read in the depths of my heart' (iv. 139). It is obvious, therefore, why Wolmar becomes an object of great awe and respect: he is father, doctor, God —the only being capable of 'restoring' Julie and Saint-Preux 'to themselves' (iv. 220).

To some extent the supporting figure of Lord Bomston also gives moral strength to the other characters, although his role is considerably reduced in the later parts of the novel. Even so, he is a 'sublime' and 'strong soul', and those who are honoured by his esteem and friendship can also feel assured of their personal worth. To be admitted to Lord Edward's intimacy is to be one of those 'privileged' souls whose moral nobility and heroism raise them above the level of ordinary men. In Saint-Preux's case Bomston also satisfies an emotional need, for friendship can act as some kind of compensation for the frustration of erotic hopes. At one particular moment Saint-Preux tells the Englishman, 'I have only you in the whole world' (iii. 96). On another occasion Bomston, like Wolmar, is the recipient of an almost divine homage. 'His sublime soul is above that of men, and it is no more permissible to resist his kindnesses than those of the divinity' (ii. 287). This again is a striking illustration of the way in which Saint-Preux is apt to feel himself to be 'nothing' before these superior beings who create the meaning of his life. At times he lets himself be fashioned and moulded as if he were some kind of inert material that needs the mind and hand of another to give it shape and consistency. No doubt, in this immediate context, he realizes that friendship cannot be more than a consolation; it is not a genuine substitute for love. But it is not a negligible factor since it is one of the two idols at whose shrine Rousseau himself—at one stage of his life—had been prepared to worship. But by the time he was engaged on the final draft of *La Nouvelle Héloïse* the intensity of his earlier enthusiasm (as revealed in the period preceding his disillusionment with Diderot) had considerably diminished.

Since personal relations have to be expressed in particular situations, there remains the problem of finding a way of life capable of giving them stability and permanence. It is thus necessary to show in what concrete manner Saint-Preux and Julie seek to escape from the dilemma of unfulfilled love and to show the precise reason for the fascination of the new mode of existence created for them at Clarens. In the first place, it has to be emphasized that the 'world' of Clarens is one that has been largely fashioned by that superior moral being, M. de Wolmar, and it is there that Julie, in particular, can satisfy her emotional needs. She lives in 'a simple and well-regulated house in which order, peace and innocence reign; in which you see united without pomp or ostentation all that corresponds to man's true destination' (iii. 184). A moral world, it is yet personal and human. Its main function is to express the key-principle of every happy existence—'order' and 'rule'. At the same time the idea of order gives a due place to the essential freedom and dignity of the human personality. The society of Clarens is one from which all discord and strife are eliminated: it is an idyllic, paradisaical world which reproduces something of nature's pristine innocence. It is, how-ever, not a mere copy of primitive nature, but a kind of second or higher nature that has been re-created in accordance with all that is best in man and society. 'The pleasant equality which reigns here re-estab-lishes the order of nature' (iv. 138). Each inhabitant of the place looks like 'a new being recently come forth from nature's hands' (iv. 77). Unlike the passionate, restless striving of instinct, the mood of this world is essentially calm and static. Everybody has his appointed place and function from which he does not move, for he lives in a society governed by 'order', 'nature', and 'reason'. The highest emotional pleasures of this world are those of contemplation. If Julie and Saint-Preux experience moments of self-distrust, they are eventually dispelled by the existence of this ordered and innocent world whose security is guaranteed by the watchful presence and wisdom of M. de Wolmar.

Because the marriage on which this society rests is one of esteem rather than love, it is a relationship in which husband and wife, far from being completely absorbed in each other, are able to direct their energies and feelings outwards and to find satisfaction in fulfilling their obliga-tions to society. Such a moderate and disciplined affection stands in sharp contrast to the selfish pretensions of erotic passion with its permanent threat of anxiety, satiety and *ennui*. The difficulty with passionate love is, as we have seen, that if it lives and is created in the moment, it is also in the passing of the moment that it dies; it is thus unable to overcome the very obstacle which gives it intensity and value. On the other hand, the elimination of love makes it possible for the self to remain satisfied with a world that is in some sense timeless because it does not need to evolve or be modified. Such no doubt is the fascina-tion of this way of life for Julie, since it enables her to attain that pure, innocent and peaceful existence whose charms had attracted her even during the most intense phase of her love for Saint-Preux. At the same time this mode of life enhances her sense of value by enabling her to live in the midst of *her* world—a world of which she is the ostensible centre and in which even the 'cold' Wolmar admits an emotional dependence on his wife, for if he is the real creator of this world, she is its sustaining vital principle. Saint-Preux himself can also find in this life a great sense of security and the feeling of being completely integrated into a closed society whose values and mode of existence bring peace and happiness by eliminating all conflict and dissonance from his heart. The personality becomes absorbed into a higher unity. Moreover, the acceptance of this mode of life is made all the easier because its high moral standards do not impose on its members a harsh asceticism which does violence to natural inclinations, for Julie is careful to indicate that her philosophy of the good life and her devotion to 'virtue' and 'duty' are not inconsistent with the idea of enjoyment. If she 'abstains', it is only to 'enjoy' (iv. 216). She advocates a kind of tempered and rational hedonism—an 'epicureanism of the reason' from which only the violent, absolute claims of human passion are rigorously excluded. That Rousseau himself is associated with this way of life is clearly shown by the way in which Julie reproduces ideas which he had intended to develop in *La Morale sensitive ou le Matérialisme du sage*.[1] It is clear, therefore, that the whole of this idyllic society lies very close to Rousseau's own heart and that he is here confronting the erotic fantasies of his early 'romantic' mood with a more sober and rational ideal that seems to offer a greater chance of a stable happiness. However, our previous psychological analysis will also have shown that this new-found idyll corresponds to a primitivist, almost regressive aspect of his temperament; he seeks to escape from the anxiety of absolute erotic passion by attaining a tranquil mode of existence that is completely devoid of inner tension and conflict. But it now figures as a consciously elaborated, if imaginative ideal which seeks to overcome the torments of extreme passion by taking refuge in a kind of dream-world—an idyllic society in which emotional conflicts have no place.

That this primitivist element is a conscious ideal and not simply the impulsive expression of some piece of abnormal psychological mechanism is revealed by the most remarkable example of the supreme emotional satisfaction that is made possible by this ordered and peaceful world—the famous *matinée à l'anglaise* described in the fifth part of the novel (iv. 54 ff.). The keynote of this scene is the extraordinary calmness and silence which permeate the whole atmosphere and penetrate the most sensitive aspects of personal experience. It is essentially an

---

[1] Cf. *supra*, p. 17.

intimate society, from which all distracting influences are excluded. Its members have attained a peace which comes from a kind of self-sufficiency. They are content to be in one another's company and would find the presence of an outsider embarrassing and irksome. It is, in the most profound sense, the meeting-place of true friends. Even language seems superfluous and communication, when it is necessary, is made through silent gestures. The elimination of speech is facilitated by the three friends' knowledge that their hearts are completely open to one another. This helps to explain the moral quality of the emotional content-ment found in this intimate society. As Julie herself says, 'the whole charm of the society reigning between us is in this openness of heart which puts all feelings and thoughts in common with the result that each, feeling himself to be what he should be, shows himself to all as he truly is'. Saint-Preux, in particular, is able to feel that he has become in some way transparent to the others' gaze. Purged of all feelings of guilt, he no longer needs to conceal secret thoughts; he is at one with himself and his friends. 'Between the three of us', he says, 'we again begin a society which is all the more charming as there remains nothing in the depths of our hearts which we wish to hide from one another' (iv. 54–55). Nobody fears the secret hostility of other persons or the disturbing emotions aroused by memories of a guilty past. At last the insecure Saint-Preux feels himself to be justified. Knowing that Wolmar can see into his heart and detect no evil thought, he rests content with the esteem of both husband and wife. Moreover, this new way of life is not a mere piece of escapism; it has been achieved by a 'new elevation', and would have been impossible had he not recognized that 'he had to be what he was in order to become what he wants to be'. He derives a specifically moral satisfaction from the thought that this new-found peace has come after an inner struggle in which erotic love has been subordinated to a keen attachment to 'all that is great and beautiful'. The restless striving of the passionate self has at last been stilled, and, with the departure of all importunate strangers, true friends can at last abandon themselves to the peculiar charm of this intimate society.

The particular fascination of this scene lies in the fact that it expresses a contemplative, not an active ideal. The elimination of all striving and noisy pursuit of practical ends produces a state of rapt contemplation and leads to an intimate mood of reverie, in which each is alone but also happy in the company of his friends. This is no solipsist dream, but a state of purest intimacy. 'We want to be recollected (*recueilli*) so to speak in each other.' The climax of this experience comes when, for two privileged hours, the three friends remain in 'this motionless ecstasy', absorbed in a 'universal self-communion' and conscious of nothing save their intimate and apparently interpenetrating emotions. The whole scene is full of a quasi-mystical exaltation which is all the more valuable for being without any outward expression. The essential fact is that in this *recueillement* all is reverie, silence, innocence, and peace; but it represents a happiness which comes from fulfilment and not from the mere absence of conflict; all truly personal feelings find their supreme satisfaction in this intimate society.

A scene like the *matinée à l'anglaise* shows how earnestly Rousseau has sought to idealize and spiritualize the purely psychological impulses associated with the idea of the *ménage à trois*. It is no longer accepted as an irrational situation imposed on him in spite of himself; for Jean-Jacques–Saint-Preux can feel that he is the conscious and intelligent participant in a rational and valid ideal shared by a group of intimate and worthwhile friends. Moreover, the intimate group of the Wolmar household forms part, as is now seen, of a larger and nearly self-sufficient society which brings peace and security to its members. This ideal corresponds to a very persistent theme in Rousseau's outlook— to that 'insularity' of which Amiel has already spoken and which expresses itself as a predilection for self-enclosed 'islands' or island-like communities separated from the turmoil and confusion of the outside world.[1]

However, when it is set within the context of Rousseau's personality as a whole, or simply within the framework of the novel's main structure, it may be doubted whether this ideal does offer a permanent solution to the problem of love. True, it eliminates the dangers of erotic passion and perhaps gives a form of happiness which is greater and more durable than that offered by passionate experience; it removes all the anxiety and insecurity involved in the pursuit of the erotic absolute. Yet, as far as Saint-Preux himself is concerned, it remains essentially a *pis aller*, because he has never actually repudiated his early feelings for Julie; he has been induced to accept this way of life as a mere substitute for a fuller mode of being: he becomes a friend because circumstances have prevented him from being a husband. But it was always as Julie's husband that he had wanted to see himself. By allowing himself to be

---

[1] Cf. H. F. Amiel, 'Caractéristique générale de Rousseau', in *J.-J. Rousseau jugé par les Genevois d'aujourd'hui* (1879), pp. 23–65. On the 'economy' of this community see some fascinating pages in Jean Starobinski (op. cit., pp. 129 ff.) who also stresses the self-sufficient character of Clarens as well as the role of 'transparency' in its personal relations. Pierre Burgelin (op. cit., p. 286) also insists that 'Clarens remains the model of a society of hearts without mystery'. The name 'Clarens' also suggests 'light'.

dominated by stronger personalities, Saint-Preux has perhaps escaped from certain emotional difficulties created by his erotic feelings for Julie, but only at the cost of henceforth mutilating his psychic life. After Julie's marriage he is no longer a complete person, but a being who exists for others and strives to fashion himself in accordance with their wishes and standards. This attitude is made all the easier because a genuine part of his personality and certain of his emotions can readily identify themselves with this new mode of existence. But the later emphasis of the novel on the role of Julie and Wolmar reflects just as personal a preoccupation on the author's part as did the earlier descriptions of erotic passion. Certain aspects of Julie and Wolmar are as integral to Rousseau as Saint-Preux himself. As far as the actual novel is concerned, it would have been quite easy to complete the story in four parts, as Rousseau seems originally to have intended. For example, it would have been quite logical for the novel to end with the scene of the lake, and, if the *matinée à l'anglaise* had been allowed to precede that incident, the ultimate affective emphasis of the story need not have remained in doubt. Yet, even in the earlier version, Rousseau apparently thought of introducing a catastrophic conclusion by allowing the main characters to suffer death by drowning. Already, then, it seems that the idyll of Clarens was not envisaged as a permanently satisfactory answer to the problem of erotic passion.

In spite of its idealistic aspects, the 'innocence' and 'order' which are the peculiar qualities of Julie's married state suggest a kind of retreat from the full implications of real life. The delicate equilibrium of the Wolmar household is maintained only because certain *relative* human feelings are held to be completely adequate for human happiness; such a view involves an elimination not only of the erotic (whose suspension might be accepted for the reasons already given) but also of the *absolute*. One-sided and egoistic though it may have been in certain respects, Saint-Preux's passion did express something of that intense striving through which every fully awakened being struggles to confer an individual, unique value on his existence. Passion is a form of action, a movement towards a goal. In other words, it can become the basis of a kind of *faith*, even though it is tied to a finite and worldly object. It is precisely this drive for absolute self-expression which is frustrated by the idyllic but static perfection of Clarens. The life of Clarens may satisfy the voice of moral conscience and bring deep emotional peace, but it involves a contemplative, not an active ideal, and, as such, runs counter to a vital human impulse.

Even Julie recognizes this in her own way since her dissatisfaction with her 'perfect' way of life assumes a particular form: it does not spring from a definite desire for the unattainable but from a kind of satiety with this happiness which has ceased to evolve and develop. It is true that Julie's life is in one way complete, that the 'whole universe' is gathered around her and that she has a sense of genuine personal fulfilment. 'I see nothing that does not extend my being and nothing that divides it; it is in all around me, there is no part of it that is far from me; my imagination has nothing more to do, I have nothing more to desire: to feel and to enjoy are for me the same thing; I live in all that I love, I am satiated with life and happiness' (iv. 258). Yet this self-sufficiency is somehow inhuman and cloying in its effects, so that one day she will make the startling admission that 'happiness bores her' (iv. 265). If the establishment of heaven upon earth means the end of all personal development, then the perfection of the idyllic life of Clarens has been bought at too great a price. The presence of *ennui* shows very clearly that her happiness rests upon the frustration of the desire for the absolute. There is an element in her personality which is still un-satisfied—even in the midst of a perfect society. She may think quite sincerely that Saint-Preux's attempt to identify this absolute with the movement of human passion was mistaken, but she cannot claim to have done more than elude the erotic; she has not actually overcome it since her marriage to Wolmar was not of her own choosing. In her heart there still remains *un vide immense* which she certainly did not experience in the tormented days of her love for Saint-Preux, but which now permeates and diminishes this apparently fulfilled existence as wife and mother and squiress in a perfect society. 'A secret langour steals into the depths of my heart, which I feel to be empty and *gonflé*.' The very fact that she is led more and more into a lonely contemplative mysticism is a striking confirmation that her actual mode of life cannot satisfy all her heart's needs.

Julie realizes that to limit existence to the idyllic life of Clarens is to violate a fundamental psychological law of human nature, which associates desire with imagination. The fact that imagination always tends to outstrip actual achievement continues to provide man with an incentive for renewed effort. 'Woe to him who has nothing more to desire! He loses so to speak all that he possesses. People derive less enjoyment from what they obtain than from what they hope for, and they are happy only before they are happy' (iv. 263). The attainment of a completely fulfilled desire would mean the end of man's development as a human being. 'The land of chimeras is the only one worth living in; such is the nothingness of human affairs that, apart from the Being who exists through himself, there is nothing beautiful save what is not.' For a fully awakened person, what does not exist may be more real and valuable than the actualities of his immediate existence. No doubt to make erotic impulse the absolute aim of life is to mistake its true purpose, since passion can never be an absolute goal, but such an attitude does does contain an imaginative element which, through the very fact of pursuing an unattainable end and providing short-lived periods of ecstasy, opens up a fascinating, if dangerous, possibility of existence. The life of virtue, for all its moral worth, neglects this living element of absolute desire and imagination, and so fails to satisfy all man's needs. The more rational detachment of a Wolmar is also beyond the reach of most people, for it can belong only to a superhuman being who is really outside existence, living in a kind of god-like self-sufficiency which makes him unreal in the human sense.

It is not inappropriate that, when once Julie has exhausted all the existential possibilities open to her, she should seek the supreme felicity of the next world, for it is there that she will be able to escape the effects of time's destructive influence. Her death is an accident and yet also a logical result of the implications of her own life. She herself admits this in a curiously prophetic utterance. The passage already quoted, in which she speaks of her 'satiety' with life and happiness, concludes with a striking apostrophe to death. 'O death, come when thou wilt! I fear thee no more, I have lived, I have forestalled thee, I have no more new feelings to know, thou hast nothing more to take from me' (iv. 258). Her last letter to Saint-Preux qualifies this statement to the extent of admitting that she had never really faced the possibility of exploring erotic love in all its fullness. Her love has resisted all her efforts to overcome it and it can henceforth be only a temptation to utter disaster, both to herself and those around her. Death will also remove this one great danger to her life. All other possibilities having been fulfilled, her life henceforth can only 'decline'. If she dies now, it will be in the fullness of time and in the knowledge that she is securing the eternal prolongation of her present happiness, which, because it develops no more, ceases to have a purely earthly meaning.[1] The security, hope, and peace of mind which she has won through the sacrifice of love to virtue

---

[1] Moreover, as Jean Starobinski points out (p. 147), through her death she solves the problem of attaining an immediate, absolute awareness of God, since she will henceforth cease to be confronted by the obstacle of *objets sensibles*.

and which must always remain a precarious conquest will, through her death, be preserved against deterioration and destruction. Moreover, she dies in the firm belief that her personality will survive as a living presence in Clarens itself, inspiring those who remain to a higher and more spiritual mode of existence. In particular, M. de Wolmar will, we are led to believe, be won over to religious faith. By her death Julie thus has the best of both heaven and earth.

Yet her death does show that, from an absolute point of view, she was not completely happy. Had she lived, the erotic absolute might have continued to fascinate her, perhaps with growing power. Her death is a drastic way of escaping from this dilemma, and, from this point of view, Albert Schinz seems justified in speaking of it as 'suicide'.[1] In a sense, therefore, the novel reverts to its starting-point, for the initial question of erotic love which seemed to have been resolved through the virtuous life of Clarens threatens to re-emerge within the still more dangerous context of marital fidelity and virtuous friendship. The conclusion suggests that Rousseau experienced some uncertainty concerning the absolute values of a personal existence whose principal contradictions could not be easily resolved, even by a life of virtue. The new element now introduced is that of religious experience, but this immediately removes the problem from the realm of purely finite and human considerations.

La Nouvelle Héloïse remains a particularly instructive document from the point of view of Rousseau's own personality, for it shows that to the question: Where is happiness to be found? he could not return a simple answer. The attribution of absolute value to erotic passion does not merely fail to take into account the restrictions imposed by 'society' on all attempts to live out 'nature's' ideals, for the contradictions inherent in passion itself, and especially its inability to overcome the limitations of temporal experience with—as far as passion is concerned—its exclusive concern with the ecstasy of 'the moment', are inseparable from certain unusual psychological needs, which impel him towards a different and quieter kind of happiness more dependent on presence than possession, on contemplation than physical desire. Yet the transformation of Julie into an ideal, almost maternal figure is not completely satisfying in itself, for even she has to acknowledge some dependence on a more austere moral figure of M. de Wolmar. Moreover, her final letter to Saint-Preux foreshadows the possible disruption

---

[1] Op. cit., p. 131. Cf. also Wolmar's observation to the dying Julie: 'You are glad to die; you are very happy to leave me' (iv. 304).

of the whole complex pattern by the very passion which it seeks to overcome and which Julie and Saint-Preux had believed to be held in check for ever. In fact, none of the particular answers given to the question of where happiness is to be found is adequate in itself, although each corresponds to some abiding element in the personality, so that erotic passion, contemplative love and disciplined morality continue to co-exist in an uneasy alliance until the very end.

The introduction of religion represents a final attempt to overcome the difficulties created by the presence of these conflicting but inter-dependent elements of Rousseau's personality, and the last part of the novel undoubtedly reflects his growing preoccupation with religious questions and the consequent hope that difficulties that cannot be over-come at the human level will perhaps be resolved in terms of the divine.[1] Yet as long as religion participates in the limitations of finite human existence and is not transported to the ethereal regions which Julie eventually reaches, it betrays a certain ambiguity. The religious theme in *La Nouvelle Héloïse* cannot be restricted to the dogmatic affirmations of the dying Julie, for though, as Rousseau himself says, these fore-shadow his own later profession of faith, they represent the intellectual elaboration of his spiritual convictions rather than their living sub-stance. Indeed, the view of God given in the novel reveals something of the duality inherent in the human relations. If at certain times He appears as the great consoler, the object of quietistic reverie and the final goal of all nostalgic aspirations to a kind of primordial emotional unity, He sometimes assumes a sterner form as the embodiment of ethical power—the all-seeing eye, the immutable presence that is ever on the watch for moral lapses on the part of his erring children, and, discouraging any escape into facile emotion, constantly exhorts them to strengthen their will and face the harsh tasks of daily life. The direct confrontation of these two conceptions is never explicitly made but it is easy to detect their sporadic appearance at different moments in the story, and this in itself is enough to prevent the acceptance of any one mood as the decisive answer to the problem of Rousseau's personal happiness.

[1] We recall also that it was during this time (1758) that he was beginning work on the *Profession de foi.*

5

THE LETTERS TO M. DE MALESHERBES

ORIGINALLY conceived by Rousseau as an outlet for frustrated emotions and only later modified with a didactic moral intention, *La Nouvelle Héloïse* could not lead to a permanent alleviation of inner tension, for the genuinely 'personal' aspects of the work found only indirect, symbolic expression in an imaginative literary setting which was vastly different from the circumstances of his actual life. Yet the absence of physical constraint and the possibility of indulging in moods that owed little to everyday circumstances allowed him to avoid many of the psychological pitfalls which beset his later efforts to undertake a more deliberate and straightforward analysis of his personality; through his novel he was able to relieve his inner contradictions without having to harmonize them in the light of a unified and coherent image of himself as he really was or felt that he ought to be. He identified himself with the three main characters in such a way as to let him abandon himself to the sensual, emotional, and moral impulses of his nature without having to face the responsibility of translating them into action. Although he was thereby allowed to indulge in day-dreams and longings, the choice of a definite literary medium like the novel also had a serious drawback: it served to obscure self-understanding not only by forcing him to embody his feelings in supposedly independent characters, but also by making him subordinate personal considerations to the exigencies of literature and philosophy.

So far, then, Rousseau had not attained any clear and settled form of self-awareness, any fixed image of himself as a definite person. Concerned primarily with trying to resolve the problem of his existence by means of a practical reform, and subsequently striving to satisfy his overwhelming 'need for love' through the intimacy of friendship, he was finally induced, by the failure of these efforts, to seek emotional solace at the level of imaginative fantasy. But the presence of a powerful moral element in both the symbolic and didactic aspects of *La Nouvelle Héloïse* suggests that he would not be likely to remain content with a merely escapist attitude towards his inner life; he still felt compelled to seek the truth about himself. Moreover, the imaginative impetus of the novel having once spent itself, his sporadic efforts to make his personality an object of explicit reflection became closely related to his role as thinker and writer. Because he opposed the values of contemporary society, he continued to see himself as the representative of a 'heroic' morality which rejected the false values of the age. In so far as the 'reform' had tried to reconcile principles and conduct, it had confirmed him in his view of himself as an apostle of 'virtue'. Nor need we assume that this was merely a pose adopted for the purpose of impressing other people. Strongly marked from his earliest years by the Calvinistic puritanism of Geneva, he naturally sought support at times of inner stress in a moral attitude which seemed to give his character stability and permanence by subordinating petty individual anxieties to the authority of objective principles. The disinterestedness involved in sacrificing individual desires to *les devoirs de l'humanité* invested him with a kind of moral superiority: as 'the servant of humanity', he was basing his life on an ideal of 'truth' and 'virtue' which protected him against the vagaries of individual experience. Not that he expected gratitude from his fellow-men, for he believed that any teacher of truth is inevitably rejected by the 'mob'; but the courageous writer of steadfast integrity finds his reward in the approbation of true men (*CG* ii. 124). A man of merit must put aside purely 'personal considerations' since he works for the 'public good'. Because he 'clings neither to glory nor fortune', he is convinced that his writings are permeated by 'humanity, freedom, patriotism and obedience to the laws' (ii. 242). Even after his bitter quarrel with Diderot, he insists that 'God, his fatherland and the human race' remain his principal concern (iii. 33). From this point of view he sees friendship as a positive danger. He tells Mme de Créqui in 1758 that 'all the preferences of friendship are thefts made from the human race and our fatherland. All men are our brothers, they must all be our friends' (iv. 82). To Dr. Tronchin he was to write: 'Two or three persons, who are wrapped up in one another, scarcely concern themselves with the rest of the universe, and they are almost proud of an act of injustice which benefits their friend.' To sacrifice the personal satisfaction derived from particular friendships is to show a capacity for wider and bolder attachments (iv. 276). 'O how much virtue', he writes on another occasion, 'do we need to reconcile justice with humanity, and to know how to be a friend without ceasing to be a man!' A few years later (1762) he was to tell Malesherbes that his 'interest in the species was enough to sustain his heart' (vii. 77).

Persistently throughout this period he dwells on his role as the 'defender' and 'friend of truth' and 'humanity'. His firm adherence to the principle is also revealed in his adoption of the motto (borrowed from Juvenal), *Vitam impendere vero*, which now begins to appear on his letters and books.

His personal life at this time tended to confirm him in his attitude. He had certainly been vouchsafed a glimpse of heaven, first of all, on the plane of mere fantasy when—during the composition of his novel —he had lived in the company of 'perfect beings after his own heart', and, afterwards, in actual experience when he had been momentarily overwhelmed by his passion for Mme d'Houdetot, but, far from bringing him personal fulfilment, both imagination and passion had led to a violent disruption of his existence: he had quarrelled with his friends, had been accused of ingratitude, ·and, in the case of Mme d'Houdetot, had felt himself to be guilty of something worse than disloyalty. The sense of guilt had also been increased by the appearance of an inguinal hernia which he attributed (perhaps mistakenly) to the physical effects of love-making.[1] To add to his physical troubles the beginning of 1758 saw him tormented by a sudden recurrence of his retention, and at one moment he thought that he had not long to live. Although he was convinced that his friends had dealt unjustly with him, he could not forget that he himself had behaved treacherously towards Saint-Lambert. Still more profoundly embedded in his mind was the nagging thought of the way he had abandoned his children. Everything, therefore, moved him to seek rehabilitation through the reassertion of moral principles capable of restoring his weakened self-esteem.

If a public profession of 'virtue' could not go beyond his writer's role, he did, nevertheless, find a vicarious satisfaction in defending the cause of threatened morality. D'Alembert's article 'Geneva', by recommending the establishment of a theatre in Rousseau's native city, provided him with a wonderful opportunity of coming to the defence of ancient morality; inspired by a genuine sense of virtuous elevation, he identified himself whole-heartedly with his role of 'citizen of Geneva'. I am here concerned with the *Lettre* only in its bearing upon the development of Rousseau's self-awareness, but even when considered from this limited viewpoint, it throws valuable light upon his state of mind at this period. Its strongly puritanical, moral note has, of course, been

[1] Dr. Elosu (op. cit., pp. 22 ff.) attributes this to the collapse of his abdominal muscles. Cf. Rousseau's own letter on the subject: *CG* iii. 322 (10 May 1758), and *Conf.* 446, 489.

frequently noted by critics. Love of the theatre reveals the insidious influence of that false and corrupted sensibility which, by subjecting its victims to the domination of love, passion, and fantasy, undermines their attachment to life's practical duties, and especially to the simple virtues and 'antique simplicity' still found in people like the Montagnons. True patriotism, virtue, reason, and loyalty would be fatally weakened by the establishment of a theatre in a small state like Geneva. In teaching his compatriots a lesson in morality Rousseau was also perhaps giving a warning to himself, for, as Professor Hendel observes, his experience with Sophie may have convinced him of the danger of romanticizing in art.[1]

That in a more specific way the *Lettre* served to reinforce his conviction concerning his literary role is well brought out in a note inserted towards the end.

> If my writings inspire me with some pride, it is because of the purity of intention which dictates them, because of a disinterestedness of which few authors have given me the example and which very few will want to imitate. Never did personal consideration sully the desire to be useful to those who have put my pen in my hand, and I have almost always written against my own interest. *Vitam impendere vero*: that is the motto I have chosen and of which I feel myself to be worthy. Readers, I may deceive myself but I would not wittingly deceive you: fear my errors and not my bad faith. The love of public good is the only passion which induces me to speak to the public: I then know how to forget myself and if somebody offends me, I say nothing about him lest anger should make me unjust. . . . Sacred and pure truth, to which I have devoted my life, never will my passions tarnish my sincere love for you; neither self-interest nor fear can affect the homage I offer you, and my pen will never refuse you anything except what it fears to grant to vengeance.[2]

Later on he was to affirm the same point in his letters where he depicted himself as 'the defender of God's cause and the laws of truth', as 'the only author who has ever written for the true good of society'. In paying 'homage to truth', he has 'given glory to God and spoken for the good of men'.[3]

That the work also involved a more subtle psychological identification of the author's feelings with its subject-matter is indicated by Rousseau himself, although the process was perhaps more obvious to

[1] C. W. Hendel, op. cit., ii. 30.
[2] *Lettre* (ed. Fuchs), pp. 176–7, note.
[3] *CG* vii. 283–5, 316, 335; viii. 41, 178.

him when he was writing the *Confessions* than when he was actually composing the *Lettre*.

The injustices of which I had been a mere spectator irritated me; those of which I had become the object saddened me, and this sadness without gall was that of a too loving, too tender heart which, deceived by those it had thought to be of its own stamp, was forced to withdraw into itself. Full of everything that had just happened to me and still agitated by so many violent movements, my heart mingled the feeling of its pains with the ideas which the meditation of my subject had produced in me, and my work was affected by this medley of feelings. Imperceptibly I depicted Grimm, Mme d'Épinay, Mme d'Houdetot, Saint-Lambert, myself (*Conf.* 495–6).

This personal involvement with his work no doubt explains Rousseau's tendency to project himself into some of the literary characters whose role is discussed in the *Lettre*. What is especially striking is the way he treats certain characters, who are traditionally held to be ludicrous or reprehensible, as the innocent victims of unjust public opprobrium. Already his description of Thyestes reminds the reader of himself. 'He is not a courageous hero, he is not a model of virtue, but neither is he a scoundrel; he is a weak and yet interesting man through the very fact of being human and unhappy' (ed. Fuchs, p. 42). More striking is his famous description of Alceste where the imaginative identification is obvious. Alceste is 'an upright, sincere, estimable man, a true *homme de bien*', who is treated with ridicule simply because his merits are unacceptable to the society of his day; his crime is to 'detest the morals of his age and the wickedness of his contemporaries'. He is a man 'who, precisely because he loves his fellow-men, hates in them the evils they inflict on one another and the vices resulting from these evils' (p. 49). Was it not Rousseau's sincerity and frankness (he implies) which had turned his friends into enemies? Such indeed is what he would like to believe. In Alceste's contempt for petty self-interest and devotion to the 'human race' he sees a reflection of his own personality. 'This habit [of concentrating on the good of the human race] elevates and enlarges his ideas, destroys in him all the base inclinations which feed and sustain pride; and from this conjunction springs a certain courage, a pride of character which allows the depths of his soul to be exposed only to feelings worthy of occupying them' (p. 52).

The *Lettre* thus reveals a curious dual tendency in Rousseau's sporadic efforts to see himself as a certain kind of person. As far as his literary role is concerned, he continues to adopt a more or less 'heroic' attitude which conforms quite closely to the moral ideas imbibed from his Genevan and Plutarchian background, although its effectiveness as a guiding principle for his inner life is limited since it remains too impersonal and rational to satisfy the more spontaneous and emotional aspects of his sensibility. At the psychological level, the more subtle kind of mood connected with his imaginative projection of himself into literary characters was also to prove disturbing, for it served to separate him decisively from his environment and to reinforce the conviction, to which he was already very prone, that between him and the world no reconciliation was possible.

A particularly interesting example of Rousseau's attempt to harmonize these divergent tendencies is contained in the curious *Lettres Morales* written for Mme d'Houdetot in 1757–8. What is especially relevant to our immediate task of clarifying the development of his self-awareness is the close connexion he establishes in them between the elaboration of an objective 'philosophy of life' and the evolution of a particular image of himself as a certain kind of person. Here we find not merely a review of moral ideas but a kind of personal moral stock-taking.[1] In this respect they represent an important transition from the didactic works of the early period to the subjective writings of the last years. In particular, they serve as an instructive prelude to the first of his personal writings, the *Quatre lettres à M. de Malesherbes*. Cured (he thinks) of his 'blind passion', he can now abandon himself to the 'enlightened' feelings stimulated not by the desire for physical possession, but by a deep concern for the 'perfection of her soul'. If he could not be her lover, he at least hoped to be accepted as her moral adviser. If Sophie becomes 'as perfect as she can be', he himself will achieve far more than a physical contentment. The letters, however, will try to present 'his own profession of faith' rather than 'give her lessons'.

Their general tenor shows that the main problem is still the same as that which had haunted him during the composition of *La Nouvelle Héloïse*—that of human happiness. Happiness is the aim of human existence, but where, in the midst of so many uncertainties and contradictions, is it to be found? Rousseau insists that no 'invariable rule' is provided by reason, passion, or the human heart. (In the same way Wolmar, Saint-Preux, and Julie had of themselves been unable to draw an infallible guiding principle from their own personal resources.) In a favourite phrase he says men run the risk of dying 'without having

---

[1] The letters are published in *CG* iii. 345–74. (They are referred to in *CG* ii. 220, 269: 5 Dec. 1757 and 28 Jan. 1758.) They are partly summarized by F. C. Green, op. cit., pp. 213–18, and by C. W. Hendel, op. cit., i. 305–16.

lived'. The difficulty with traditional answers to this problem of happiness is that philosophers teach others the art of being happy while failing to apply it to their own lives. To become involved in 'this vast labyrinth of human reasonings' is to be doomed to ignorance. In fact it is not in the philosophers' reason but in our own hearts and the achievement of an ultimate 'self-contentment' that the answer to the problem really lies; happiness is an internal, intimate feeling that can never become an object of public show and discourse. Taking up the theme of his first work, Rousseau insists that this age of philosophy and culture has produced nothing but dissension and confusion. 'Each sect is the only one which has found the truth, each book has as its exclusive content the precepts of wisdom, each author is the only one who teaches you what is good' (351). Every art has been discovered save that of being happy. Indeed, how can we hope to 'reason' our way to wisdom if we fail to understand 'those primitive truths' which must serve as the foundation of all the rest? The so-called 'systems' of our day are merely injudicious generalizations from some comparatively 'trivial fact' which will never bear the philosophical weight placed upon it. A main source of error is the habit of looking for truth outside us, whereas the real starting-point should be *man himself*; knowledge is essentially a *human* problem. This does not mean—as Locke and his French disciples taught—that human truth is located in sense-experience, which is a particularly untrustworthy source of knowledge; when reason seeks to restrict itself to sense-experience, it is soon caught up in contradiction and error. Newton and Locke easily refute Descartes's artificial separation of the two substances of body and mind, but equally grave difficulties confront their own views of these questions. Ultimately we are driven back to the Cartesian starting-point: 'I think, therefore I exist.' To discover the true basis of his life a man must adopt an attitude of humility, look into himself and so learn to rely on the promptings of his heart and 'inner feeling' rather than rational arguments based upon external reality. In a favourite expression already used in *La Nouvelle Héloïse* and destined to be given a prominent place in *La Profession de foi du Vicaire savoyard*, a man must 'retire into himself' and there listen to 'this inner voice which judges him in secret'.[1] At certain privileged moments he will also be able to receive inspiration from 'the contemplation of moral beauty and the intellectual order of

---

[1] In the dedication of the Second *Discours* he had exhorted the Genevans 'to retire into their inmost heart and consult the secret voice of their conscience'. The phrase *rentrer en moi-même* already occurs in a letter to Mme Dupin, *CG* i. 184 (9 Apr. 1743).

things' as well as from the opposite feeling of 'secret anxiety' at the sight of his own wretchedness (360).

By withdrawing into himself in this way he will find his primordial, essential nature and so discover that the most authentic promptings of his 'natural inclinations' are towards goodness. Is not the fact of man's fundamental goodness proved by the 'cry of remorse' which follows from the violation of his moral convictions and the 'virtuous peace' which comes from a 'soul satisfied with itself'? The wicked man is unhappy; the good man is happy with 'an unchangeable satisfaction'. Indeed, Rousseau appeals to the universality of this principle, which illustrates the 'astonishing uniformity of men's judgement', as a further proof of its validity. In each soul there is 'an innate principle of justice, on which, in spite of our own maxims, we judge our actions and those of others as good or bad, and it is to this principle that I give the name of conscience' (366). Once this moral basis of our life is known, we shall not seek to dissipate our existence on all around us but begin

by becoming ourselves again, retiring within ourselves, circumscribing our soul within the limits that nature has given to our being; let us begin, in a word, by gathering ourselves together in order that, as we seek to know ourselves, everything that constitutes us may present itself to us at the same time. As for me, I think that the one who knows best of what the human self consists is nearest to wisdom; and that just as the first outline of a drawing is made up of the lines which complete it, man's first idea is to separate himself from all that is not himself (369–70).

Contrary to the popular view, solitude will be a virtue, for it will help a man to effect this separation of his true being from the artificial elements of his environment. Rousseau is not here advocating a life of monastic seclusion since genuine solitude can be attained even in the midst of the world. The secret is to learn to be alone without boredom and to cultivate the habit of contemplation. Nobody can hope to philosophize or to know himself unless he first achieves this inner withdrawal. Although physical isolation from the world is not indispensable, Rousseau suggests that it is especially in the country that true solitude can be cultivated, for rural objects induce a mood of *recueillement* and *rêverie*. He concludes by indicating more precise ways of attaining this type of moral ascesis, suggesting that the man who finds this solitude should let his mind be filled with pleasant memories and affections, that he should perform sincere but unostentatious works of charity and lead a simple life. In several respects these concluding recommendations recall the type of life already described in connexion with the idyll of Clarens.

The main points of Rousseau's arguments in the *Lettres morales* have been reproduced less for their interest as a first sketch of certain parts of *Émile* than for the light they throw on the development of his personal life at this time. The lesson of inwardness is intended as much for himself as his reader; henceforth he does not wish to exist as a man inwardly divided but as one who has at last been able to establish his happiness on a firm basis: no longer at the mercy of ephemeral impulse or fortuitous circumstance, he will at last enjoy the peace of a harmonious personality undisturbed by external threats.

The personal implications of the *Lettres morales* are very interestingly revealed in the few pages explicitly devoted to an analysis of his own character, and from this point of view they represent a vital stage in the development of his self-awareness. We have already seen how his consciousness of inner conflict and the world's lack of understanding had convinced him that he was in some sense a being apart, and that, although the reform of the 1750s had given a decisive practical expression to the belief that he must henceforth base his life on standards and principles unacceptable to most of his contemporaries, the emotional upheaval provoked by his break with Parisian society, as well as his active exploration of this new way of life, had at first prevented him from carrying out a more detailed and careful examination of his own personality. But the outcome of his infatuation with Mme d'Houdetot and the sense of having fallen short of his own moral standards, with its concomitant sense of guilt and unworthiness, now made it necessary for him to deepen the examination of his own life and penetrate its real character.

One of the first results of this process of self-analysis was to convince him of an essential feature of his personality which, though it had been an integral part of his sensibility from his earliest years, now began to force itself upon his attention with renewed insistence. This was the idea that between his personal feelings and external circumstances there was a kind of antithetic relationship which always set them in opposition to each other.[1] In periods of material prosperity he had always been unhappy, whilst physical adversity had been accompanied by a sense of inward contentment. In fact, the feelings derived from the 'state of his fortune' were always different from the emotions accom-

---

[1] The idea was to play an important role in the *Confessions*. Cf., for example, 171–2, and *supra*, p. 21.

panying his deeper view of himself; in poverty he experienced 'a feeling of happiness and peace', in prosperity 'an importunate disquiet'. He admits that his natural bent for a 'contemplative life'—a bent that had been fostered by his withdrawal from the world—had developed a conviction that he had to find within himself 'le contre-poids de sa destinée', and this conviction, in its turn, was related to 'the secret judgement which he passed unthinkingly on the actions of his life and the objects of his desires' (361).

The immediate effect of this contradiction between external and internal reality was to increase his feeling of solitude. Because he was endowed with feelings that could never be shared by others, he felt compelled to 'withdraw into himself with the painful awareness that he could find no heart which would respond to his' (CG iii. 125). But this feeling of isolation also convinced him that his character could not be judged by principles applicable to other men who, for the most part, lived in the world of 'appearance' and 'opinion', not of 'being' and 'nature'. No doubt he had often been guilty of grave lapses, but he was certain that he possessed an essential self whose intrinsic worth placed it beyond the imperfection of individual acts. These wrong actions were not those of his inmost being but of a kind of peripheral self still dominated by the false values of the world—in short, by a self that had not yet dared to discover its own true quality. As he pondered the implications of this view, Rousseau was more and more persuaded of his essential goodness and innocence: if he had not been 'virtuous', he had always been 'good' inasmuch as his whole personality had never actively willed the evil. The main point about 'goodness' (as opposed to 'virtue') was that it expressed an intrinsic quality, an essential characteristic of every man in so far as he was part of 'nature': it represented 'the absolute goodness which made a thing what it was by its nature' and thus, as far as man was concerned, the ultimate guarantee that he was a God-created being. No doubt this was not a new principle, even as far as his personal life was concerned, but it seems that it is only during this period that it emerged as a definite and permanent element in his view of himself. The conception of man's essential goodness was something of a banality in eighteenth-century thought, as numerous critics have pointed out, and may be traced back to the Renaissance. It is worth noting, however, that the idea does not occur directly in Rousseau's first writings; even in the second Discours it appears only in a footnote, and, as Professor Lovejoy suggests, Rousseau's account of man's historical evolution from the primitive stage could be interpreted on the basis of the contrary assumption.[1] If society came into being with all its attendant evils, was this not because at one stage of his existence man, of his own accord, had chosen to follow the wrong path? Certainly there would now be no point in trying to return to the primitive condition and the savage state that man had left behind him for ever. But even this type of existence has a lesson for modern man who is so pathetically disorientated in his search for true values; primitive man is happy because he has learned to identify himself with the intrinsic quality of his existence—in a word, to be himself. The task of the civilized man is to recreate this 'natural' condition at a higher level, to become what he ought to be by virtue of his intrinsic 'original' potentialities as a human being. But to achieve this he has to separate true 'goodness' from the artificial self created by his participation in modern social life. Rousseau was now convinced that his unique function as man and writer was to reveal this 'goodness'. He differed from others because the frequentation of society had not affected the fundamental integrity of his personal existence; he had passed through the dangerous hazards of social life without having suffered any permanent damage to his essential self. Henceforth, he would refuse to base his sense of values on 'social' criteria which had little or no relevance to his inner life. If at times he had been led into grievous error, was this not due to a supine acceptance of social values which had caused him to act against his own true nature? In the same way, he had often been persuaded to applaud actions which his conscience ought to have condemned, but he at last realized the truth: 'I believed that I could feel within myself a germ of goodness which compensated me for bad fortune and a germ of greatness which raised me above good fortune; I saw that it is vain to seek our happiness afar off when we neglect to cultivate it within ourselves; for, although it comes from outside, this happiness can be made tangible only in so far as it finds within us a soul capable of savouring it' (CG iii. 362). That is why Jean-Jacques was persuaded that, in spite of the many vicissitudes of his life, he had not really lost his pristine innocence. Already in 1757 he could affirm defiantly to Mme d'Épinay that he 'never did harm to anybody'.[2] To Mme d'Houdetot he wrote: 'Let people show me a better man than myself. Let them show me a more loving, sensitive soul, one that is

---

[1] Cf. A. O. Lovejoy, 'The Supposed Primitivism of Rousseau's "Discourse on Inequality"', in Essays in the History of Ideas (Baltimore, 1948), pp. 14–37. See also A. Schinz, La Pensée de Jean-Jacques Rousseau, Part II, chap. i, pp. 135 ff.

[2] CG iii. 86. Cf. also ibid. 147.

more enamoured of the charms of friendship, more affected by the honest and the beautiful, let them show me that, and I will say no more' (iii. 173–4). In 1758 he told the same correspondent: 'I consult my heart and remain calm. I have never done harm to anyone and I shall not begin so late' (iii. 278).

This preoccupation with his inner worth obviously does not involve a mere abandonment to individual caprice; Jean-Jacques will constantly seek to reassure himself that what he wants for himself is what he *ought* to want and what he has a right to ask. The sense of personal value is thus inseparable from a process of reflection aimed at securing a consistent and comprehensive view of his personality. The reform of 1756 had been mainly a personal *act*, not a detached and theoretical analysis of his own character—a movement towards the recovery of personal freedom and the adoption of a specific mode of life rather than a statement of abstract principles. In the *Lettres morales*, on the other hand, Rousseau is clearly making an effort at personal introspection and analysis which foreshadows the later letters to Malesherbes and the *Confessions*. He now seeks to justify himself as a *certain kind of person*, and especially as one who has a legitimate claim to esteem. In this respect, the development of his attitude shows very plainly how his reactions to life are determined by the desire to see himself as a certain *ideal* type of man; however objective the ultimate criteria of his moral judgements may be, the impulse to moral action seems to involve a view of himself as a certain ideal person whom he has not yet become but who corresponds to his real, if potential, self.

All this represents a very important stage in Rousseau's personal development, and one that was destined to exert a profound influence upon his subsequent life. It was not a question of evolving a mere 'philosophy' of existence but of effecting as it were a genuine internalization of value, of appropriating inwardly the truths of which he was such an impassioned advocate; his attempt to discover an unshakeable basis for human existence in general was inseparable from a desire to evolve a philosophy which would also satisfy his own inner needs. The search for moral values and the desire for personal happiness were thus indissolubly connected. Already in 1754 he admitted that 'however happy I may be in my relationships with others, it would be difficult for me to be as content with anybody as I am with myself' (ii. 64). The pull of ambition and literary creation, as well as the desire to establish intimate relations with others, had checked this inner preoccupation, but with the advent of misfortune he had been thrust back into himself until he had at last attained absolute confidence in the quality of his own being. 'Whoever has the courage to appear always what he is will sooner or later become what he must be' (*CG* iii. 101). Only in this way could he feel that he was truly 'restored to himself'.

The *Lettres morales* show that this growing need to 'draw on his own substance' is accompanied by a psychologically significant tendency to derive the meaning of his existence from its relation to his past life. During the years of literary and social ambition, he had constantly been looking ahead, but now that his literary career was drawing to a close, he was more and more inclined to dwell on his past. Indeed the dichotomy already observed between inner feeling and outward circumstance was largely due to his efforts to penetrate the meaning of his earlier life: he believed that it was during 'the first forty years' of his life that its true quality had been most adequately revealed, his subsequent absorption in the world's activities having been a period of decline and misfortune. But as he 'advanced towards the end of his career', he was forced to recognize this important truth: 'My existence is only in my memory, I live only on my past life, and I cease to attach value to its duration since my heart has nothing new to feel.' It is from the past that 'he henceforth derives his whole being'. But what is important in the past are not so much the physical events themselves as 'the various affections they have caused me' (iii. 362), for they lie behind 'this hidden force' which is his essential moral nature. The immediate basis of his life thus depends directly upon the earlier feelings which have produced it; in this sense the past becomes more real than the present, for a present which—as he believes—will henceforth cease to evolve and take on new meaning remains conditioned by a previous value; what he is now is the result of what he has been, and henceforth his existence will rest firmly on the memory of those earlier feelings.

Not all memories are admitted to this privileged position for, although the past is held to provide a firm basis for present attitudes, the activity of his memory remains partly dependent on the influence of a state of mind that is reluctant to dwell on anything disagreeable: it is only pleasant memories which help him to escape from the anxiety of the present. Moreover, these feelings have the additional function of confirming him in his idea of himself as good and worthy. His honesty will not allow him to gloss over obviously blameworthy actions, but he will interpret them as irrational aberrations which were in some way inessential and transient aspects of his personality: it was only the happier feelings which expressed his real self.

By itself memory cannot fill the emotional void created by his with-drawal of interest from the external world; still less can it compensate for the frustrations and disappointments of his own existence. Since, moreover, it is emotions rather than events which carry the real meaning of the past, there inevitably occurs a kind of split between fact and feeling. No doubt the strongly antithetic nature of the relationship now existing between inner disposition and outward circumstance was not so obvious in the happy past, but even then his emotions often failed to find an adequate outlet in the circumstances of everyday life: they often remained mere idealistic aspirations which were never fulfilled in actual experience. He is therefore tempted to go back to these earlier feelings and subject them to a process of imaginative elaboration which makes their idealistic possibilities the basis of a new world having only a tenuous connexion with the real past. This new world will still be closely tied to his inner life and shaped in accordance with his personal needs, but it will extend beyond the limits of his actual experience.

The profound influence of Rousseau's imagination—and not merely his memory—upon his subsequent personal development is often revealed in a complex and ambiguous way. In one respect, imagination certainly works in conjunction with memory, and thus helps to confirm the idealization of the past. When it is given freer reign (as in *La Nouvelle Héloïse*), it makes the past a mere starting-point for the weaving of more elaborate fantasies which ultimately have only a very remote connexion with the events of his personal life. At other times—and in this respect Jean-Jacques recalls the attitude of his fictional character, Saint-Preux—his imagination has a more disturbing role; directly related to his anticipation of the *future*, it is now set in motion by the unrealized but still realizable possibilities of his existence; it thus becomes inseparable from all those complex emotions which impel him beyond the immediately given; in this way it invariably involves at least some feelings of acute anxiety. It is no longer a question of pleasant image-laden day-dreaming, but of an activity in which the image-creating element is subordinated to affective responses of a more tormenting kind. As early as 1743 Rousseau had spoken of his 'sad inclination to anticipate' future evils. Often this anxious imagination is associated with his physical ailments, as he admits, and sometimes leads to hypochondriac moods. His 'incorrigible imagination' is also apt to affect his relations with other people, inducing him to fear the worst possible consequences from his friendships. His correspondence and personal writings are full of references to this imagination which is 'disordered', 'disturbed', 'cruel', and 'frightened'.[1] It thus helps to prevent him from establishing a firm and settled attitude towards the world and his own life and drives him to a constantly renewed examination of every situation in which he finds himself. Whereas his creative imagination enables him to forget himself in the 'land of pleasant chimeras' and so leads to a certain serenity and contentment which are independent of the frequently harsh demands of immediate reality, his anxious imagination induces him to make certain aspects of his actual experience an occasion for the elaboration of frightening possibilities which frequently have only a very slight connexion with probability. 'My cruel imagination', he says (*Conf.* 219), 'always goes ahead of my misfortunes.' At the same time this anxiety will at certain moments increase the urge to escape from unpleasant immediacy into the happier world of chimera and fantasy. The general effect of both forms of imaginative activity will of course be to limit his capacity for establishing direct relations with the world around him. His friendships and affections will constantly be seen through a screen of subjective feeling which often conceals from him the real character of the persons with whom he is dealing. In the end he will come to think that the world of his imagination is actually superior to that of ordinary experience and that toying with imaginative possibilities is preferable to the more mundane task of coping with the problems of everyday existence. In any case, there develops a progressive weakening of his capacity to appreciate the real features of the external world which now tend to be modified through the influence of imagination, memory, and personal feeling.

Nevertheless, this increasing preoccupation with his own life is not volatilized into mere emotional escapism, for his introspection involves a search for personal value. He is eager to distinguish the essential from the superficial self, and, if this striving after personal reality becomes associated with a certain kind of feeling, it is only because he experiences an overwhelming need to place his life on a firm basis capable of bringing him the peace and happiness he so much desires. Henceforth he is resolved to sacrifice everything to this single object: freed from all concern with a literary future and a life of fame and glory, he is determined to make 'the short time which remains to him' an occasion for 'enjoying the happiness of living' (*CG* iii. 309). It is probably this concern with personal happiness which helps to explain Rousseau's

---

[1] Cf. (*inter alia*) *CG* vi. 325; vii. 9; *Conf.* 219; 348; 626–7. Cf. the references *supra*, p. 21.

far-reaching decision (made in 1760) to abandon his career as a writer. *Émile* was to be his most extensive but also his last work.[1] He proposed 'to confine himself for the rest of his days to the narrow and peaceful circle into which he was born' (*Conf.* 515). But if this step was intended as a mere preliminary to a deeper and more immediate form of intimate enjoyment, it had a disturbing personal implication, for it threatened to deprive him of a valuable outlet for the expression of mental and emotional energy by throwing him back upon his own conflicting inner resources. Indeed, although this period shows progress in his efforts to see himself as a definite kind of person, the elaboration of a more coherent view of his character was not without its dangers and difficulties. The passages of self-examination in the *Lettres morales* reflect, for example, a certain desire to relieve emotional stress, and they contain an element of idealization which is closely connected with his feeling of the world's hostility. This tendency shows a marked, if sporadic, development at this time. The subtle pressure of his desire to justify himself against the charge of misanthropy has already been indicated in the *Lettre à d'Alembert*, while his correspondence shows the same sensitiveness to criticism and a disturbing inclination to see hidden hostility where it perhaps did not exist. In 1759, for example, the famous Genevan doctor Théodore Tronchin had been tactless and unkind enough to ask whether 'the friend of humanity was no longer the friend of man'. Jean-Jacques replies to the question with some warmth and sees in the doctor's query the influence of 'secret informers'. In spite—or perhaps because of—his break with Diderot (and it was undoubtedly this incident which Tronchin had in mind), Jean-Jacques insists that he is still 'the friend of the human race', but he adds darkly: 'The friend of truth also finds malevolent people everywhere, and I have no need to go and look so far' (*CG* iii. 201). Another letter addressed to Lenieps in the same year is even more revealing, and suggests a definitely obsessive preoccupation with the theme of persecution.

In Paris [he writes] I have hidden enemies who will not forget the wrong they have done me; sometimes the offended person forgives but the offender never does. You must realize how unequal is the struggle between them and me. Scattered throughout society, they can spread any rumour they wish, without my being able to know about it or defend myself against it. . . . They

---

[1] Details will be found in letters to Pastor Vernes, 29 Nov. 1760 (*CG* v. 271–2) and to his friend Lenieps in Dec. (ibid. 270). The intention is reaffirmed in other letters: v. 291; vi. 130, 137, 282. Cf. also v. 272 note.

M

satisfy their vengeance whilst pretending to be generous. Beneath the cloak of friendship they conceal their dagger and kill a man while pretending to pity him. 'Poor citizen! He's not so bad at heart, but he has a bad head.' They utter a few obscure, puzzling words which are soon picked up, commented on and disseminated by the philosophers' apprentices. In secret councils is prepared the poison which they are determined to spread in the public mind (*CG* iv. 223–4).

Here we have a clear indication of the theme which is to become an *idée fixe* in his later life—the belief that others' animosity is inspired by the knowledge that they have wronged him. His insistence that this hostility also takes the form of sham generosity was also to become a favourite topic in the *Dialogues*. For the moment it will be enough to emphasize his inclination to see himself as a good man persecuted by a wicked world.

In view of his decision to abandon writing it was perhaps natural that he should be particularly anxious about the fate of *Émile* and tend to identify his better self with the essence of this work. It was on this book, he was convinced, that his true 'glory' as a writer and his reputation as a man would ultimately rest. The publication of *Émile*, therefore, was a personal as well as a literary event. Increasingly ready to separate his 'real', inner self from the public figure seen by his contemporaries, Rousseau also acknowledges that the other's hostile gaze has the power to disturb his peace of mind by arousing in him an awkwardness and embarrassment which add still further to the misrepresentation of his true personality. At the same time he feels a certain need to be known in his true character, so that if people will not accept the immediately observable individual (who in any case falls short of the 'ideal' but essential Jean-Jacques), they will at least be confronted by the objective embodiment of the ideal self in the form of a book that was not written for any materialistic or self-seeking motive but simply in response to a disinterested desire to teach humanity truths essential to its happiness and well-being. These truths differed from the message of other writers because they were drawn from the author's own heart, from the quintessential self which not only showed the connexion between Jean-Jacques and the nature of 'man' but actually presented a far more faithful picture of his soul than the false image perceived by those who knew him in 'society'. That is why, as he tellingly puts it in the *Confessions*, he chose 'to write and conceal himself': had he tried to reveal himself more directly, he would certainly have been despised or misunderstood. On the other hand, by hiding the physical everyday self he would give a more adequate portrait of the ideal being upon whom the whole value of his work and personal existence ultimately depended. It was, therefore, particularly unfortunate that the publication of *Émile* should have been accompanied by conditions likely to aggravate an anxiety to which he was also for less important psychological reasons so readily exposed. By 1761 his state of anxiety was probably exasperated not only by the continuance of a rural seclusion which deprived him of any real human affection but also by the lack of any reliable information about the printing of *Émile*. Having been somewhat reluctantly dissuaded by Mme de Luxembourg from entrusting the work to his usual publisher, Rey, he allowed his 'frightened imagination' to run riot at the thought that he was dealing with strangers. He was suddenly convinced of the publishers' collusion with the Jesuits to falsify his writings and produce a mutilated version of *Émile*. Overcome by his fears, he wrote a panic-stricken letter to Malesherbes, the *directeur de la librairie*, begging his help to unmask such a diabolical plot; at all costs, he thought, his honour and reputation must be preserved against this dire threat. It seems highly probable that this inner torment was increased by his physical condition at the end of 1761, for his urinary troubles were always worse in cold weather. On 18 November he communicated his suspicions to Malesherbes; he was sure that the delay was due to the machinations of the Jesuits 'who were absolutely determined to suppress the work' or else 'to mutilate and falsify it according to their fancy'. Two days later he realized his mistake and retracted this accusation—an 'abomination' produced, he insisted, by his 'disordered imagination'. Towards the end of the month his suspicions reappeared—provoked perhaps by an extremely painful accident, a catheter having broken off in his urethra. He again wrote desperate letters repeating his earlier charges against Duchesne and the Jesuits. Thanks to the good offices of Malesherbes and his new friends, the Maréchal and Maréchale de Luxembourg, who speeded up the publication of his work, these fears were overcome, and by Christmas he was able to deplore the 'iniquities, follies and impertinences' of which he had been guilty. 'It is with a shudder that I look at myself and see how contemptible I have become' (vii. 8). His main concern was henceforth to regain the 'esteem' he had so rashly lost. The kindly Malesherbes tried to reassure the unhappy Jean-Jacques of his good will, attributing his aberrations to 'an acute sensitivity, a great depth of melancholy and an inclination to see objects by their blackest side, but an equal readiness to abandon himself to truth and justice when confronted by them' (vii. 10). It seems that this letter (written on 25 December 1761) was the immediate occasion of the first of the four letters written to Malesherbes in January 1762.[1]

The letters to Malesherbes were thus composed after a period of considerable physical and psychological strain, and at a time of his life—Rousseau was now nearly fifty, an age which psychologists increasingly recognize as a critical one in a man's life—when he was experiencing a number of reasons for wanting to undertake a general review of his existence. Perhaps we ought not to take too seriously his talk of suicide, but a letter like the one intended for his friend Pastor Moultou reveals his tense condition (vii. 3). His conviction too that the Parisian philosophers and their friends attributed his retreat from the capital to 'obstinacy', 'pride', and 'the shame of going back on his word' was also linked to the more upsetting thought that even the kindly and liberal Malesherbes must have formed an extremely unfavourable impression of his behaviour. 'Sensitive to this error in a man for whom I had so much esteem, I wrote him four successive letters in which, while explaining the real motives of my behaviour, I gave a faithful description of my tastes, inclinations and character, and all that took place in my heart' (*Conf.* 569).

The particular circumstances giving rise to the letters as well as the pressure of the various factors operating in his personality during the preceding years show that they were produced and inspired by a certain complexity of motive. The effort at self-analysis and the desire to see into the meaning of his own acts are clear enough, but self-examination is inseparable from self-justification. Here for the first time we see the emergence of a fundamental tendency which is to dominate the personal writings of his last years: the urge to write is not inspired solely by a desire to search out and know his own character, but by a need to destroy a false image of himself which he thinks is implanted in the minds of other people and which has been deliberately created by critics and enemies. If his writings reflect an ideal Rousseau purged of his

---

[1] For a concise and extremely useful survey of the events leading to the writing of these letters, see Gustave Rudler's edition of the *Lettres à M. de Malesherbes* (London, Scholartis Press, 1928). The text of the letters, which were all written in Jan. 1762, is given in *OC* i. 1130–47. Although the irrationality of Rousseau's fears is obvious, their pathological significance ought not to be exaggerated. The publication of *Émile* was surrounded by a certain amount of mystery, and the extraordinary importance attached by Rousseau to his work naturally made him apprehensive of danger. His belief in the Jesuits' animosity towards him was probably not ill-founded, but at that particular moment—on the eve of their expulsion from France—they were undoubtedly preoccupied with other matters.

human limitations and inspired by all that is best and noblest in his mind and heart, the opinion of others is, on the contrary, determined by a false conception of some 'bad' Rousseau who has been created from the prejudices, errors, and malevolence of ill-informed or malicious persons. Since, moreover, he is constantly haunted by the thought that this false image may be imposed (through various machinations of his enemies) on the writings he wishes to be handed down to posterity, he is all the more anxious to communicate to some loyal, esteemed friend an explanation of his true character. His self-analysis and his efforts to reconstitute the 'true' Rousseau are thus constantly influenced by a desire to correct erroneous estimates of his conduct and rebut unfounded charges. This preoccupation partly helps to explain a certain simplification in the psychology of these letters and his silence or reticence on some topics which have already figured prominently in his earlier life and work. At the same time the process of self-examination and justification is bound up with a third and rather different preoccupation: an active desire to express himself and relieve his inner tensions through the act of writing. He hopes thereby to obtain a more secure and stable basis for his life, since these letters, being a kind of declaration of personal faith in his own life, offer a valuable means of redirecting his actual existence. Therefore, throughout our study of this work, we shall have to take into account the influence of the three interacting functions of self-analysis, self-justification, and self-expression.

I do not propose to give here a detailed chronological summary of the letters, since this has already been provided by Professor L. A. Bisson;[1] nor do I wish to develop their pre-Romantic implications, however important these may be from the point of view of subsequent literary history in the way they foreshadow the reverie, nature-worship, and religious feelings of the French Romantics; this aspect of the letters having already been dealt with by Professor Bisson, I propose to consider them solely in the light of Rousseau's developing self-awareness and his efforts to come to grips with the problem of his own personal existence. The four letters are not all dominated by the same precise intention: the first two take the form of psychological analysis, whilst the third (the most interesting from the 'Romantic' point of view) attempts the more constructive task of sketching the ideal dominating his present mode of existence and so prolongs in certain respects the

[1] Cf. L. A. Bisson, 'Rousseau and the Romantic Experience', in *The Modern Language Review*, xxxvii, No. 1 (Jan. 1942), 37–49.

idyllic dream of the perfect life at Clarens; it is this letter which gives once again his positive conception of happiness. The fourth is more concerned with justifying his present way of life against the charge of anti-social behaviour and so attempts to define his attitude towards other people, whether they are considered in terms of humanity, friendship, or posterity; here Rousseau takes up a theme already discussed in the earlier correspondence with Dr. Tronchin. The letters thus tend to elaborate three essential themes—an analysis of his inner life involving an attempt to explain the apparent contradictions of his character, the description of his positive personal ideals, and a justification of his behaviour against the charge of an anti-social bias. The passages of psychological analysis are particularly interesting because they enable us to see Rousseau's own systematic and over-all view of his character against the wider background of conscious and unconscious motivation so far examined in connexion with his general personal development.

The first letter seems at the very outset to aim at a more objective examination of his character, for he there attempts to see himself from the outside and to approach his own personality by way of the false picture which he deems to exist in other people's minds. As he says of these letters in the *Confessions*, he was worried by the thought of 'leaving such an unjust opinion of me in the minds of honest folk' (569). As we shall see, this was to become an overriding preoccupation in all Rousseau's personal writings, and especially in the *Confessions* and *Dialogues*: he feels a constant need to break down this false image because he considers it to be based on a thoroughly inaccurate knowledge of his true character. The need to refute this erroneous conception also impels him towards greater sincerity and self-knowledge— towards an understanding of his real qualities and motives. Hence the letters proceed by a dialectical movement which swings between these two poles of the 'false' and 'true' Rousseau: they constitute a kind of inner dialogue in which he first of all gives the wrong explanation only to refute it by an account of the motives which really have (according to him) inspired his behaviour. It is plain that the two conceptions to some extent condition each other and neither can be considered in isolation.

The significant point that emerges from his observations concerning other people's reactions is the way in which he attributes their error to a fundamental insufficiency in their own characters: if they do not know the real Jean-Jacques, it is because they are intrinsically incapable of doing so. (Later on he is to treat this insufficiency as actual malevolence.) Their lack of understanding is clearly derived, he suggests, from their habit of judging others by their own standards; it is particularly men of letters who 'judge my feelings by theirs'.[1] This reveals the firm grip on Rousseau's mind of the conviction that in some fundamental way his own personal existence was incompatible with the life of the world around him; he was more and more convinced not merely that his life was different from that of other men, but that it had some intrinsic quality which necessarily made it so. It is in this essential conviction, whose growth we have already traced from his earliest days, that are to be found all the wisdom and the folly of Rousseau's last years. The sense of being different no doubt helped him to probe more deeply and sincerely into his own personality than would have been the case if he had been content to live in conformity with contemporary values, but his rejection of the world was also connected with a personal inability to adapt himself to social life; the anxiety associated with his reactions to his environment was tied—in part at any rate—to certain irrational feelings, the true character of which he himself was often unable to acknowledge, so that, though often remarkable in its perspicacity and persistence, the effort to know himself as he truly was often encountered the presence of unusual psychological obstacles which prevented him from seeing not only the reality of his immediate situation but the personal outlook of those very people who, in his view, so lamentably failed to understand *him*.

He considers it to be characteristic of public opinion that it should have completely misunderstood the reasons for his withdrawal from the world, wrongly attributing it to a ridiculous vanity; he insists that he is too much concerned with his own happiness to inconvenience himself for the sole purpose of getting himself talked about by others, and that it is scarcely credible that a man who has waited until the age of forty before making himself known to the world should go and spend his days in solitary boredom simply for the sake of 'acquiring the reputation of a misanthropist'. He insists that his retreat from society is largely determined by purely personal considerations and is not due to any heroic determination to live in accordance with lofty principles. 'I was born with a natural love of solitude which has only increased as I came to know men better. I am far more content with the chimerical beings I gather around me than with those I see in the world; and society, for which my imagination fully compensates me in my retirement, completes my dislike of all those that I have left behind' (1131).

[1] Cf. also *Conf.* 639: 'They have always judged my heart by theirs.'

Contrary to what M. de Malesherbes supposes, he is not 'unhappy and devoured by melancholy'; it was only in Paris—and in times of so-called prosperity and social success—that he was overcome by these feelings. The recent agitation experienced in solitude was unjustified and irrational, as he admits, being produced by his 'disordered imagination', but it was also inspired by a worthy motive: a concern for his honour and good name in the eyes of posterity.

It is this reference to his 'natural love of solitude' which is most revealing, for he now tends to treat his solitude as a kind of innate characteristic, whereas he had previously been inclined to see it as something imposed upon him by circumstances. In *Mon portrait* he says: 'I am lonely only because I am sick and lazy; it is almost certain that if I were healthy and active, I should be like other people' (1125). Indeed two years after these letters he was to say the same thing to Boswell about his melancholy: 'I was born placid. I have no natural disposition to melancholy. My misfortunes have inflated me with it.'[1] Now, however, he plays down the factors which affected his earlier reactions to society. But he first gives the correct psychological explanation: 'For a long time I was myself mistaken concerning the cause of this invincible dislike I have always experienced for human intercourse; I attributed it to the vexation of not being quick-witted enough to show in conversation the little wit I had, and, by a natural reaction, to regret at not occupying in the world the position I thought I deserved.' Immediately, however, Rousseau rejects this accurate explanation of his earlier behaviour in favour of another which he thinks gives a much truer account of his reactions: he insists that his 'natural taste for solitude' is not due to anxiety but to his devotion to 'the indomitable spirit of freedom which nothing has been able to overcome, and before which honours, fortune and reputation itself are as nothing to me'. His apparently selfish attachment to his own pleasure and independence, therefore, merely expresses an essential law of his own being which becomes invested with a certain moral *value*. Freedom, implies Rousseau, involves an act of liberation and personal honesty and thus approaches an ideal. When a man penetrates the confusing and artificial aspects of his own nature, which are first of all wrongly accepted under the influence of his own ignorance and distorting social pressure as the expression of his real self, he attains an awareness of his true, essential personality; fidelity to his own intimate being will be a

[1] Cf. *Boswell on the Grand Tour: Germany and Switzerland, 1764*, ed. F. A. Pottle, London, 1953.

source of intense satisfaction and pleasure, which now emerge not as merely selfish impulses but as genuinely moral qualities. For a moment it looks as though Rousseau is going to restore the heroic image he had formerly associated with his Genevan life, but, with a certain honesty, he at once restricts the moral scope of this new principle. The 'freedom' he now desires is not the noble principle so often lauded by traditional moralists, but simply an expression of his basic *paresse*. Hence, as he says, the freedom he seeks is largely of a negative kind, the creation of circumstances which enable him to refrain from action when he wishes; freedom does not mean doing what he wants but abstaining from doing what he does *not* want. He admits that to the irksome obligations of social life he prefers the pleasures of 'intimate friendship' which, coming from the heart's spontaneous feelings, are superior to all forms of imposed duty. Gratitude and similar states of mind place a restriction on the self by forcing it to do what it would not do of its own accord; he has no taste for an active life, because activity means adapting himself to the needs of a given situation instead of being able to follow the un-solicited promptings of his own nature. His ultimate aim, therefore, is the enjoyment of an *immediate* leisure and repose. In other words, he is once again attempting to express—though in a more systematic and self-conscious way—those *expansive* emotions which had been so cruelly frustrated in his Parisian days.

If he can feel that he is really himself only in this spontaneous upsurge of uninhibited emotions, he realizes the impossibility of returning to the worship of his former 'idols' of friendship and love. Not only does he renounce the dream of 'unreserved intimacy' with a friend, but he also excludes the thought of those 'erotic transports' which had played such a great part in the inception of *La Nouvelle Héloïse*. In fact, from this point onwards, the erotic theme plays a rapidly diminishing role in Rousseau's life; whether it is because advancing years and the progress of his malady produced a decline of sexual interest or whether his experience with Mme d'Houdetot, his first and only love, convinced him of the futility of ever hoping to feel again the same emotions, Rousseau ceases to dwell on this aspect of his nature. True, the *Confessions* will have a good deal to say on the subject, but only in connexion with a phase of his life that is now over. If he still delights in the company of 'chimerical beings after his own heart', they tend to lack the erotic vividness of his earlier dreams.

If, when compared with the complex pattern of *La Nouvelle Héloïse*, the *Lettres à M. de Malesherbes* seem to have a much simpler intention, this is only to be expected since the earlier work offered a merely indirect, symbolic expression of his personality that was often subordinated to a different literary and philosophical purpose. The letters, on the other hand, represent a direct, deliberate attempt to see his personality as a whole, and as such they are ultimately meant to inspire a still greater effort at self-realization. This leads to a certain simplification of the personal image; he consciously chooses those aspects of his being with which he wishes to be specifically identified; in order to be himself, he has to reject the merely fortuitous aspects of his character which can have no permanent place in his future life. The aspiration to a personal goal causes him to suppress, for example, the feelings of anxiety and guilt by which he is so frequently tormented, as well as the heroic moral ideal which no longer has the same importance now that he has chosen a life of solitude in which the expansive needs of his 'free' self will play a determining role. Nevertheless, moral feeling is too deeply ingrained in his character for him to be able to rest satisfied with a life of merely hedonistic pleasure. He feels a certain need to justify himself morally, for only thus can he permanently banish the image of the false Rousseau. In order to recover the esteem of those who have been misled by the opinion of others and his own aberrations, he has to establish the authenticity and essential 'goodness' of his true being, for only a good man would really be justified in separating himself from the society through which most people express their obligations to life and the world.

Although the charges directed against him are in his view quite unfounded, Rousseau cannot escape from the thought that his life is still marked by certain inconsistencies. Whatever he may now say, he has to admit that his past behaviour has involved certain contradictions; he cannot deny, for example, that at one phase of his life he did seek fame and glory, pursue an active social life, and flourish as a literary man. Why, then, did such an 'indolent' man spend so much time and energy on writing books for the edification of others? Why did a man with such a 'natural love of solitude' so earnestly seek the company of the *salons*? He realizes at the end of his first letter that all has not yet been explained. 'I shall depict myself without pretence and modesty; I shall show myself to you such as I see myself and such as I am.' His very solitude will help him to achieve this deeper self-analysis for 'nobody in the world knows me better than I do'.

It is interesting to note that, whereas the first letter had concentrated almost entirely on the opposition existing between his own view of himself and that held by other people, this renewed effort at self-analysis concentrates on a different type of contradiction—that which he feels to exist *in his own nature*. Here again he takes up a theme briefly discussed in the *Lettres morales*, where he established a significant dichotomy between the quality of his feelings and the nature of his physical circumstances. This sense of contradiction had always been an important element in Rousseau's nature, but it is only in the later phases of his life and in his personal writings that he seeks to clarify it. Most of the elements involved in his inner conflicts have already been examined in our earlier analyses, but it will be interesting to see how he himself now relates them to his immediate situation. He confesses that he is quite unable to account for the opposition between his lazy, timid reactions and his tendency to enthusiasm and irascibility, but he at least proposes to 'give by means of facts a kind of historical account which may serve to make it conceivable'. In this way he anticipates the *Confessions*, for, instead of engaging in a direct psychological analysis of his immediate condition, he tries to explain his character through a reconstitution of his personal development and a revaluation of himself which will allow the reader to judge the truth of the matter. Of his childhood he mentions only 'this heroic and romantic taste' imparted by his reading of Plutarch and seventeenth-century novels; he attributes to this early influence his completely unrealistic estimate of other people's characters, since he at first imagined that the actual world contained men who were like his literary heroes; the inevitable disillusionment brought about by later experience developed such an aversion to contemporary life that he sought compensation in an imaginary realm created in accordance with his own emotional needs. This highly selective account of his early years maintains complete silence on the subject of his father's influence and all those other factors to which attention has already been called. However, his general point that his early inability to adapt himself to real life drove him to take refuge in an imaginary world undoubtedly presents a true account of one fundamental aspect of his nature. What others might consider to be a deficiency of character, he treats as a mark of superiority; if he cannot find happiness in the world, is not this (he implies) because the world has no objects which can 'satisfy his heart'? If for several years he remained attached to society in spite of this heart-felt conviction, it was because of his failure to distinguish between 'nature' and 'opinion'; he allowed his real character to be obscured by the false values of contemporary society, which produced a completely incorrect assessment of his true personal needs. Yet, even in those years of self-deception, his attitude was not free from ambivalence because 'his heart was constantly at variance with his mind', and he continued to love those whom he had so many valid reasons for hating. The 'illumination' on the road to Vincennes provided a decisive solution to this problem since he then saw clearly for the first time that the hateful aspect of human nature was not an integral part of its original structure but a corrupt and perverted covering produced by the pressure of the social system. The whole purpose of his literary work had been to expound the implications of his fundamental idea that man is naturally good;[1] once humanity had grasped this essential truth, it would see that the real source of its misfortunes lay not in itself but in its situation. As far as he personally was concerned, it simply remained for him to apply this important discovery (which had been for a time a predominantly intellectual conviction) to his own life which must henceforth be 'courageously' directed in accordance with his principles. That was why he had carried out his 'reform' and withdrawn from society into the country. Maybe since then he had 'drifted' a little from this original resolve, but not too far; to reconcile 'goodness' with 'happiness' he had only to reaffirm his independence. Once he had shaken off the tyrannical influence of false friends and finished with the irksome task of publishing his remaining works, he would be able to enjoy his freedom, convinced that his duty to himself was quite consistent with the attainment of personal happiness.

Rousseau here makes very evident the existential function of his psychological analysis, for he wants to transform this new self-awareness into a means of strengthening his resolve to continue in his present way of life. By providing his immediate desires with a more solid basis in his own moral nature, he can go beyond a merely theoretical knowledge of his own character and discover a sound incentive for future action, even though it be an action which is largely restricted to his own existence. His earlier teaching concerning the incompatibility of true 'humanity' and contemporary 'civilization' had been followed by a highly significant personal act—a great effort of will through which he had thrown off the world's corrupting influences and been 'restored to himself'; he had come to see that his errors did not stem from his 'good' self but from the artificial being created by his environment. That is why he is now convinced that nobody 'is better than he'. With the

---

[1] The idea developed only slowly in Rousseau, as has been suggested (cf. *supra*, p. 161), but there can be no doubt that it is one of the essential ideas of his final 'system'.

attainment of true self-knowledge he at last understands the 'goodness' of his character. Other men will be unable to understand him because, being the victims of their social situation, they will inevitably judge his heart by theirs. Nevertheless, he ought to be admired for what he has done, since this apparently selfish action has a higher moral value than his socially conscious contemporaries will allow. Here we may note that, although the letters began with the modest disclaimer that his behaviour was less noble than some had supposed since his reform was aimed at producing conditions for personal 'enjoyment', their general tenor now seems to imply that the happiness he is seeking confers on him some kind of moral superiority.

He is plainly not quite satisfied with this argument, and the ambivalence and uneasiness of his attitude is noticeable in the fourth and last letter, which seems to show that all his contradictions are not resolved. In spite of himself Rousseau cannot forget other people nor can he overcome this persistent tendency to see himself through the eyes of others. Certainly the number of persons for whose feelings he really cares has been considerably diminished by his increasing contempt for 'opinion'; but the necessity of earning proper esteem is still recognized. He has for himself 'a high esteem', he insists, and his subsequent argument shows that he is also anxious for the esteem of his friends. In this fourth letter he returns to a theme that had already preoccupied him in his earlier correspondence with Dr. Tronchin. Whatever he says to the contrary, a difficulty still remains, and his honesty compels him to admit its reality: How is it that a man who is so 'good' and 'loving' shuns the society of his fellow-men? Is he not—by his withdrawal into the country—committed to a life that is devoid of social value? Apart from the fact that country-folk engage in activities that are far more socially useful than the busy but selfish intriguing of unprincipled city-dwellers, Rousseau calls attention to a point that was already implicit in his earlier argument—that his life is justified by its *exemplary* value. Is he not offering men an example of the way of life they ought to lead, and is he not showing them the error of their present ways? Rousseau seems to suggest that the life of every 'good' man, however bizarre it may appear to most people, must have some moral value by the mere fact of expressing true human nature. Unlike most other men, he has retained something of that original goodness with which God endows at birth each of his creatures; retreat from the world has helped him to see more clearly the significance of his life's development and the meaning of his real, primordial character. As for correcting the world's abuses, he maintains that he can do this far more easily in his present situation than if he were actively engaged in civilized life. He could not have spoken out in a forthright denunciation of the theatre if he had been living in Geneva. Moreover, he earns his living in a way that suits him; he is harming nobody and making some contribution to society. Is that not enough?

The psychological crux of his whole situation is stressed in the following significant passage:

> I have a very loving heart, but one which can be self-sufficient. I love men too much to have any need of choosing amongst them; I love them all, and it is because I love them that I shun them; I suffer less from their ills when I do not see them. This interest in the species is enough to sustain my heart: I have no need of particular friends, but when I have them it is essential for me not to lose them, for when they detach themselves from me, they break my heart (1144).

As far as the loss of his old friends is concerned, he soon disposes of any possible objection to his behaviour by insisting that these so-called friends were really secret enemies who wanted to tyrannize and enslave him—hence his love for 'men in general'. In spite of Rousseau's neat way of resolving his difficulties, the essential dilemma is revealed in his very first words—that he has a 'loving' heart which is nevertheless 'self-sufficient'. To most normal people genuine love excludes self-sufficiency since it involves the free confrontation of two independent personalities which nevertheless admit a reciprocal attachment. Self-sufficiency involves, on the other hand, a contraction of personal existence and a diminution of individual value. If the mystic seems to be exempt from this general human condition, it is only after he has undertaken a rigorously ascetic discipline capable of allowing him to stand alone before God. Rousseau, of course, refuses to accept all idea of such a discipline since his aim is to 'enjoy', not 'deny' himself. In fact the whole of our preceding analysis will have revealed that his overwhelming 'need for love' made him quite unfitted to live in a state of self-sufficient detachment from his fellows since it filled him with a constant hunger for more immediate emotional gratification. Even those obscure feelings of anxiety and guilt from which he so frequently suffered had some relation to other people and might well be interpreted as a sign of his failure to establish satisfactory relations with his fellows. However much he might affirm his own self-sufficiency, he remained profoundly dependent on others, although the contradictions of his nature often prevented him from consciously acknowledging that need.

In particular his stress upon his 'goodness' shows that he wishes to justify himself in the eyes of his friends as well as his own, while his earnest efforts to prove the socially useful nature of his present life also show that he is not indifferent to others' judgements. At a deeper emotional level his striving for a self-sufficient happiness involves him in such a violent suppression of his expansive need for other people that the subsequent delusions of persecution, as we shall see, are in some ways only the distorted and subconscious expression of this hidden, unsatisfied impulse.

The third letter already shows that Rousseau cannot remain satisfied with mere psychological analysis; he has to relate his character to a specific mode of existence and the concrete conditions of his immediate happiness. Because it is in such perfect conformity with his true character, this way of life will reveal his 'moral state'. It is this third letter which—as Professor Bisson emphasizes—anticipates so many features of the later Romantic Movement. Here, however, I am not concerned with these wider implications of Rousseau's attitude but simply with their bearing on his personal life and later writings. As he himself suggests, his main interest was to provide his life with some positive basis and so to remove the threat of disintegration and incoherence. Instead of feeling that his existence was being dissipated among a series of unrelated and inconsistent activities, he sought to establish it on a firm basis that was in harmony with his real character. Once, therefore, he had attained a clearer view of his personality in the first two letters and explained his essential needs, it was only natural that he should seek to adapt it to a specific mode of existence. The essential satisfaction derived from this outlook was that the happiness he had now attained was truly *his*—even though it was far from complete. The evils and misfortunes by which his life had been constantly beset were 'the work of nature', something imposed upon him in spite of himself and against which his freedom was powerless; his happiness, on the other hand, was the result of his own efforts and something for which he had actively striven. The reason for this was that he had learned to seek happiness within and not outside himself. For many years he had been mistaken concerning this vital fact until the 'reform' of 1756 had suddenly revealed the truth. Then he had wisely made a definite personal choice which had 'restored him to himself' and put him within physical reach of this new goal.

In this third letter Rousseau takes up again the problem so earnestly examined in *La Nouvelle Héloïse* and the *Lettres morales*: Where is true happiness to be found? He is more and more convinced that the difficulty is not to find objective principles capable of providing some universal criterion for the attainment of happiness but to effect a personal appropriation of truth as he sees it. Although happiness is principally an individual matter, a state of mind that he must create for himself, this cannot be achieved without the help of a favourable environment which imposes no restrictions on the free expression of spontaneous inner need. As the *Lettres morales* had already taught, true freedom and happiness do not mean a futile dispersion of the self amid the multifarious activities of the world, but the physical circumscription of existence and the deliberate cultivation of solitude. The letters to Malesherbes reaffirm this ideal, but in a way that places a stronger emphasis on the principle of an immediate enjoyment which avoids the tormenting anxiety associated with a hazardous future or the futile yearning for an irrecoverable past. He realizes that it is 'folly to torment himself for an age which he will not reach'. That is why he has 'forsaken everything and hastened to enjoy (himself)'. This, henceforth, will be his absolute goal: the attainment of an immediate personal enjoyment in which his whole personality can find an expansive expression of its most intimate emotions and which will form both the psychological and the moral basis of his existence.

Enjoyment for Rousseau will differ from the kind of pleasure experienced by other people, because its absolute character gives it an *intensity* which is lacking in the emotions of everyday life. The physical restriction of which we have just spoken thus becomes the prerequisite for a broadening of personal existence: he circumscribes himself only to extend his inner being. Now at last Jean-Jacques is determined to give free reign to that expansive side of his nature, the force of which he had always acknowledged but which he had been hitherto compelled to restrain. Enjoyment of this kind is not a merely static emotion but the dynamic aspect of a personal existence which henceforth identifies itself with the expansion of its most intimate possibilities. This expansion, it need scarcely be said, does not take the form of practical action, but of an infinite desire which can never be confined to the objects of everyday experience.

The peculiar fascination of this new form of happiness lies for Rousseau in its spontaneity. He had always been tormented, as we have repeatedly seen, by inner divisions and contradictions which he attributed to the tension involved in his relations with his environment. The intense and uninhibited quality of this new happiness helps him to overcome all sense of inner division and to feel that he is truly himself in all completeness and unity. Although he does not reach the point of abandoning external reality in favour of some completely escapist solipsism, he constantly requires his environment to provide conditions which will facilitate the emergence of expansive feelings. This means that they must be such as to eliminate all idea of the anxiety aroused by the thought of his fellow-men (and he deems rural solitude to be admirably suited to this end); then, he must be supplied with a background of 'pleasant' objects which prepare him for the movement of expansive liberation. In this way all inner struggle is eliminated; there is no anxiety, no inner division—nothing but the spontaneous upthrust of a personal existence which is completely identified with its own sense of unity.

The ultimately important factor in this experience is undoubtedly Rousseau's own state of mind, for happiness will come only to the man who has been able to achieve the most intense form of self-realization. But this kind of expansive fulfilment of personal existence is inseparable from a new consciousness which is directed not only upon the self but also on the external world. In order that this personal experience may not become a mere succession of fleeting moments, a new realm of objectivity is uncovered and the inner self encounters the reality of physical nature. This dual movement of the personality inwards towards its own existential possibilities and outwards towards the hidden structure of the non-self is not analysable in terms of a reflection which moves in the world of separation and differentiation. Yet the distinction between the self and the outer world is certainly not abolished even though it is obscured, since the personality, while undergoing a process of transformation which ultimately involves a heightened self-awareness and the development of all its own emotional and intellectual capacities, also discovers a new and richer meaning in the external reality in which it moves.

But what did I enjoy when I was alone? Myself, the whole universe, all that is, all that can be, the entire beauty of the world of sense, the whole imaginable content of the intellectual world: I gathered around me everything that could flatter my heart; my desires were the measure of my pleasures. No! never have the greatest voluptuaries known such delights, and I have obtained a hundred times more enjoyment from my chimeras than they have from realities (1138-9).

This experience cannot be fully explained in terms of a merely spatial relationship between the self and the world, for in addition to the

N

intimate interpenetration of subject and object there is a blending of the actual and the potential, the real and the imaginary. If the expansion of the self facilitates the enjoyment of its deepest potentialities as it moves away from its limited, everyday existence towards a more comprehensive expression of its being, the sensuous and spiritual beauty of the world also shows it to be a system whose unity reflects its relation to the Creator: it thus becomes more than a collection of beautiful physical objects since this exalted experience reveals its intellectual and spiritual as well as its sensuous meaning. Although we cannot expect too precise a description of the process, it seems clear that all the various dimensions of experience are involved—the senses, emotions, intellect and imagination. In short, both the self and the external world are now seen to possess abundant possibilities of meaning to which the unawakened consciousness of the ordinary observer remains for ever blind.

The complex nature of the relations existing between the self and the objective world is plainly revealed by Rousseau's treatment of nature in the third letter, where he anticipates his even more subtle treatment of the theme in the *Rêveries*. He admits that his first concern is to overcome the anxiety provoked by the thought of 'servitude' and 'domination'. He seeks to escape from men and lose himself in a lonely refuge where nothing can disturb his inner peace. At the same time, the emotional satisfaction thus obtained from his retreat into nature is not simple: although one part of his personality is content to let itself become absorbed in an attitude of rapt contemplation and 'admiration', there is also the mood of 'observation' and discovery which provides an outlet for more affirmative feelings; he delights in the thought that he is the first possessor of a virgin territory that for so long has lain intact and unknown. In his feelings for nature there is a curious blending of emotional and sensuous enjoyment, an effacement and also an affirmation of his personality before a reality other than his own.

The gold of the broom and the purple of the heather struck my gaze with a richness that touched my heart; the majesty of the trees which covered me with their shade, the delicacy of the shrubs around me, the astonishing variety of the grasses and flowers which I trampled underfoot kept my mind continually alternating between observation and admiration: the concourse of so many interesting objects vying for my attention and drawing me incessantly from one to the other, favoured my dreamy, lazy mood, and made me often say to myself: 'No! Solomon in all his glory was not arrayed like one of these' (1140).

Yet the delights of the physical scene are not enough to hold his attention indefinitely, and he is soon led to 'populate' his natural surroundings with 'beings after his own heart'. Here he refers—though more discreetly than in the *Confessions*—to the mood which had given birth to *La Nouvelle Héloïse*. He says nothing about his erotic frenzies, but stresses the idealizing activity of an *imagination* which allowed him to find so much pleasure in this 'charming society' of his own creation. 'I fashioned a golden age in accordance with my fancy and filling these fine days with all the scenes of my life which had left me pleasant memories, and with all those which my heart could still desire, I was moved to tears at the thought of humanity's true pleasures, pleasures so delightful and so pure, and yet henceforth so far from men' (1140). The experience of real nature is thus amplified and prolonged by the elaboration of imaginative possibilities drawn from his own life. At such times fleeting thoughts of 'Paris, his time and his petty notoriety as an author' were not enough to disturb the 'exquisite feelings' of which his heart was full.

Because the enjoyment of physical nature is so closely bound up with his own subjective needs, it is apt to become absorbed into the illimitable, absolute nature of human desire. Once vouchsafed a glimpse of infinite beauty, the heart is suddenly 'saddened' by 'the nothingness of its chimeras', for it realizes with anguish the enormous gap separating possibility from reality. In this respect Rousseau assumes on his own account the mood of Julie whose satiety with happiness had produced a feeling of 'inexplicable void' in her soul. 'Even if all my dreams had turned into realities, I should have imagined, dreamed, desired yet more. I found within me an inexplicable void which nothing could have filled; a certain heart-felt longing for another kind of enjoyment, of which I had no idea, but of which I felt the need. Well! that too was enjoyment, since I was pervaded by a very active feeling and by an alluring sadness of which I should not like to have been deprived' (1140).

Rousseau does not accept this sense of 'nothingness' as ultimate, since he turns away from his inner feelings to contemplate the universal order, not as a mere aggregate of physical objects, but as the work of its divine creator. This indescribable experience is the ultimate limit of his feeling for nature. Here he seems to go beyond the subjective enjoyment of the merely emotional or sensuous possibilities of nature, for he attains a specifically religious and metaphysical mood in which his inner being, identifying itself with the spiritual meaning of 'the universal system of things', finally prostrates itself in a final act of adoration before the incomprehensible majesty of God.

Some critics have been inclined to see in this attitude a clear example of Rousseau's 'pantheism', but in spite of ecstatic moments in which his personality merges with 'the system of the universe', it would be inaccurate to describe his experience as 'pantheism', since the proper use of this term suggests an identity of substance between the world and God. Rousseau's soul certainly feels an affinity with the universe because both are God's creation, but this does not mean that they *are* God. Although the genuinely transcendent reality of the world in relation to God tends to be obscured by Rousseau's emotional approach, it is doubtful whether he is denying that they have a separate existence or saying more than that the earth's beauty suggests the presence of God in this world.

In the *Quatre lettres à M. de Malesherbes*, therefore, we find Rousseau's first systematic attempt to see his character as a whole and to give his self-consciousness a stable and coherent form by eliminating or explaining the contradictions of his character in the light of its more fundamental attributes. In spite of moments of 'inexplicable void', he feels that he has at last found a mode of being capable of achieving 'his life's true happiness, a happiness without bitterness, vexations and regrets, and to which he would willingly have limited his existence'. It is significant that he professes to be no longer absorbed in memories of the unfulfilled longing of his youth or even with the more Julie-like yearning for a lost innocence. During his sleepless nights he now meditates on a less remote and less exalted past; he recalls 'his lonely walks, those fleeting but delightful days I spent completely alone with myself, with my good and simple housekeeper, with my beloved dog, my old cat, with the country birds and forest does, with the whole of nature and its inconceivable author' (1139). He has now learnt that happiness comes not from a hopeless rumination of the past or anxious hopes for the future but from a frank acceptance of all the spontaneous but limitless enjoyment of an 'eternal' present.

6

TOWARDS THE *DIALOGUES*

It is impossible to say whether the way of life outlined in the four letters to Malesherbes would have provided a permanent solution to Rousseau's personal problems, for the events following the publication of *Émile* in 1762 brutally awoke him from his idyllic dream of a lonely and peaceful rural existence. Certainly, the kindly interest and tactful friendship of the Maréchal and Maréchale de Luxembourg, of which he speaks in the last of the letters, brought him considerable happiness in these years by strengthening his self-esteem and providing the emotional support of which he stood in such great need. At Montmorency he planned to lead a life of 'absolute retirement' and 'independence', devoted—as far as writing was concerned—to the composition of his memoirs. We do not know whether these new contacts would have been strong enough to overcome the psychological difficulties already apparent in the letters to Malesherbes, but his life at Montmorency did encourage the hope that he was at last in a position to enjoy 'the charms of this simple, even life apart from which there is no happiness for me' (*Conf.* 527).

Ironically, this peaceful retreat was but a prelude to years of acute mental crisis, for the period between the publication of *Émile* (1762) and the writing of the *Dialogues* (1772-6) was to be one of the most troubled in Rousseau's life. It is at this time that we witness a progressive deterioration in his mental condition and the onset of definite delusions of persecution; the psychological climax, precipitated by the quarrel with Hume, led to intermittent but persistent periods of mental unbalance, the ultimate literary outcome of which was the writing of the dialogues entitled *Rousseau juge de Jean-Jacques*. Yet it is not at all certain that such a crisis would have arisen without the influence of the very real persecution to which Rousseau was subjected by ecclesiastical and civil authorities. Even the person most strongly predisposed to mental aberration has to find himself in a situation likely to bring on a sudden breakdown before the crisis actually occurs; although a psychosis may be partly determined by an individual's heredity and early history, he has to feel himself confronted by what he considers to be an unsympathetic or unmanageable environment before the abnormality becomes manifest. The events following the publication of *Émile* were naturally likely to arouse anxiety in a much less sensitive man than Rousseau. Forced to flee from France under the threat of arrest and imprisonment, he led—after 1763—an extremely unsettled existence; it is enough to recall here his flight to Switzerland, his eventual stay at Môtiers under the protection of the King of Prussia, his polemic with the Archbishop of Paris and quarrel with the Genevan authorities, the 'stoning' at Môtiers, his expulsion from the Île de Saint-Pierre, and his subsequent journey through France to England, his friendship and then his quarrel with Hume, his panic-stricken departure from Wootton and his flight back to France, his various wanderings and mental crises there until his final return to Paris in 1770. In addition to official persecution, he also suffered from Voltaire's treacherous attacks—and especially the *Sentiment des citoyens*—which certainly did nothing to ease Jean-Jacques's lot during these troubled years.

Although it lies outside the purpose or competence of the present study to make an exact clinical diagnosis of Rousseau's mental condition, it is impossible to understand the development of his subsequent attitude towards the problem of personal existence without some account of this much-discussed question of his 'sanity'; since his conscious efforts to solve this problem were, in some degree at least, inseparable from his general mental condition, it is necessary to try to estimate the effect of these various mental and emotional strains upon his ultimate attitude towards both himself and the world.

It may be said at once that it is not possible to give a simple answer to the question: Was Rousseau insane? chiefly because the term 'insanity' is a legal rather than a genuinely scientific concept. Although the existence of Rousseau's mental abnormality can scarcely be doubted, it is not easy to define or classify it accurately. His illness has been variously diagnosed as 'neurasthenia' (Dr. Regis, Dr. Möbius, Émile Faguet), 'psychasthenia' or a form of 'anxiety-disorder' (Janet), 'hysteria' (Renouvier), 'higher degeneracy' (Drs. Magnan, Sérieux, and Briand), and 'urinary disorder' (Drs. Poncet and Le Riche). Louis Proal, in his extended study of Rousseau's psychology, follows Dr. Magnan in seeing his case as one of 'degeneracy', using this term in a strictly limited sense to denote a 'lack of harmony or balance among the intellectual faculties'—a tendency to which certain highly emotive temperaments are particularly prone.[1] Others have tried to link up Rousseau's condition with the various phobias to which he was subjected (fear of the dark, horror of crowds, and so forth). As we have seen, the psycho-analysts place particular stress upon the sexual deviations, some of them treating his condition as one of repressed homosexuality.[2]

Unfortunately the precise meaning of some of these technical terms is often in doubt, and certain types of classification which were once common in psychiatric circles (neurasthenia, psychasthenia) have now been discarded or given a much more restricted meaning. Rousseau's case is also complicated by the presence of a large number of aberrant symptoms; it is fairly easy to find signs of anxiety, hysteria, and hypochondria, while the existence of definite phobias is also very evident. Some observers, struck by the prominence of one or other of these symptoms, have sought to make it the most important principle of interpretation. It seems, however, that some caution is necessary here since most mental disorders, whatever the precise name given to them, contain a whole constellation of symptoms, the predominance of a particular type of syndrome being accompanied by a number of subsidiary abnormalities which are often the sign of other well-known maladies. (Anxiety, for example, is a feature of neurotic and psychotic conditions other than those known technically as 'anxiety-neuroses'.) It would thus seem that the most useful method of approaching the Rousseau case is the one which, while recognizing the existence of various minor aberrations, seeks to characterize his mental condition in the light of the most persistently abnormal reactions of his adult life. From this point of view the most striking and obvious aspect of his later mental condition is the rapid development of the notion of 'persecution', which culminated in the formation of definite 'delusions'. To the 'delirium of persecution'[3] accompanied by systematic delusions, modern psychiatrists give the name 'paranoia', and, if in the subsequent discussion we speak of Rousseau's paranoid reactions, we are referring simply to his persistent tendency to become obsessed with such ideas.

The present work uses the term 'paranoia' in a purely descriptive sense and leaves unresolved the question of its precise aetiology. As I have insisted in earlier analyses, interest will not be focused on an

---

[1] Cf. Louis Proal, *La Psychologie de Jean-Jacques Rousseau* (Paris, 1923).

[2] See especially, R. Laforgue, *La Psychopathologie de l'échec* (Paris, new ed., 1950), pp. 97 ff. Cf. *supra*, p. 27.

[3] The word 'delirium' is used here in its French psychiatric sense of 'delusional state' (cf. Henderson and Gillespie, op. cit., p. 341).

attempt to trace back this abnormality to a precise cause but on the
bearing of the delusions of persecution upon Rousseau's self-awareness:
the paranoid tendencies will be examined in relation to his conscious
attempt to see—and ultimately to choose—himself as a certain kind of
person; what will interest us particularly will be the connexion of his
paranoid condition with the fundamental structure of the self as it is
expressed in a radical personal *intention* and in a conscious and deliberate choice of personal value. From this point of view it will be far better
to try to see these abnormal reactions within the context of the personality *as a whole* than as the manifestation of a particular 'disease'. This
way of looking at the problem also accords with the views of those
modern psychiatrists who treat paranoia primarily as a *disorder of the
personality*—as an abnormality which springs from the distortion and
hypertrophy of certain characteristics of temperament which, through
the strains and stresses of life, are thrown into unusual prominence and
impel the personality to react in a rigid and irrational way; they are the
pathologically exaggerated expression of reactions which form part of
'normal' everyday life; the incompetent workman who blames his tools
or the vexed traveller who curses the missed train are simple instances of
paranoid reactions. It is only when such delusions become systematized
that they assume psychotic significance. As Bleuler puts it, paranoia
comes 'always from affectively determined errors which spring up in a
way similar to the daily experience of normal persons, but which are
fixed and extended'.[1]

It is also important to recall that it may often be only a *part* of the
personality which is thus affected. Louis Proal's study performs a useful
service in correcting earlier misunderstandings when it calls attention
to the important fact that Rousseau's 'lack of balance' resulted only in
a partial 'delirium' involving a limited aspect of his personal attitude,
namely, his relations with other people. Hence it is quite reasonable to
separate his 'genius' from his 'madness' since the two aspects of his
personality need not and—in certain important ways—will not coincide. This view seems to be confirmed by more recent studies of
paranoia. It is interesting to note, for example, that far from indicating
any general deterioration of intelligence, paranoia often occurs in
persons of high mental ability; their main error is to exercise their considerable powers of reasoning, including logical analysis and deduction,
on faulty premises, the initial mistake being a failure to perceive the
real nature of their situation and the feelings of other people towards

[1] Quoted in Henderson and Gillespie, op. cit., p. 343.

them. This first erroneous perception is usually due to some deep emotional disturbance which makes them incapable of forming a correct estimate of their environmental conditions. Hence, although the abnormality assumes the form of a false belief, it would ultimately seem to be due to a disorder of *affect* or *emotion* rather than of intelligence.[1] This view would be confirmed by the fact already noted that the mental faculties may remain unimpaired; the paranoiac is psychically incapsulated, the rest of his personality being quite capable of normal functioning; provided that no contact is made with the persecution theme, he may seem no different from other people.

Although this disorder affects only one part of the personality, it is a condition which can show a steady deterioration. As Rousseau's case clearly reveals, the range of delusions tends constantly to widen so that, in the end, the subject may feel himself to be the victim of a well-nigh universal persecution. This conviction, in its turn, may evoke a feeling of such utter helplessness that a still more abnormal type of response is brought into being in order to deal with this desperate situation.

One of the most precise explanations of paranoia remains that put forward by the psycho-analysts, who follow Freud's famous analysis of the Dr. Schreber case.[2] There it is pointed out that the delusions of persecution are first directed upon formerly loved and revered persons who have exerted an important influence on the subject's emotional life. Thus it is significant that Diderot, Grimm, d'Alembert, and Hume were all men towards whom Rousseau had directed feelings—often very intense feelings—of affection, gratitude, and admiration. Freud goes farther than this and insists that the longed-for person becomes the persecutor because he is the object of a forbidden wish—namely, homosexual desire. It is only fair to point out, however, that many psychiatrists, while acknowledging the basic 'projective' mechanism at work in this psychosis, refuse to attribute it solely to homosexual desire and insist that the forbidden thought may have another origin (e.g. feelings of guilt and worthlessness, a sense of inferiority).[3] Whatever be the

---

[1] Cf. loc. cit. The shrewd judgement of Rousseau's contemporary, Corancez, is also worth quoting. 'He always started from a principle which was the product of his wounded imagination, a principle which he could not seriously examine; but the consequences he drew from it were all within the rules of the soundest logic, so that you could not help being extremely surprised to see him, on the same fact, both so wise and so mad' (cf. Musset–Pathay, op. cit., i. 257).

[2] Cf. Sigmund Freud, *Collected Papers* (trans. A. and J. Strachey, London, 1948), iii. 385–470.

[3] Cf. Henderson and Gillespie, op. cit., p. 385. 'The causation of paranoid conditions is probably not by any means a uniform one.'

precise feeling by which the subject is obsessed, it does seem to be a general feature of paranoia that its victims are primarily concerned with an attempt to escape from an intolerable tension by attributing to other people sentiments and attitudes which help to divert their own mind from a preoccupation with disturbing emotions. The secret thoughts and emotions from which the paranoid personality seeks to escape may, of course, be sexual in origin, but there seems no reason to exclude other impulses.

Because paranoia is a disorder of personality, its origins can often be traced far back in the subject's life; it is a state of mind which develops over a period of years and depends for its final emergence upon a number of elements involving both the self and the environment. As Rousseau's case suggests, no single factor is absolutely decisive by itself since it is a question of a cumulative, dynamic process extending right back to the first years. In this respect it will be sufficient to recall significant aspects of our previous analyses: the role of Rousseau's innate temperament—while doubting the existence of paranoia as an 'inherited' psychosis, psychiatrists admit the possibility of a predisposing 'paranoid' temperament—with its great instability and proneness to cyclothymic changes of mood; his highly developed sensibility which from the first made it difficult for him to establish adequate object-relations with his environment; important developmental influences such as his mother's premature death, his early dependence on an erratic father, the impact of the Genevan environment with the subsequent creation of irrational feelings of anxiety and guilt; the unfortunate 'spoiling' influence of his aunt and her servant; his transplantation to alien surroundings (and especially to Paris); his early experiences of 'injustice', about which he says so much in the *Confessions*, and the frustration of his first efforts to win recognition from his contemporaries. All these factors reinforced a tendency to unhealthy subjectivity and reverie which led him to see the immediate world in an unsympathetic light.

The sexual deviations already described—masochism, exhibitionism, and onanism—also indicate early maladaptation, and though their specifically sexual quality tended to diminish in later years, they created an obsessive need to be the *object* of another's attention. In spite of an almost pathological shyness and timidity before certain social situations Rousseau clearly betrayed an excessive emotional dependence on other people, and it was chiefly through being the object of their attention that he sought to attain a satisfactory mode of self-evaluation: he could be adequately aware of himself as a worthwhile person only when he believed that he was recognized as such by others. The attitude of withdrawal was thus related to an intense, but indirectly expressed, desire for self-affirmation which, in its turn, eventually led to an almost compulsive need to command attention; it is this trait which helps to explain the abnormal 'pride' of which he was so often accused. At times he would frankly admit his desire to be the object of attention. His adoption of Armenian dress in 1763 could be partly justified by his embarrassing malady, but it clearly satisfied at the same time a psychological need by making him stand out from his fellow-men as a bizarre and unique figure who could not fail to arouse considerable public interest. 'I have a pride well nourished by my approbation', he says again.[1] The difficulty of expressing this need directly (he desires to be noticed and yet experiences anxiety at the thought of being confronted by others) perhaps helps to explain the psychological inspiration behind the personal writings, where he avoids direct personal contact with the public and yet is able to reveal himself to it through the medium of writing. In fact it is Rousseau himself who aptly summed up his attitude when he said that he hid himself in order to write.

Nor ought we to forget the importance of purely cultural pressures in determining the onset of Rousseau's paranoid delusions.[2] Undue emphasis upon his early history is apt to obscure the important fact that, apart from any question of real hostility and persecution and a general lack of sympathy for his viewpoint, his adult perception of real moral defects in the society of his day made it difficult for him to turn to his environment for any kind of support against inner strain; he could feel no sense of solidarity with contemporary values, and after he had broken with the *philosophes* he felt himself to be out of tune with the 'progressive' ideas of the time. The cultural standards which enabled others to correct deviations from normal behaviour and outlook he found quite unacceptable, and his conviction that a man's real nature was incompatible with the 'social' self of his day isolated him still further from those around him. There is no doubt that this sense of being cut off from his contemporaries was an important factor in building up inner tension and anxiety. He was a 'foreigner' who had inadvertently wandered into a society that did not—or professed not to—speak the same language as himself.

[1] Cf. *supra*, p. 42.
[2] G. Vallette also points out that the geographical and historical situation of Geneva as a tiny Protestant republic surrounded by powerful Roman Catholic neighbours (and possibly enemies) predisposed its citizens to a 'persecution-complex'.

Rousseau's own account also makes clear that he was given to neurotic illness at a comparatively early age. The malady from which he suffered at Chambéry in 1736 was plainly psychological in origin (as he himself later admitted) and was probably due to the unsatisfactory nature of his relations with Mme de Warens and a feeling of guilt towards the dead Claude Anet, whose coat he had coveted.[1] Once he had changed his environment he began to recover rapidly and was soon well enough to indulge in a brief, sensual liaison with Mme de Larnage.

All these considerations, when taken together, create a somewhat disturbing impression, but they cannot be said to form by themselves a rigid paranoid pattern. Their appearance tends to be sporadic and is to a large extent offset by other normal factors to which attention has been called. In other words, they are not really sufficient to explain the fundamental *intention* of Rousseau's life at this stage of its development, although they bring to his self-awareness a number of elements from which he will never afterwards be completely free. It would be rash to accept the conclusion of a critic like Dr. Demole who sees the first definite paranoid symptoms in the 'famous' illumination on the road to Vincennes. Certainly, the influence of the Parisian phase was extremely important inasmuch as Rousseau's efforts to impose himself by an effort of will encountered a profound inhibition of his self-assertive powers which ultimately led him, through his consciousness of an unsympathetic environment, to withdraw into an unhealthy subjectivity marked by definite feelings of inferiority. But, as we have seen, he did make some efforts to overcome the limitations of his situation and to affirm himself in terms of moral values whose implications went far beyond his own individual case. Although the intense personal feeling of the first *Discours* was partly due to his resentment against a society which had frustrated so many of his desires and ambitions, this is scarcely enough to make of its theme a 'clearly characterized *idée delirante*' or to prove that his intellectual gifts simply enabled him to give his psychosis a deceptively rational basis. Because it was his ideal, moral self as well as his emotions which were involved, he could have argued with some justification that his own personal reactions were far less important than the basic facts to which he was calling attention and which affected the lives of all his contemporaries; he was not speaking simply for himself but for 'man'.

---

[1] It will be recalled that he believed himself to be afflicted with a 'polypus in the heart'. Cf. also the comments of J. Starobinski (op. cit., p. 171), who rightly calls attention to the 'expressive' function of Rousseau's psychosomatic illness.

More relevant than the 'illumination' for the first marked appearance of paranoid symptoms was the quarrel with Diderot, for it was at this time that he began to believe in the existence of a 'plot' or 'league' against him. It will be recalled that his chief charge against Diderot was that the latter wanted to dominate and humiliate him. Unable to feel that he was the absolute object of the other's undivided attention, Rousseau easily swung to the other extreme of believing that he was being thoroughly despised—and he could bear all feelings save contempt, which touched his self-esteem at its most sensitive spot. But once he had severed his relations with the d'Épinay circle, even the unnatural effects of these unfortunate circumstances were considerably diminished. Likewise, the pathological fears he was later to experience in connexion with the publication of *Émile* did not last, and cannot be taken as proof of a permanent paranoid condition.

Perhaps a more typical indication of Rousseau's developing paranoid tendencies is provided by his relations with d'Alembert. After a period of friendly relations during his 'Encyclopaedist' days when Rousseau seems to have been prepared to accord to d'Alembert the respect due to a leading French intellectual, he made the publication of the article 'Geneva' the occasion for a sustained attack upon the suggestion that a theatre should be established at Geneva. Although the clash of principle and argument was sharp, the publication of the *Lettre à M. d'Alembert sur les spectacles* in 1758 did not have a harmful effect upon their relationship and no personal animosity was aroused either by Rousseau's *Lettre* or d'Alembert's official reply. As far as Rousseau was concerned, the *Lettre*, although addressed to d'Alembert, contained little personal reference and was mainly devoted to an exposition of the author's views on morality and art.[1] On d'Alembert's side too there was no ill feeling. Just before the publication of his work, Rousseau wrote to warn his protagonist of the forthcoming production. D'Alembert replied with a friendly note in which he affirmed: 'Far from being offended by what you may have written against my article "Geneva", I am, on the contrary, very flattered by the honour you have done me; I am very anxious to read your work and profit by your observations' (*CG* iv. 10). That these declarations of interest were not idle words is proved by the practical steps which d'Alembert took to advance Rousseau's work; it was he who aroused Malesherbes's interest and so helped to secure the work's entry into France; he even offered to act as official censor.

[1] Moreover, Rousseau was really hitting at Voltaire whom he considered (probably correctly) to have been responsible for the idea of establishing a theatre at Geneva.

Again, when Rey, Rousseau's publisher, wrote to d'Alembert asking
him to facilitate the introduction of the *Lettre* into France, d'Alembert
immediately sent another letter to Malesherbes in which he declared:
'You can accept my word for it that there is nothing in this book which
can prevent its sale' (ibid. 49). When official approval was finally
obtained, Hémery, the inspector of the *Librairie*, noted in his *Journal*
that 'although this book is against M. d'Alembert, he was nevertheless
made its censor'.[1] D'Alembert's published reply to Rousseau's work,
his *Lettre à J. J. Rousseau, citoyen de Genève*,[2] although polemical, was
without any trace of personal animosity, and both his reaction at the
time and his later behaviour suggest that he was in no way offended by
Rousseau's essay. He continued to take a friendly interest in Rousseau's
work and in 1760 we find the abbé Trublet reporting d'Alembert's
anxiety to see Rousseau's letter to Voltaire on Providence.[3] In 1760
Rousseau and d'Alembert were again in contact on the subject of the
abbé Morellet's detention in the Bastille. As Rousseau was at this time
the friend of Mme de Luxembourg, he was asked to solicit her help in
securing the abbé's release. This he did and with good effect—much to
d'Alembert's delight. Later Rousseau was to accuse d'Alembert of
having made this event an excuse 'not for supplanting him but suc-
ceeding him' at Mme de Luxembourg's. There is, however, nothing in
Rousseau's correspondence or behaviour to suggest that he seriously
entertained the thought at the time of the incident; it may well have
entered his mind a few years later when he thought that he had other
reasons for suspecting his former friend of dire treachery. In any case,
Rousseau clearly continued to set some store by d'Alembert's literary
opinion, for he was careful to have his name inserted on the publisher's
distribution list. In 1761 d'Alembert wrote to give his impressions of
La Nouvelle Héloïse, in which he found 'this heart-felt eloquence, this
warmth, this life which characterizes your works and shines out especially in this one'; he made a few friendly suggestions for improving the
book, advising the suppression of the notes and a few pages. Rousseau
was 'charmed' with d'Alembert's letter; the praise and the 'frank and
judicious criticism' made him cherish both 'as the language of friendship' (*CG* vi. 2). In his turn d'Alembert sent to Rousseau a new edition
of his *Éléments de musique*, accompanying the book with a letter
expressing the hope that he would soon have another work from

---

[1] Cf. J. P. Belin, *Le Mouvement philosophique de 1748 à 1789* (Paris, 1913), p. 151, n. 4.
[2] *Œuvres de d'Alembert* (18 vols., Paris, 1805), v. 306–67.
[3] *CG* v. 141.

Rousseau. Later on Rousseau saw in this action further proof of d'Alembert's duplicity, for in the *Confessions* he roundly accused him of using material which he himself had provided for the *Encyclopédie*. At the time there was no suggestion of any such lack of good faith. After the publication of *Émile* d'Alembert wrote to Rousseau a long letter in which he complained bitterly of the persecutions to which Jean-Jacques had been subjected 'because he gave men plans for a reasonable religion'. 'This misfortune, which I am impelled to share with you through the influence of friendship and the greatest esteem, leaves me strength to speak only of yourself and to offer you, in your present position, any assistance I can give to alleviate it' (vi. 294–6). As King Frederick's friend, he then offered to help Rousseau to settle in Prussia; if he did not like the idea of frequenting the Court, he could find a retreat at Neuchâtel where the Earl Marischal was now living; Rousseau could rest assured in the meantime that the merits of *Émile* were such that the voice of 'honest folk' would rise above that of 'hypocrisy and fanaticism'. He concluded: 'Hate (nothing is more just) the bulk of mankind as it deserves; but love a few men and deign to place me in that number.' When he wrote the *Confessions* Rousseau was to treat this letter as further proof of d'Alembert's treachery, since he sent it unsigned. (D'Alembert was frequently in the habit of not signing his letters, as Voltaire himself mentions on one occasion;[1] if he did not sign this one, it would not be because he had any sinister intention towards Rousseau, but was simply the expression of his usual caution.)

It was about this time that Rousseau's attitude towards d'Alembert began to change. In this respect it is worth mentioning that there were not wanting sympathizers who sought to convince Rousseau of the *philosophe*'s hostility towards him. The pastor Moultou aggravated his suspicions by telling him that Voltaire and d'Alembert were stirring up trouble for him in France and Switzerland. 'They are anxious to set you at loggerheads with our ministers in order to have their own back on you' (*CG* viii. 21). More and more overwhelmed by the thought of persecution, Rousseau's sense of isolation increased. 'No man in Europe will undertake my defence', he laments (viii. 105). The secret machinations of 'two exiled priests' he deemed to be particularly dangerous because, in addition to drawing up an 'indictment' against him, they went to Paris and put themselves 'under the protection of d'Alembert who gave them shelter in his own home'.[2] Although a few of Rousseau's

---

[1] Voltaire, *Œuvres* (ed. Moland), xlviii. 218.
[2] Ibid. and cf. *Conf.* 506.

sympathizers like Moultou were willing to encourage these suspicions, others such as Mme de Verdelin refused to believe that d'Alembert had aligned himself with Rousseau's enemies; she, at any rate, was of the opinion that d'Alembert had done his best to persuade the public and Rousseau's friends that he regretted the event. As the mental pattern began to take shape, Rousseau refused to change his attitude. Hearing that d'Alembert had been offered the post of tutor to the son of the Empress Catherine, he told the Earl Marischal: 'M. d'Alembert has philosophy, learning and much intelligence, but if he brought up this little boy, he would make him neither a conqueror nor a sage but a Harlequin'—and that, in his eyes, was enough to condemn him! The sensible and kindly Lord Keith refused to accept such a suggestion; having met d'Alembert during the latter's visit to the King of Prussia, he had formed a very favourable impression of him. 'I must do him justice', he wrote to Rousseau, 'he (d'Alembert) speaks of you in a friendly manner and with the greatest consideration.' In fact, a general review of their relationships up to this period suggests that d'Alembert was very well disposed towards Rousseau and that the latter's growing suspicions were without any real justification. Curiously enough, Rousseau was the first to acknowledge the injustice of his distrust, for in 1764 we find him admitting to Watelet that he had made a serious mistake. 'M. d'Alembert has sent his kind regards to me on several occasions. I appreciate this kindness on his part. I have behaved badly towards him. I blame myself for it. I think that I have done him an injustice and I am sure that my heart is not unjust, but I confess that unprecedented and innumerable misfortunes and calumnies—and these were the least of my fears—have made me mistrustful and credulous about evil' (*CG* xii. 74). Perhaps still conscious of the injustice of his past thoughts, he instructed Duchesne on 2 December 1764 to put d'Alembert's name on the distribution list for the *Lettres de la montagne*. Meanwhile, Watelet hastened to assure Rousseau that d'Alembert was grateful for Rousseau's acknowledgement of his error. 'He is far from believing that you are in any way to blame. I answer for his feelings towards you, feelings with which I am well acquainted, just as I should answer for yours, concerning which he has never been in doubt' (ibid. 137). A confirmation of d'Alembert's good intentions towards Rousseau is also to be found in his correspondence with Voltaire, where we see him trying to placate the latter's anger and pointing out that if Rousseau has been guilty of rudeness, it is because he is a sick man. 'I know that Jean-Jacques has behaved badly towards you . . . but

I cannot think that you would try to torment him in his solitude, where he is already unhappy enough by reason of his health, his poverty and especially his character.' Above all else, d'Alembert urges Voltaire to maintain an attitude of 'calmness' and 'dignity', for it would be regrettable if there were discord 'in the camp of philosophy at the very moment when it was going to capture Troy'. In short, until 1766 and the outbreak of the quarrel with Hume, d'Alembert's attitude toward Rousseau was fairly consistent. Although out of sympathy with his ideas and perhaps occasionally exasperated by the oddity of his behaviour, he did all he could to help him and never forgot that he was a sick man deserving of pity and the help of the *philosophes* who ought to support him against the common enemy. The idea of d'Alembert as a persistent and often fanatical hater of Rousseau—still accepted by some critics[1]—has little or no basis in fact. His friendly and well-intentioned attitude did not change until the outbreak of Rousseau's quarrel with Hume. I have, however, outlined the development of their early relationship, not in order to justify d'Alembert, but to show the insidious growth of Rousseau's paranoid suspicions, which were at first accompanied by frequent remissions and the return to moments of lucid and fair-minded judgement.

It will also be clear that the quarrel with Hume was not a sudden and inexplicable outburst of completely irrational behaviour, but the result of a long process of mounting anxiety and tension which had already had a partial outlet in his suspicions of the Jesuits and d'Alembert. But Rousseau's relations with the latter were not intimate or frequent enough for him to become the object of the extraordinarily intense emotions aroused by his feelings for Hume. It was not until his sojourn in England that the paranoid tendencies declared themselves in an unmistakable way. No doubt Rousseau's visit to that country, of which he had always thought ill and for whose inhabitants, language, and climate he had never shown much sympathy, was well calculated to provide an occasion for acute inner conflict. Immediately upon his arrival he had been the object of great public interest and admiration and this, following a successful short stay in Paris where he was also fêted and treated with some acclaim, was at first very likely to enhance his sense of worth and self-esteem, which must have been seriously impaired by his recent experiences of unrest and persecution. When he was suddenly taken from the busy English capital to Mr. Davenport's lonely house at Wootton, where he was left a good deal with his own

[1] For example, H. Guillemin in *Cette affaire infernale* (p. 142).

thoughts, he may have undergone a powerful emotional reaction. No doubt he was genuinely anxious to escape from the social obligations imposed by city life, but, as we have seen, he derived a particular satisfaction from the thought of being the object of others' attention. Now that he had to live alone, Rousseau's thoughts began to dwell upon himself with fatal effect. After treating him as a seven days' wonder, the newspapers became either critical or indifferent. Abandoned to his own resources, Jean-Jacques began to experience a resurgence of the anxiety and insecurity by which he had so frequently tormented in the past. Inevitably his fear and resentment fastened upon the very man who had done all he could to bring him to England and upon whom he now felt an almost filial dependence. It may be said at once that, if later on Hume was to be guilty of some impatience and lack of tolerance with the sick Rousseau, there was absolutely no foundation for the latter's wild and fantastic charges against his former friend.[1] The interest of the whole incident lies almost exclusively in the light it throws upon Rousseau's psychological condition at the time.

The tragedy of the whole affair lay in Hume's failure to recognize the fundamental nature of Rousseau's need. Thrust into the solitude and strangeness of a foreign country, Rousseau felt a powerful resurgence of his overwhelming 'need to love and be loved'; his constant sensitivity to hostility and criticism, aggravated by the real persecution of the previous years, led to a corresponding increase in his desire for emotional comfort and reassurance: he looked upon Hume not merely as a protector of his material interests and well-being, but as the recipient of his intense needs for emotional *épanchement*. Bernardin de Saint-Pierre suggests that Rousseau was sympathetically disposed to Hume before he actually met him partly because his Christian name was precisely the one adopted by his father in accordance with the post-Reformation Genevan custom which required each member of a coterie to adopt a Biblical name.[2] Certainly Rousseau's subsequent attitude suggests that in some ways he was prepared to look upon David Hume as a kind of father-figure, a less exalted M. de Wolmar in whose bosom he could alleviate all his anguish and unhappiness. From the very moment when he landed in England Jean-Jacques had given vent to a typical outburst in his new friend's presence, and he must have been shocked and dis-

---

[1] For the text of the letters we have preferred to follow J. Y. T. Greig's edition of *The Letters of David Hume* (2 vols., Oxford, 1932), to which may be added *New Letters of David Hume* (ed. R. Klibansky and E. C. Mossner, Oxford, 1954).

[2] Op. cit., p. 39.

concerted to find that the Scotsman Hume and the reserved English gentleman Davenport were not only unaccustomed to indulge in the French compliments which Rousseau—for all his contempt for *la politesse*—found so much to his liking, but also quite unable to reciprocate his own great need for *épanchement*. Hume could do no more than tap his weeping friend on the shoulder and utter a startled and embarrassed 'My dear sir! My dear sir!'—a gesture that was later to be interpreted as a proof of actual disapproval and criticism!

The harshness of the weather (snow was still on the ground when he arrived at Wootton) probably helped to increase Rousseau's disquiet and physical discomfort by provoking an acute attack of retention,[1] but a much more important factor in precipitating an emotional crisis seems to have been the necessity of having to rely on the company of the cantankerous and disgruntled Thérèse in a house where the servants did not speak his language or he theirs. His *gouvernante* did not take long to quarrel with Davenport's servants and she no doubt pestered Rousseau with her complaints; she was, moreover, only too ready to encourage his morbid suspicions when she saw a means of securing some advantage for herself. Like many people of low intelligence and extreme ignorance she had a highly developed animal cunning which she knew how to use with good effect. It is one of the curious paradoxes of Rousseau's life that this 'stupid female', as Mme de Verdelin called her, should have gained such an extraordinary ascendancy over a man who was in so many ways her superior. From the very moment of their arrival in England, she had threatened to bring trouble to Rousseau. Although Hume described his new charge as a 'very modest, mild, well-bred, gentle-spirited and warm-hearted man as ever I knew in my life', he was clearly not impressed by his female companion. Rousseau's insistence that Thérèse should 'sit at table' with Mr. and Mrs. Townsend, two of Hume's wealthy contacts who had offered Jean-Jacques the hospitality of their house, was enough to secure a rapid withdrawal of that invitation. She was reported as being 'wicked and quarrelsome, and tattling, and is thought to have been the chief cause of his quitting Neuchâtel'.[2] Hume also repeats Rousseau's own admission that she is 'so dull that she never knows in what year of the Lord she is, nor in what month of the year, nor in what day of the month or week; she can

---

[1] Corancez pointed out that these attacks were often followed by a period of mental aberration. This was certainly the case with his earlier suspicions against the publishers of *Émile*.

[2] *Letters*, ii. 3, 8.

never learn the different value of the pieces of money in any country'. Yet all this did not alter the startling fact that 'she governs him as absolutely as a nurse does a child'. After Rousseau's violent break with Hume, Richard Davenport was to record that 'his Gouvernante has absolute power over him and without doubt more or less influences all his actions'.[1] Thus her constant quarrels with the servants at Wootton, as well as her general mood of dissatisfaction, may well have helped to increase Rousseau's state of unrest and disquiet. The result of all this was that with almost inexorable fatality the earlier pattern of reaction reappears, but with still clearer definition: a period of intense and spontaneous affection is followed by a mood of suspicion and resentment.

Being thrust into an intensely introspective mood by the writing of the *Confessions* upon which he was now busily engaged, he was soon reduced to a state of mind in which the slightest suggestion of neglect or criticism was immediately taken for a proof of extreme hostility. The press's sudden loss of interest in him, as well as his discovery of the rather poor joke of 'the King of Prussia's letter' (actually written by Horace Walpole), served to increase his disquiet and undermine his self-confidence. No longer fêted by his fellow-men, he now sees himself as a man who is 'alone, without support, without friend, defenceless, abandoned to the rashness of public judgements and to the effects which are their usual sequel, especially in a people which does not like foreigners' (*CG* xv. 171). He is, he tells Mme de Verdelin, 'the most wretched of men'. London opinion is, he believes, only too ready to heap insult and dishonour upon a man who until then has enjoyed the highest 'esteem' and 'consideration' of 'honest people and the public'. It is surely significant, he thinks, that England is the only country in which such disfavour has been shown to him. Because of the displacement of emotion to which attention has already been called, Jean-Jacques becomes more and more sensitive to these slurs upon his reputation, for it is with his good name as a man and a writer that he henceforth identifies his ideal self. With remorseless logic he is led to a conclusion against which his mind at first rebels: if (as is clear) everyone is now turning against him, were not those first signs of approbation and acclaim part of a sinister plot to defame him in the eyes of the world? If he was so well treated at the beginning of his stay in England,

[1] Cf. *New Letters of David Hume*, p. 221. Rousseau's physical isolation at this time must not, of course, be exaggerated, for he certainly made friends at Wootton; he became particularly fond of Mary Dewes, the niece of one of his neighbours, Bernard Granville; but these and other contacts were not enough to offset the insidious influence of Thérèse and his own tormenting emotions.

was this not simply a feint to put him off his guard and so prepare the way for his ultimate degradation, nay, his actual destruction? But who could have been responsible for such an idea? There was only one possible answer: the man who had made such a show of befriending him in the first place—David Hume. After all, it was Hume who had really been responsible for bringing him to England; it was Hume's friend, Richard Davenport, who had offered him the hospitality of his country house. Above all, it was to Hume that he had looked so anxiously for the emotional support which might have helped to keep his morbid fears in check. When no such consolation is forthcoming, Rousseau, suddenly sensing and fearing hostility all around him, becomes absolutely convinced that Hume's silence and lack of effusion are certain evidence of his guilt and breaks off all communication with him. Eventually he sends to Hume the vast paranoid letter of 10 July 1766,[1] which forms one of the most curious psychological documents of his stay in England.

In spite of the changed circumstances of his life, Rousseau's fundamental preoccupations were not essentially different from his earlier reactions, and it is interesting to compare his charges against Hume with his previous accusations against Diderot. The main difference is that Hume is now held to be a far more evil and demonic character than Diderot. Yet the basis of the charge is the same: Hume's object, from the first, was to lure Rousseau into his power and, when he was once trapped, to degrade and humiliate him by making him appear as the recipient of ignoble charity. Hume is held responsible for all his misfortunes, including the unfavourable comments which begin to appear in the English press. It is in the attacks upon his reputation that Rousseau finds the hostility of these false friends to be particularly reprehensible, for their sinister intentions had assumed the mask of benevolence. He sees his worst suspicions confirmed by the memory of various small incidents. It was no mere accident that the son of Dr. Tronchin—the *jongleur* and friend of his arch-enemy Voltaire—should have lodged in the same house as Hume! Why, even the lodging-house keepers were being encouraged to show him 'hatred and disdain'! Once the main suspicion is firmly implanted in his mind, the idea of a plot having ever wider ramifications becomes rapidly more real and frightening. It is interesting to note how Rousseau derives the conviction of universal hostility from an initial assumption that degradation takes the form of *dependence* on others. This had been his early grudge against

[1] Cf. *CG* xv. 299–324, and *Letters*, ii. 385–401.

Diderot—that the latter had shown a displeasing air of superiority! Now he is tormented by the thought of living in another man's house, of receiving financial assistance—even from a king. Having always been very sensitive to this question of material gifts,[1] he henceforth sees Hume's and others' benefactions as a means of transforming him into a 'monster of ingratitude'. It is the feeling of being at 'another's discretion' that lies at the root of all Rousseau's fears; to be in another's power is to be exposed to universal opprobrium. That Hume himself always had this intention is conclusively revealed (he thinks) by the statement made during his sleep—'I've got Jean-Jacques Rousseau'.[2]

The very absence of any direct evidence in support of his suspicions is transformed in Rousseau's mind into a further proof of a hostility that is all the more terrifying for being hidden. He gradually moves from the idea of degradation and humiliation to that of active persecution; he begins to stress the element of mystery and subterfuge in the plot; 'black vapours' are arising everywhere to choke him. He is ready to interpret even the most friendly gestures as sure signs of treachery; he is surrounded by 'secret traitors' and 'perfidious friends' who are working to dishonour and destroy him.[3] For the first time too we see the definite emergence of the idea of 'subterranean' hostility; his enemies are 'moles burrowing underground'. He comes to the point of treating a mere look or expression as a sufficient indication of malevolence and lays great stress on the fact that Hume has piercing eyes. As the delusions become more intense and systematized, Rousseau himself is contrained to admit that this concourse of events is truly 'astonishing'. He is overcome by a panic-stricken sense of helplessness. As the plot grows in ferocity and extent, so does Rousseau feel his own powers of resistance weakening. He is terrified by the 'unnatural' behaviour of his enemies, since it is 'not in nature' for men to be so cruel. These terrible adversaries must be the 'blind instruments' of some evil vengeance and would be guilty of conduct that was quite incredible were it not so obviously real.[4]

Even when Rousseau has managed to escape from England, he obtains only a brief respite from his delusions and thereby confirms the general psychiatric view that paranoid symptoms tend to increase

---

[1] Cf. *supra*, p. 88.

[2] Cf. *CG* xv. 156, 228. It is interesting to note that Rousseau here reproduces an idea already present in his earlier view of friendship: cf. *CG* iii. 132, and *supra*, p. 89.

[3] Cf. *CG* xv. 154–62.　　　　　　　　　　　　　　　　　[4] Ibid. 309–24.

rather than diminish in intensity. That a mere change of scene cannot effect a radical cure is due to the obvious fact that the basic cause of the delusions still remains, the most insignificant incident being enough to revive them. After his return to France a brief remission is followed by a recurrence of delusions which now become more firmly implanted than before. Indeed the years between his return to France and the writing of the *Dialogues* show an almost catastrophic deterioration in Rousseau's mental condition. After a short sojourn with the sensible and tactful Marquis de Mirabeau, Rousseau, or 'Monsieur Renou' as he now calls himself,[1] accepts an invitation to stay with his 'sister' (Thérèse) at the château of the Prince de Conti at Trye. In July 1767 he begins to suspect hostility on the part of the prince's servants, and fears that eventually their machinations will lead to attacks from the local inhabitants. Then, in September, his old friend, Coindet, who had been indefatigable on his behalf, becomes an object of suspicion (xvii. 251). More important, his intimate friend, Du Peyrou, with whom Rousseau had previously deposited his papers, comes to see him, falls ill, and in a delirium accuses Jean-Jacques of trying to poison him. Rousseau takes the sick man's ravings seriously, quarrels with him, and refuses to go on with the idea of allowing Du Peyrou to publish his complete works. In 1768 he has another spasm of persecution-mania in Lyons and Grenoble. In August he becomes involved in a complicated affair involving an ex-convict, Thévenin, who falsely alleges that Rousseau has owed him nine francs for the last ten years. Instead of treating this accusation with the contempt it deserved, Rousseau in great distress immediately demands an official inquiry into the whole affair, since he is convinced that his enemies are confronting him with this 'false witness' for sinister reasons of their own. A little later a certain 'sieur Querenet', one of Conti's servants, is accused of plotting against him. Then in 1770 he writes an extremely long letter to M. de Saint-Germain, which provides the final and most unmistakable proof of his paranoid condition. In this document, which anticipates both in language and ideas so many of the themes later developed in the *Dialogues*, he goes beyond the notion of being persecuted by particular persons to that of a universal official conspiracy with the Duc de Choiseul at its head. This represents the psychological culmination of Rousseau's delusions of persecution, although he was to give them a more extended and

---

[1] However, it ought to be pointed out that the idea of changing his name was suggested by his host, the Prince de Conti, who feared the authorities' reactions to Rousseau's reappearance in France.

dramatic expression in the *Dialogues*, perhaps the most remarkable piece of written evidence that Rousseau has left us of his later mental condition.

In this letter[1] we see the careful elaboration of a theme that had already impinged fitfully on his self-awareness, but which now forms part of a definite pattern—the idea that there is an unbridgeable chasm between 'the most loving of men' and the one who is 'the horror of his fellow-men'. (The letters to Malesherbes already reveal Rousseau's concern with the idea of a 'false' and 'evil' Jean-Jacques who exists in the heart of his contemporaries and whom many wish to pass off as the authentic Rousseau.) The bearing of this theme upon Rousseau's personal development can scarcely be overstressed, for it affects almost all his later introspection; it is in this letter to Saint-Germain that it emerges as a veritable obsession. Henceforth his personality is split between these two images: the good, innocent man he feels—and imagines—himself to be and the evil Jean-Jacques created by the malevolent minds of his enemies, the man who is the object of universal opprobrium, 'the talk of the people and the plaything of the mob'. Being absolutely isolated, he is powerless to ward off the most malicious attacks and answer the most terrible accusations. The idea that he is a poisoner, already haunting him during Du Peyrou's stay with him and perhaps symbolizing in some way his secret sense of guilt (for to be poisoned is to be polluted), also re-emerges here in all its starkness.[2] The man whose heart is as 'transparent as crystal' and who never knew a hateful or spiteful thought is accused of the blackest crimes. Equally striking is the idea which is to play such a dominant role in the *Dialogues*—that he is not allowed even to defend himself, because he is surrounded by 'an impenetrable veil of mystery' and iniquitous 'works of darkness' which prevent him from knowing the exact nature of his 'crimes'. Everybody is familiar with his guilt—except himself. The hopelessness of his situation is mainly due, he thinks, to the official support now being given to the 'plot'; it is not merely individuals like Mme de Boufflers, Mme de Luxembourg, Tronchin, d'Holbach, d'Alembert, and a host of others who are hounding him to his doom, but the whole world of authority with, at its head, the minister Choiseul, who, believing (quite mistakenly, thinks Jean-Jacques) that he has been insulted in his writings, is now bent on his destruction.

[1] For the text, see *CG* xx. 233–62.
[2] The importance of this theme has already been stressed by Jean Guéhenno, op. cit. iii. 247 ff.

Nothing has been omitted from the execution of this noble enterprise [of destroying him]: the power of the great, the resources of women, the ruses of their satellites, all the vigilance of their spies, authors' pens, mud-slingers' voices, the encouragement of my enemies, malicious searches into my life in order to besmirch it, into my conversation in order to poison it, and into my work in order to falsify it; the art of disfiguring everything, so easy to those in power, of making me hateful to every order, of defaming me in every country. ... They have let loose upon me spies of all sorts, adventurers, men of letters, *abbés*, soldiers, courtiers. Emissaries have been sent to various countries to depict me with the features that have been marked out for them (*CG* xix. 255).

The vividness of his delusions is interestingly confirmed by an analysis of the images Rousseau uses to describe his enemies. A study of this imagery reveals that, although they have a common persecutory basis, their emotional tones are apt to vary. To some extent perhaps the intensity of his language can be explained by his inability to forget, even in his paranoid moments, that he is still a writer who wishes to create the most striking impression possible; but when due allowance is made for this, the reality of his suffering cannot be doubted, and the presence of this powerful affective element testifies to the strength of his delusions. In their most extreme form the persecutors are identified with various kinds of animals and birds who take an almost sadistic pleasure in tormenting their helpless victim; these ferocious attackers appear in the shape of 'wolves', 'tigers', and 'rooks'.[1] Sometimes the savagery of their attacks assumes 'infernal' proportions and his enemies are no longer birds and animals, but devilish creatures bent on the most terrible cruelties. This type of reaction occurs only in his moments of most intense emotional stress, when he is exclusively preoccupied with the hostility of his environment. Generally speaking, the absence of direct evidence of open hostility makes him emphasize the secret nature of his attackers' activities; his enemies remain hidden, intent upon surrounding him with an air of mystery, secrecy, and silence. They are frequently 'underground' or engaged in 'subterranean manœuvres'; they are 'moles' burrowing 'under the earth'; or else they are 'spies', malevolent and watchful, working continually in the dark and all the more dangerous for being 'unseen'. His terror is increased by his belief that, though these enemies make him feel their hostile presence, they keep their victim in ignorance not only of their real activities but of the reason for their hatred; they are engaged in casting a 'net' around him,

[1] The tone of some of Rousseau's references suggests that his attitude involves at times a regression to more primitive and infantile modes of emotional response.

and in trapping him within their 'meshes'. And still the victim is unaware of the cause of this malevolence. At times Rousseau's imagery assumes an almost Kafkaesque note of nightmarish fear with its emphasis on the 'work of darkness' and the inexplicable animosity of these hidden forces. Occasionally his language takes on a more claustrophobic quality, especially when he becomes less obsessed with the idea of direct aggression than with that of enforced captivity. His enemies wish to 'bury him alive in a coffin';[1] they seek to 'gag' or 'stifle' him, denying him even the freedom to breathe or else reducing his existence to a living death. Here we witness a curious transposition of an idea which had already appeared in Rousseau's mind, for a letter addressed to the Berne authorities during his stay on the Île de Sainte-Pierre had appealed for permission to undergo a kind of voluntary imprisonment.[2] But at that time imprisonment has been associated with the idea of security and protection against misfortune, whereas it is now linked up with the idea of a living death. Permeating all these ideas in the consciousness that he is the victim of a 'plot', 'league', and 'conspiracy' which becomes ever wider in its scope until the authorities themselves, as well as private persons, are drawn into this universal desire to torment a helpless victim with all the vicious cruelty of which men are capable.

It is the growing influence of these delusions which helps to explain the psychological significance of Rousseau's reactions to Hume. In this respect, to place exclusive emphasis upon the previous psychic determinants of his present conduct (as certain psycho-analytical interpreters do) is to overlook the importance of his conscious efforts to adapt himself to the tensions of the immediate situation; he reacts to what is felt to be a hostile challenge from the environment by a form of conduct which he hopes will help to modify it in a favourable sense. Irrational though Rousseau's attitude may seem to be when judged by normal standards, it expresses an effort to overcome inner conflict and anxiety and to readjust himself to difficult circumstances. The complex nature of his dependence on others meant that he could never find a direct outlet for his need of affection; if he sought an eventual ecstatic satisfaction of his desire for *épanchements*, it was only after he had first assured himself that he was the exclusive object of another's feelings: it was the other—not Jean-Jacques—who had to take the initiative, for Jean-Jacques was prepared to transform himself into an object only on condition that the other's subsequent reactions actively encouraged his own sense of personal worth and facilitated the enjoyment of highly sub-

---

[1] Cf. *CG* xix. 247, 277, 318.   [2] Cf. *CG* xiv. 207.

jective emotions. But if the other upon whom he was emotionally dependent did not behave in the appropriate way, then Rousseau was compelled to have recourse to a different, more desperate kind of strategy: the appeal for sympathy and affection having failed, he had to provoke him by more aggressive means. The other is attacked and reviled, but in a way that is intended to elicit the contrary reaction: he is repelled in order to be brought closer. Painful, heart-rending estrangement will be followed (Jean-Jacques hopes) by rapturous reunion. The other is accused of being a devil so that he may ultimately reveal himself as an angel. When we study carefully the long accusatory letter of 10 July 1766, we feel that the figure of the evil Hume is conjured up in order that it may be exorcised by *le bon David*. Although a part of Rousseau is obsessed by thoughts of the 'blackest of men', another part of him is engaged in a desperate attempt to bring forth the 'best'. 'No! No! David Hume is not a traitor; if he were not the best of men, he would have to be the blackest.' The challenge thrown out to Hume —'prove yourself to be the best or the worst'—is but a tortuous means of obtaining emotional reassurance and renewed affection. Moreover, if Hume can pass this stern test, will not Jean-Jacques himself be assured of his own worth as a man whose 'goodness' has produced the most intense emotional reconciliation of which any two people are capable? There is thus a close link between his feelings for Hume and the process of self-evaluation. In each case these paranoid reactions, though containing an element of regression to more primitive modes of response, have a prospective function as an attempt of the personality to adapt itself to the intolerable strain of its immediate environment and ultimately to move on to a more secure mode of personal fulfilment.

It is worth noting that Rousseau's apparently settled conviction that Hume's sole intention of bringing him to England had been to degrade him by placing him in a position of humiliating dependence on his benefactor was sometimes shaken by moments of doubt concerning the reasonableness of such a belief. This had already been apparent in earlier letters. On 25 May he had told Mme de Verdelin that 'he was not absolutely convinced' of Hume's perfidy, although 'he was every day more persuaded of it' (*CG* xv. 241). The result was a 'horrible perplexity' which he would be only too happy to resolve 'with tears of joy', if Hume would give the requisite signs of affection. As these proofs are not forthcoming and Hume (the cunning man!) merely continues to busy himself with unimportant trifles like obtaining a royal pension for his friend, Rousseau becomes more and more certain of his duplicity.

Yet even in the letter of 10 July Rousseau gives a pathetic indication of
his bewilderment. 'Everything is equally incomprehensible in what is
happening. Behaviour like yours is not natural, it is contradictory and
yet it has been proved to me.' Then follows a dialectical statement of
his position rather similar to the earlier one; on each side of him there
looms up an abyss;

> I am the unhappiest of men if you are guilty; I am the most base if you are
> innocent. You make me desire to be this contemptible object. Yes, the state
> in which you would see me, prostrate, trampled beneath your feet, crying for
> mercy and doing everything to obtain it, loudly proclaiming my indignity,
> and paying the most dazzling tribute to your virtues, would be for my heart
> a state of utter joy after the oppressive and death-like condition in which you
> have placed me.

Then he concludes by asking Hume to 'justify himself if he is innocent'
and remain silent only if he is guilty. Even after proffering the wildest
charges, Rousseau still hopes—in his heart of hearts—that Hume will
be able to give him the emotional support he so desperately needs.
However terrifying and distressing the delusions of persecution may
be, they seem to have as one of their main functions the relief of a
fundamental anxiety which can be calmed only through the most
intense and affectionate expression of feelings on the part of the person
who is accused in this way. If reassurance is forthcoming after such
devastating and violent accusations, cannot Rousseau feel henceforth
that he has really won the absolute affection of which he is in such
great need? The last quotation also suggests that Rousseau may have
hoped to obtain through Hume some kind of relief from the persistent
feeling of guilt and worthlessness which even his growing conviction
of his essential 'goodness' had not been able to eradicate. If Hume's
piercing eyes had at first suggested those of a hostile accuser, might
they not be transformed into the Wolmar-like gaze of a man who sees
into his heart only to approve of its essential worth? He hopes that the
all-seeing eye—whether of the divine or earthly father—will bring him
peace and unity.

Rousseau's dramatic departure from Wootton and his panic-stricken
return to France, as well as the great publicity given to the quarrel by
Hume's decision to publish all the relevant documents, are apt to
obscure the peculiarly personal and intimate nature of Rousseau's first
reactions. Had it not been for Hume's violent letters to his friends, as
well as Davenport's subsequent failure to contact Rousseau at Spalding,
the latter might well have returned to Wootton and even sought to

re-establish relations with Hume. (Even after his return to France he thought of going back to Davenport's house and would perhaps have done so had he not discovered that Walpole, whom he judged—after 'the King of Prussia's letter'—to be his avowed enemy, was in contact with the ambassador.) Davenport at any rate was not convinced that Rousseau's decision to leave Wootton was final. Hume's essential mistake in the whole affair was to have treated Rousseau's wild accusations as questions which could be decisively answered by an appeal to objective facts: by publishing details of the quarrel and transferring the whole matter to the arena of public argument and debate, he obscured the subjective and essentially private nature of Rousseau's whole attitude.[1] The latter was not concerned with Hume's character as such, but with eliciting a particular type of response. Hume (quite understandably perhaps in the circumstances) treated the charge of 'villainy' as a direct attack upon his person: he failed to see that Rousseau was merely striving—though tortuously and only half-consciously—to relive his old dream of an 'unreserved intimacy'; he wanted to struggle through the darkness of hostility and misunderstanding to the pure light of perfect friendship, while at the same time assuaging those tormenting thoughts of which his conscience was still afraid.

The whole gigantic edifice of Rousseau's delusional system emerges finally as a desperate attempt to regain a stability and equilibrium that had been so seriously undermined by the events of the previous years. The obsessive preoccupation with others' hostility was not intended to serve as a mere screen to conceal his own feelings of inadequacy and guilt, but as a positive basis for a new affirmation of his own 'goodness'. If he was persecuted by all, was it not *because* of his goodness? Was it not because others knew him to be innocent and good that they took such fiendish pleasure in pursuing him with their hatred? Persecution, therefore, was not a mere aberration, but an essential condition for the renewal of his efforts at self-realization. It created as it were the stable background against which the striving for personal fulfilment could be carried on.

Moreover, it is important to recall that in spite of moments of extraordinary emotional tension and unbalance, Rousseau did not remain in a permanent state of anxiety. At first sight the vast letter to Hume suggests the idea of a man whose whole life is dominated by a single

---

[1] This fundamental point is brought out by Bernardin de Saint-Pierre who says (op. cit., p. 65) that Rousseau blamed Hume 'for having betrayed my confidence and made private quarrels public'.

fixed idea, but when Davenport visited him soon after his arrival at Wootton, he found him 'perfectly gay, good-humoured and sociable', and so confirmed Hume's own earlier impression that Jean-Jacques was 'the best company in the world'.[1] Although Rousseau's panic-stricken flight to Spalding suggests the behaviour of a man nearly demented through fear, the local rector who spent several hours a day with him during his stay in the town found him 'cheerful, good-humoured, easy and enjoying himself perfectly well, without the least fear or complaint of any kind'. It is clear that even at times of greatest stress Rousseau could enjoy periods of remission from his torment.

Apart from any question of mere mood, it would be unjust to interpret this period of Rousseau's life solely in terms of the psychopathological elements so far examined. In the first place, his 'abnormality' often covers a number of varying, complex states of mind, in which psychically determined elements are often blended with deliberate, if sometimes indirect efforts at self-awareness: 'unconscious' and 'conscious' factors make up a shifting pattern of personal response which is not amenable to some simple psychiatric 'explanation'. As the Hume episode very clearly shows, Rousseau's reactions cannot be properly understood as the strictly determined end-product of an earlier psychic history since apparently irrational behaviour is often seen upon closer inspection to involve serious attempts at modifying his immediate situation and affecting a change in the attitude of other people; this movement towards others is also bound up with a readjustment in his evaluation of his own personality, which further complicates the meaning of the Hume incident. Naturally this does not imply that Rousseau was fully conscious of all the factors inspiring his conduct; nor need we deny that, as his inner anxiety and tension increased, there was a greater abandonment of freedom and a diminished capacity for attaining true insight. But the systematic delusions of the last years were the culmination of a long and complicated history of individual responses to particular situations—a history in which no single psychic factor was absolutely decisive. Moreover, even when due allowance is made for the pressure of earlier psychological influences, we have to remember that Rousseau's *total* personality involved far more than his abnormal reactions. Indeed, if we compare his case with clinical instances of psychopathological obsession, we are struck by the comparatively limited role played by persecution in his complete life-pattern and by the way in which the abnormal symptoms become absorbed into some

[1] *Letters*, ii. 65, 165.

deeper personal intention. Although his self-awareness is inevitably influenced to some extent by these abnormal pressures, it is not completely dominated by them; what is particularly remarkable is his readiness to accept an abnormal psychic condition, the true significance of which he himself cannot understand, as a challenge to existential decision and action; we may agree that Rousseau's beliefs concerning persecution contain unmistakable delusional elements, but, far from letting himself remain the passive victim of forces greater than himself, he seeks in his quieter moments to confound his 'persecutors' by confronting them with the authentic, quintessential Jean-Jacques. Striving to establish his true reality in his own eyes, he often confronts real persecution with genuine nobility and courage, as, for example, after the condemnation of *Émile* in 1762 when he sustains himself with the thought that he is 'the defender of God's cause and the laws of virtue'. Having 'given glory to God and spoken for the good of men', he can take not a little heart from the thought that he is 'an author of another kind who dared to tell men solid truths capable of making them happy if they knew how to heed them' (*CG* viii. 178). At such times he felt that he was being sustained by an aspect of his personality which went beyond the limits of his own individual existence. Even when the idea of real persecution became confused with paranoid delusions, it is probably no exaggeration to say that he was still impelled towards renewed efforts to attain a deeper sincerity and a more stable attitude towards existence. In spite of his frequent hesitations, false starts, and wanderings into strange by-paths he moved steadily, if slowly, towards a personal goal—the exploration and understanding of his own being.

Perhaps at no point can we say that Rousseau achieved a fixed and settled attitude, for the quest was one which in a sense could never be complete. In any case, it was not a question of establishing a strictly logical or rational outlook or of rounding off some abstract metaphysical system, but of coming to terms with the concrete tasks of everyday life, and of finding a philosophy which allowed him to confront its hazards and uncertainties with courage and firmness. There was a constant passage from the plane of intimate introspection to that of practical living, from reflection to action. It is thus dangerous to interpret his drive towards self-expression in terms of any single mood, for each was modified by contact with ordinary life. At one moment trying to ward off the dark and terrifying shadows conjured up by his delusions, he may at another abandon himself to the simple joys of rural life, happily walking and botanizing in some peaceful corner of the countryside.

Of one very radical effect of his general position there can be no doubt: he was henceforth quite convinced that no genuine help would come from anybody but himself. This period is marked by a very powerful reinforcement of those subjective tendencies which had already declared themselves in earlier years. Now, however, it is not a question of mere escapism, but of a serious and carefully pondered belief that he was 'left to himself for all resources' (*CG* xix. 267). The few occasions when he had been able to enjoy undisturbed contentment in lonely but picturesque places merely confirmed his previous conviction that true happiness could be found only in the enjoyment of his own state of mind. He had been especially impressed by this during his short stay on the Île de Saint-Pierre when he imagined that he had at last found a perfect haven for the rest of his life. During difficult moments of his sojourn at Motiers he had reiterated this same resolve to 'withdraw into himself' (xiii. 43). At last had come the time to 'devote to himself so much solicitude lost in the cause of other people's happiness'. Henceforth 'it is only on his own substance that he must feed' (xix. 212). This preoccupation is to become a recurrent leit-motif in the personal works and reflects a sentiment he had already expressed didactically in a letter to Mlle Henriette, the young woman who had turned to him for epistolary moral guidance. True contentment does not come from dependence on others but from a philosophy which 'detaches us from everything and restores us to ourselves'. 'Be sure', he tells her, 'that you will be satisfied with others only when you no longer need them, and you will enjoy society only when you cease to find it necessary.' The great secret of happiness is to be 'self-sufficient' (*CG* xi. 59). A few months later (November 1764) he returns to the same point: 'I cannot repeat too often that I know neither happiness nor contentment in estrangement (*éloignement*) from oneself: on the contrary, I am daily more convinced that people can be happy on earth only in so far as they draw further away from things and nearer to themselves' (xii. 29). Three years earlier (1761) he had already affirmed that 'there is no enjoyment more delightful than the enjoyment of oneself' (vi. 304).[1] So convinced was he of the truth of this that at one stage, when

---

[1] The didactic works echo the same theme. 'Whoever does what he wants is happy, if he is self-sufficient' (*Émile*). 'Supreme enjoyment is satisfaction with oneself. . . . No, God of my soul, I shall never reproach Thee for having fashioned me in thine own image, so that I may be free, good and happy like Thee' (*PF*, ed. Masson, pp. 191–3).

he felt overwhelmed by his suspicions of Hume and the attitude of the English press, he decided to 'abandon all correspondence, concentrate on himself and be dead to the public for the rest of his life; it only remained for him to be occupied with himself—that was enough for the rest of his days' (xv. 241).

Although this determination 'to live for himself and to be satisfied with being happy' (xix. 106) is developed to some extent as a means of protecting him against hostility and persecution, it also has a more positive role, and really continues the movement towards self-expression initiated at the time of the reform of 1756. In no sense does Rousseau intend to set himself up as an otherworldly ascetic, or as a man who has decided to follow a severe mental and moral ascesis, for he is constantly affirming that he wants to live a life of immediate enjoyment. 'We work only to enjoy.' He proposes to live 'from day to day', extracting from each hour all the contentment he can. His all-absorbing preoccupation is with 'peace of mind'—'peace is worth more than anything'.[1] His frightened imagination will, he hopes, remain quiescent, being now relieved of all worldly cares and in any case no longer terrified by the thought of a horrible fate which he henceforth accepts as inevitable. His enemies' onslaughts leave him unmoved because he is not living outside himself, but in accordance with his own deepest and most spontaneous impulses. No longer does he depend on his mind but on his *sensibilité*, that fundamental, intimate part of himself which had, whether he willed it or not, directed his most earnest desires from his earliest days. He now realizes that, when properly understood, sensibility is not a merely self-centred aspect of the personality, but a source of genuine peace and contentment. The defect of reason is not that it is evil in itself, for it has the 'goodness' of all genuinely human attributes, but, being dependent upon other aspects of the self, it can become the instrument of 'pride' and 'passion' and so be diverted from its true function. At certain moments of his career—for example, at the time of the composition of the *Lettre à d'Alembert*—Rousseau had been inclined to stress the moral value of reason, but even then he had never supposed it to be completely autonomous and capable of possessing value in its own right: it was inseparable from 'virtue' and 'conscience'. Now, however, as he grows older and the need for a personal philosophy becomes more insistent, he feels increasingly incapable of adopting any kind of narrow rationalism. Immediacy demands a deepening of the inner, sensitive self—not subjection to the impersonal principles of

[1] *CG* xi. 240; xvii. 146; xviii. 22, 135, 231, 368.

P

universal reason. When Mlle Henriette casts doubt upon the value of *sensibilité*, he is moved to make an emphatic protest: 'How can we have a soul and not take pleasure in it? It is our soul which is the true source of pride and self-esteem.' To another correspondent, the Marquis de Mirabeau, he makes a still more personal application of his principle. 'However badly you may think of sensibility considered as a man's sole sustenance, it is the only one which I have left: I no longer live except through my heart' (xvii. 102). Looking back upon his life, he sees that it is indeed his heart—and not his mind—which has been his soundest guide. 'All the harm that I have done has been through reflection; and the little good I may have done has been on impulse. That is why I confidently abandon myself to my inclinations: they are so simple and so easy to follow' (xvii. 3).

In view of all this it is not surprising to find him occasionally adopting a strongly anti-intellectual attitude. Although his own brilliant *Lettre à M. de Beaumont* and the *Lettres écrites de la montagne* show that his mind could—when necessary—be as sharp as ever, he speaks of a growing aversion to 'all that goes by the name of literature'. He even refers with contempt to his own publications and tells the astonished Boswell that his books are so much 'nonsense'. No doubt we must allow for an exaggeration due to false modesty or depression, for had such a judgement come from anybody but himself, how violent would have been his protests! Yet, as far as his own personal happiness is concerned, he does betray a marked distaste for intellectual effort. 'I always found it painful to think; now I can think no more' (xvii. 102). He wants to empty his head and, as he puts it humorously, 'stuff it with hay' (xiii. 207). 'Reason is killing me; I should like to be mad in order to be sane' (xi. 193). 'I no longer read anything', he declares (xviii. 47, 129), and he makes exception of only a few romances (of which he had always been fond) and travel-books. The thought of literature is unbearable because of the unhappiness and trouble brought upon him by his own books, and in 1767 he sells off his library to Louis Dutens without much apparent regret.[1] Why should he spend his time reading and writing when he feels quite incapable of producing any new ideas? Days of creative thought, he is convinced, have gone for ever (xviii. 134). Henceforth he must seek another and, as he believes, more satisfying source of contentment.

In abandoning himself to his sensibility, Rousseau is convinced that he is following a course of action which is not only personally reward-

---

[1] Cf. *CG* xvii. 289–91.

ing but morally praiseworthy. As we have seen, sensibility is not a merely physical and sensuous aspect of human life, for it is deeply rooted in the intimate emotions of the heart: it is only when the sensuous and affective ('moral') aspects of the self are in harmony that true happiness is possible for man. Rousseau believes that when he follows his heart, he is avoiding the dangers of false *amour-propre*—whether in the domain of inhuman reflection or overweening passion. Through separation from the noisy, multifarious pleasures of the world and the vexatious boredom of society, a man can discover 'this divine moral sense' which makes him really himself. We recall in this respect the 'divine model' or 'effigy' which, in *La Nouvelle Héloïse*, Rousseau had attributed to every human being as the sure proof of his spiritual origin. That is why, on becoming truly ourselves, we can experience this 'exquisite' sense of personal elevation and fulfilment. At first sight it seems to be a purely internal, emotional experience. 'If nature has made you the rare and fatal present of a heart that is too sensitive to the need to be happy, do not seek to satisfy it by anything outside it: it is only upon its own substance that it must feed' (xix. 212). But sensibility is far more than a merely subjective feeling, it is a higher kind of moral emotion. 'This moral sense so rare among men, this exquisite feeling for the beautiful, the true and the just keeps the soul of whoever is endowed with it in a continual ecstasy which is the most delightful enjoyment of all.'

The renewed emphasis upon the value of sensibility and the heart also reinforces the earlier tendency to dwell with some complacency on the idea of his essential 'goodness'.[1] If, by giving way to his feelings, Rousseau becomes in some fundamental way himself, then plainly he is—on this view—fulfilling his existence as God intended that he should, for what God created must be good. Here again, he is convinced that 'goodness', however personal and individual, is no merely selfish attribute but part of a quality which pervades the whole of God's creation. No doubt this emphasis becomes inseparable later on— and perhaps already at this period—from certain psychopathological overtones, but it also represents an important aspect of his drive towards personal sincerity as well as a deeply felt element in his philosophy of existence.

The general character of his basic attitude is fairly clear, but his particular reactions still show some instability. The movements of withdrawal and affirmation already observed in his earlier life continue

[1] Cf. *supra*, p. 161.

to reveal themselves, although the specific mode of their expression is determined by the pattern of his later development. At times he affirms that there is nothing for him to do but *resign* himself to his 'fate' and to detach himself from all that is not of immediate interest: the forces of evil are so great that it would be useless for him to try to evade them; all he can do is to break off communication with the external world. His greatest wish, he now declares, is to be forgotten by the public and to be able to lose himself in a 'happy obscurity'.[1] 'The public is dead for me; its mad judgements have killed it in my heart', he declares after the discovery of Hume's 'perfidy'. 'I know of no other good than peace of soul and days ended in rest, far from the wild tumult of men; if the wicked will not forget me, it matters little; I have forgotten them.' 'Obscurity, peace, precious rest, where are you? Ah! if I were to find you in these mountains, I should never leave them for the rest of my life. I am trying to lose all memory of the past' (viii. 106). A little later he repeats the same wish. 'The sole good for which I yearn is rest' (ibid. 148). If in Great Britain he thought of living in the Welsh mountains or the wilds of Derbyshire, it was because of his growing passion for seclusion. For a time he thought that he had found peace at Wootton, for he tells one of his Genevan correspondents, d'Ivernois, in May 1766:

I warn you for the last time that I no longer wish to remind the public that I exist, and that for my part it will hear no more of me for the rest of my life. I am at rest: I want to try to remain so. Because of my desire to be forgotten, I write as few letters as possible. Apart from three friends (of whom you are one), I have broken off all other correspondence, and nothing will induce me to take it up again (xv. 244).

Subsequent events were to show that this resolution was not maintained, partly because his peace was constantly being disturbed by the dissatisfied Thérèse, and partly because one side of his personality still needed to feel itself the object of others' attention.

This yearning for peace and obscurity, though frequently suggesting a genuine mood of resignation, reveals a curious state of uncertainty. At times he seems quite determined to submit, in his own favourite phrase, to 'the yoke of necessity'; having experienced 'the nothingness of things', he 'grows calm in his resignation'. 'I am silent, I wait, I resign myself.' He 'fears and desires nothing'.[2] He is often comforted by the thought that Providence is using him for its own mysterious

---

[1] *CG* xv. 19, 52. [2] *CG* xvii. 193; xviii. 8, 21, 370.

purposes and that, in some obscure way, he is a man of destiny. Sometimes, however, the feeling that he is the victim of forces greater than
himself leads to a more sombre mood. It is particularly in the *Confessions*
that we find the recurrent theme of suffering through 'destiny'. He
believes that 'his birth was the first of his misfortunes'. Later on it was
his 'fate' to lose his friends and be marked out for a uniquely unhappy
existence. Eventually he was convinced that 'a blind fate was dragging
him to his doom' (*Conf.* 525).[1] His private correspondence reflects the
same idea, for he is 'destined to suffer for the rest of his life' (*CG* ix. 97).
All this serves to show how the belief in continued unhappiness and
loneliness begins to form part of a fixed and rigid pattern which, in
spite of bursts of optimism and hope, he is increasingly powerless to
control. Obsessed by the thought that he is the object of universal
hostility and persecution, he abandons all hope of improving his lot.
If this renunciation of hope brings, as he says, a certain peace, it is not
the quiet, confident resignation of a man who has truly found himself,
but of one who is about to plunge into utter despair.

Nevertheless, it would be quite unjust to exaggerate the extent of
Rousseau's pessimism, for his most melancholy moments tend to
provide a further incentive to self-examination as well as to renewed
efforts to obtain inner peace. Far from being an evil, solitude is a
necessary condition for the enjoyment of that independence without
which tranquillity is impossible. He therefore comes back to the topic
which had also been discussed in the letters to Malesherbes—freedom.
Only a lonely and free retreat can provide him with the contentment
he so desperately desires. But the freedom he wants is of a highly
personal kind: the freedom to abstain from doing what he does not
want to do. He does not seek some kind of heroic freedom, but simply
the opportunity to abandon himself to his essential *paresse*. Only in
this way can he attain true 'peace of soul', that supreme good to which
he constantly aspires throughout these years of mental distress.

That this mood forms part of a deep personal intention is also
revealed by the way in which it links up with another aspect of the
reform of the 1750s: to attain authentic selfhood and inner unity it is
necessary for him to overcome in some way the divisions and distractions of *time*. By 'concentrating' his being within himself, he hopes to
find some kind of absolute satisfaction, some ultimate value, which will
free him from the vagaries and uncertainties of clock-time. In so far as

[1] Cf., on this tendency to invest events with 'fatal' meaning, J. Starobinski, op. cit.
p. 60.

a man tries to fulfil himself in society, he seeks an indefinite, quantitative extension of his being through the enjoyment of 'heaped up pleasures' (xix. 213). But this entails a dispersion and fragmentation of personal existence which moves away from its true centre and plunges into the relative, artificial values of contemporary life instead of developing its intrinsic qualities. Abandoning a desperate and soul-destroying search for empty distractions, the man who wants to attain a properly stable equilibrium will aspire to a more durable condition—'a permanent state that is not made up of distinct acts'. Rousseau had already been fascinated by this ideal during his early days with Mme de Warens. In *La Nouvelle Héloïse* he had lauded the attractions of the 'eternal present', and the charm of *la matinée anglaise* had been largely due to the unique opportunities it provided for attaining a state of timeless contemplation and communion. Obviously such an ideal could never be more than asymptotic in the conditions of everyday existence since by its very nature it was a privileged experience, but it is one which Jean-Jacques, as he becomes more and more isolated from the outer world, consciously accepts as a personal ideal capable of satisfying his deepest inner needs.

His flights into 'the land of chimeras'—including the chimera of a timeless existence—did not exclude an attitude which was far too realistic to remain satisfied with vague emotional yearnings, however entrancing the objects which inspired them. Happiness involved, as he fully realized, the translation of dreams into the particular circumstances of everyday existence. He had long been convinced of the benefits of unpretentious living and at this time he constantly insisted on the benefits of 'a simple, lonely and free life'. During the tormented Parisian years he had never been able to forget the idyllic life he had spent with Mme de Warens, and *Le Verger* of 1739 had depicted the charms of a peaceful, rural life far from the 'frivolous tastes of foolish mortals'. The *Epître à Parisot* had expressed a similar sentiment with its eulogy of 'a good book, a friend, freedom, peace'. This modest dream had been largely forgotten during the Parisian phase, but it had never been completely given up, and the reform of 1756 had once again brought him back to a quieter life amid rural surroundings. Perhaps he had subsequently 'drifted' from this mode of existence, as he admitted to Malesherbes, but the love of it had never died in his heart. Now that he had repudiated all connexion with 'philosophers'— henceforth looking upon himself as *un bon homme*[1]—he quite naturally

---

[1] Cf. *CG* vii. 228; xvi. 327.

sought the 'simple, sane life' of the country. In this way he could simplify the conditions of his material existence. In any case, he had never belonged to any party and had never considered himself a professional writer: he was merely a man who spoke up for the truth as he saw it. His literary career (he believed) having set a personal example of virtue and integrity, he was now quite justified in following this secluded, unaffected mode of life. Moreover, being the son of a Genevan artisan, he was quite ready to earn his living by music-copying, for this was a trade which he thought to be in perfect conformity both with his principles and his inclinations.

Although he turns from time to time to his old 'idol' of friendship and makes plans for a lonely retreat sustained by the thought that he is 'faithfully loved by a single friend', he eventually accepts the futility of this dream. 'For eight years I have sought a soul among men; now I look no longer, and my lantern is put out' (xx. 171).[1] If others reject him then he must draw upon his own 'substance' and become 'self-sufficient' (xyi. 248). No doubt he still believes that he was meant to be 'the best friend that ever was' (*FA*, 1124), but 'fate' having decreed his isolation from others, he is now concerned with remaining 'completely where he is' (xi. 240). Everything is conspiring (he thinks) to make him pursue the mode of being by which he had always been fascinated—that of reverie and contemplation. Earlier on he had sternly rebuked a young correspondent for his 'taste for the contemplative life'. 'It is only an indolence of soul, blameworthy at any age and especially at yours. Man is not meant to meditate, but to act; the industrious life which God imposes on us can be nothing but acceptable to the good man's heart' (iii. 328). Julie too, it will be recalled, had been tempted by, and blamed for, her inclination to religious quietism.[2] But Rousseau is now convinced that his exceptional character and circumstances justify him in following a bent which at other times and in other cases ought to be condemned. After all, he considers that his life's work is finished and that he is approaching old age as the object of universal persecution. Is he not thus justified in directing his efforts towards the search for peace and self-knowledge? Reverie is a state of mind well suited to a man whose greatest pleasure is to take lonely walks across the countryside. He is little more, he says, than *une machine ambulante*, but, as long as he can walk, he will find pleasure in living. 'It is a pleasure which men will not take away from me because its origin is within myself'

---

[1] The image of the 'lantern' is a favourite one. Cf. *infra*, pp. 254, 277.

[2] *Supra*, p. 137.

(xix. 111). One of his objections to winter is that he has to replace these bracing activities by domestic pleasures such as playing the spinet, singing old, and especially Genevan, airs in his 'cracked voice', or else in following some simple hobby such as the collecting of old prints. With the arrival of spring he feels free and alive once more: only then can he savour to the full a day-to-day existence devoid of worry and made up of gentle emotions, simple physical activities, and the delights of reverie and contemplation.

For all its manifold attractions, reverie constitutes only one element in a much wider pattern, and it would be extremely misleading to see Jean-Jacques as a man completely absorbed in melancholy introspection. Not only does his reverie often have a markedly euphoric character, as M. Monglond rightly points out,[1] but his very concern for immediate gratifications brings him back again and again to the concrete, practical pleasures of daily life. The kind of life he would like to live were he completely free to choose would be, he tells a correspondent, M. de la Tourrette, in 1770, as follows:

> If it were given to me to choose an even, gentle life, I should want in every day of mine, to spend my mornings working, either at copying or on my herbarium; to dine with you and Mélanie; then to feed for an hour or two both my ear and my heart on the sound of her voice and harp; then to spend the whole day walking with you *tête à tête*, while botanizing and philosophizing according to our fancy (xix. 346).

Even when he refers to lonelier activities it is plain that his reverie was to be no systematic and soul-absorbing occupation. Already at Môtiers he had told Mme de Boufflers of the pleasures of his 'limited' day-to-day life 'without care for the morrow'. Frightened by 'any kind of care', he now realizes that

> remaining where I am, I spend delightful days, wandering without worry or plan or business, from wood to wood and rock to rock, ever dreaming, and thinking not at all. I would give anything to know botany; it is the real occupation for a perambulating body and a lazy mind ... (xi. 240–1).

At Wootton his pleasures were not very different.

> I like to dream, but freely, letting my thoughts wander and without being bound to any subject. . . . This idle, contemplative life which you don't approve and which I don't excuse, daily becomes more delightful to me; to wander alone, endlessly and incessantly, among the trees and rocks which surround my abode, to dream or behave as irresponsibly as I like, and, as

---

[1] A. Monglond, *Vies préromantiques* (Paris, 1925), p. 52.

you say, to gape at crows; when my brain becomes overheated, to calm it by analyzing some moss or fern; finally, to abandon myself without restraint to my fancies which, thank Heaven, are all within my grasp; that for me is the supreme enjoyment, to which I imagine nothing to be superior in this world for a man of my age and condition.[1]

Rousseau very sensibly realizes that to forget the painful interests of the past he must discover some new activity capable of taking his mind off unpleasant thoughts. In 1763–4 he begins to show enthusiasm for botany—a pastime 'very suitable to a perambulating body that is forbidden to think', and the 'real amusement of a lonely man who goes for walks and wants to think of nothing'.[2] He had always been prone to short-lived enthusiasms for people and things, but he now believes that he has at last found a hobby which will satisfy him for the rest of his life, and apart from brief periods of discouragement and loss of interest he never abandons it for long. 'I am very happy to have acquired a taste for botany: this taste changes imperceptibly into a child's passion, or rather into a useless and futile twaddle, for I learn to-day only by forgetting what I learned yesterday; but no matter: if I never have the pleasure of knowing, I shall always have that of learning, and that is all I need' (xv. 338). This is an activity eminently appropriate for a man who abandons himself to his natural 'laziness'. 'My child's passion distracts me, keeps me busy, consoles me' (xviii. 8). Not the least of its attractions is that it allows him to indulge in his all-consuming love of walking. At the same time it brings a precious 'serenity of soul' by keeping at bay all 'hateful passions', and especially the thought of other men's animosity. Apart from this subjective satisfaction, botany also brings him close to God's handiwork. 'The study of nature detaches us from ourselves and lifts us up to its Author' (xvi. 44). 'Each day I want to be moved by the wonders of Him who made men to be good, and whose work they have so unworthily degraded. The plants in our woods and mountains are such as they originally came forth from his hands, and it is there that I love to study nature, for I confess to you that I do not find the same charm botanizing in a garden' (ibid. 293). Freed from all utilitarian and pragmatic purposes, 'this fine, entrancing study' constitutes 'the true amusement of a lonely man' and Rousseau is prepared to say of himself that 'he owes his life to plants' (xix. 24). Botany allows him to exist in harmony with his own being and God's world around him.[3]

---

[1] *CG* xvi. 246–7 (to the Marquis de Mirabeau).   [2] *CG* xii. 54, 110.
[3] Cf. also *Conf.*, Book XII (641), for a long account of his attitude towards botany.

This practical, down-to-earth acceptance of the simple life presents a striking contrast to the tormented feelings of his paranoid moods, but it is too heavily charged with escapism to offer a permanent solution to the fundamental problem of his personal existence. In spite of its many delights, botany tends to be a diversion rather than an end in itself, a pleasant but ultimately inadequate means of banishing inner conflicts. For a time it enables him to take his mind off the idea of persecution by offering him an opportunity for the unreflective enjoyment of his sensibility and the pleasures of a simple life. But ultimately it leaves the dilemma of the 'persecuted' man unresolved, for it is not accompanied by a truly consistent form of self-awareness. It is thus significant that the phase of his life that has just been examined was characterized not merely by the onset of paranoid delusions and the search for simple pleasures, but also by the composition of the *Confessions*.

7

ROUSSEAU JUGE DE JEAN-JACQUES

In spite of his many misfortunes, Rousseau felt that he was still left with one resource of which his enemies had as yet been unable to deprive him: his ability to write his own justification and so to prove to posterity the falseness of the accusations levelled against him. The urge to write his own apologia became all the more pressing for being bound up with the other complex motives already evident in the *Lettres à Malesherbes*—the desire for self-analysis and self-expression. This tendency had already made a fitful appearance in the *Lettres morales* of 1757–8, whilst his earlier life had also been marked by a number of introspective phases. The half-humorous, half-serious self-portrait published in *Le Persifleur* dates back to 1749; the still earlier *Epîtres*, addressed to his friends Bordes and Parisot, were composed in 1742–3; the *Mémoire présenté à M. de Sainte-Marie pour l'éducation de son fils* (1740) also contains several interesting passages of self-analysis, whilst the personal implications of *Le Verger de Mme de Warens* of 1739 are equally obvious. It seems, however, that it was his publisher Rey who first suggested, in a letter of 31 December 1761, that Rousseau should write the story of his life and use it as a preface to an edition of his collected works. The day before the receipt of this letter Rousseau had already begun the first of the four letters to Malesherbes and was thus engrossed with the problem of his personal life. At first he returned a non-committal answer to Rey, but the thirty-eight fragments which make up *Mon portrait* and may date from 1762, show that he was preparing to write his *Confessions* two years before he actually began a chronological and systematic review of his life in 1764.[1]

From the outset he is convinced that he is composing a work remarkable for its outspokenness and sincerity. Already in his first letter to Malesherbes he had proclaimed his intention of depicting himself 'without pretence and modesty' and he now returns to the same theme. 'I have much to tell', he writes to Duclos, 'and I shall tell everything; I shall not omit one of my faults, not even one of my bad thoughts.

---

[1] Cf. *FA* 1120–9 and 1839–44. See also, for chronological details, Hermine de Saussure, *Rousseau et les manuscrits des Confessions* (Paris, 1958).

I shall depict myself as I am; the evil will almost always obscure the good; and, in spite of that, I can scarcely believe that any of my readers will dare to say to himself: "I am better than that man was" ' (*CG* xii. 222). Moreover, the writing of the *Confessions* is an undertaking worthy of a man who, like Jean-Jacques, is determined 'to be occupied with himself for the rest of his days' (xv. 242); only a man who had decided to 'concentrate himself absolutely within himself' could ever hope to complete such a project. Of one thing he is quite certain: he is composing a unique work. 'No man', he tells Mme de Verdelin, 'has hitherto done what I am proposing to do, and I doubt whether any other will do as much after me' (ibid.). He writes to the Earl Marischal in a similar vein. 'I shall do what no man has done before me, and probably what no one else will do afterwards. I shall tell everything, the good, the ill, everything. I feel that I have a soul which can show itself' (xv. 338). Or again, 'I shall be doing a unique and I dare to say a truly fine thing' (xiii. 264), because, as the final version puts it, he is engaged on 'a work unique through its unexampled veracity', and all the more remarkable for having been written by 'the best of men' (*Conf.* 516).

It is particularly in the first preface to the *Confessions* (later omitted in favour of the shorter and more dramatic statement of the definitive text) that Rousseau sets out most fully his initial conception of his task. He stresses that he is not concerned with the mere narration of his personal history and the simple chronicling of events, however interesting or unusual these may be, but with 'the secret history of his soul' or, as he puts it in a letter, 'the history of his most secret feelings'. It is this absolute honesty about his 'real life', that is, 'his state of soul', which in his eyes gives his work its inimitable value.

He considers that he is especially fitted for such a task by the peculiarly infallible memory with which he is endowed. His recollection of incidents which happened long ago may sometimes be faulty, but he is quite sure of one point:

I may make omissions in facts, transpositions and mistakes in dates; but I cannot be mistaken about what I have felt, nor about what my feelings made me do—and that is the main thing. The proper object of my confessions is to give exact knowledge of my inner being in all the situations of my life. It is the history of my soul that I have promised, and to write it faithfully I have no need of other memoirs; it is enough for me (as I have done hitherto) to withdraw into myself (*Conf.* 278).

Moreover, eschewing any preconceived idea of himself as 'a certain type of man', he will eliminate a rapid, synoptic view of himself in favour of the gradual, dynamic unfolding in time of a psychic life that is not cramped by any artificial unity. He will record his feelings without really judging them, and will often write in a way that astonishes himself. It is then for others to judge—if they dare. The example of one completely truthful man will be a challenge to others to be honest with themselves and to affirm—if they can—that they are better than 'that man' Jean-Jacques Rousseau.

He knows that this is not an easy task as—in his opinion—the failure of other men's efforts at self-portraiture shows only too clearly; the most honest person is prone to self-deception when he is writing about himself. The difficulty is this: that nobody can write a man's history but that man himself, because only he knows his 'inner mode of being' and his 'true life'; yet as soon as he begins to write about himself, he disguises his life instead of revealing it, and, on the pretext of producing an autobiography, makes his own apologia. 'He shows himself as he wants to be seen, not at all as he is. At best the sincerest people are truthful in what they say, but they lie by their reticences, and what they suppress makes such a difference to what they pretend to confess that in uttering only a part of the truth they say nothing at all' (*FA* 1149). The illustrious Montaigne is a striking example of this kind of dishonesty, for he admits only to pleasant faults. No doubt he gives us a likeness of the original, but it is, as it were, only in profile, not full-face. 'Who knows but whether some scar on his face or a disfigured eye on the side he has hidden from us would not have completely altered his features?'

Apart from this difficulty, which is common to all autobiographies, Rousseau insists that his own efforts at self-portrayal face the further complication of dealing with a unique subject. 'I am not made', he says in the final version, 'like any of the men that I have seen; I dare to believe that I am not made like any of those that exist. If I am not better, at least I am other' (*Conf.* 5). Already his striving for complete honesty and frankness distinguishes him from the rest of humanity which 'has hitherto known no other man who has dared to do what I am proposing to do'. In a deeper sense his character is so differently constituted from that of his fellows that it will be extremely difficult to give a satisfactory explanation of its many idiosyncrasies. He will seek to overcome this very considerable obstacle by stripping off all the acquired and artificial aspects of his character in order to expose the first spontaneous manifestations of its original nature and so present the portrait of 'a man as he was within' (516).

He is convinced that his *Confessions* will also fulfil a 'useful function' because, in spite of his uniqueness, he is a human being who carries within himself that 'inner model' which is the mark of every true man.[1] If he is a being apart, it is perhaps because he is closer to genuine humanity than other people. Now the majority of men have difficulty in knowing themselves because they lack adequate guidance concerning the standards that ought to govern their understanding of themselves and others; having no adequate *pièce de comparaison*, they fail to appreciate the real nature of their own motives and those of their fellows. What better illustration of this could be provided than the host of inaccurate attempts to describe Jean-Jacques himself? Have not others always been prone, as he already told Malesherbes, to judge his heart and mind by their own? Was not this the reason for their egregious misunderstanding of the real Rousseau? Instead of this 'imaginary, fantastic creature' men will henceforth be able to see the true Jean-Jacques and so have before their eyes the prototype of a *real* man. They will thus be provided with 'the first criterion for the study of men' (*Conf.* 3).

It is evident, however, that Rousseau also has a more personal motive for writing his confessions, and the first preface already shows his preoccupation with the fundamental idea which dominates all his personal writings from the *Lettres à M. de Malesherbes* to the *Rêveries*: the need to destroy the false portrait which other men are constantly substituting for the authentic original. Only through the most daring self-revelation will he be able to remove this false image from other people's minds. As he says in the final text of the *Confessions*, this task is all the more urgent because of his belief that 'his name must live': he 'must transmit with it the memory of the unfortunate man who bore it as he really was and not just as his enemies untiringly toil to depict him' (400). This means of course that his work is not entirely free from the apologetic bias he blames in his predecessors, for he hopes that this frank portrait will ultimately secure his justification. This emerges clearly in the final apostrophe to the reader, which echoes the sentiment expressed in his correspondence: 'But let every reader imitate me and withdraw into himself, as I have done, and let him say in the depths of his conscience if he dares: "I am better than that man was." '

He also seeks a more subtle satisfaction, for he hopes to intensify the enjoyment of the present moment by adding to it the memory of his past life. 'By surrendering myself both to the memory of the previous

[1] Gf. *supra*, p. 130.

impression and to the present feeling, I shall doubly portray the state of my soul, namely, at the moment of the event's occurrence and at the moment when I described it; my uneven and natural style, now rapid and diffused, now restrained and wild, now serious and gay, will itself form part of my story' (*FA* 1154). Writing thus becomes a personal act having value for his immediate existence through the mere fact of offering a form of self-expression.

While throwing very interesting light on the intention of the *Confessions*, this early preface omits any direct mention of certain important considerations which emerge more clearly from the narrative itself. It has been said that this first preface was suppressed because of Rousseau's growing desire to write his own apology: first of all concerned with describing himself in his 'humanity', he then yielded to more subjective feelings. However, I am not convinced that the earlier version of the *Confessions* gives an essentially different impression from that of the final text, for it is clear that both the intensely personal and the more general purpose were present from the very beginning and persisted to the end. Perhaps he came to feel the inadequacy of any objective explanation, believing that any long preliminary explanation of his precise purpose was liable to create confusion and that it was far better —once the brief initial challenge had been issued—to confront the reader with the confessions themselves: his actual method of presenting the 'secret history of his soul' as a reality unfolding itself from within was bound to go beyond any purely formal, abstract analysis of his aims. It would then be to the reader 'to assemble these elements and determine the being they constitute; the result must be his work' (*Conf.* 175).

Even so, the final narrative does furnish us with an important indication which is not to be found—at least explicitly expressed—in the long first preface. The latter already shows how secretly dependent Rousseau was—for all his defiant affirmations of independence—upon other people's approval: his overwhelming need to reveal himself as he believes he really is becomes inseparable from the feeling that he is the *object* of another's attention and esteem. Although he has long since outgrown the crude exhibitionism of his adolescence, a more complex and subtle form of the same basic urge to be known and seen still dominates a good deal of his personal writing. More especially—and this is what the first preface does not mention—the idea of being seen by others 'as he really is' is related to his efforts to seek an alleviation of the heavy burden of guilt which seemed to become more oppressive with the years. Revealed as he truly is, he becomes—or hopes to become—absolved from tormenting feelings of remorse and unworthiness. He admits that one of the reasons for writing his confessions was to relieve the anguish associated with the memory of his crime against the servant-girl Marion. 'I have never been able to take it upon myself to unburden my heart in a friend's bosom. . . . This weight has thus lain without relief upon my conscience, and I can say that the desire to deliver myself from it in some way has contributed a good deal to my resolve to write my confessions' (*Conf.* 86). He felt a similar guilt over his desertion of the epileptic music-master Le Maître. Yet clearly this hypersensitivity to youthful sins covers a still deeper feeling of guilt, compounded no doubt of far more serious misdeeds like the abandonment of his children and of obscure and irrational feelings of guilt and unworthiness.

In their attempts to allay such feelings, the *Confessions* make use of a theme that had already appeared at a critical moment in *La Nouvelle Héloïse*: a person can attain unity and a feeling of positive happiness and fulfilment by becoming as it were *transparent* to the other's gaze. In its ideal form this experience can have religious meaning, for to be open to the other is—in the most complete sense—to be open to God. Even at the human level transparency has a kind of purifying function. We have already seen how the fear of persecution is often associated with the notion of darkness and a primordial—almost primeval—horror of the unknown dangers that lie concealed in the hostility of another's gaze. To the darkness of guilt and hostility he opposes a soul that is, in a recurrent phrase, 'as transparent as crystal'. 'I should like', explains Rousseau, 'to be able in some way to make my soul transparent to the reader's eyes, and for that purpose I am seeking to show it to him from every viewpoint, to illuminate it from every perspective, to bring it about that no movement passes unnoticed by him, in order that he can judge for himself the principle producing it' (*Conf.* 175). Earlier on he had made a similar point when he wrote: 'In undertaking to show myself completely to the public, I must not allow any part of myself to remain obscure or hidden: I must hold myself incessantly before its eyes, so that it can follow me in all the aberrations of my heart and all the corners of my life; it must not lose sight of me for a single moment' (59). Ultimately, to be transparent means to be a complete self, to attain that perfect unity which allows the personality to exist without break or fissure—to be at one with itself in a pure and untroubled translucency. The *Confessions* thus reproduce in a much more subtle form something of that nostalgic yearning for primordial unity which we have seen to be at the basis of Rousseau's 'primitivist' character. The dream of complete personal unity involves the ideal of a perfect fusion of the image of himself as seen by others and his own awareness of his personality as he really believes it to be.

This striving for self-realization unfortunately encountered an insuperable psychological obstacle: the darkening of his mind during the composition of the last books of the *Confessions* made it increasingly difficult for him to consider other people as anything but enemies and persecutors, while, after his return to Paris in 1770, the banning of the reading of the *Confessions* to select audiences created such anxiety and despair that he was ultimately impelled to think once more of preparing yet another written justification of his conduct. The result was the dialogues entitled *Rousseau Juge de Jean-Jacques*, which he began in 1772 and upon which, according to his own account, he spent a quarter of an hour daily until 1776.

Once it was completed, he became obsessed with the problem of disposing of the manuscript; his main concern was that it should not fall into his enemies' hands; he even hoped that it might eventually reach the king himself.[1] On 24 February 1776 he decided to place the manuscript on the high altar of Notre-Dame, being convinced that in this way Providence would ensure its survival. Unfortunately, on that particular day, he found himself shut off from the high altar by an iron grill which he could not open. He immediately fled panic-stricken from the church and 'wandered all day long through the streets, not knowing where he went, until weariness and darkness compelled him to return home exhausted and stupefied with grief' (980). Further reflection convinced him that this set-back was perhaps not a misfortune after all, since it was unlikely that his manuscript would ever have reached the king. He then deposited copies with the abbé Bonnot de Condillac and a young Englishman, Brooke Boothby, whom he had formerly met at Wootton and who happened to visit him in Paris at this time. Suspecting soon afterwards the integrity of his confidants, he began to doubt the wisdom of this fresh step. In April he wrote a circular letter addressed 'to every Frenchmen who still loves justice and truth'.[2] Practically nobody accepted it. 'All, after reading the inscription, declared, with an artlessness that made me laugh in the midst of my

---

[1] Rousseau has given his own account of the affair in the *Histoire du précédent écrit* appended to the *Dialogues* (*OC* i. 977–89).
[2] Cf. for the text *OC* i. 990–2.

grief, that it was not meant for them. "You are right," I said as I took it back, "I indeed see that I have made a mistake". That is the first frank utterance I have heard from a Frenchman's mouth for fifteen years' (321). Yet the effect of this final incident was to allay his hysteria and panic and, 'by convincing him that his fate was irremediable, it taught him to struggle no more against necessity'.

The *Dialogues* seek to solve the problem of self-awareness by an approach that is different from the one used in the *Confessions*, where the meaning of his character and consciousness was illuminated indirectly through a faithful adherence to the chronological method: whereas he had there allowed his personality to unfold itself in the very act of development, he now has recourse to a method which ultimately seeks to present the reader with a full-faced, static portrait free from all obscurity and ambiguity. No doubt the psychological starting-point is similar to that of the previous personal writings for he is still obsessed by the need to destroy the false portrait which he believes to exist in the public's mind and which, in his opinion, bears no relation to the real Jean-Jacques. He now admits that the *Confessions* had a similar purpose.

When he saw himself disfigured amongst men to such a degree that he was considered a monster, his conscience, which made him feel that there was more good than evil in him, gave him the courage, which perhaps he alone had and will ever have, to show himself as he was; he believed that by fully manifesting his soul's interior and revealing his *Confessions*, such a frank, simple, natural explanation of all the oddity people have found in his behaviour, bearing its own testimony within itself, would make them feel the truth of his statements, and the falsity of the horrible and fantastic ideas which he saw being spread around him without being able to discover their origin (903).

The deliberate exaggeration of the portrait of the 'evil' Rousseau is clearly designed to throw into sharp relief the subsequent emergence of the 'good' Rousseau. From the very outset, therefore, the *Dialogues* are dominated by the black and white antithesis between the false and the true Rousseau, although it is naturally the 'good' Rousseau who is to emerge triumphant.

This idea probably explains the choice of the dialogue-form which, says the author, provides him with the easiest way of discussing 'the pros and cons of this difficult question'. This does not mean that the *Dialogues* have greater literary value than the *Confessions* (the opposite is true), for the former do not discuss an issue that is really in doubt;

they are a device created solely for purpose of presenting a case (Rousseau's innocence), the justice of which has been decided beforehand. His obsession with the idea of persecution prevents him from reproducing the lyrical, poetic charm, as well as the penetrating psychological insight of the *Confessions*; nor does he succeed in making his interlocutors vivid personalities existing in their own right, since they are mainly an excuse for the elaboration of a personal apology. The intensity of his inner conflict and his obsession with the idea of persecution make it impossible for him to stand at a proper 'aesthetic distance' from his work and exercise any kind of adequate self-criticism.[1] The many literary defects are largely due to Rousseau's inability to master the artistic demands of his particular medium; there are various digressions which distract and irritate the reader at certain particularly important stages of the argument. Yet, when all this is admitted, the *Dialogues* remain a most valuable document for the understanding of Rousseau's state of mind at this period of his life. What is particularly striking is the sudden transition from diffuseness to a few pages of sheer brilliance, and one of the most remarkable features of the work is that the terrible paranoid nightmare is frequently illuminated by flashes of extraordinary lucidity and insight.[2]

The general function of the *Dialogues* is easily grasped when we consider the main characters. The two interlocutors are 'Rousseau', an allegedly impartial observer who, though apparently eager to find out 'the truth' about the 'Jean-Jacques case', is really benevolently disposed towards him, and 'the Frenchman' who is at first extremely hostile to Jean-Jacques, not out of malice but because he is the innocent dupe of calumny. The chief development of the work is the gradual conversion of the Frenchman from animosity to sympathy as he learns more and more about Jean-Jacques's true character. However, the real protagonists are not these official spokesmen, but two beings who never appear in person—the implacable enemies, 'our gentlemen' with their constant companion the 'evil' Jean-Jacques, and the 'innocent' Jean-Jacques who has been so basely attacked in this way. The main interest of the *Dialogues* lies in the emergence of the real Jean-Jacques as the author wishes us to see him. In order to achieve this purpose Rousseau tries to stand outside himself, to see himself impartially as the person he really believes himself to be. But this method of approach, though aiming at objectivity, soon shows us that we are not dealing merely with

[1] He himself admits as much in his preface.
[2] On the *Dialogues* see Robert Osmont's penetrating introduction in *OC* i. 45–72.

'the judge of Jean-Jacques', but his ardent apologist—the passionate advocate of an unjustly condemned man.

This effort at self-portraiture thus involves a curious splitting of the author's personality, not only between the visible 'Rousseau' and his interlocutor 'the Frenchman', but also and more fundamentally between the good 'Jean-Jacques' and the evil figure presented by the 'gentlemen'. Moreover, these various personal projections still have to be related to the living author himself as well as to the wider and more difficult question of whether any man through reflection and writing can become identified with the object of his own consciousness. But apart from this general issue, Rousseau's use of the dialogue-form creates serious psychological limitations, since it is obvious from the very first that the 'wicked' and the 'good' Jean-Jacques partly condition each other. Other people treat Rousseau as 'wicked' because (for reasons to be examined) they really know him to be 'good'. But this good Rousseau is also evoked as a riposte to the evil figure. In fact both the 'wicked' and the 'good' Jean-Jacques must ultimately be related to the complete Rousseau, though not necessarily as simple elements in a composite picture.

The *Dialogues*, then, along with the *Rêveries*, represent Rousseau's last effort to fix the main outlines of a personality which he still felt to be Protean and contradictory. He is driven on by an intense anxiety which seeks desperately to eliminate all contradictions; but the pressure of psychopathological delusions often gives way to a positive effort at self-awareness, for by describing his essential character in its basic unity, he hopes to see himself in a pure transparency as a living, stable individual with whom he can henceforth be identified. Whereas the *Confessions*, through leaving the various personal contradictions unresolved, abandoned the final judgement to the reader himself, the *Dialogues* aim at producing a definite and completely satisfactory answer to the problem of his life's meaning.

The simple antithesis between the 'good' and 'evil' Rousseau is apt to create the misleading impression that the 'good' Rousseau is simply a compensatory fantasy created in response to paranoid delusions. In this respect we recall our earlier point that Rousseau's choice of himself, even in these extremely unfavourable psychological conditions, cannot be interpreted as a merely mechanical response to abnormal impulses. He may be unaware of the 'real' meaning of his delusions, but he continues to accept them as convictions to which he must respond; they constitute a challenge to further self-exploration and as such they show that his personality is not merely psychically determined by its past but also orientated towards the future. The *Dialogues* are not just a piece of idle speculation but a personal act, an act of self-justification no doubt, but also one of self-expression and self-realization. In seeking to be aware of himself as a certain kind of person, Rousseau is induced to *become* himself and choose himself in a new way.

As we are here concerned mainly with the problem of this evolving self-awareness, it will not be necessary to give a strictly chronological analysis of the *Dialogues*. It is enough to say that the three main aspects are roughly indicated by the subject of each dialogue.[1] In the first we have an elaborate account of the 'wicked' Jean-Jacques who is the object of such universal persecution. The second refutes this black account by presenting the real Jean-Jacques, the innocent and good man as he appears to an impartial observer content to rely on his own common sense and unbiased judgement. The third and last dialogue deals with Jean-Jacques the writer and the true meaning of his works; it finally appears that Jean-Jacques is the man of his writings, so that the author and the living person can be none other than the same being. Unfortunately the main ideas are often obscured by rambling digressions which make the author lose sight of his principal topic. Thus the obsession with persecution and the 'plot' against him plays a large part not only in the first, but also in the other two dialogues, each of which contains long discussions of the theme. The reader is sometimes irritated by these verbose repetitions and digressions which are liable to occur at a moment when Rousseau is saying something really interesting either about himself or his works. On the other hand, it would be wrong to ignore the many examples of skilful and subtle argument contained in the *Dialogues*, for these are constantly breaking through the more tiresome pathological pages. It is characteristic of Rousseau that moments of acute insight and wisdom should occur in the midst of long paranoid reiterations. The reader's chief regret is that so much dialectical skill is devoted to the refutation of a viewpoint that is without any firm contact with the facts of his everyday life.

One of the most curious and significant aspects of this work is that its many discussions of the universal 'plot' were taking place at the very time when the general public was beginning to lose interest in the person

---

[1] Rousseau's own sub-titles are: I. *Du système de conduite envers Jean-Jacques, adopté par l'administration avec l'approbation du public;* II. *Du naturel de Jean-Jacques et de ses habitudes;* III. *De l'esprit de ses livres et conclusions.* All quotations are taken from *OC* i. 657–992.

of the author.[1] In spite of his desire for 'obscurity' and 'rest', Rousseau felt a continual need to reveal himself to others and to be the object of their attention in a way that allowed him to achieve an adequate consciousness of himself as a man redeemed and justified by their acknowledgement of his real 'goodness'. As we have stressed throughout, he feared the other only because he needed him, and after the failure of the *Confessions* to fulfil their object, he was more anxious than ever before to convince the public—and posterity—of the baselessness of the false portrait which he believed to be firmly accepted by the popular mind. He sought to destroy this illusion in two ways: first, by showing that the portrait painted by *nos messieurs* contained features which were so contradictory and inconsistent with one another that they could not belong to a single person, so that the image of the 'wicked' Jean-Jacques was annihilated by its own internal contradictions and absurdities; secondly, by confronting this fantastic and unreal portrait with a description of the actual Jean-Jacques he hoped to show not only how this portrait was altogether more credible in its own right, but how it also corresponded to the impression created by a reading of the works actually written by Jean-Jacques.

The general nature of Rousseau's argument (as opposed to the psychological analysis) is well illustrated by the first *Dialogue*. The Frenchman sums up the viewpoint of Jean-Jacques's enemies when he describes him as a 'monster', a 'bear', a 'serpent', and 'reptile', a 'hypocrite' who is 'the horror of the human race', 'the laughing-stock', and 'plaything of the mob', a veritable 'scourge of humanity'; the epithets bestowed upon the unfortunate Jean-Jacques range from vilification to ridicule. But, protests the interlocutor 'Rousseau', the works written by this man are full of the loftiest idealism and the most passionate love of virtue and cannot have been produced by *une âme de boue*; the only possible explanation is that they must have been written by someone else, for the noble writer and the public monster cannot be the same person. But (it appears later) the works attributed to Jean-Jacques are really by him; the man and the author are the same person. This leads to the first genuine doubt: since the literary works certainly exist, does it not follow that perhaps after all the 'monster' described by 'our gentlemen' is not as real as they would have us believe?

---

[1] Cf. A. Monglond, *Vies préromantiques*, pp. 19 ff. The Parisians had shown a keen interest in Rousseau when he returned to them in 1770 and the subsequent reading of the *Confessions* maintained public curiosity for a few months. Towards 1775 he was being largely ignored by the general public.

Rousseau is not content merely to stress the contradictions just indicated; he develops a further point which helps to prepare the way for a more positive approach to the problem of the real 'Jean-Jacques'. Although the figure of the monster is generally accepted by the public, everyone (including 'our gentlemen') agrees that during the first forty years this man who is now so hated and feared was loved and esteemed by all who knew him. His life is 'cut into two parts which seem to belong to two different people' (112). During 'the first forty years' he led a contented, if obscure, existence, spending his time in a quiet retirement which was occupied only by study and his affectionate devotion to a few intimate friends who respected and loved him for what he was—a sensitive and shy man who shunned society in favour of a life of peaceful seclusion. If they had been put into practice the ideas that filled his mind at this time would have brought about 'the happiness of humanity'. The public sees in this same man, whom it never knew in the days of his obscurity, a fierce misanthropist with a heart and head full of black and wicked thoughts. Surrounded during 'the first forty years' by nothing but love and consideration, Jean-Jacques is now hated and despised; his earlier life, in so far as it is known, is treated as a mere mask which enabled a very cunning hypocrite to hide his base character; if he won 'public esteem' and 'the benevolence of all who knew him', it was solely because of this clever hypocritical concealment. Such is the conclusion which his enemies wish to impose on the public.

Rousseau considers that it is not difficult to indicate the precise moment of this separation of his life into two distinct parts: his misfortunes began with his decision to be an author and the subsequent achievement of fame and glory. Not that he was ever a 'professional' writer who gained his living by administering to public demand; he was a man who, belonging to no party, wrote simply to express certain very intense, personal convictions concerning the nature of contemporary life; his sole authorities were justice and truth, his sole aim the betterment of humanity. But this was precisely the cause of his unhappiness: the idealism of his attitude was so directly opposed to the outlook of an age dominated by purely mercenary motives that it encountered nothing but suspicion, hostility, or incomprehension: his contemporaries refused to accept the sincerity and independence of a writer whose values were so fundamentally incompatible with their own.

What makes his present position particularly distressing is Rousseau's belief that he is not always confronted by open hostility but by a hatred which really sets itself up as 'benevolence'. The 'Frenchman' suggests that *nos messieurs* deliberately exaggerate the picture of the evil Jean-Jacques in order to save the public from still further corruption. The more repellent the portrait, the greater the likelihood of 'honest' people shrinking from all contact with the living original. The principal aim is 'to get him loathed in order to prevent him from doing harm'. The apparent iniquity of inventing crimes to blacken the criminal still further is explained by his enemies' desire to protect humanity from such a dangerous 'beast'! Moreover, this 'benevolence' not only reveals the persecutors' wonderful 'generosity' and 'commiseration', but also illuminates the most extraordinary feature of their victim's unhappy position. The 'gentlemen' wish to spare his feelings by refusing to let him know the extent of his own baseness: they have deprived him of 'all that makes life bearable'—honour, justice, companionship, esteem—but while holding him up as an object of hatred and ridicule, they have managed to keep him in ignorance of what is really happening. He is often surrounded by a false show of friendliness and esteem, but all the time his friends are falling away from him and he is conscious of increasing isolation, of being 'without support' as a man absolutely 'alone in the world'. It is largely through this terrible sense of being surrounded on all sides by 'mystery' and 'darkness' that Jean-Jacques is eventually led to recognize the frightening nature of his position. He is quite unable to locate the source of the attacks against him; as he seeks desperately to break through the barrier of silence and mystery, he realizes with horror that he is shut in by 'a triple wall of darkness'. He is, in another favourite expression, 'buried alive among the living'.[1] Persons who might have helped him are either suborned or prejudiced against him; he no longer has any friends and is hemmed in by 'venomous spies' and cunning villains who are ready to exploit the slightest sign of weakness. More terrifying than anything else is the feeling of being constantly watched by unseen, sinister eyes. Nor are the attacks limited to his person. A characteristic device of his enemies, and especially of the 'good David Hume', was to have his portrait painted in such a way as to make him look like a hideous Cyclop. The mere fact that it was the illustrious Ramsay who was commissioned with this task made the effect seem all the more devastating! More important still, not only is all Jean-Jacques's correspondence meticulously examined by his enemies who also make every effort to lure him

---

[1] On the subject of Rousseau's paranoid imagery see *supra*, p. 207, and the letter to Saint-Germain where he uses similar expressions.

into uttering some rash and compromising statement, but his writings are seized and falsified. Every outlet has been blocked, and to achieve their aim, his enemies have had recourse to a double expedient: on the one hand, pernicious writings which are actually the work of others are treacherously attributed to him, whilst, on the other hand, his own works are garbled and produced in such a manner as to obscure or distort their real meaning. In this way it is hoped that not only the present generation but posterity itself will hold Jean-Jacques in horror. Once he has passed from the living tomb which is his present life, the real man will thus be lost for ever.

Rousseau's obsession with the theme of persecution—already so obvious in the previous years—now attains truly nightmarish proportions. The force and intensity of the delusions are such as to bind the earlier paranoid tendencies into a single, all-embracing theme. It is not merely the public but the whole world of official authority which is engaged on this terrible task of systematic and unrelenting vilification. Jean-Jacques is not even left with the final resource of many paranoiacs, an appeal to the police, for the police themselves are also in the plot. The following passage gives a characteristic indication of Rousseau's mental condition at this time:

He believes that all the disasters of his life, from the moment of his fatal renown, are the result of a plot which was formed a long time ago, in great secrecy, by few people, who found the means of bringing in one after the other all those whom they needed in order to carry it out: the great, the authors, the doctors (that wasn't difficult!), all influential men and 'light' women, all recognized authorities, all those who are in charge of the government, all those who direct public opinion. He claims that all the apparently accidental and fortuitous events relating to him are merely successive developments which have been planned beforehand and arranged in such a way that everything which is to happen subsequently already has its place in the picture, and must have its effect only at the appointed time. All that fits in well enough with what you yourself have told me and with what I believe I have seen under various guises. According to you, it is a means of showing kindness towards a scoundrel; according to me, it is a league whose precise object I cannot determine, but whose existence cannot be denied since you yourself have taken part in it. He thinks that, from the moment when this work of defamation was undertaken, they decided—in order to facilitate the success of the enterprise—to graduate it, to begin by making him hateful and wicked, and to end by making him ridiculous and contemptible (781).

Yet Rousseau still cannot believe that all men are so wicked that they would wittingly participate in such a monstrous act of injustice. In the last dialogue there is a long development which tries to 'explain' the universality of the plot by showing it to be a kind of 'epidemic' or 'contagion' which has infected the most innocent members of the public. Is not the Frenchman himself, who is, after all, an honest fellow, a striking example of the way in which quite worthy people can be contaminated by skilful and unscrupulous propaganda on the part of a few determined but clever men? Rousseau explains the origin of the plot as the work of a relatively small faction (the 'philosophers') who, through malevolence, guile and a variety of ruthless methods, have taken advantage of public ignorance of the true facts about Jean-Jacques in order to achieve their own sinister purposes; they create a climate of opinion which is so hostile to innocence that even those few persons who are still well-disposed towards Jean-Jacques no longer dare to raise a voice of protest. The result of all these machinations is that Paris itself has been transformed into a 'solitude that is more frightful than the caves and woods, for he finds in the midst of men neither communication, consolation, counsel, understanding, nor anything that might help him to find his way in a vast labyrinth where they let him see in the darkness only false paths which lead him still further astray' (713).

More interesting than Rousseau's explanation of the plot's universality is his account of the motives inspiring such uncharitable behaviour. He admits his bewilderment and terror before the existence of this widespread, malevolent persecution of an innocent man and, on one occasion at least, acknowledges the impossibility of finding a normal and reasonable explanation; it is all so dark and mysterious that he can never hope to trace it to its original source. Although the ultimate explanation may be lacking, the intensity and persistence of the attacks can be partially accounted for in terms of a principle already invoked in the *Lettres à Malesherbes*—the tendency of other men to judge Jean-Jacques's feelings by their own.[1] Under the pressure of the violent emotions now agitating his mind he gives this principle a wider and more systematic explanation than previously. Ironically enough, Rousseau applies to his enemies a principle that modern psychiatrists would now use in his own case—the idea that the Jean-Jacques persecuted by them is not the real man but the projection of their own minds. He seems to see in the ferocity of his enemies' attacks a desperate attempt to quieten their own guilty consciences: they are unable to admit their error and injustice in persecuting a man they really know to be innocent. Our hatred, he insists with some force, is always greatest

[1] See *supra*, p. 173.

against those whom we have wronged and whose forgiveness we dare not or will not ask; by increasing our animosity we still the voice of doubt and make our own injustice seem righteous.

Rousseau thinks that a good deal of the persecution is ultimately due to the *philosophes'* resentment against a writer whose lofty ideals expose the insufficiency and egoism of their own standpoint. In the third dialogue he delivers a fierce attack upon the *philosophes*, reproaching them for 'secret' and 'depressing' doctrines based on materialistic and immoral principles which are calculated to undermine the foundations of society and 'destroy all religion and free will' as well as the whole fabric of moral life;[1] believing in neither good nor evil, but only necessity, they prevent people from 'returning to repentance'. The aim of this atheistic viewpoint is to obtain power and to replace the tyranny of the Jesuits by another that is more uncompromising still. This also serves to explain the mutual hatred of the two factions. 'These two organisations, both domineering and intolerant, were therefore incompatible, since the basic intention of each was to rule despotically. Each wanted to reign alone; they could not share power and reign together; they mutually excluded each other' (967–8). What wonder then that a man like Jean-Jacques who taught the most sublime moral truths, upheld belief in God and hope in immortality, insisted upon the value of 'those innate feelings which nature has engraved in every heart to console man in his misfortunes and encourage him to seek virtue', and refused to attach himself to any party, what wonder that such a man should be the object of inhuman persecution! He taught that justice had a basis other than materialistic self-interest and that 'the moral order of which we can have no idea here below has its source in a different system, which we seek in vain on this earth but to which one day everything will be restored' (972). The more Jean-Jacques wrote, the more sharply did he throw into belief the worthlessness and corruption of those philosophers and writers who merely sought their own profit. In this way Rousseau explains—to his own satisfaction at least—the sharp cleavage created by the 'first forty years': the sight of a good and innocent man bent solely on the propagation of useful truths was so exceptional and so disturbing to their equanimity that other writers were left with no other resource than the defamation of this man whose example they so much feared. Hatred of Jean-Jacques is thus interpreted as an indication of his enemies' own inadequacy.

He realizes that it is not enough for him to expose the unworthines

[1] Already in *Émile* Rousseau had referred to the contemporary *doctrines désolantes*.

of others' conduct; to the false picture painted by his enemies must be opposed the portrait of the real man as he appears to the unprejudiced mind of an observer prepared to follow 'good sense' and 'sound judge-ment' rather than base passions, 'the heart's desires' and the hostile reports of others. Rousseau had carefully prepared the ground for this positive approach to Jean-Jacques's character, since very good reasons had already been advanced for casting doubt on the validity of the 'wicked' portrait. It is mainly in the second dialogue that we witness Rousseau's attempt to draw the picture of the true 'Jean-Jacques'. The personality whose intimate history had been so carefully traced in the *Confessions* now appears before us as a more or less complete self whose very existence is a living refutation of the calumnies spread by its persecutors. But this definitive portrait cannot emerge until Rousseau has found an adequate unifying principle capable of giving his character a permanent coherence. As he now reviews his life in the light of the terrible attacks that are being made upon it, he thinks he has at last discovered the secret of his existence, the guiding thread which links up the happiness and the wretchedness, the virtues and the defects of his behaviour. It is also at this point that the kind of 'choice' of himself made by Rousseau stands in marked contrast to the attitude charac-teristic of religious—and especially Christian—'conversion'. Certainly the initial decision to 'withdraw' and 'retire' into himself, so frequently insisted on by Rousseau in all his personal writings, could well be accepted by most religious people, but whereas orthodox Christian conversion usually leads the individual to view his past life with remorse (since it is a period of sin for which he must 'repent'), Rousseau con-siders that salvation must come from a re-appropriation of his pristine character. If his true character was revealed in 'the first forty years' of innocent happiness, it seems natural for him to seek refuge in an attitude which does not allow him to be 'remade' or 'reborn' through some qualitative change of inner being, but 'restores him to himself' in his original purity. The Jean-Jacques who now confronts his enemies is not *essentially* different from the man who for forty years knew no greater happiness than to be himself, and who by now going back to this early period can once more find contentment in the recovery of his pristine in-nocence. The fundamental truth upon which Rousseau now insists with great force is that, first and foremost, he is the man of his *temperament.* Some people, as he admits, have the power to rise above their tempera-ments, to create, as it were, a new character. Not so Jean-Jacques, who cannot do violence to the spontaneous inclinations of his innate sensibility: he is and always has been 'the man of nature'. 'Of all the men I have known, Jean-Jacques is the one whose character derives most completely from his temperament alone. He is what nature made him; education has modified him only very little. If, from the very moment of his birth, his faculties and his powers had been completely developed, from that time people would have found him to be more or less as he was in his maturity, and now, after sixty years of suffering and wretchedness, time, adversity and man have changed him very little. Whilst his body has grown old and broken, his heart remains young; he retains the same tastes, the same passions as in his early years, and until his life's end he will not cease to be an old child' (799–800). Ultimately this means that his character must be understood in terms of his natural sensibility. How mistaken are those people who see him as a cunning, calculating seeker of personal advantage! Never could he be so clever or so base, for he is 'a simple, sensitive and good man' who is content to be himself.

This explanation of his character in terms of innate temperament and sensibility has the great merit (in Rousseau's eyes) of enabling him to establish a radical distinction between 'appearance' and 'reality'. The great error of most men is that they seek happiness in mere 'appearance', and 'do not care about reality' (936) whilst he seeks his in *le sentiment intime*. 'Counting for nothing the appearance of things and for very little the opinion of men, he seeks his happiness within' (864). But Rousseau's belief that he is resolving the conflict between appearance and reality by a simple, unadorned portrait of himself as he is in his unsophisticated immediacy overlooks the vital point that he is thereby making an active *choice* of himself as a certain kind of person—as an 'innocent' and 'good' man into whose heart there never entered a deliberately evil thought or the wilful urge to hurt another. As M. Starobinski well points out, the whole effort to demonstrate his reality as an unreflective being depends on a persistent effort of reflection.[1] These countless pages of feverish, anxious refutation of calumny show how incapable Jean-Jacques really is of *being* himself: his unremitting efforts to prove that he is 'a simple, good and innocent man' merely show that this is the being he *wishes* and *wills* to be.

It is also evident that this choice of himself as good and innocent is partly dependent on the idea of himself as a persecuted man. In a certain sense, he accepts persecution as the objective guarantee of his innate goodness. By associating all thoughts of evil and guilt with others' attitude towards him, he prepares the way for the view of

[1] Op. cit., p. 263.

himself as good and innocent. He is good because others are wicked. In this respect we may say that he chooses—though not necessarily in a fully conscious and explicit manner—to be persecuted. In a word, the 'wicked persecutors' and the 'innocent Jean-Jacques' are two inseparable panels of the same diptych.

Even so, Rousseau is still perspicacious and honest enough to realize that nobody's guilt can be completely projected on to others, however evil they may be. It is, therefore, necessary for him to 'explain' it—at least partially—in terms of his own character: he has to account for the disquieting fact that, in spite of his 'goodness', he has sometimes been led to commit actions of which he is now ashamed. These lapses, he insists, can be explained quite simply by means of his temperament. His actions have always stemmed from his sensibility and not from his reason—from his 'heart' and not from his 'will'. Once the original feeling has spent itself, he loses all capacity for action; even though the desire may still be strong, his conduct is 'null'. His natural *paresse*, upon which he had insisted from his early years,[1] makes him incapable of carrying through any really sustained action and especially of overcoming obstacles. Being good, he cannot of course deliberately will evil, but he has to recognize that 'goodness' is not the same as 'virtue', and alas! though he has always been good, he has not always been 'virtuous' —if by 'virtue' is meant a strong, rational will that is able, if necessary, to resist and overcome the needs of the heart. He will always admire— perhaps passionately admire—'virtue', whilst admitting his inability to practise it himself. Deterred by obstacles he has (as he admits) often failed to do what he ought to have done: he has 'abstained' when he should have acted. The fact remains, however, that he has never committed a deliberate crime, but has merely been guilty of 'sins of omission' (825). This is the secret of his nature—a secret so woefully obscure to those who have sought to compare his character with their own. Like his fictional hero Saint-Preux, he is a 'weak', 'frail', but never a 'wicked' man. He sums up:

This man will not be virtuous, since he will not overcome his inclinations; but by following them, he would never do anything contrary to what the man who listens only to virtue would do by overcoming them. Goodness, commiseration, generosity, these first impulses of nature, which are merely emanations of self-love, will not be raised in his mind to austere duties, but they will be his heart's needs which he will satisfy more for his own happiness than through a principle of humanity which he will never think of reducing

[1] Cf. *supra*, p. 50.

to rules. The instinct of nature is less pure perhaps, but certainly surer than the law of virtue: for often one may be put into contradiction with one's duty, but never with one's inclination, in order to do ill (864).

Jean-Jacques then is a man 'who is without malice rather than good, a sound but weak soul, who admires virtue without practising it, who ardently loves the good and rarely does it' (774), but he is also a man 'whose heart never knew a criminal or hateful thought'. Nobody was ever more enthusiastic than he for 'the great, the beautiful and the generous'. But the predominance of his heart over his mind, and his feeling over his will means that, in spite of 'occasional lofty and great feelings', he remains 'nothing' through his behaviour (811).

The all-powerful influence of his temperament, which involves not merely an incapacity for action but also a veritable *paresse de penser* (for if he has sometimes 'thought deeply', it has always been with a certain reluctance), explains his tendency to allow himself to be subjugated by personalities stronger and more determined than his own; in a more general way it also accounts for his temporary corruption by 'society'. Being a man of sensibility, he had not the strength of will to resist the insidious influence of contemporary social values and, against his deepest convictions, he allowed himself to be unfaithful to the spontaneous promptings of his natural goodness. Instead of being himself and of identifying himself with his own nature he was tempted to 'compare' himself with others—to use a false reflection which made him dissatisfied and ambitious and took him farther and farther away from his original nature.

To this explanation of his conduct he adds another factor of a more specifically psychological kind. If he has acted in a way that was inconsistent with his deepest conviction, it was because of the influence of his natural 'shyness' and timidity which, in social situations, always seemed to inhibit him, even though his sensibility, if left to its own impulse, might have led to praiseworthy conduct. Too often he has been the victim of a terrible *mauvaise honte*. Many of his alleged misdeeds, wrongly imputed by others to sinful pride, were simply 'the singularities of an ardent temperament held in check by *un naturel timide*'. This shyness, which, as we have seen, bedevilled his life from the earliest years,[1] allows him to be petrified by the awareness of others' critical scrutiny. In spite of himself his will is paralysed by the 'insulting', 'impudent', 'cruel', 'mocking', and 'malevolent' looks of others, so that his noblest impulses may be stifled at their very source. This experience

[1] Cf. *supra*, p. 44.

becomes all the more painful because these baleful looks make him feel what is for him the most terrible of all things—that he is an object of 'contempt'.

Now the effect of all this is to reinforce the conviction already implanted by the thought of persecution—that he is now absolutely alone. Always conscious of himself as a 'being apart', he now treats this separation as quite irrevocable, and throughout the *Dialogues* he is constantly referring to himself as a 'friendless stranger' who is 'without relations, without help' and who, being thrust still further into loneliness by his shyness and *humeur sauvage*, henceforth has 'only himself as his sole resource'. All consolation must be drawn from himself and not from outside: he will 'withdraw' and 'retire' into himself to find perhaps a happiness worthy of 'a simple, sensitive and good man' like Jean-Jacques.

An important consequence of this acceptance of himself as a 'man of temperament' is his determination to identify true personal 'being' and 'reality' with the principle of *enjoyment*. All the factors so far examined incline him to this choice. The pressure of his delusions and his inner anxiety make it necessary for him to avoid, as he is constantly reminding us, all 'painful' and 'unpleasant' thoughts: rejecting 'all painful feeling', he naturally turns away from the attitude most likely to create discomfort, and especially anxious concern with an uncertain future, as well as the activities of other people. By concentrating on enjoyment he is able to remove the burden of reflection, to escape the anxiety of 'possession'. Through 'being' rather than 'possessing' he can identify himself with the experience of the present moment, of that 'present which alone is in our power' (822). Now he can 'enjoy himself in his own existence'. He speaks pityingly of those for whom 'the torment of possession would poison the pleasure of enjoyment'. The great advantage of this attitude is that it provides an experience which is *spontaneous*, *immediate*, and *absolute*. Heart, feeling, sensibility, all converge on an intensely personal experience which exalts 'being' and 'enjoying' at the expense of 'having' and 'doing'. It also has the great advantage of seeming to provide Rousseau with a life which, by being under his own control, at last places him beyond his enemies' reach. Indirectly his enemies have helped him to obtain this satisfaction since they have forced him to remain in a situation where, undisturbed by the thought of having to adapt himself to the demands of social life, he is lucky enough to find the 'yoke of necessity' harmonizing with the promptings of natural inclination.

Since 'enjoyment' cannot by its very nature remain general and abstract, but has to express itself through a specific personal attitude, Rousseau soon realizes that it is inseparable from his earlier liking for *contemplation* and *reverie*. Later on in the *Rêveries* he will invest this experience with a deep metaphysical significance, but its importance as an intense personal experience is already apparent in the *Dialogues*. Always opposed to energetic activity—except when it was inspired by some powerful but short-lived impulse—he feels that he can now devote himself to the cultivation of his natural feelings, and especially to 'those great and ravishing contemplations which form life's best enjoyment' (729). These moods of reverie and contemplation, needless to say, are not part of some spiritual discipline, but a means of enabling him to enjoy the possibilities of an immediate existence freed from the influence of *prévoyance* and 'unpleasant' thoughts. In spite of the priority accorded to enjoyment as an actual experience, Rousseau devotes a certain amount of reflection to elucidating the characteristics of reverie. Already in the *Confessions* his account of his short but idyllic stay on the Île de Saint-Pierre had revealed what deep satisfactions could be obtained from the mood. Now, as the feeling of isolation and proscription becomes more intense, he turns yet once again to ponder the implications of this early experience. Moreover, his withdrawal into the country in 1756 had given him still earlier opportunities of abandoning action for a life of contemplation and the *Lettres à Malesherbes* offer us a glimpse of the lonely walker who allows himself to be carried away by the ecstasy of his meditations. At first, however, the mood tended to be without any particular form or structure, so that Rousseau was more content to savour the living experience than to analyse its precise meaning. It is only now that he begins to appreciate the full significance of these early raptures.

As we may expect, the initial justification for the cultivation of reverie lies in the simple fact that, in the words of the second dialogue, 'the contemplative life turns a man against action' (822): his most earnest endeavours to achieve happiness having convinced him that he will never find in the real world those objects worthy of one who is 'intoxicated by his contemplation of the charms of nature' and whose 'imagination is full of virtues, beauties and perfections of all kinds', he is inevitably led to depend more and more on the creations of his own mind, especially when he feels such an overwhelming need to shun all painful ideas. At last Jean-Jacques is provided with a heightened sense of his own existence and given an opportunity of indulging in those

R

expansive feelings to which he has always been sensitive, and to these
is now added the thought that they are being experienced by a man who
is aware of himself as one who has the right to enjoy them. The very
lack of external restraint also permits him to build up his own inner
world and to live with the 'fictions of his own heart'. That is why his
soul feels free to abandon itself to the dream of perfection by which it
is constantly haunted.

Yet Rousseau himself is aware that contemplation, if it is not supported by something other than its own subjective impulse, is liable to
evaporate into a vague dreaming or, in his own language, to become
'dry and abstract'. To prevent this he must have some recourse to the
external world, but to an external world that is properly attuned to his
own inner needs. It is particularly in a sense-experience freed from all
thought of the world of men that Rousseau finds pleasurable support
for his reveries. 'The concourse of the objects of sense makes his
meditations less dry' and so brings illusion closer to reality. In an
interesting passage Rousseau tries to explain in greater detail the relationship existing between himself and the external world through
reverie.

However pleasant it may be, reverie exhausts and tires in the long run: it
needs relaxation. We find this by letting our head rest and by completely
abandoning our senses to the impression of external objects. The most trivial
sight has its own charm because of the repose it obtains for us; and provided
that the sense-impression is not completely absent, the slight movement
which it evokes is enough to keep us from a sluggish torpor and to sustain
within us the pleasure of existing without exercising our faculties. The contemplative Jean-Jacques, at any other time so inattentive to the objects
around him, often needs this kind of rest, and then savours it with a childlike sensuousness of which our sages have scarcely any inkling. He notices
nothing except some movement by his ear or before his eye; but that is
enough for him. It is not only a fair, a review, an exercise or a procession
that amuse him, for a crane, a capstan, a ram, the working of some machine,
a passing boat, a turning mill, a ploughman, men playing bowls or battledore,
the flowing river, the flying bird, all hold his gaze. A display of trinkets, old
books open on the Parisian embankments and of which he reads only the
titles, pictures on the walls, at which he gives a dull-eyed glance, all such
things hold his attention and amuse him when his exhausted imagination needs
repose (816–17).

The mood of reverie attains a truly ecstatic intensity when it combines with the imagination, for it then becomes a veritable 'passion'.
Frustrated by immediate circumstances, Jean-Jacques projects his

dreams into 'ethereal regions' and into 'an order of things very different from that in which he sought' the fulfilment of his 'cherished illusions'. Once again he acknowledges how his early upbringing had misled him concerning the nature of the real world, but, while admitting his error, he cannot give up his enthusiasm for his first ideals:

This man, intoxicated by his contemplation of nature's charms, with his imagination full of various models of virtue, beauty and perfection of all kinds, would for a long time look for all that in the world. Through the intensity of his desire he would often believe that he had found what he was seeking; the slightest appearances would seem to him to be real qualities; the slightest protestations would take the place of proofs; in all his attachments he would always believe that he could discover the feeling he experienced within himself; constantly disappointed in his expectations, and still cherishing his error, he spent his youth in the belief that he had given substance to his fictions; scarcely could maturity and experience finally reveal them for what they are, and in spite of the errors, faults and expiations of a long life, perhaps only the concourse of the most cruel misfortunes has been able to destroy his cherished illusions, and make him feel that what he is looking for does not exist on this earth, or exists only in an order of things quite different from that in which he has been looking (821–2).

Hitherto life itself had been enough to bring him back from this idealistic world to more matter-of-fact considerations, but the firmly rooted conviction that he is the victim of a universal plot now fixes him irrevocably in the mood of imaginative fantasy. He there finds not only an escape from the tormenting feelings aroused by the thought of his persecutors, but a more positive satisfaction derived from the companionship of fictitious beings 'after his own heart'. The life of fantasy is simply a compensation for the love that has been denied him in this life. Yet what a wonderful compensation it is! How exalted the passion it inspires! 'These visions perhaps have more reality than all the apparent goods by which men set so much store' (814). He lives with 'chimeras', with 'happy fictions' which bring delight and ecstasy unknown to those living in the humdrum world of everyday life. In the middle of the second dialogue Rousseau, writing with impassioned eloquence on the pleasures of the imagination, is carried away by a remarkable lyrical fervour.

Although he is deprived by cruel hands of this life's goods, he is compensated by hope in the future, while imagination gives them back to him in the present moment itself; happy fictions take the place of a real happiness; but nay, he alone is firmly happy since worldly goods may at any moment slip from him who holds them; but nothing can take away those of the imagination from whoever knows how to enjoy them. He possesses them without risk or fear; fortune and men cannot deprive him of them (814).

To appreciate the quality of this experience we have only to recall the man

who, passing beyond the narrow prison of personal interest and petty earthly passion, rises on the wings of imagination above the mists of our atmosphere; he who, without exhausting his strength and powers in struggling against fortune and fate, knows how to leap up into the ethereal regions, hover there and keep himself up by his sublime meditations, can in this way defy the onslaughts of fate and the mad judgements of men. He is beyond their attacks; he has no need of their approbation in order to be wise, or of their favour in order to be happy (815).

If sensuous elements are necessary to complete this experience, it is only to prevent mere monotony. That is why an agreeable natural setting is so desirable, since

nature is clothed for him in the most charming shapes, and is adorned in his eyes with the most vivid colours, is filled for his use with beings after his own heart; and—which are the more consoling in misfortune: profound but exhausting conceptions, or cheerful fictions which delight and enrapture him who abandons himself to them in the midst of felicity? He reasons less, it is true, but he enjoys more; he does not lose a moment of enjoyment; and as soon as he is alone, he is happy (816).

Although the emphasis is upon immediate enjoyment, present feeling may be stimulated by meditation upon the past or future, provided only that all painful and unpleasant elements are rigorously excluded. Sometimes, for example, he indulges in personal reminiscence, but only of those periods of his life when he was truly happy; he is continually 'going back to the happy times of his childhood and youth, and he has often relived them in his memories'. At other times, he prefers to contemplate a remote future when all his present misfortunes and unhappiness will be transformed into sweetness and light, but 'more often, allowing his senses to combine with his fictions, he forms beings after his own heart; and living with them in a society of which he feels himself to be worthy, he soars into the empyrean, in the midst of the charming and almost angelic creatures by which he is surrounded' (858).

This last quotation already shows that the world of contemplation is not a purely narcissistic one, for Jean-Jacques readily admits that absolute solitude is a 'sad condition contrary to nature'. In certain moods he needs the presence of the physical world itself, as we have seen, suitably embellished through the activity of his imagination and inner life. But he also requires—and the point is particularly revealing—the idealized presence of *other people*. 'Affectionate feelings sustain the soul, the communication of ideas enlivens the mind.' Furthermore, 'our *self* is not entirely within us'; man cannot 'enjoy himself without the co-operation of other people' (813). That is why even in his most ecstatic imaginative flights he likes to be aware of other people, although they are merely the creation of his heart's desire. Pleasant fictions take the place of real companions, but his imaginative activity is such that he has the illusion of not being completely alone. The introduction of these 'fictions' seems to give his imaginative experience some kind of substance and limits the feeling of absolute solitude.

In one sense the whole attitude of contemplation—in so far as it is inspired by a need for emotional compensation—is contradicted by the very factors which inspire it. Driven into solitude, Rousseau still experiences the overwhelming need of his life—the need to love and be loved. Once more we encounter the psychological paradox already discussed in connexion with the letters to Malesherbes—the paradox and contradiction of the 'self-sufficient' heart which is nevertheless so 'loving'. In spite of his isolation, there still remains this persistent need of others, whether in the form of friendship or love. The other person is there, even though he is nothing more than a phantom in Jean-Jacques's own brain, and he is there because of the demands of that 'heart which the need for love had always devoured' (819). This is a persistent leitmotif of the *Dialogues*. Providence never intended him to be alone, and all his misfortunes spring from the 'need to attach his heart' (810). Heaven meant him for the 'delightful intimacy' of true 'friendship'. Of this he has not the slightest doubt. His liveliest and most hopeless passion was to be loved; he firmly believed that he was made to be loved. Had he found the affection he so desperately needed, it would have given 'fresh stimulus to his faculties'. His misfortune was precisely to have failed to find such sympathy and understanding. If he now lives alone in his mood of reverie, it is to be 'with the friends he has created for himself'. 'He needs other people only because his heart needs attachment; he gives himself imaginary friends because he has not been able to find real ones' (824).

His attitude towards the external world reveals the same concern. He frankly—and rather surprisingly—admits that his love of nature, about which he writes so eloquently, is nothing but a 'substitute' for 'the attachments he needs so much'. 'He would have given up the substitute for the thing itself had he been free to choose, and he is reduced to conversing with plants only after making vain efforts to converse with men' (794). His love of birds and animals also springs from the same frustrated need: he seeks in them what he cannot find in men. How little do people understand him when they interpret his infinite patience with animals and birds as a proof of his misanthropy! The ultimate need of his heart is an expansive one, but when he seeks to extend his feelings to those around him, he can find no soul worthy of responding to his own.

In these revealing observations Rousseau shows that the main problem of his life was not to discover a new attitude towards the world, nature or even God, but to solve the difficult problem of personal relations. His apparent devotion to the ideal of solitude, as well as his cultivation of contemplation and reverie, are nothing but attempts to find a substitute for this overriding need of others. Often compensatory mechanisms of this kind will produce a satisfaction that far outweighs the happiness that was originally sought in the more direct expression of emotional needs, but, in this case, there is no genuine 'sublimation' of the fundamental need of others' affection. The way in which others intrude even into the midst of his fantasies shows how desperately tormented he still was by his first impulse.

The insufficiency of the hedonistic, subjective mood of reverie is also demonstrated by the persistence of the theme of persecution. As we have already insisted, the 'persecutors' not only symbolize certain deep but inadmissible feelings within himself, for they are also a disguised expression of his need for others. In the last resort his account of the plot is but a desperate appeal to others to see him as he really is and so to give him their esteem and affection. Nowhere does Rousseau show more clearly the close interdependence of his own self-evaluation and his need for others than in the final exhortation to 'the Frenchman':

If we join with him to form a sincere and open fellowship, he will—once he is sure of our honesty and esteem—open his heart to us without any difficulty; and receiving in ours the effusions to which he is so naturally inclined, we shall be able to draw from them precious memoirs whose value will be appreciated by other generations and which will at least put them in a position to discuss fully questions which are today resolved on the strength of his enemies' word alone. . . . All he wants is the hope that his memory will one day be re-established in the honour it deserves. . . . Let us add to that the pleasant feeling of seeing two honest and true hearts opening out to his (974–6).

A close examination of both the persecution-theme and the constructive attempt to see himself as a man of 'nature and temperament' suggests that this far-reaching but desperate effort to attain a stable form of self-awareness will fail to achieve its purpose. He cannot remain permanently satisfied with this image of himself because, as we have seen, it does not express his complete personality. This idea that he can remain content with 'being' himself overlooks the vital fact that it is really a disguised effort to *become* himself. Illuminated, it is true, by brilliant flashes of insight, his search for his real self cannot properly overcome the fundamental anxiety which gives rise to it. Whatever he may say, he cannot find ultimate contentment in the enjoyment of the present moment, in a hedonistic philosophy of existence which ignores the problem of guilt. Indeed, his own continual efforts to assimilate morality to pure emotion, and to resolve the problem of guilt in terms of innate sensibility, fail to overcome the half-conscious conviction that this approach to life is not quite satisfying to the whole man. In spite of the tenacity of his efforts, the very persistence of the persecution-theme proves that Rousseau has not been able to give himself complete absolution.

Perhaps the most significant indication of the disturbing influence of these conflicting pressures upon his present self-awareness lies in the distinct hypertrophy of the ego so apparent in the *Dialogues*. There is not only a firmer relationship than hitherto between his idea of himself as a 'good', 'innocent' man and the systematization of the delusions of persecution (and consequently a much sharper cleavage between the false portrait of the 'wicked' Jean-Jacques and the true notion of the 'good' man), but a sudden heightening of the feeling that he is an absolutely unique man placed in an absolutely unique situation. It is easy of course to trace the development of this idea in his previous history, but it now acquires a much greater and an almost pathological importance. The universality of the plot against him itself constitutes a situation without parallel. The persistent thoroughness with which his enemies seek to inform themselves about the most remote and intimate aspects of his life 'from his birth to the present day' is a striking proof of the extraordinary situation in which Jean-Jacques now finds himself. Here we witness 'a case that is unique since the beginning of the world and one which gives rise to a completely new law in humanity's code' (707). The way in which he has been hemmed in by 'walls of darkness' that are 'impenetrable to his gaze', as well as the efforts made to 'bury him alive among the living', form 'perhaps the most singular and astonishing enterprise that has ever been carried out' (706). 'Such an odd position is unique since the beginning of humanity's existence' (765). He is, he repeats, in 'a unique and almost incredible position' (826). The very existence of such an amazing plot, which would never have been hatched against an ordinary man, is itself a striking proof of the uniqueness of his own nature. If the plot is unparalleled, it is only because the man against whom it is directed is altogether different from other men. Such indeed is the conclusion to which 'Rousseau' is inevitably led: this man is indeed 'unlike anybody else he knows; he requires a separate analysis, one made solely for him'.

Ultimately he derives a certain comfort from the thought of his exceptional nature. As he appears—in his own mind—to attain clearer insight into the true meaning of his unique situation and character, he experiences a certain assurance, or, at least, some degree of resignation before his fate. Faced by such universal hostility, he realizes that active resistance is useless and that there is nothing for him to do but 'put out his lantern' and 'withdraw completely into himself' (792). He can now find satisfaction in the thought of his innocence and goodness. 'I thus grow old amongst all these madmen, without any consolation from anybody, without nevertheless losing courage or patience, and, in the midst of the ignorance in which they keep me, I raise to heaven as my sole defence a heart that is free from deceit and hands that are innocent of all evil' (719, note 1). The religious conviction that one day, in the next life, true order and justice will be restored brings him some further consolation. If we cannot call this new state of mind a genuinely stoical one, he himself realizes—as he nears the end of his last dialogue—that he can begin to regard 'with indifference the fate that awaits him during the rest of his short life' (949). Partly responsible for this achievement are his enemies who have finally over-reached themselves in their implacable hatred against an innocent man.

They have used all the resources of their art to make him the unhappiest of beings; through trying one method after another, they have exhausted them all, and, far from achieving their aim, they have produced the opposite effect. They have made Jean-Jacques find resources within himself which he would not have known but for them. After doing their very worst, they have put him in a position where he has nothing more to fear, either from them or anyone else, and they have enabled him to regard all human events with the utmost indifference (951–2).

Moreover, will not Providence 're-establish order' and allow innocence to be vindicated? (954). Perhaps it is too much to hope for compensation in this earthly life, but God will surely look after his own in the next.

At a more mundane level he can obtain considerable satisfaction from the thought that he has at last found a way of life and 'a constant mode of being' which, being in complete conformity with his real character, prove its unity. The 'man of nature' that he is requires above all things a simple life that allows him to follow his natural inclinations. Rousseau recognizes that he was never meant to occupy a high social rank.

Nature made him only a good artisan, sensitive, it is true, to the point of rapture, intensely fond of beauty, passionately attached to justice, and, in brief moments of effervescence, capable of vigour and elevation, but a man whose usual condition was and will be mental inertia and mechanical activity and who, in a word, is rare only because he is so simple. One of the things of which he is glad is to find himself in his old age more or less in the rank into which he was born, without ever having risen or fallen very much in the course of his life. Fate has put him back where nature had placed him; daily he congratulates himself on this conjunction of circumstances (849–50).[1]

The second dialogue stresses the harmony existing between his character and his present way of life. If he leads 'an even, gentle life', it is because of his good and innocent character. The spontaneous impulses of his personality help him to follow without effort 'this simple, industrious, almost mechanical life'. This mode of existence may, in the first place, have been imposed upon him by necessity since his primary concern was to escape from the vigilance of his enemies, but he now sees that he is adopting a way of life which allows him to 'yield unresistingly to the inclinations of his nature' (849). He has become a man who delights in simple work and pleasure; he gains his living by copying music 'at so much a page' and thus shows what a good 'artisan' he is; he takes an innocent pleasure in an amateurish botanizing, which allows him to remain close to the nature he loves so much and provides him with opportunities for lonely and delightful rambles. If he is occasionally persuaded to undertake some more austere piece of literary work, it is with the sole object of conferring benefits upon others, as, for example, when he was asked to draw up a constitution for Poland. Generally speaking, the charm of this 'constant way of life' lies in its

[1] He made the same point to Bernardin de Saint-Pierre (op. cit., p. 65). 'I have neither risen above nor fallen below the condition into which I was born: I am a workman's son, and a workman myself. I am doing what I have done since I was fourteen years of age.' That is why music-copying was so much to his taste.

undisturbed regularity, innocence and peace; more particularly, it enables him to 'abstain from action' and all irksome tasks, and so leaves him free to indulge in those imaginative reveries and flights of fancy by which he sets so much store. Liberated from the tormenting influence of false pride, he can now at last enjoy the immediate present and follow the natural inclination of his heart and senses. Far from abandoning himself to some hermit-like asceticism, Jean-Jacques is free—within the limits of his solitude—to express those 'tender and expansive feelings' by which he is so often filled. The 'uniformity of this mechanical life' well befits a man who delights in 'walking always alone, thinking little, dreaming much and working almost automatically' (849). Yet none of these activities is carried out systematically, for he is concerned mainly with expressing the spontaneous promptings of his natural sensibility. Therein lie the charm and fascination of this simple mode of life.

Rousseau is unwilling to admit that this is a purely selfish mode of existence. He does not lead a completely lazy life, since he is 'hard-working in his own way', though it is work done in submission to 'the necessity of things and not the will of men'. Certainly he does not pretend to be a 'sage'; he is a 'man of nature' who indulges in expansive emotions. He does not even claim, as we have seen, to be 'virtuous', but this very sincerity ought, he thinks, to command respect. In a world of false values and ruthless self-seeking Jean-Jacques's life may, in a sense, be held to have an *exemplary* value. Although his case is unique, it is also a prototype of what a genuine 'man of nature' can and ought to be. This does not mean that others must copy his actual way of life, but by his existence they are challenged to be more sincere with themselves and others. Is not Jean-Jacques a striking example of a man who has bravely defied current conventions and so shown to men the only way of finding happiness?

He realizes that it is not enough to demonstrate the correlation between physical behaviour and real character; it is also important to study the connexion between character and thought, between a man's personal life and his view of the world. This becomes particularly relevant in the case of a writer who has made public profession of a specific philosophy. The *Dialogues* place great emphasis on the idea that a bad man cannot produce a genuinely moral book and they use this argument to try to destroy the fiction of the 'evil' Rousseau. The moral elevation of books like *Émile* and *La Nouvelle Héloïse*, with its hymn to virtue, can only be the work of an author who is himself uplifted by similar feelings. Now Jean-Jacques is certainly the author of these works, so that it only remains to show how, as the true pattern of his behaviour and character unfolds itself, he is the man of his books, and in some fascinating pages which are tantalizingly interrupted and finally cut short by paranoid digressions, Rousseau attempts, in the third dialogue, to summarize the spirit of his 'system'.

Already at the beginning of the first dialogue he had explained the chief 'object' with which the innocent Jean-Jacques's writings are concerned—an 'ideal world like ours and yet quite different' (668 ff.). By 'ideal' world is meant not a completely transcendent realm of being, but one which is the perfected expression of human life as it might be found here below in its 'natural' and 'primordial' state, if it were freed from the distortions and limitations imposed upon it by 'society'. The inhabitants of this world, Rousseau is careful to insist, are not 'perfect' for they have many 'faults'. For example, they are not 'virtuous' since virtue presupposes the capacity to overcome natural inclination. On the other hand, they can trust their 'passions' because they are 'simpler' and 'purer' than those of ordinary people; they have a more delicate *sensibilité* and so are capable of more refined and exquisite enjoyment than that experienced in everyday life. This ideal world is thus the world of 'nature' and 'sensibility' as it was originally created by God and as He intended it to be. Nature is what man 'really' is, not as a matter of historical fact, but from the point of view of the authentic possibilities of his own essential being. However distorting the mask which civilization attempts to fit upon human life, there can be no doubt that the first movements of nature are 'always good and right' (668), even though the soul may not have the strength to overcome the obstacles that hinder its free development; this will in fact be the source of the 'faults' still attributable to the inhabitants of the ideal world. But this incapacity to overcome obstacles is quite different from the vices of modern man. In this ideal world primitive passions always refer ultimately to the uninhibited expression of primordial nature; as such they cannot be harmful in their effects, for they have an absolute value transcending the purely *relative* significance of civilized feelings. The inhabitants of Rousseau's world are content to be themselves and to trust the passions which make them 'great and strong souls'. In this way they are better able to maintain their pristine integrity. Since their faults are never due to 'wickedness' or a deliberate desire to harm others but simply to their inability to overcome obstacles, they will often be 'guilty', but never 'wicked'. These people will not be lost in otherworldly mysticism, but will know the real contentment which comes from an intimacy based on the true 'art of enjoyment' (rather than possession) and on a proper appreciation of the pleasures of the heart and senses. Indifferent to riches and still more to the false values of 'opinion', they will allow their lives to be dominated and limited by 'nature' and 'reason'. It may be that this world will contain writers, but their sole reason for taking up the pen will be the conviction that they have 'some happy discovery to proclaim, some fine and useful truth to disseminate, some general, pernicious error to oppose, some point of public usefulness to establish' (673). Writing for them is not a trade; they will have no desire to thrust themselves into *le tripot littéraire*, for they do not feel 'this ridiculous urge to be for ever scribbling on paper'.

In describing the inhabitants of this ideal world Rousseau is obviously painting a portrait of that 'man of nature', Jean-Jacques himself; in depicting these ideal people he is merely describing his own 'original' character. Like this ideal world's inhabitants, when he had once been vouchsafed a vision of beauty and goodness, he could not remain satisfied with the mediocrity and ugliness of the world as it was. By some remarkable dispensation of Providence he had been born with a temperament which enabled him eventually to throw off the corrupting influence of civilized life and to live in accordance with his own true 'nature'. No doubt he was fortunate to have been born and brought up in a society free from many of the evils characteristic of the large states of the West. Chance brought him to the source of all corruption, to the modern Babylon, Paris, where on one hot October afternoon, as he was dazzled by his vision of a new heaven and a new earth, he was suddenly able to understand the cause of modern man's unhappiness and the means by which he might still hope to attenuate it. Inspired by an intense inner persuasion, he was prompted to give not only to the country in which he was then living, but to humanity at large, an insight into those principles of 'truth', 'justice' and 'nature' upon which all authentic human existence should be based. But he was soon led to see that his own personal existence ought to accord with his principles, even though this meant the abandonment of society and a retreat into solitude. The effect of this step upon his personal fortunes was quite disastrous since he immediately became an object of envy to those 'friends' who were jealous of both his literary success and moral courage. This act of 'reform' merely served to provoke all those people —and they were the majority of his contemporaries—who were made uncomfortable by the truths he was expounding; they could not bear to face the fact that their lives were resting on a sham. The result was that he, the apostle of goodness who had sacrificed his personal comfort to the duty of proclaiming the truth to his fellow-men, was hounded from one country to another and at last made the object of a universal plot which, ironically enough, owed its persistence and ferocity to the uniqueness and innocence of its victim. There must be no doubt on this point: Jean-Jacques is, like the inhabitants of his ideal world, 'a being from another sphere', one who can never be understood by his fellows, even though he merely exemplifies in his own life those qualities which should belong to the character of every true man.

If Jean-Jacques's account betrays a certain idealization of his past life (for example, the 'reform' is explained largely in terms of moral principle and not as a means of obtaining psychological relief from anxiety), this is largely because of his desire to present his life and work as a unified whole; he believes that there can be no serious inconsistency between his *essential* character and his basic thought. With a persistence which owes something to paranoid desperation he sets up and tears down all the arguments that have been arrayed against his life and work, so that in the third dialogue it remains only to show that the 'spirit' of his writings is in perfect harmony with his character and his way of life; the man, his conduct, and his philosophy will then be seen to form a perfectly consistent and homogeneous whole. It is not necessary to reproduce here all the points as they are set out in the *Dialogues*, for they have been frequently quoted in discussions about the 'unity' of Rousseau's 'system'. There is little doubt that those critics who, like Lanson, use these arguments to justify the basic unity of his thought are acting in complete conformity with Rousseau's own intention when he declared that he had created 'a united system which might not be true but which contained no contradiction' (930); it was based on 'his great principle that nature made man happy and good, but that society depraves him and makes him wretched'. 'Men' indeed might be 'wicked', but 'man is good'. *Émile*, especially, 'this book which is so much read, so little understood and so ill appreciated, is only a treatise on man's natural goodness, intended to show how vice and error, foreign to his constitution, are introduced into it from the outside, and imperceptibly cause it to deteriorate'. In his early writings he was more concerned to destroy the false prestige attached to 'the instruments of our understanding' and to show how the false glamour attributed to 'pernicious talents' led to contempt for 'useful virtues'. 'Everywhere he has shown us the human race better, wiser and happier in its primitive constitution; blind, unhappy and wicked, as it goes farther away from it. His aim is to set right the errors of our judgement in order to slow down the progress of our vices, and to show us that where we seek glory and brilliance we find only error and misery.' But he does not propose to lead men back to primitive life, for 'human nature never retrogresses, and we can never go back to the times of innocence and equality when once we have left them'. The only hope is to halt the moral deterioration of large states and to prevent small and relatively uncorrupted countries from adopting the errors and the vices of the large ones. It is, he insists, a gross misrepresentation of his views to suggest that he wishes to overthrow the existing order, for nobody has a greater aversion than he for 'revolutions and leaguers of all kinds' (935). His real role is that of 'the painter of nature and the historian of the human heart', for as a 'historian' he has indicated the main phases of this progressive deterioration of man under the growing influence of 'civilization' and, at the same time, he has torn aside the mask which conceals man's 'original' nature in order to depict it in its potential perfection. Moreover, he has pointed the way to happiness by showing men that they must 'withdraw into their hearts in order to find there the seeds of social virtues' (687).

What is particularly interesting is the way in which Rousseau's emphasis upon the ideal aspects of his system links up so closely with his belief in the close interdependence of his character and thought. Although the truths he teaches ultimately concern the happiness of 'humanity', they could only be proclaimed by a man who had first of all experienced them in himself. He puts this very forcefully when he writes: 'Whence could the apologist and painter of nature, to-day so disfigured and calumnied, have drawn his model save from his own heart? It was necessary that one man should paint his portrait in order to show us in this way the primitive man' (936). If Jean-Jacques was able to perform this exceptional task of humanity's educator, it was only because he had known how 'to seek in the calmness of the passions these first features which have vanished from the multitude'. This in its turn involved the rediscovery and 'restoration' of himself by a considerable effort of will and not a little anguish as he listened to the 'inner voice' speaking to him 'in the silence of the passions'. Only because he had discovered his own personal authenticity was he able to distinguish the 'natural' man from the factitious social being we normally see around us. This is why he feels justified in saying that he has expounded 'the true system of the human heart' (697). Only a writer inspired by 'noble enthusiasm' would be capable of carrying out such an undertaking; only a 'good' man who drew his inspiration from his own heart would be able to infuse into his work the intense idealism so expressive of its personal origin.

It is evident from Rousseau's own account that he did not consider this indissoluble link between his personality and his work to be a simple one. In each case, it was necessary to penetrate beneath the deceptive surface of 'appearances' in order to grasp the real 'being' of both 'man' and 'Jean-Jacques'. In fact, the more closely Rousseau approaches his own authentic self, the more vividly is he aware of the true 'nature of man'. His own exceptional position is due mainly, he believes, to the contradictions created by the corrupting influence of 'society' and in no way involves any intrinsic defect in 'nature' itself. He himself is unique not in relation to 'nature' but to other men who are still living under the thrall of social artifice: as far as nature is concerned, he is merely paradigmatic. The proof of this is to be found, he believes, in the fundamental unity and harmony of an existence which —unlike that of people who live always 'outside' themselves—is in complete accordance with his own essential being.

As he ponders this fundamental question of the interdependence of his ideas and personality as well as the more limited question of the relation between his individual existence and the world of men, he is convinced that the ultimate principle capable of illuminating the whole issue is the vital distinction between 'self-love' (*amour de soi*) and 'pride' (*amour-propre*). Self-love expresses an ultimate quality of human existence, the vital principle which makes a man what he is: it is the manifestation at the personal level of the principle lying at the heart of the whole of God's creation—of the 'goodness' of any being that exists in accordance with its own true nature. But if *amour de soi* is the absolute principle of human existence, its particular form in ordinary life need not always be a complete expression of all man's potentialities; his nature—compounded of senses, heart, mind, and soul—lends itself to countless variations. Yet when for some special reason—for example, the peculiar nature of the relationship that is being brought into effect at any given moment—a limited facet of the personality is required to express itself, it will always reveal something of the original quality animating existence as a whole, though it will not always do so in the same way. With the growth of 'society' the simplicity of true *amour de soi* is obscured by the inordinate development of some limited aspect of the self (for example, the 'passions' or 'reason'), which often assumes a kind of tyrannical control of the personality, ultimately deposing self-love as the mainspring of human conduct. The tragedy of modern man is that he is alienated from his 'original' nature and subordinated to something less than his true self, so that he is constantly living outside himself in a permanent state of conflict and contradiction. In a word, *amour de soi* degenerates into *amour-propre*. Whereas the former is content to exist in its own right, it is characteristic of the latter that it should be constantly *comparing* itself with other things and persons. 'Pride' too makes the self the object of 'love', but in a false and artificial way which ignores any genuinely intrinsic quality it may have: unlike the 'self-love' which involves a spontaneous expression of 'the heart's needs' and so leads to 'goodness', 'commiseration', and 'generosity', pride is concerned with a particular and limited impulse, the satisfaction of which depends on the possession or domination of something other than the self—as in the case of a 'passion' which brings a man into conflict with his fellow-men and his own deeper nature. Certainly abandonment to self-love will not lead to untrammelled freedom, but the 'yoke' it accepts will be that of 'necessity' and not the arbitrary 'will of men'. It may be diverted from its object by various 'obstacles', but this will never lead to envy and thus impair the real stability of the self. *Amour de soi*, therefore, confers a genuine unity on the personality, while *amour-propre* leaves it unhappy and divided.

There seems no valid reason for disputing the sincerity of Rousseau's attempt to capture in these pages the spirit of his 'system'; as he looks back upon his life's work, certain fundamental principles seem to stand out clearly in his mind; towards the world and the problem of man's happiness he considers that he has taught a consistent doctrine. It may be objected that he takes no account of the gradual development of certain ideas—such as those of man's 'natural goodness' and the distinction between *amour de soi* and *amour-propre*—which were clarified over a period of years: the system, as historians of his thought have made clear, did not spring full-panoplied from his brain. But ultimately this is a point of merely historical interest which does not really affect the validity of his thought as a finished entity: the question of its worth is largely independent of its actual formation.

A more vital point is to decide whether this attempt to prove the close identity of Rousseau 'the man' and Rousseau 'the thinker' adequately expresses the whole truth of his work as a didactic system or the complete authenticity of his existence as a human being. Certainly our previous analyses, while stressing the close link between thought and personality, have rejected any facile identification of the two in purely autobiographical or psychological terms: in each case, Rousseau was concerned with a problem of value—whether personal or philosophical —which always sought to transcend the merely accidental and particular aspects of experience. The whole project of the *Confessions* rested on the assumption that his real self had not been adequately expressed by the physical actions and circumstances of his life, while his philosophical 'system' constantly stressed the need to go beyond the factual to the ideal, beyond 'what is' to 'what ought to be'; the nature of both 'Jean-Jacques' and 'man' thus remained potential rather than properly fulfilled aspects of actual experience. But if he was so passionately concerned with the fate of 'man' in the modern world, it was only because he had first of all experienced the urgency of the problem within his own heart. Indeed, he believed that, since his contemporaries were so blind to the real meaning of 'nature', it was only in the depths of his own intimate self that he could hope to find a means of correcting widespread error.

As he approaches the end of his career, he considers that the problem of his individual existence—in both its factual and ideal aspects—is inseparable from the broader cultural problems already discussed in his writings. The 'good' Jean-Jacques in conflict with his 'persecutors' is not very different from the position of 'man' at odds with 'society'. If he strips his own case of its merely fortuitous and extraordinary features —for it is *his* unique destiny to be the object of *universal* persecution— we shall find the dilemma of any 'good' man in contact with an evil 'world': Jean-Jacques is simply a particular example of innocent 'self-love' oppressed by the sinister forces of 'pride'. It is significant, for example, that when he describes himself as a man prepared to accept the 'yoke of necessity' while shunning the 'arbitrary will of men', he is merely echoing a theme which had figured prominently in his discussion of political problems, for the precise object of the 'law' and the 'general will' had been to protect the individual against the tyranny of his fellow men. In his last years, therefore, Rousseau sees himself as a striking example of the 'man of nature' who has at last learnt to be himself.

Although we may readily grant the relevance of his efforts to correlate his personality and his thought, a close examination of his arguments suggests that his efforts to bestow unity and stability upon his existence as man and thinker involve a certain simplification of both his personality and his work. As we have already seen, this final attempt to portray himself as a 'man of nature' is not simply a description of

S

himself as he is but as he *chooses* to be. This explicit acceptance of himself as a certain type of man is the result of a choice aimed at eliminating those complex, disturbing elements which stood in the way of a unified and integrated view of his personality. If his self now seems to be more harmonious and consistent, it is only because he has succeeded in projecting inadmissible feelings of guilt on to the figures of his 'persecutors'. But the constant presence of these figures is a striking proof of the terrible power of forces which he himself thinks have been tamed for ever. In fact, by reducing the substance of his personality to the 'goodness' and 'innocence' of pure 'sensibility'—to the expression of a spontaneous, undiluted *amour de soi*—Jean-Jacques has merely thrust into his subconscious all those moral and psychological factors which until then had prevented the completion of an acceptable self-portrait.

Since this view of himself is supported by an examination of the 'spirit' of his writings, it is perhaps inevitable that they too should be interpreted in the light of his now all-powerful sensibility. It is significant, for example, that he presents *La Nouvelle Héloïse* as a simple hymn to virtue, an idyll full of unsophisticated moral fervour, whereas it really contains, as we have already seen, many deep tensions and contradictions which reflect the complexity of his own struggle for personal fulfilment. Assuredly Rousseau had always insisted upon the luminous simplicity of the 'nature' which had been obscured by the artificiality of civilization, but, in a world corrupted by false 'social' values, the recovery of this simplicity was a difficult task that could be achieved only by a considerable effort of will. Just as Rousseau, while still living in society, had been compelled to sustain his integrity by an appeal to the heroic moral principles of an older tradition, so would those contemporaries who still wished to save their souls have to re-create that 'nature' which no longer offered itself to them in a direct and straightforward manner. The whole concept of 'nature' was in fact complicated by the subtle interrelation of its factual and ideal aspects. Historically and geographically, 'nature' might seem to contain a kind of primitive simplicity, but though a consideration of natural models remote from us in space and time (as in early historical or prehistorical 'primitive' life) could offer a salutary lesson to modern man in so far as they represented people and communities which were content to exist in accordance with their own intrinsic nature, they could never be mere patterns for imitation. Nature was an ideal *towards* which as well as *from* which we had to move: it represented an ideal which had to adapt the simplicity of its 'primitive' forms to the moral and social needs of the fully developed individual. It was an ideal that—in the modern world—could be achieved only through a co-operative 'social' effort inspired by an awareness of man's maturest needs.

But Rousseau, in the *Dialogues*, had abstracted himself from this social context. He saw himself as a man who no longer needed to be 'virtuous'. By an accident of birth he had been born with a temperament which absolved him from the necessity of striving for the 'virtuous' perfection which was—or should be—the object of other men's lives: his particular disposition had prevented him from being permanently corrupted by society and he had never really lost the pristine innocence of 'the first forty years'. Henceforth separated from men, he had—in order to be both 'good' and 'happy'—merely to abandon himself to the impulse of his temperament. But he could sustain this image of himself only through a simplification of his personality and his work, so that Rousseau's error in the *Dialogues* does not lie in a deliberate falsification of facts, but in the omission of those elements which conflict with his conscious view of himself as a man of sensibility. Inevitably his need to thrust anxiety-provoking thoughts from his conscious mind by means of an identification of his 'good' or 'ideal' self with the 'spirit' of his writings leads him to exaggerate the unity of both his character and his work. Just as he is induced to concentrate on those aspects of his nature which refute the idea of the 'wicked' Jean-Jacques, so does his account of his writings throw into relief those aspects which are in direct opposition to the false interpretations of his calumniators. Hence, this element of simplification, of which I have just spoken.

In spite of the important place accorded to the discussion of his 'system' Rousseau does not devote much time to a consideration of purely abstract and intellectual questions, and, as the *Dialogues* draw to a close, we are again reminded of their significance as a *personal act*. However tortuous and indirect the expression of certain themes, the work is not intended primarily as a mere explanation of his life and work, but as an active *appeal* to others to modify their attitude towards Jean-Jacques. Just as the vast paranoid letter to Hume had been a desperate attempt to obtain emotional solace and reassurance, so are the *Dialogues* offered as an active challenge to others to revise their opinion of him. Rousseau's behaviour after the completion of his work shows very plainly that its composition was intended as an act, not just a literary exercise or a fruitless piece of introspection. The image of himself as a man of temperament forms part of a wide existential pattern which, by compelling others to accept it as a portrait of his authentic self, will at last allow him to feel justified in his own eyes as well as theirs. It is not only Jean-Jacques, but others who must finally set their seal on this effort at self-justification. If his contemporaries will not respond to this appeal, then as a last expedient he will direct his efforts at posterity. As the pathetic cries of the *Dialogues* themselves often indicate, the tragedy of his life was primarily bound up with the problem of personal relations, with the difficulty of solving this 'desperate need for love' which had haunted him from his earliest years. However earnestly he might seek to compensate for this misfortune by building up in his own mind the image of a 'good', 'innocent', and, ultimately, self-sufficient Jean-Jacques, this fundamental need still remained active, though it could henceforth express itself only in very indirect and distorted ways.

Then, quite surprisingly, after a period of intense and almost hysterical anxiety, he began to experience something of that resignation to which he had already referred in the *Dialogues*. It was the very extremity of his trials and misfortunes which had led him to abandon all hope and realize the futility of further struggles. The lack of adequate response to his circular letter addressed to 'every Frenchman loving truth and justice' seems to have convinced him that he must 'no longer struggle against necessity'. He begins to ask himself: 'What harm has this plot done you? What has it taken from you? What crime has it made you commit? As long as men do not tear from my breast the heart that is enclosed therein in order to substitute for it, during my lifetime, that of a dishonest man, in what way will they be able to change my being or affect it adversely? In vain will they fashion a Jean-Jacques to their own liking, Rousseau will always remain the same in spite of them.' In other words, his essential being does not in any way depend on 'opinion' and cannot be altered by others. He concludes:

I have then completely made up my mind; detached from all that appertains to the earth and the mad judgement of men, I resign myself to being for ever disfigured by them, without relying any the less on the reward of my innocence and suffering. My happiness must be of another kind; I must no longer seek it among them, and it is no more in their power to prevent it than it is for them to know it. Destined to be in this life the prey of errors and lies, I await the hour of my deliverance and the triumph of truth without any longer looking for them amongst mortal men. Detached from all earthly affection, and even delivered from the anxiety of experiencing hope on this earth, I no longer see any influence through which they can disturb the peace in my heart. . . . Whatever men may do, Heaven in its turn will carry on its work. I do not know the time, the means or the manner. What I do know is that the Supreme Judge is powerful and just, that my soul is innocent, and that I have not deserved my fate: that is enough. To submit henceforth to my fate, to persist no longer in struggling against it, to let my persecutors dispose of their prey as they wish, to remain their plaything for the rest of my sad old age, to hand over to them even the honour of my name and my future reputation (if it pleases Heaven that they should dispose of them) without being any longer affected by anything, whatever happens; that is my final resolve. Let men henceforth do all that they wish; after I have done what I had to do, even though they torment me for the rest of my days, they will not prevent me from dying in peace (986–9).

8

LES RÊVERIES DU PROMENEUR SOLITAIRE

THE note of resignation on which Rousseau ended his *Histoire du précédent écrit* did not mean that the personal problem raised by the *Dialogues* had thereby been resolved; he was merely making a kind of despairing renunciation of all hope of ever finding out the truth about his extraordinary situation. This 'resignation' revealed no genuinely rational attempt to face the reality of his situation, for it was the result of emotional exhaustion and a natural reaction to a period of intense agitation and anxiety. Although he could feel that the *Dialogues* had given a detailed account of himself and his present way of life, Rousseau's inability to understand the real significance of his obsession with the theme of persecution meant that, as soon as the immediate effects of his emotional fatigue had worn off, he would be faced again with familiar questions about the nature of his personality and existence.[1]

His return to Paris in 1770 and his establishment in the Rue Plâtrière in June of that year foreshadowed the end of his many wanderings, for, apart from a change of residence in the Rue Plâtrière itself, he was to make only one more move before he died: this was on 20 May 1778, when he went to live on the estates of the Marquis de Girardin at Ermenonville. Indeed, the outward circumstances of his life

---

[1] Some of the material in this chapter is drawn from an article, 'Subjective and Objective Elements in Rousseau's *Rêveries*', in *French Studies* (vii, No. 1, Jan. 1953, 1–17). In addition to the text, introduction, and commentary in *OC* i, there are important editions of the *Rêveries* by J. S. Spink (Société des textes français modernes, Paris, 1948) and by Marcel Raymond (Textes littéraires français, Droz, Geneva, 1948), both with valuable introduction and notes. The literary consequences of certain psychological data have already been examined in the well-known article by Robert Osmont, 'Contribution à l'étude psychologique des *Rêveries du Promeneur Solitaire*. La vie du souvenir. Le rythme lyrique' (*Annales de la Société Jean-Jacques Rousseau*, xxiii. 1934). For the biographical background of these last years see A. Monglond, *Vies préromantiques* (Paris, 1925), pp. 14–89. See also two important articles in the *Annales*: Marcel Raymond, 'Deux aspects de la vie intérieure de J.-J. Rousseau', xxix. 1941–2, 6–57; Basil Munteano, 'La Solitude de Rousseau', xxxi. 1946–9, 79–168.

as they are revealed in the anecdotes and memoirs of friends like
Bernardin de Saint-Pierre, Eymar, and Corancez contain little of
dramatic import. We see Jean-Jacques leading a simple, modest
existence, devoting his time to the copying of music (until 1776 when
advancing age compelled him to give up this occupation), the composition of music (especially between 1774 and 1777 when he sketched with
Corancez a pastorale in four acts entitled *Daphnis et Chloé*), some literary activity (a translation of Tasso, the *Considérations sur le gouverne-
ment de Pologne* in 1771–2, the *Dialogues* between 1772 and 1776, and
the *Rêveries du promeneur solitaire* from 1776 until a few weeks before
his death on 2 July 1778). His relaxations consisted of playing on the
spinet, singing Genevan airs, having an occasional meal with friends in
his own home, drinking coffee in the Champs Élysées, going for long
walks, sometimes with Thérèse or a companion, more often by himself.
Until 1773 he spent a good deal of time botanizing, but he then took
no more than a desultory interest in the subject until 1777 when a
sudden burst of enthusiasm again sent him over the countryside in an
eager search for plants and flowers. Botany was the chief occupation of
the last months of his life and on the eve of his death he had been out
on one of his expeditions. His last years were thus spent in peaceful and
fairly regular habits, the only outward signs of abnormality being the
onset of anti-social moods often marked by suspicion and distrust of
his friends, some of whom, like the unfortunate Dusaulx, were cast
from him.[1]

In spite of this apparent calm Rousseau's inner life continued to be
haunted by the old tormenting thoughts and emotions. To obtain
relief he once again began to confide some of his intimate musings to
paper but in a much less feverish manner than when he composed the
Dialogues. He now wrote like a self-conscious artist anxious to obtain
the maximum poetic effect, even when he was dealing with particularly
private emotions. These *Rêveries*, the last and most beautiful of
Rousseau's writings, were probably begun a few months after his disappointment with the *Dialogues*, the first *Promenade* apparently being
composed at the end of the summer of 1776.[2] The others (ten in all,
including one that was unfinished) were written at various intervals
between then and 12 April 1778. According to Bernardin de Saint-
Pierre, Jean-Jacques had for some time been toying with the idea of

---

[1] Bernardin de Saint-Pierre reported the same characteristic. 'There are days', explained
Rousseau, 'when I want to be alone. . . . I fear intimacy. I have closed my heart' (p. 67).
[2] Cf. Spink and Raymond, op. cit.

writing a work on old age and adversity.[1] Professor Spink also suggests that discussions with the same friend may have caused Rousseau to turn once again to his beloved Plutarch, even though he had to abandon the reading of this author because of the many 'wounds' it reopened.[2] Various thoughts and observations written down on the back of playing-cards also show that the idea of the *Rêveries* had been in his mind for some time before he actually undertook any systematic composition; he probably carried these cards with him on his rambles and jotted down odd thoughts as they occurred to him.[3]

A study of the final text of the *Rêveries* suggests that this work, like all the personal writings since the *Lettres à Malesherbes*, was composed in response to a number of motives. In spite of all his previous efforts at self-analysis Rousseau was not convinced that he had yet discovered the complete truth about himself. 'What am I myself? That is what remains to be found out' (995). He proposes to examine himself with the detachment of a scientist. 'In some respects I shall carry out upon myself the operations performed by physicists upon the atmosphere in order to know its daily condition. I shall apply the barometer to my soul, and these operations, well directed and often repeated, could furnish me with results that are as certain as theirs.' On second thoughts, however, he realizes that such a rigid plan is impracticable. He will hope 'to ascertain the modifications of my soul and their successions', but not quite in the carefully controlled and methodical manner of scientific experiments. 'I shall be satisfied to keep the register of the operations without seeking to reduce them to a system.' What he produces will not be a precise record but 'a shapeless journal' which is nevertheless 'a faithful register of my lonely walks and the reveries accompanying them'.[4] He also insists that he is not seeking a merely theoretical knowledge about himself, for he hopes—in the light of his newly

---

[1] Op. cit., p. 126. Rousseau was not satisfied with what Cicero had written on the subject.

[2] To the name of Plutarch should be added, as M. Raymond points out (*OC* i, p. lxxxi), that of Montaigne. Cf. *Rêv.* 1001: 'I am carrying out the same enterprise as Montaigne, although with an aim contrary to his.'

[3] For the text see J. S. Spink, op. cit., pp. xxi–xxv and *OC* i. 1165–72.

[4] Enlightening comments on Rousseau's use of the term *rêverie* are given in M. Raymond's introduction (*OC* i, pp. lxxv–lxxviii). 'La rêverie est un laisser-aller de l'esprit qui se poursuit passivement, "sans diversion et sans obstacle" ' (lxxviii). As such it differs from 'meditation' which is a more concentrated and systematic form of attention, and 'contemplation' which suggests a preoccupation with the objective world. ('Contemplation' indicates a study of the world as an entity, 'observation' being concerned with detail.) Rousseau does not always use the terms with great precision, and the description of reverie also owes a great deal to art.

acquired self-awareness—to effect some kind of moral improvement within his own personality. If he is spending his last days in 'studying himself', it is 'to prepare in advance the account that I shall soon have to give of myself'. It would thus seem that he is no longer completely satisfied with the image of himself (so elaborately developed in the *Dialogues*) as a 'man of sensibility'. 'If, through reflecting on my inner states, I succeed in putting them into better order and in correcting the evil which may still remain in them, my meditations will not be entirely useless and, although I am no longer good for anything on earth, I shall not have completely wasted my last days' (i. 999).[1] As he puts it at the end of the third *Promenade*, 'I shall be happy if, through the progress I have made, I learn to leave this life not better (for that is not possible) but more virtuous than when I came into it' (iii. 1023). The writing of the *Rêveries*, therefore, is not to be a mere pastime or still less a purely literary exercise, for it involves an earnest attempt at self-examination and self-realization.

Unfortunately Rousseau still feels that all his efforts to find happiness are threatened by the relentless hostility of his 'persecutors'. It has been suggested by some critics that in the *Rêveries* he has partially recovered from the psychosis of the previous period. The material of this work is certainly richer and more varied than that of the vastly longer *Dialogues* which return with monotonous frequency to a limited number of themes; the greater artistry is also not in doubt, for here Rousseau has succeeded in creating a wonderfully poetic atmosphere and a delicately cadenced style which transcends in aesthetic value (though not always in psychological interest) almost all that he wrote in the *Dialogues*.[2] To some extent this enhanced artistic power is due to a lowering of the heavily charged emotional tension of the *Dialogues*, but I should not be inclined to see in this fact a proof of Rousseau's greater mental balance. We have already insisted that paranoia is mainly a disorder of temperament which affects only part of a man's character, leaving his mental and much of his affective life intact; it is only when he is put into contact with the complex of emotions animating his delusions that his abnormality becomes manifest. In many parts of the *Rêveries* Rousseau does succeed in directing attention away from the thought of persecution as he seeks positive compensations for his loneliness and isolation and the objective content of the work is thereby

---

[1] The roman numeral in the references to the *Rêveries* indicates the *Promenade*.
[2] For an examination of the relation between the stylistic and psychological aspects of the *Rêveries* see the article by R. Osmont quoted above.

considerably widened in scope, but this does not mean that the paranoid tendencies have been overcome; the very fact that they are now resignedly accepted as part of his everyday normal existence shows them to be so deeply rooted in his mind that he will henceforth never be free from them again. Indeed a close examination of the purely psychological aspects of the *Rêveries* (as they appear, for example, in the eighth *Promenade*) will give some reason for believing in a gradual but steady deterioration of his mental condition during these last years.

The by now familiar theme of persecution appears in the very first paragraph which evokes the old antithesis between the 'good Jean-Jacques' and the 'wicked persecutors'.

Here am I, then, alone on the earth, having no brother, neighbour, friend or companion but myself. The most sociable and loving of human beings has been outlawed by a unanimous agreement. In the subtleties of their hatred they have sought what torment could be the most cruel for my sensitive soul, and they have violently broken all the bonds which tied me to them. I should have loved men in spite of themselves. They have been able to elude my affection only by ceasing to be men. There they are then, strangers, unknown persons, nothing to me since they have wished it thus (995).

In the eighth *Promenade* the theme of persecution almost reaches the intensity of the *Dialogues*. At times too Rousseau's phraseology recalls the style of the earlier production, as when he speaks of his enemies surrounding him with 'mystery' and 'darkness'. He is still preoccupied with the idea of defamation and ridicule, for he remains, in the eyes of his persecutors, a 'monster', 'poisoner', 'murderer', the 'horror of the human race', and the 'plaything of the mob'. Even passers-by, he is convinced, would 'spit upon him' if they could and 'a whole generation' would take great delight in 'burying him alive' (i. 996). He now lays greater stress upon the 'devilish' nature of his enemies' activities. Full of a 'burning hatred which is as immortal as the demon inspiring it', they delight in devising 'hellish ruses' which are only too characteristic of their 'infernal spirit' (viii. 1077). When they seek to conceal the true quality of their feelings, they 'plunge into the ground like moles' (1059), happy to hatch their evil schemes in subterranean darkness. At other times they set a constant watch upon him, so that the most harmless passer-by may suddenly reveal his real attitude as he looks at Jean-Jacques with eyes full of sinister malevolence. Living as he now does upon his senses, he is particularly susceptible to others' looks, to their 'fierce', 'insulting and mocking glances'. How too often does a human face wear a 'grinning, deceitful mask' which seeks to conceal

the most violent animosity! The persecutors' intentions remain unchanged, for they still seek to degrade and ridicule him, to cover him
with 'defamation, depression, derision and opprobrium'. The cumulative effect of all this is to convince him that the 'league' is now
'universal, without exception'. It is true that individual enemies may
die, but collective bodies continue to exist, and it is they who will
maintain their assaults upon Jean-Jacques's good name. The Oratorians
and the doctors are two particularly hostile groups, the former especially, as 'churchmen and semi-monks', will be 'for ever implacable' since
they charge him with their own iniquity.

The sequel to the first *Promenade* shows how difficult it was for him
to forget other people. Although he speaks of his detachment from
men, the thought of them remains active within him, often taking the
form of the belief that 'they' are always preoccupied with him, wherever he is and whatever he is doing. If he does occasionally find happiness, it is always 'in spite of them'. Occasionally he returns to the
theme that had played such a prominent part in the *Dialogues*—the
idea that other men are concerned with a Jean-Jacques of their own
creation. People 'obstinately see me as other than I am' and instead of
his real self they direct their attention upon 'the J.J. they have made for
themselves after their own heart in order to hate him at their ease' (vi.
1059). Yet it is in this very *Promenade* where his paranoid tendencies
show themselves so clearly that the more normal desire for companionship and affection often breaks forth. The same contradiction is
apparent throughout the *Rêveries*: fleeing from all contact with his
fellows, he none the less cannot refrain from feelings of delight and joy
at the sight of innocent children's gambols; the simple humanity of the
poverty-stricken old soldiers of the Invalides evokes a movement of
sympathy and generosity in spite of his determination to be alone. A
particularly interesting example of the ambivalent nature of his reactions
to other men is provided by the seventh *Promenade* when he describes
his reactions to the unexpected discovery of a stocking-manufacturer
in a lonely part of the Swiss mountains; he himself says that 'he cannot
express the confused and contradictory agitation which he felt in his
heart at this discovery' (vii. 1071). He is suddenly filled with a 'feeling
of joy' at the idea 'of finding himself amongst his fellow-men at a time
when he thought that he was completely alone'. But immediately this
joy gives way to the 'painful feeling' that in the Alps themselves he
cannot 'escape from the cruel hands of men determined to torment him'.
Convinced on the one hand that both his inclination and his duty impel

him to remain 'wrapped up in himself', he yet experiences a need for others; in spite of his incapacity for action and his profound aversion to all kinds of obligation and restriction, he cannot resist the attraction of those simpler human emotions which often bring a man into spontaneous and happy relationship with his fellows. Even when he imagines that he is no more than a spectator, he cannot help sharing in other people's happiness. Often he likes to be the unobtrusive observer who is the hidden cause of the joy he sees around him: when he bought the poor street-seller's apples to distribute to the young 'savoyards', he witnessed 'one of the sweetest sights that can flatter the human heart— that of seeing joy, combined with the innocence of age, spread all around me' (ix. 1093).[1] Nothing gives him a greater thrill than to see the 'happy faces' of children and ordinary folk delighting in the simple pleasures of life. 'Innocent joy' is for him the most precious of all feelings. Although such pleasures must be mediated through the senses, they also have to contain a 'moral' element which enhances the enjoyment thus procured by bringing him into a direct emotional relationship with others. In spite of his resolve to remain henceforth 'detached from men and everything else', Jean-Jacques continues to the very end of his life to be haunted by a desire for the presence of others. The *Rêveries* thus confirm the testimony of his friends and his own earlier writings that he had a remarkable gift for understanding and sympathizing with the outlook of humble people.

These simple, expansive impulses were not enough to enable him to overcome the conflict and torment provoked by the thought of his persecutors. At any moment these ordinary folk, for whom he feels a genuinely human sympathy, may suddenly be transformed into secret enemies or else into spies whom his adversaries have sent to keep watch on him. The greeting exchanged with the old military pensioners soon gives way to the frightening thought that these men have been converted into implacable enemies who henceforth look upon him with 'the most violent hatred' (ix. 1096). Even they are soon absorbed into this mood which causes his mind to be for ever haunted by the thought of evil persecutors trying to defame and humiliate the 'good Jean-Jacques'.

Even though the reappearance of more normal human feelings sometimes enables Jean-Jacques to draw closer to his fellow-men, the paranoid symptoms are powerful and persistent enough to make it impossible for him to find a permanent solution to the problem of his personal existence in the sphere of human companionship. There he

[1] He also related the story to B. de Saint-Pierre (op. cit., pp. 90–91).

tends to remain a spectator, vicariously enjoying pleasures which can never form a completely integrated aspect of his own life. He is too completely withdrawn into himself, too convinced of his own desperate solitude to be able to establish satisfactory relations with others.

There are two important factors which help to diminish the effects of his persecutory anxiety. Although his enemies are—he believes—as implacable as ever, their refusal to leave him the slightest 'glimmer of hope' has caused them to 'exhaust all their resources' and at the same time allowed him to pass from a state of acute agitation to one of relative calmness. What was intended as the final torture has been transformed, by a strange reversal of fortune, into a means of consolation and inner peace. 'Freed from any new fear and delivered from the anxiety of hope' Jean-Jacques has at last (he thinks) been able to achieve that resignation of which he had already spoken at the end of the *Dialogues*. In this respect the *Rêveries* amplify the mood of the *Histoire du précédent écrit*. Thanks to his enemies he has now learned 'to submit to his fate without kicking any more against necessity' (i. 996). Henceforth he will be able to 'bear the yoke of necessity without murmuring' and to submit to his fate 'without reasoning or resisting'. He can now return to 'the order of nature' and become 'what it meant him to be'. Not a little comfort can be drawn from the religious conviction that these sufferings to which he has been so persistently subjected have been in some mysterious way willed upon him by Providence. 'God wants me to suffer and He knows that I am innocent' (ii. 1010). That is why 'I have resigned myself unreservedly and again found peace'. In the second place, although he realizes that his enemies' attitude is still as determined and ruthless as ever, he now feels liberated from the thought of his tormentors. Their physical reality is unchanged, but they no longer have the power to disturb his mind and penetrate his inner thoughts. He does not think of them as human beings, for they are often as 'nothing' to him, having become depersonalized and reduced to soulless automata, 'mechanical beings' moved only by physical impulse and whose actions can be understood only through the laws of motion; they are nothing but 'differently moved masses, deprived as far as I am concerned of all morality' (viii. 1078).[1] It is useless for him to worry any more about this desperate need for love which has hitherto dominated his existence; he is still the most 'loving' of men, but since men are henceforth 'nothing' to him, there is no reason for him to cling any longer to his old chimera.

[1] Cf. *CG* xx. 190, where he calls them *pagodes*, i.e. 'small Chinese ornaments, with nodding heads', and by extension, 'grotesque figures'.

Thanks to his enemies he has now learnt to accept the lesson of those inner contradictions and divisions which have exerted an ever growing influence upon his self-awareness. Especially does he recall memories of the 'social' Rousseau, who, after being temporarily subjugated by his life in higher society, has at last regained his natural mode of existence. The thought of those days is enough to remind him of the curious contrast he always experienced between his outward physical circumstances and his inner feelings. During the periods of material prosperity he was almost always unhappy, whilst poverty and neglect were accompanied by a sense of peace and security. At the beginning of the eighth *Promenade* he makes some interesting observations on this curious paradox:

The various periods of my brief prosperities have left me almost no pleasant memory of the intimate and permanent manner in which they affected me, and, on the contrary, in all the troubles of my life, I constantly felt myself filled with tender, touching and delightful feelings which, while pouring a wholesome balm on the wounds of my bleeding heart, seemed to transform pain into pleasure; I recall only the pleasant memory, freed from the ills I experienced at the same time. It seems to me that I have enjoyed more fully the sweetness of existence, that I have lived more completely when my feelings, compressed, so to speak, around my heart by my destiny, were not being evaporated outside on all the objects of men's esteem, which have so little merit in their own right and which form the sole occupation of people who are believed to be happy (viii. 1074).[1]

One of the reasons for earlier conflict may be traced to the evil influence of society which made him seek his happiness through 'pride' rather than in the spontaneous impulse of 'self-love'. If, in his old age, he attains a certain serenity in spite of his terrible isolation and suffering, it is because he has at long last regained something of his original character which brought him so much contentment during the 'first forty years' when he was 'trusting, loving and kind'. All of these themes had already appeared in the *Dialogues*, as we have seen, but in the *Rêveries* Rousseau remains less exclusively tied to a single mood and often allows his mind to dwell upon possibilities which have only a remote connexion with the principal paranoid reactions. These latter certainly persist, but as a constant accompaniment rather than as the main theme of the work.

Henceforth he is determined to accept his utter solitude, for 'he is a hundred times happier in this loneliness than he would be if he were

[1] Cf. *supra*, p. 21.

living in the midst of them' (998). It is time for him to 'put out his lantern'[1] and 'withdraw into himself' (viii. 1078). 'I rely henceforth only on myself'; 'reduced to myself alone', 'I have only myself as my sole resource' (1080). But encouraged by the thought that his happiness lies within himself, he draws no little comfort from the knowledge that his own personality offers abundant material for meditation and exploration. Cut off from his fellow-men, he now 'feeds on his own substance, but it is inexhaustible' (1075). Having in this way learnt to withdraw into and be 'occupied with himself', he is prepared to reopen the question of the meaning of his own existence. Unlike the *Dialogues* which are almost completely dominated by the desire to define his personal problem as that of a 'good' and 'innocent man of nature' in conflict with the machinations of the 'gentleman', the *Rêveries* actually emphasize the question: 'What am I?' in a way that enables him to draw out the positive implications of his lonely situation. Solitude is not a mere condition of separation (although to the very end Rousseau cannot overcome the anguish of isolation), but a state of individual self-awareness which leads ultimately to an affirmation of the self as a reality valid in its own right. His existence now has an absolute meaning for him, whatever the interpretation put upon it by other people.

Haunting the solitude of the lonely walker is the dream of complete personal fulfilment. He wishes to be 'fully himself, and himself without distraction and without obstacle, and in a state in which he can honestly say that he is what nature intended him to be' (ii. 1002). Indeed, as he looks back upon the past, he cannot forget 'that unique and short time of his life when he was fully himself without admixture and without obstacle, when he could truly say that he had lived' (x. 1098–9). These were fleeting moments whose reality is now guaranteed only by the often uncertain testimony of a failing memory, but they are the criterion by which all his present efforts at self-fulfilment must be judged. His mind reaches out beyond the oscillations and contradictions of his personality to a stable form of happiness—'a state in which his soul finds a solid enough basis to rest completely thereon and to gather together its whole being' (v. 1046). What he seeks is 'a permanent state' capable of providing him with 'that full, perfect and sufficient happiness' for which he has so often yearned but which he has never attained.

Moreover, this 'permanent state' must overcome not only the contradictions of his own nature but the fragmentation of the self in time. The temporal problem had not been an acute one in the *Dialogues* since

[1] Cf. for this phrase *Dial.* 792 and *CG* xx. 188 (cf. *supra*, pp. 221, 254).

external reality was there endowed with a kind of rigid if sinister permanence which reflected back to him a static double image—the 'evil' Jean-Jacques existing in the minds of the 'gentlemen' and the 'good' Jean-Jacques as he appeared to his own unclouded consciousness. The *Rêveries*, on the other hand, show us a self which—when it escapes from its obsession with universal hostility—is forced to grapple with an outside world that is constantly exposed to the destructive influence of time. 'Everything is in a continuous flux on earth; nothing preserves a constant, settled form, and our affections which are attached to external things pass away and change like them. Always ahead of or behind us, they recall the past which exists no more or anticipate a future which often is not to be: there is nothing solid to which the heart can attach itself. Therefore, here below we have scarcely anything but passing pleasure; as for lasting happiness, I doubt whether it is known' (v. 1046). That is why the hearts of most men remain 'anxious and empty'. The need to overcome this limitation of temporal existence acts as a powerful incentive to the quest for a sort of absolute, timeless fulfilment of the self in terms of values which transcend the vagaries of finite existence and yet preserve its concrete immediacy. It is not a question of abolishing time through some kind of otherworldly mysticism, but of dominating it in a way that endows its finite nature with a timeless plenitude. The 'moment' is thereby transformed into a kind of 'eternal present'. He seeks happiness in the form of 'a simple and permanent state which is not at all vivid in itself, but whose duration increases the charm to the point of finding supreme felicity in it' (v. 1046). Or, as he puts it expressively in the same *Promenade*, it is 'a condition in which time is nothing for the soul, in which the present still endures without nevertheless registering its duration and without any trace of succession, without any other feeling of privation or enjoyment, pleasure or pain, desire or fear than that of our existence alone and this feeling is able to fill it completely' .(ibid.).

Apart from the general difficulties involved in any attempt to achieve an ideal of this kind, Rousseau is faced with certain psychological hazards peculiar to himself, and until the very end a number of psycho-pathological elements are bound up with his search for personal happiness. The need to deepen intimate existential possibilities which had hitherto lain dormant or undeveloped leads to an intensification of personal consciousness which, as well as weakening his grasp on external reality, produces a definite distortion or exaggeration of elements within his own personality. This last phase of his life produces a marked 'hypertrophy of the ego' which replaces a properly balanced relationship with other people by an unhealthy preoccupation with the self as an object of thought and feeling. Rousseau is the more easily induced to retreat into self-absorption by his firmly rooted conviction that, as the object of a universal plot, he is excluded from the fellowship of other people. Moreover, he still clings steadfastly to the idea, already apparent in the *Confessions* and *Dialogues*, that his life and situation are remarkable for their uniqueness. The persecution to which he is subjected forms 'the most iniquitous and absurd system that the infernal spirit could ever have invented' (viii. 1077). Consequently he must submit to 'the saddest fate ever suffered by a mortal' (vii. 1073). Not only is he absolutely different in character from other men, but his condition is one which 'perhaps no other man would be able to face without terror'; he is 'in the strangest situation in which a mortal has ever found himself' (ii. 1002).

This determination to be 'occupied with himself' ultimately impels him to relate his striving for complete self-awareness to an ideal which he had intermittently pursued from his earliest years and which now re-emerges with particular vividness: the thought of attaining an absolutely pure and undivided selfhood and of feeling that he is completely and utterly himself 'without hindrance or division' is inseparable from the dream of luxuriating in an existence that is completely independent of any reality other than its own. The greatest bliss of which he deems any human being to be capable and which must surely (he thinks) be the crowning feature of the good man's life in the next world is to be *self-sufficient*. Fortunate is he who has been able to obtain a glimpse of such happiness in this world! This indeed is the great aim of his last years, the ultimate criterion by which the success or failure of all his efforts to attain self-fulfilment must ultimately be judged.

Rousseau hopes that the act of creating a work like the *Rêveries* will help him to draw nearer to this ideal, since writing has the great advantage of allowing him to be both subject and object: it helps him to create something which is himself and yet more than himself through its objectivity and permanence. Since he thereby opens up endless possibilities of re-reading his own thoughts, he will henceforth be provided with a means of self-communion which requires no other element but himself and his written words. He will be able to hold up more than a mirror to his own consciousness since what he sees is not a mere

T

physical reflection of his personality but a substantial embodiment which, in the truest sense, *is* himself and yet—because of its literary form—constitutes a reality capable of resisting all the vicissitudes of fortune and the assaults of time. The problem of grappling with others' existence is likewise transcended because Jean-Jacques now feels that he is creating his *alter ego*, the unique other with whom he can remain in personal contact. Moreover, he hopes in this way to overcome the gap which exists between present and past existence. Hitherto, as we have seen, his real wretchedness was partly due to his feeling that the happiest periods of his life were those of his early years, from which he now seemed to be for ever cut off; moments of tranquil recollection were too few and brief to provide him with a permanent means of identifying himself with his past life. Now, however, he hopes to create a kind of permanent incarnation of his own past experience and at the same time protect himself against all the uncertainties of the future. Moreover, he is opening up a relationship in which he can participate whenever he wishes. In this respect he is developing an idea which had already appeared in his first introduction to the *Confessions*.[1] The past is to become integrated into the present and to constitute an extra dimension of immediate experience. 'If', he says, 'I remain, as I hope, in my present frame of mind, the reading [of my reveries] will remind me of the pleasure I enjoy in writing them and, by thus bringing past time into being once again, will, so to speak, double my existence. In spite of men I shall still know how to savour the charm of companionship and I shall live with my decrepit self in another age as though I were living with a friend less old' (i. 1001).

Since the act of writing is tied so closely to the inner substance of the author's personality, it will be impossible to assess the value of this final effort at self-realization until we have explored the actual content of the *Rêveries*. But it will be already clear that Rousseau's last attempts to attain a stable form of self-awareness are going to be carried out within the limits of his own subjective experience. Still sustained by the thought of himself as a 'good' and 'innocent' man who has been terribly wronged by evil-doers, he now believes that he has been 'purified in the crucible of adversity' (i. 1000).[2] In himself he can find 'barely any traces of a reprehensible inclination', for 'never did premeditated evil

---

[1] Cf. *supra*, pp. 228 ff.

[2] 'Mon cœur s'est purifié à la coupelle de l'adversité.' We find the same phrase in the long letter to M. de Saint-Germain (*CG* xix. 257) where he says: 'Aujourd'hui que j'ai eu le tems de mettre par ma raison les iniques œuvres des hommes *à la coupelle* du temps et de la vérité. . . .'

ever approach his heart' (viii. 1075).[1] As far as others are concerned, he refuses even to be judged by them since, 'all earthly affections' having been 'torn' from his soul, he is left with this unalloyed goodness which makes him both lonely and unique.

Yet, as he delves more deeply into himself, he realizes that self-knowledge is not as easy to attain as he had at one time supposed. The most 'mechanical actions' may be determined by causes of which we are quite unconscious. He meditates upon a simple incident at the beginning of the sixth *Promenade* where he relates how his initial pleasure in giving money to a little boy encountered on one of his usual walks turned into such a vexatious duty, as soon as he saw that this generosity was expected from him as a matter of course, that almost unwittingly he found himself seeking another road. He suddenly sees that 'the real, first motives of most of my actions are not as clear to myself as I had for a long time supposed' (vi. 1051). Although Rousseau is often unwilling to accept the full implications of his own insights (as when he admits his own insufficient virtue), the *Rêveries* are full of penetrating remarks which indicate an extraordinary effort at self-analysis and sometimes anticipate the findings of modern psychology. Unusual sincerity and perspicacity thus mingle with surprising blindness, the result being a curious mixture of shrewd psychological insight and pathological delusion.

His natural inclination to look for happiness within the resources of his own being is strengthened by his belief that the mental and emotional deterioration of old age makes it difficult for his soul to escape from 'its senile envelope'. Lacking his former expansive power to transport himself into another world through the ecstasies of his imagination, he is thrust back more and more into the domain of personal *memory*. Even his imaginative flights contain far more 'reminiscence than creation' (ii. 1002).[2] 'I no longer live except through memory', he declares. Although memory may now replace the more creative aspects of imaginative activity, it can never, in a man of Rousseau's character, be free from all imaginative content. The very fact that he is now turning towards the past as a means of escape from the anxieties of the

---

[1] Cf. also his statement to Dusaulx (quoted Monglond, op. cit., p. 48). 'I was a man, and I have sinned: I have committed grave faults which I have fully expiated, but never did crime approach my heart. I feel that I am as just, good, virtuous as far as any man can be on earth: that is the reason for my hope and my security.'

[2] Cf. *OC* i. 1770, where it is pointed out that 'reminiscence' according to Condillac is an *involuntary* memory. See also M. Raymond's article, 'Deux aspects. . . .', in *Annales*, xxix, 1941–2, pp. 6–57.

present suggests that his reminiscences will be partly inspired not only by his own consciously confessed escapist needs but also by those emotional drives which lie beneath the surface of his immediate awareness. He seeks, for example, to live within a world of memories embellished and idealized by various emotional and imaginative influences. The past is recalled and re-created in such a way as to provide support for a view of himself as a wronged or innocent man or else as an unhappy man who was once contented in his surroundings. The memory theme is here linked up with the idea of the happy 'first forty years' which played such an important role in the *Dialogues*. The recollection of his happiness with Mme de Warens or on the Île de Saint-Pierre will give substance to the idea of his innocence by filling it with a kind of concrete content and relating it to the memories of his past life.

Unfortunately this piece of escape-mechanism is defeated by its own methods. Since memory is not entirely dependent on the conscious will, the images evoked are not always those which the mind consciously seeks, but represent involuntary memories originating in the deeper affective levels of the psychic life. The influence of involuntary memory is further increased by the simple fact that the idealization of the past results partly from an effort to avoid a mental conflict which, if admitted to consciousness, would give rise to persistent fear and anxiety. Since, however, Rousseau's idealized memories are tied to factual memories, they also tend to revive feelings of guilt and remorse associated with the unhappy past. That is why the *Rêveries* are not limited to the idyllic accounts of Mme de Warens and the Île de Saint-Pierre but also include anguished memories of the servant-girl Marion and his abandonment of his children. The intrusion of these unhappy memories is sufficient to disturb the peace which Rousseau seeks to achieve through the process of idealization.

Sometimes he attempts a purely *imaginary* solution to the problem of finding personal happiness. By withdrawing from the sphere of both present and past experience, he tries to create a state of mind which will remove him completely from the source of emotional conflict. He again has recourse to the familiar device of constructing a fantasy world inhabited by 'imaginary beings' and the 'children of my fancies whom I have created after my own heart and intercourse with whom sustains my heart's feelings' (viii. 1081). In this way he is able to indulge in emotions associated with 'the happy, gentle life for which he was born'. Sometimes the imaginative activity is more complex and seeks a solution which recognizes and tries to overcome the ambivalence of certain feelings. To escape from the dilemma of an attitude which asserts that happiness can be attained only through solitude and self-sufficiency and which also admits the necessity of human relationships, Rousseau invents the curious device of imagining himself as a man endowed with the magic power of Gyges's ring and so able to become an invisible and omnipotent observer of his fellow-men upon whom he can wreak his benevolent but capricious will (vi. 1057–8). Such moments, however, offer no more than a temporary escape from his unhappiness; not only is the pressure of immediate environment and conflicting emotions too great to be ignored, but his imagination itself is losing much of its former power to sustain him in the world of his illusions.

Since subjective feeling cannot by itself provide the means of attaining permanent happiness, Rousseau is compelled to go beyond purely psychological data. Neither the delusional system, which fashions a distorted image of other people in accordance with the self's subconscious impulses, nor the more normal escape-mechanisms of memory and imagination are able to guarantee their own reality; the personality has to discover a deeper level of consciousness capable of supporting it against the shifts and changes of everyday life, and this, in its turn, involves a modification of its relationship with the outside world: the enhancement of self-awareness inevitably leads to a more sensitive perception of external reality. The first and most obvious point of contact between the self and the world is the realm of sense-experience, for Rousseau accepts the current eighteenth-century view of sense-experience as a predominantly passive attitude through which the consciousness allows itself to be moulded by the 'impressions' which impinge upon it from outside. Jean-Jacques admits that he now enjoys the charms of 'sensation' more readily than those of pure memory and imagination. He frequently admits his dependence on his senses; he is 'always too much affected by the objects of sense' (ix. 1094) and, 'dominated by my senses, whatever I may do, I have never been able to resist their impressions' (viii. 1082). 'I no longer have anything but sensations' and 'my ideas are nothing but sensations' (vii. 1068). This means that his aspiration towards self-sufficiency is at the mercy of his senses which, by relating him to the external world, ultimately involve him to some extent in circumstances beyond his control. Whilst his inner anxiety compels him to move towards the world of sense, it prevents him from adopting a consistent attitude towards the very sense-experience upon which he becomes increasingly dependent. Sometimes he considers that his senses constitute his life's torment:

hostile looks are enough to intimidate him and, as long as men can act upon his senses, he feels that he is within their power. This susceptibility also reacts upon his imagination which, constantly affrighted, exaggerates the dangers threatening him. At other times he acknowledges that sense-experience can be a source of intense happiness. Great is his delight when he is surrounded by pleasant natural objects which allow him to abandon himself to 'light but pleasant sensations'. The pleasures of botany spring largely from 'the cheerful objects' which he encounters in his expeditions. This ambivalence is to be explained not merely by the contradictions of sense-experience itself but also by the fact that it is often inseparable from emotional factors. Already the *Dialogues* had stressed the close bond existing between his 'physical' and 'moral' *sensibilité*.[1] To give him complete satisfaction, the delights of the senses had to be associated with those of the heart, and it is undoubtedly the contradictions of Jean-Jacques's heart which help to explain the complexity and ambivalence of his attitude towards his sensations. He repeats in the *Rêveries* his earlier assertion that sense-experience cannot be separated from 'moral' considerations. Although 'the charm [derived from the sight of happy faces] seems to be solely one of sensation', it must also satisfy 'his heart' (ix. 1093). His senses act upon his heart, but his heart also acts upon his senses, and his heart is of course the source of much emotional strain. Although the realm of sense-experience is of itself unable to bring him lasting peace, the importance of sensations is very considerable since it is through them that he is put in touch with the external world, and especially with the realm of 'nature' which gives him so much delight. There, more than anywhere else, he can obtain a gentle but satisfying stimulation of all his senses. He goes to nature 'to run his eyes over the superb and entrancing view of the lake and its shores' (v. 1045); he loves the sensuous enjoyment provided by the various landscapes he traverses while he walks, botanizes, and dreams in picturesque surroundings.

The subtle interpenetration of sensuous and emotional elements means that Rousseau's feeling for nature was by no means a simple one. Perhaps it would be more accurate to speak of his 'feelings' for nature, since he approached her in various moods.[2] It is this need to relate his experience of the physical world to his own inner needs which has led critics to interpret Rousseau as a writer who transforms the natural

[1] Cf. *supra*, p. 17.

[2] In addition to the diversity of moods, we should also recall, as Professor Trahard had done (op. cit., p. 196), the relatively limited position occupied by the feeling for nature in Rousseau's work as a whole.

scene into *un état d'âme*.[1] At such times, it is alleged, he does not distinguish between his own personal emotions and the spirit of the landscape he is contemplating. One of his main reasons for spending so much time alone with nature during his last years was his fear of persecution: he hoped to find in nature a 'common mother' who would offer consolation and refuge to her 'children' in distress. 'I see only hostility on men's faces, and nature smiles at me always' (ix. 1095). In this respect he sought to satisfy through the physical world that yearning for the 'ideal mother' which had so often affected his relations with human beings.[2] The *Confessions* had already stressed the same theme—for example, his account of his stay on the Île de Saint-Pierre contains the significant admission: 'I would sometimes exclaim with emotion: "O Nature! O my Mother! Here am I under thy sole protection; here no cunning, two-faced man can come between us"' (644). The fascination of such experiences lies in the consoling thought that nature as a 'universal' or 'common' mother constitutes a reality greater than himself, a being into which he can allow himself to become absorbed without any fear of disastrous human consequences. Probably something of the same satisfaction—expressed more symbolically—accounts for his great love of lake-water, the stillness and translucence of which represent the recovery of innocence and purity with the consequent disappearance of all guilt and inner division.[3] The love of nature thus corresponds to a profound need for a kind of primordial unity, security and innocence which overcomes the fear and anguish still associated with his reactions to the hazardous world of human relations.

Rousseau's account of his rural excursions makes it clear that this is only one of the emotional pleasures he discovers in nature; his enjoyment does not always take the form of a passive, quiescent absorption in the 'common mother'. Just as at the psychological level withdrawal from others had alternated with a need to affirm himself, so does the feeling just described often give way to a more assertive and even aggressive reaction. Already in the *Lettres à Malesherbes* he had stressed his delight at the thought of being the first to explore a particular corner of nature. He loved to find 'some wild spot in the forest, some deserted spot where nothing showing me the hands of men would indicate servitude and domination, some refuge *which I might believe I had been the first to penetrate* and where no importunate third person

[1] Cf. D. Mornet, *Le Romantisme en France au XVIIIe siècle* (Paris, 1912).
[2] See *supra*, p. 25.
[3] Cf. for this theme in other authors, G. Bachelard, *L'Eau et les Rêves* (Paris, 1941).

came and interposed himself between nature and me' (1139–40). Even the 'maternal' pleasure derived from his stay on the Île de Saint-Pierre involved the idea of himself as a Robinson Crusoe (a figure for whom Rousseau always had a great affection) who had built up his own little world on an island of which he was the king. In the *Rêveries* a similar sentiment re-emerges, associated this time with the figure of another great explorer—Christopher Columbus. As he felt himself secure in 'a refuge unknown to the whole universe, one in which persecutors would not be able to root him out', he was suddenly filled with 'a movement of pride'. 'I compared myself to those great travellers who discover a desert island, and I complacently told myself: "Undoubtedly I am the first mortal to have penetrated thus far." I almost considered myself like another Columbus' (1071). At such times he feels a particular thrill at being the master of all he surveys. Occasionally an almost erotic note creeps into his reactions as he savours his power to deflower and possess such virgin territory: he experiences a strange excitement as he 'tramples underfoot' the unresisting flowers and shrubs.[1]

Often he abandons this psychological enjoyment of nature for a more metaphysical and religious satisfaction. It is true that he can no longer rise to his former ecstasies, his soul having lost that freshness and resilience which allowed it to soar into the infinite or else 'plunge headlong into this vast ocean of nature', for he now feels that 'he no longer has enough vigour to swim in the chaos of his former ecstasies' (vii. 1066). As he grows older and lonelier, he abandons this ecstatic approach in favour of a quieter and less exalted form of silent contemplation and inner communion. If 'lonely meditators like to become enraptured at their leisure by nature's charms', it is largely because of the many opportunities thus provided for *recueillement*.

But his enjoyment of nature still remains imbued with some religious meaning. He often refers, for example, to the natural scene as the expression of the divine order and the counterpart of man's immortal being (iii. 1001). This correspondence between man's religious nature and the spiritual scheme of the universe had always been of capital importance in his philosophy. Perhaps he now seeks a less specifically religious identification of his own personality with the physical universe, but it is still one that can provide rapturous pleasure as 'he loses

---

[1] Perhaps this feeling ought to be related psychologically to the important trait emphasized by M. Starobinksi in another connexion—Rousseau's desire to be at the centre and origin of an experience (op. cit., p. 127). As Rousseau's recent editors aptly comment his feeling for nature is both 'maternal' and 'nuptial' (*OC* i. 1851). At the same time, to feel himself the originator of a totally new experience helps to banish thoughts of guilt.

himself with delightful intoxication in the immensity of this beautiful system with which he feels himself to be identified' (vii. 1062–3). Or again, 'I experience inexpressible ecstasies and delights to merge, as it were, in the system of beings, to identify myself with the whole of nature' (1065–6). At such times 'his soul wanders and hovers in the universe on the wings of imagination in ecstasies which surpass all other enjoyment' (1062). The essential charm of such experiences is that they allow him to indulge in those expansive urges to which he had always been so sensitive. He is no longer limited to the circle of his own consciousness but seems to become lost in a reality far greater than himself. His whole being spreads out towards the objects around it. 'My expansive soul . . . seeks to extend its feelings and existence on to other beings.' The same feeling was experienced at the time of a serious accident on 24 October 1776, when he was knocked down by a large dog, for as soon as he recovered consciousness, he 'seemed to fill with his light existence all the objects I perceived [around me]. Completely absorbed in the present moment I remembered nothing; I had no distinct notion of my individual nature, had not the slightest idea of what had happened to me; I did not know who or where I was; I felt neither pain nor fear nor anxiety' (i. 1005). This latter experience is of course exceptional, but its general effect is the same as the more metaphysical enjoyment of nature: he feels that obliteration of all distinction between himself and his environment and the temporary loss of all sense of personal individuality. The burden of separate existence is suddenly lifted and his whole being is, as it were, diffused into all that surrounds him. 'I never meditate or dream more delightfully than when I forget myself' (vii. 1065). It is this sense of being identified with a whole of which he now forms an integral part that provides the peculiar fascination of these experiences.

Such moods, however, appear only sporadically either in the form of reminiscence or else as emotions which are soon merged into feelings of a more specifically psychological kind. He is sometimes reminded that these expansive impulses may be less pleasurable, especially when they are not directly related to the world of nature. Thus the eighth *Promenade* takes up in almost the same phraseology an idea of the seventh but gives it a completely different emphasis. After explaining the curious contradiction already examined between his inner state of mind and his physical circumstances, he recalls how the desire for happiness led him to indulge in those expansive moods of which he had spoken in the previous *Promenade*.

When everything was in order around me, when I was satisfied with all that surrounded me and with the sphere in which I had to live, I filled it with my affections. *My expansive soul extended itself on to other objects,* and incessantly drawn out of myself by all kinds of fancies, by pleasant attachments which did not cease to occupy my heart, I in some way forgot myself, I was completely abandoned to what was alien to me and I experienced in the continual agitation of my heart all the vicissitudes of human affairs. This stormy life left me neither peace within nor repose without' (viii. 1074–5).

Certainly this was the false kind of expansiveness, but the ecstatic identification with nature is often a mere substitute for the expression of more normal human emotions, and especially for the need for others. It is true that Rousseau was still capable of a spontaneous movement towards others, as we have already observed, but he was not prepared to adopt an attitude of genuine trust and reciprocity; his heart, ever dissatisfied and yearning for more than the world could give, made him turn to nature as a substitute for human relationships, but, as is already clear from the *Dialogues*, he would readily have given up the substitute for 'the thing itself' had human love been possible for him. At certain times also, he felt little interest in nature, as he admitted to Bernardin de Saint-Pierre, and it is easy for the reader to exaggerate— under the spell of the fifth *Promenade*—the place accorded to nature in the *Rêveries* as a whole. Indeed, nowhere more clearly than in his famous description of the Île de Saint-Pierre does Rousseau show his proneness to subordinate his feeling for nature to a preoccupation with the problems of his own inner life, for he there allows his description of the island's natural beauties to give way to an analysis of his own emotional condition.

Occasionally he is content to affirm the existence of a mere analogy between his own state of mind and the atmosphere of the landscape he is describing. This had been a characteristic aspect of his earlier descriptions of nature. It will be recalled that Saint-Preux had found the melancholy atmosphere of Meillerie, with its 'sad and horrible' mood, in complete conformity with 'the state of his own soul'; as he looked round him, he 'found everywhere in objects the same horror as reigned within himself'.[1] In the same way Rousseau himself saw in the bleak Derbyshire hills a reflection of his own unhappy condition.[2] In the *Rêveries* where he speaks—for example, in his account of the autumnal

---

[1] *NH* i. (Part I, Letter XXVI).
[2] The analogy need not be restricted to sombre moods. Mountains also suggest to him ideas of majesty and grandeur (cf. Trahard, op. cit., p. 199, for other examples).

countryside in the second *Promenade*—of 'a mingling of sweet and sad impressions too analogous to my age and fate for me not to apply it to myself' (ii. 1004), he is plainly conscious of the merely subjective character of the comparison. A similar attitude dominates his account of the 'herborisation' near la Robaila (vii. 1070-1), where the wildness of the scene seems perfectly attuned to his own mood. In each case, however, it is worth noting that natural description gives way to a preoccupation with personal feelings which have no connexion with the physical scene. In the first instance he goes on to reflect upon the meaning of his present position and state of mind. 'I was meant to live and I die without having lived. . . . I grew sentimental over these reflections, I again went through the movements experienced by my soul since the time of my youth' (ii. 1004). In the second case, he admits that 'a movement of pride' soon made him forget his interest in the beauties of nature.

Rousseau's feeling for nature thus covers a number of attitudes— and it is one of the charms of his work that it ranges so freely from mood to mood—but it is doubtful whether he was prepared to remain permanently identified with any of them. His everyday experience tended to be devoid of any metaphysical or mystical significance and he remained content with the sensuous aspects of his lonely walks. More and more did he rely on his sensations to give him pleasure. At the same time, we find that religion—apart from its link with nature— occupies a definite, if restrained, place in the *Rêveries*. The explicit efforts to relate religion to the study and contemplation of nature tend to appear as reminiscences of the formative years of his religious out- look since his observation that 'meditation in solitude, the study of nature, the contemplation of the universe compel a lonely man to move incessantly towards the author of all things and to seek with a gentle anxiety the end of all he sees and the cause of all he feels' (iii. 1014) refers mainly to the early part of his life when he was 'devout in the manner of Fénelon'. If he still feels these aspirations towards nature, it is as sporadic moods which are quickly absorbed into other feelings. For example, his remark concerning 'the congruence I perceive between my immortal nature and the constitution of the world and the order I see reigning in it' gives way to a development of a markedly paranoid char- acter, and, generally speaking, the religious impulse is not strong enough to detach his mind from the delusional system. Yet the mere fact that he was in the habit of re-reading his *Profession de Foi* shows how deeply attached he remained to his religious principles, although a study of the *Rêveries* as a whole suggests that, instead of expressing a single, consistent attitude, they reveal a number of diverse and often conflicting states of mind.

Of more immediate concern to Rousseau than earlier religious ecstasies in the presence of nature are thoughts of personal immortality, which are sometimes described as the ultimate and only means of consoling him in his misfortunes. Taken within the general context of the *Rêveries*, such remarks do not seem to have any deep influence in resolving the emotional conflict to which his personality is subjected. The assertion, for example, that, if he could recapture his earlier ecstatic reverie, 'his soul would often leap above this atmosphere and anticipate communion with the celestial intelligences whose number he hopes shortly to increase' (v. 1048–9) is plainly an imaginative flight into conditions of life which, as he frankly admits, will never be realized. On the other hand, it is only fair to say that, without these religious convictions, his mental state might have been very much worse than it was and that, although the relative tranquillity of the *Rêveries* is partly due to abnormal psychological conditions, it also owes something to a more direct and personal appreciation of the religious significance of his own life.[1]

The way in which the religious impulse is being constantly absorbed into the psychological pattern is interestingly revealed in several direct references to the idea of God. When God is mentioned by name, it is either as a being whose chief concern is to be interested in Rousseau's sufferings ('God is just; he wants me to suffer'), or else—and this is more usual—as a useful means of illustrating Rousseau's own character and attitude. By a curious reversal of roles God tends to be subordinated to Jean-Jacques! He sees himself 'as impassive as God Himself' (i. 999). In a state of reverie 'one [Rousseau] is self-sufficient, like God' (v. 1047). On another occasion he imagines himself as 'invisible and omnipotent as God' (vi. 1057). As well as indicating delusions of grandeur such remarks seem to illustrate that inclination to 'omnipotence of thought' which Freud attributed to children, neurotics and primitive people and which marks a state of mind that abolishes all distinction between wish and reality: unable to find satisfaction in the everyday world, the self moves into a domain of fantastic wish-fulfilment and forgets the limitations of its real life.[2] In Rousseau's case, this

---

[1] I should hesitate, however, to say with Professor Trahard (op. cit., p. 120) that the *Rêveries* 'mark the summit of this religious thought which strives to conceive of God' and present the 'mystical climax of his spiritual life'.

[2] Cf. *supra*, p. 32, for this 'primitive' side of Rousseau's nature.

mood is only a transient one and indicates an attitude which remains largely potential and imaginary; it never goes to the point of an absolute and deliberate identification of the personality with God, so often characteristic of genuine megalomania; it is rather as though he projects on to God those thoughts and feelings which he never succeeded in expressing in his actual existence—the need to dominate his environment and to control the tormenting presence of other people, and, above all, to attain the detachment and self-sufficiency with which the idea of inner peace seems to be increasingly associated.

This tendency to what may be called 'religious projection' is not entirely new in Rousseau, even in the specific sense of which we are now speaking. I have already suggested that when he was writing *La Nouvelle Héloïse*, he at times ascribed divine-like attributes to M. de Wolmar, the omnipotent and all-wise father-figure.[1] There admittedly Rousseau was not thinking consciously of himself, but inasmuch as Wolmar symbolizes his moral self or 'super-ego', he can be identified with an actual dimension of his own personality. Indeed, if the role of God remains somewhat ambiguous in that work, oscillating between a Supreme Being who satisfies all the soul's expansive longings and a stern, all-seeing eye which is ever watchful for deviations from the path of moral rectitude, it is because He is not entirely separated from the personality of Rousseau himself. There, of course, the link between Rousseau and God remains more indirect, especially when it is mediated through other characters in the novel, but it does seem to indicate the presence of a mood that is to become more important with the passing of time.

In the *Rêveries* God as the supreme moral agent has very little significance, for Rousseau is now reluctant to submit himself to the stern demands of ethical discipline and he develops a correspondingly greater need to see God as the object of contemplation rather than moral action. The memory of the heroic 'Genevan' ideal is now little more than a dream. At most he is willing to admit the need to be more 'virtuous' and to prepare himself for the next life, but such moods show little heroic determination to modify the course of his existence. However, it must be emphasized that the type of projective identification of which I have just been speaking does not form part of his *theological* conception of God's nature, which is far more rational and still corresponds to the ideas set out in the *Profession de Foi*. We are here dealing with an unconscious or half-conscious feeling which is due to the

---

[1] Cf. *supra*, p. 141.

general circumstances of his immediate life. But he does admit that his religious meditations now turn more naturally to the 'consoling' aspects of God's existence. He had always expressed sympathy for what he imagined to be the passive, quiescent religious attitude of Orientals; in his old age he is even readier to allow his religious feelings to accord with the spontaneous impulses of his temperament. This is scarcely surprising when we recall his attachment to 'natural religion' and his refusal to accept the fact of the Incarnation or the relevance of any revealed religion. Yet this means that when the inner feelings are weakened and distorted, the religious attitude also suffers some modification and is even liable to become absorbed into the aberrant emotions themselves.

The religious element is, therefore, but a single, if complex, aspect of the *Rêveries*, and it is always important to distinguish between Rousseau's rational, didactic attitude and those moods which are of a personal and sometimes pathological origin. In any case, neither the feelings for nature nor the religious convictions are of themselves able to provide him with a fully satisfactory means of fulfilling his fundamental desire for 'a sufficient, perfect and full happiness' capable of overcoming all the limitations of temporal existence. These experiences are too partial or transitory to provide an unshakeable basis for his inner life. His constant need is for a 'permanent state' which will carry him beyond the uncertainties of time while allowing him to enjoy a kind of 'eternal present'. It is this ideal which constitutes the meeting-point at which all the various dreams of perfect self-fulfilment ultimately converge. If it could be realized, he would overcome the fatal tension between subject and object which so often threatened to disrupt his earlier aspiration towards complete self-awareness: such a state would not be completely 'objective' because it would form part of the self; on the other hand, though personal, it is more profound than the subjective states so far examined because it imbues the present moment with something of the quality of eternity itself.

As he ponders this idea which—if it were achieved—would give perfect expression to this dream of self-sufficiency, he is convinced that he must seek a level of consciousness far deeper than that of the prideful 'reflection' which moves constantly in the world of division and differentiation. Though such a highly privileged state of awareness is vouchsafed to very few men, Jean-Jacques does not think that it conflicts in any way with the possibilities of 'original' existence. He had always believed that man was essentially a 'lazy' being who delighted in the spontaneous expression of his primordial nature. No doubt the life of a truly 'moral' being was inseparable from a rational participation in society under the ægis of the 'law' and the 'general will', as he explicitly insists in the *Contrat Social*: this 'social' existence represents a higher personal unity which every human being has to win both individually and collectively through an effort of will. But in one way man is thereby striving for an ideal which 'primitive' people achieve without effort—the perfect coincidence of desire and capacity. 'Civilization' involves a 'fall' from a state of primeval innocence, from a sort of paradise in which the individual effortlessly identified himself with the intrinsic potentialities of his being. Unlike his unsophisticated predecessors, modern man has been diverted from the fulfilment of his 'original' nature by the creation of false needs and desires which have transformed *amour de soi* into *amour-propre*. While there can be no question of a historical reversion to primitive conditions which—as far as Western Europe is concerned—have vanished for ever, there is a lesson to be learnt from a consideration of the 'state of nature' which goes far beyond any of its particular historical or pseudo-historical manifestations: what primitive man does instinctively at the level of mere sensation, social man must learn to achieve with the help of more highly developed faculties—namely, identify himself with all the 'natural' capacities and possibilities of his being. Only in this way can he hope to be 'restored to himself'. In each case, the aim is the same—to experience 'the feeling of existence' which, for the primitive, is the coincidence of consciousness and sensation and, for modern man, of consciousness and a pure sense of selfhood. This goal will never be reached until man has succeeded in cutting through the tangle of pride and egotism, of false reflection and unnatural passion so characteristic of modern life, thereby recovering the basic truth than his natural state as a 'passive, mortal being' is not one of anxious, restless striving for the attainment of some practical object but to 'delight (*se complaire*) in the feeling of existence', in a fundamentally affective and so ultimately contemplative condition which precedes all active striving for particular finite ends.[1]

Rousseau had always been inclined to follow a life of contemplation rather than action. His 'lazy' temperament which made him 'quick to desire but slow to act', as well as his inveterate shyness, drove him still more deeply into himself. Although ambition had for a time diverted him from the promptings of his true nature, he had eventually returned

[1] Cf. the very important posthumous fragment reproduced in *OC* i. 1801 and already quoted and commented upon by P. Burgelin, op. cit., p. 136.

to his love of contemplation, especially after his withdrawal into the country had provided him with wonderful opportunities for solitary meditation and carefree reverie. Yet the earlier accounts of reverie (for example, those of the *Lettres à Malesherbes*), while extolling the delights of the mood, had tended to lack precision, and it was not until he wrote the *Confessions* and the *Dialogues* that he began to analyse it with greater care. In the *Confessions* he had already described the Île de Saint-Pierre as a refuge perfectly suited to his love of peaceful seclusion and idle contemplation. The *Rêveries* again deal with this phase of his life, but give it a more metaphysical emphasis.

He is now far less concerned with describing the physical details of his stay on the island than with presenting a final crystallization of his experience of reverie. The Île de Saint-Pierre is merely a starting-point for the analysis of a mood having a much deeper significance. It is true that the state of reverie can always be most easily enjoyed against a picturesque background, but it cannot be interpreted simply as a more intense version of the feeling for nature. The function of the external world is to 'fix the senses' and so to drive 'all other agitation' from the soul by gently occupying the sensuous part of his personality and relating it (though not too intimately) to the surrounding objects. 'The uniformity of the continuous movement which rocked me' [he wrote at first 'of the movement of the feeling which dominated me'] is accompanied by a corresponding mental movement taking the form of evanescent thoughts about the meaning of life or of 'some faint and brief reflection upon the instability of this world's affairs' (v. 1045). Neither the physical movement nor the 'inner movements' constitute by themselves the state of reverie, but their co-existence, which leads to a 'continuous' movement, is enough to set free the deeper level of the personality for the enjoyment of its own existence. The precise nature of this ultimate experience—the state of reverie itself—is too intangible and absolute to be described. As 'the feeling of his existence', it detaches a man from all conscious contemplation of the external world and any awareness of ordinary individuality. It is remarkable inasmuch as it brings him closer to that divine self-sufficiency after which Rousseau had always hungered. As long as this state of mind lasts, 'one is self-sufficient, like God'. 'The feeling of existence, emptied of all other affections, would alone be enough to make this existence dear and sweet to the man who can put aside all the sensuous and earthly impressions which incessantly come to distract and disturb our pleasure here below' (v. 1047).

At first sight the state of reverie seems to have the great advantage of enabling Rousseau to overcome the anguishing problem of time. He at last seems to have attained an absolute and ultimate experience in which 'time is as nothing for the soul' since he does not have to 'recall the past' or 'reach out to the future'; no longer need he be tormented by his 'affrighted imagination' which constantly anticipates future danger by 'carrying everything to extremes'; nor is he now filled with a hopeless longing for what might have been, had his past life been different. His personality has at last attained a perfect rhythm which reconciles continuous duration with temporal succession in a way that allows the self, as it concentrates on the immediate enjoyment of its own existence, to expand the *moment* into a kind of absolute plenitude that is independent of all external and adventitious circumstances. In reverie, then, he seems to have found that 'permanent state', that 'solid basis', for which he had been striving so long.

Moreover, reverie is ultimately independent of any particular natural setting, for Rousseau points out that, when a favourable physical background is lacking, certain psychological conditions may be an effective substitute. The main danger is that, in the absence of a physical background that can effectively engage the attention of the sensuous self, the personality may fall into a state of complete lethargy. To prevent this Rousseau insists that the gentle movement necessary for the inducement of reverie must be produced 'inside him' and not outside. He emphasizes the point by saying—no doubt with humorous exaggeration—that reverie can be achieved in the Bastille and even in a dungeon (v. 1048).[1] (Perhaps this was one of the reasons which led him to ask the Berne authorities to allow him to spend the rest of his days in one of their prisons!) A fertile and lonely island is, of course, the ideal setting for reverie, because it has the advantage of facilitating the return to everyday existence by enabling him to 'assimilate' the 'fictions' of reverie to the pleasant objects of the physical environment. Should, however, such conditions be lacking, the experience of reverie is not thereby rendered unattainable.

The lack of homogeneity discernible in the earlier attitude towards religion and nature is also apparent in the case of reverie. Although the 'feeling of his existence' is unique and irreducible, Rousseau admits that he is no longer capable of experiencing it in its original perfection. Moreover, it is important to recall that the perfect reverie described in the fifth *Promenade* is in fact a *memory* of a previous emotional

---

[1] Cf. also *LM* 1132 (Letter of 4 Jan. 1762) for a similar idea.

U

experience which may have become idealized and embellished through the process of later reflection. In a sense, therefore, the reverie of the Île de Saint-Pierre remains an imaginative possibility which was never experienced in exactly the same way as Rousseau describes it; it is a re-creation of the past rather than a concrete reality of the present. From this point of view it does not appear to represent Rousseau's final answer to the problem of his personal existence, even though it was to exercise such an extraordinary fascination for a later Romantic generation. A close study of the text shows very clearly the development and embellishment of the experience through the process of writing. For example, Rousseau at first describes reverie as an 'occasional' mood and then, upon further thought, makes it a 'frequent' one.[1] In any case, he realizes that he can no longer recapture his earlier bliss in all its fullness, so that he is reduced to enjoying the memory of the experience rather than the experience itself—and, as has just been suggested, the mere fact that it is a memory seems to enhance the quality of the original feeling. In any case, he will henceforth have to be satisfied with reverie of a less exalted kind. Whereas the previous state was so ethereal that the physical world seemed to dissolve away before *le sentiment de l'existence*, with the result that 'physical objects often escaped his senses', Rousseau now proposes to seek a kind of hybrid substitute in which 'abstract and monotonous reverie' is enlivened by 'charming images'. Whatever the happiness brought by this type of reverie—and he says that his physical condition and his languishing imagination make it impossible for him to attain it except on rare occasions—it is a less pure experience than the 'feeling of his existence' and can scarcely offer an adequate solution to his personal problems.

Even though reverie seems in retrospect to have been such a perfect mood, the very fact that its perfection belongs to the past—as well as his own admission that he 'is less enraptured [than formerly] by the delirium of reverie' (ii. 1002)—means that it is not now 'a simple and permanent state' but a sporadic emotion which has no power to fill his actual life. In spite of the occasional feeling of having found a kind of eternal present characterized by the sense of self-sufficiency, Rousseau is constantly flung back into temporal existence with all its disadvantages and limitations. The pleasures of memory are being constantly eroded by the flow of everyday life which bursts in upon the quiescence of reverie and *recueillement*. In fact, all the attitudes so far examined—the subjective escape mechanisms of imagination and memory, the desper-

[1] Cf. v. 1046(*d*) and manuscript variation.

ate attempts to find adequate substitutes for living relations with others, the feeling for nature, religious experience and the state of reverie—are too far removed from the source of conflict to offer a lasting refuge from unhappiness. Moreover, in spite of the difficulties created by his paranoid feelings, Rousseau's sincerity is great enough for him to remain dissatisfied with any attitude that does not engage his whole being.

Whether he explicitly acknowledges it or not, no mood can bring him permanent peace which fails to resolve the tormenting problem of guilt. Satisfying one part of his nature, these various existential attitudes leave unresolved the conflicts of his moral conscience. In spite of his oft proclaimed determination to renounce all intellectual activity, he is constantly analysing and reflecting upon his own inner life and, almost unwittingly, he is led to transfer his personal problem to the plane of philosophical speculation. Moral philosophy therefore has an important role in the *Rêveries* because it enables Jean-Jacques to indulge in his feelings and yet subject them to study and analysis. A re-reading of one of his favourite authors, Plutarch, also reminds him that individual problems can be related to those of other men, or at least to the general considerations which ought to apply to other men were they really human beings. By its appeal to general ideas, philosophy seems to lift individual issues from their particular setting and place them within the context of universal, objective principles. Moreover, Rousseau, as we have seen, was always convinced of the beneficence of the universal order, and there was in his case no question of an 'existentialist' re-creation of values which ran counter to the scheme of nature: although his own individual situation might plunge him into loneliness and suffering, he did not doubt that in some mysterious way Providence had a place for him in its ultimate scheme of things. Neither evil nor irrationality was an inherent feature of the universe as such, and since man's life was bound up indissolubly with the spiritual order that lay outside him (since there was, in Rousseau's words, 'a congruence between his immortal nature and the constitution of this world and the physical order he sees reigning in it'), it followed that the life of each individual man was inseparable from the life of the whole.

One of his main difficulties lay in the confusion created by the contemporary philosophical fashion which was content with principles having little relevance to the lives of the men propounding them. The doctrines of the *philosophes*, in so far as they were at all relevant to the needs of modern man, were 'depressing' and 'sterile' and, above all, typical of the intolerance and insincerity that characterized this sect.[1] In the third *Promenade* he again castigates the thinkers whom he had attacked so bitterly in the *Dialogues*. Not only are their professed ideas quite unsuitable to people who are in need of help and comfort, for we cannot even be certain of their real opinions. In so far as their outlook has any personal application, we may be sure, he implies, that it is inspired by selfish and unworthy motives. As for him, he needs a 'philosophy' which is objectively valid, and yet truly *his*; it has to embrace both 'the eternal truths admitted by all time, by all the sages, recognized by all the nations and engraved in ineffaceable characters in the human heart' and the particular needs of his own personality; it has to be 'consoling' as well as 'true'. That is why in these last years he has been more concerned with moral than with metaphysical truth. A system of thought which deals with non-human truths must remain dry and abstract and largely irrelevant to human existence. Rousseau himself needs a philosophical viewpoint which contributes to his overriding concern with personal *happiness*. Indeed, this had always been the general emphasis of his thought, and now that he was fast approaching the end of his life he felt a still more desperate need to find a philosophy which had value for a man who was 'feeding on his own substance and finding all his pabulum within himself'. His early conviction that he was unfitted for social life had already thrust him back into himself and helped him 'to know the nature and destiny of his being with more interest and care than he had found in any other man' (iii. 1012).

I have found many who philosophized much more learnedly than I, but their philosophy was, so to speak, foreign to them. Wanting to be more learned than others, they studied the universe to know how it was ordered, just as they might have studied some machine they had noticed out of sheer curiosity; they toiled to instruct other people, not to throw light on their own inner selves. . . . As for me, when I desired to learn, it was to know myself, not to teach others; I have always believed that before instructing others, one had to begin by knowing enough for oneself; and that of all the studies I have tried to make in the course of my life among men, there are scarcely any that I would not have made equally well if I had been imprisoned alone on a desert island for the rest of my days (1013).

Hence his attitude is clear: 'their philosophy is for others; I need one for myself'. His previous thinking already represented 'the most zealous and sincere researches which have perhaps ever been made by any

---

[1] Cf. *supra*, p. 241.

mortal' (1017). With the production of the *Profession de Foi* he at last reached 'the fundamental principles which were adopted by my reason, confirmed by my heart and which all bear the stamp of inner assent in the silence of the passions'. Although his ideas are supported by the previously observed correlation between man's 'immortal nature' and the external order, Rousseau ultimately derives his chief consolation in suffering from the conviction that he has found 'a whole body of doctrine that is so solid, so consistent and formed with so much meditation and care, so well suited to my reason, my heart, my whole being, and strengthened by the inner assent which I feel to be lacking in all the rest' (1018). It is this feeling which makes him so certain that he has found a truth capable of supporting him in his terrible misfortunes.

After giving the history of his intellectual evolution, Rousseau still acknowledges that the question of personal appropriation remains to be considered. It is not enough to have true knowledge, it is also necessary to make it part of one's daily life. To achieve this end he resolves henceforth to allow his existence to be circumscribed 'within the narrow sphere of his former knowledge'. In other words, he does not propose to embark on any more philosophical ventures, but will concentrate on acquiring 'the virtues necessary to his state'. Here we witness that curious process of expansion and contraction which marks Rousseau's inner life during these last years. After indulging in expansive feelings which seem at times to carry him into the celestial regions themselves, he withdraws into himself and focuses his whole attention on his inner spiritual and moral centre. He is induced to do this by the thought that he must soon lay aside his mortal body and take with him into the next life the 'soul' that has been shaped and tested by the trials and tribulations of his earthly existence. Clearly the acquisition of 'virtue' will be of more value to him in his last days than the search for impersonal knowledge. If he cannot leave life 'better' than he entered it, he can become more 'virtuous'. That is why the particular philosophical preoccupations of the *Rêveries* are mostly of a moral kind.

In so far as philosophy seems to do justice to both the subjective and objective aspects of human existence—in so far, that is, as it seeks to satisfy man's inner feelings and, at the same time, put him into contact with universal principles, Rousseau appeals once again to his idea of the 'conscience' or 'moral instinct' that had figured so prominently in the *Profession de Foi*. The *dictamen de la conscience* and the impetus of the moral instinct have always been enough, he insists, to solve his personal problems, since his conscience has never lost its 'pristine integrity' (iv. 1025). Now conscience has the advantage of being intensely personal (each man's conscience is his own) and yet infallible (for it gives direct insight into the objective meaning of every moral situation and so raises it above the level of merely subjective decisions). In his present situation Rousseau feels all the more justified in trusting his moral instinct as his innocence and goodness allow him to abandon himself almost without reserve to the natural inclinations of his temperament.

How, then, is he to account for the feelings of guilt and remorse by which he is constantly haunted? How is it that such a 'good' man has been led into wrongdoing? Rousseau explains that his past misdeeds were never due to a deliberately evil intention, for 'he has in his heart the seeds of no harmful passion' and he has only to 'withdraw into himself' to ascertain that 'he is without any evil inclination in his heart'; all his past errors were the result of shame, shyness, and embarrassment—in other words, of psychological impulses which have no genuinely moral significance, even though they can influence a man's conduct in certain circumstances. This view, already put forward in the *Confessions* and *Dialogues*, is confirmed by his references to the familiar idea that true character is the expression of *amour de soi*, whilst aberrations are due to the activity of *amour-propre*—that unnatural feeling which lets the self be dominated by passions and self-interest and which is ultimately the product of an artificial social environment.

However consistent Rousseau tries to make it, he cannot remain permanently satisfied with such a viewpoint. It may not be difficult to be 'good' because 'goodness' largely consists in following nature and the moral instinct, but does not true morality also require, as he has previously admitted, the practice of virtue? Now this is something he has never been able to carry out, so that, although he thinks that his unique situation justifies him in abstaining from action, he admits that this is a 'weakness' and that it is his duty to be more 'virtuous' than he is. Ought he not then to admit that it is not enough to attribute wrongdoing to mere shyness and shame, since virtue requires us to overcome the influence of such feelings?

Nowhere is the ambiguity of Rousseau's attitude revealed more clearly than in the fourth *Promenade*, which takes the form of an apparently rigorous logical and impersonal examination of the problem of lying. Like all the *Promenades*, however, this one owes its inception to personal events in the author's own life—in this case, to a reading of Plutarch and the chance encounter of the quotation *Vitam vero im-*

pendenti in 'one of abbé Rozier's journals', which, by reminding him of
the motto so proudly inscribed at the head of his own writings, makes
him ponder once again the problem of truth and falsehood. He is now
aware that, in spite of his previous resolve to tell everything about himself in the *Confessions*, self-knowledge is a more difficult pursuit than
he had at first imagined: he realizes—and the point is a vital one—that
it is not enough to *want* to be sincere with oneself in order to be so.
His disquiet is further increased by the intrusion of a painful memory
concerning an incident in his youth—the 'frightful lie' which had
resulted in an innocent servant-girl, Marion, being accused of and condemned for a theft which Jean-Jacques himself had committed. Yet he
had felt no real hostility to this girl and no desire to hurt her: his act had
been due entirely to 'false shame'. It was *un délire* which was the result
of his 'shy nature' overcoming 'all his heart's wishes' (iv. 1024–5). One
beneficial consequence of this incident was, he thinks, the profound
aversion for lying he has experienced ever since that time. Indeed, so
great has been his subsequent passion for truth that he has never
hesitated to 'sacrifice my security, my interests and my person with an
impartiality of which I know of no other example among men'. Nevertheless, he is conscious of having lied gratuitously on a number of
occasions when such an action seemed quite pointless since it brought
no profit to himself. At such times he had lied with such *gaîté de cœur*
that he afterwards experienced no remorse or repentance for his ill-
doing. How then could a man like Jean-Jacques, with his extraordinary
devotion to truth and his sensitive conscience and sound moral instinct,
have been led into such bizarre and inconsequential behaviour?

At this point Rousseau seeks to resolve the personal problem in the
light of general principles about truth and deception. In this way
clarification will, he hopes, also bring reassurance. In the course of
his ingenious, if sometimes sophistical, argument he is careful to choose
those principles which are likely to be most consoling for his own
state of mind. He affirms that he has read 'in a book of philosophy'
that 'to lie is to conceal a truth that ought to be made plain' and that,
consequently, 'to keep silent about a truth that one is not obliged to
utter is not to lie'. It thus seems to Rousseau that any man who 'in such
a case' is not content to remain silent, but actually says what is contrary
to the truth is not really lying, since he is doing harm to nobody!
Clearly Rousseau's conception of truth-telling and lying is defective
since he ignores the fact that lying involves a positive intention to
deceive; lying may involve also the concealing of truths that ought to

be revealed (as he says) but this is only one aspect of a more fundamental question attitude which involves distortion and falsification as
well as mere concealment. However, Rousseau conveniently ignores
this wider issue in order to hasten on to his 'consoling' but unacceptable
conclusion that a man is not really lying when he is not hurting anyone.

He then goes on to establish a fundamental distinction between two
kinds of truth—'general and abstract truth', which is 'the most precious
of all goods' since it is 'the eye of reason' without which man must be
for ever blind, and 'particular and individual truths' which, having a
purely utilitarian function, are not always good since they may vary in
their effects, being sometimes harmful and sometimes quite indifferent.
Here again Rousseau conveniently chooses a principle which allows
him to draw a conclusion that satisfies his emotions rather than his
intellect. He argues that since 'useless and otiose truths' have no moral
significance, we 'profane the sacred name of truth' if we apply it to such
'examples'; when truth is deprived of all utilitarian importance it is not
something that is 'due', and to suppress it is not to lie. Plainly, this
dubious conclusion depends largely on an unsound premise since the
facile distinction between 'general' and 'particular truths' is not as
obvious as Rousseau supposes. He himself ignores any such objection
and insists upon the idea that truth-telling depends primarily on the
question of utility. But how is utility to be understood? How is a man
to distinguish between what is due to others, to himself and even to
truth itself?

Characteristically, Rousseau does not seek to resolve this difficulty
in the light of the principles just enunciated but invokes a new principle
that many readers familiar with his outlook might well have expected
to see appear much earlier—namely, the idea of the moral instinct or
conscience. He affirms that, whenever he has been confronted by moral
difficulties, he has always listened to the voice of conscience, to that
infallible *dictamen* which can always be relied upon to illuminate the
most impenetrable darkness. Who, more than Jean-Jacques, has been
fortunate enough to preserve the full purity of this moral guide? Now
as soon as his argument moves back to the plane of personal experience,
Rousseau seems to show an honesty which was markedly lacking in the
more abstract discussion, for he seeks to extend his argument by introducing an idea which at first seemed to be rigorously excluded by his
emphasis on the role of utility: this is the principle of *intention*. However, he does not thereby repudiate the early notion but tries to combine the two in such a way as to allow him to retain both! False speaking

becomes lying, he maintains, 'only through the intention to deceive and even the intention to deceive, far from being always connected with the intention to harm, sometimes has a completely contrary aim' (1029). This leads him to a further conclusion. 'To lie for one's own advantage is imposture, to lie for others' advantage is deceit, to lie in order to hurt is calumny—and that is the worst kind of lie. To lie without profit or prejudice to oneself or others is not to lie: it is not lying but fiction.' Inasmuch as it does not concern justice, fiction is quite harmless and without moral significance. Rousseau seeks to amplify his point by considering at some length the question of literary fiction, thereby eluding the more fundamental moral aspects of this problem while seeming to take it seriously. Once again, his apparently 'objective' treatment of the whole idea conceals, as Félix Gaiffe points out in his acute analysis of this *Promenade*, a deep-seated desire to justify himself.[1]

It is not necessary to follow Rousseau in his criticism of Montesquieu's use of 'fiction' in *Le Temple de Gnide*, for this is a point of minor importance; more interesting is his attempt to give us a portrait of the genuinely 'truthful man'. He insists—with some force and insight—that there is a certain type of person whose truthfulness conceals a ruthless self-interest. As long as he is speaking about matters which do not concern him, such a man may be scrupulously accurate in all he says, but once his own interest is involved he quickly abandons this detached and impartial attitude. The truthful man is quite different from this kind of person:

... In perfectly indifferent matters, the truth which the other then respects so much moves him very little, and he scarcely has any scruples about amusing a social gathering with invented facts, from which there results no unjust judgement either for or against anybody living or dead. But any discourse which contributes to somebody's advantage or detriment, esteem or contempt, praise or blame against justice and truth is a lie which will never approach his heart, mouth or pen. He is firmly truthful, even against his own interest, although he takes very little pride in being so in idle conversation. He is *truthful* in that he does not seek to deceive anybody, is as faithful to the truth which indicts him as to that which honours him and never deceives anyone for his own advantage or his enemy's hurt. So the difference between my truthful man and the other is that the man of the world is scrupulously faithful to any truth which costs him nothing, but no further, and that mine never serves it more faithfully than when he must sacrifice himself for it (iv. 1031).

[1] *J.-J. Rousseau et les 'Rêveries du Promeneur Solitaire'* (Paris, 1936), pp. 88–96.

For such a man 'truth' and 'justice' are synonymous, and the truth which he 'adores' does not—any more than the morality he practises—consist of obedience to petty rules and formulae, but in giving each man his due 'in things which are really his'. If the reader had any doubts about the identity of this man, Rousseau would soon dispel them when he tells him that his hero is very jealous 'of his own esteem'—'that is the value that he can least do without, and he would experience a genuine loss if he acquired others' esteem at the expense of *that* value'. This true man is obviously none other than Rousseau himself who is merely summing up his own character when he says: 'He will sometimes lie in indifferent matters . . . [but] in all that appertains to historical truths, human conduct, justice, sociability and useful enlightenment, he will guarantee from error both himself and others as far as lies within his power. Any lie outside all this is according to him no lie' (1032).

This portrait, which is really a self-portrait, prepares the way for an abandonment of the field of general principle and a return to the circumstances of his own life. When he stresses that the 'criminal lie' uttered against Marion led to a high-minded devotion to truth, it is clear that even the preceding abstract discussion had really had a personal aim and the complicated structure of logical argument had been merely intended (as Gaiffe rightly says) as a means of bringing peace to a troubled conscience; his tortuous dialectic 'is only a desperate struggle against remorse'.[1] Certainly the last section of the *Promenade* reveals him trying to apply his general principles to his own particular case. He is now convinced that his crime against Marion was an exceptional act which left such 'ineffaceable remorse' in his soul that he was thereafter 'guaranteed not only against any lie of this kind, but against all those lies which might in any way at all affect the interest and reputation of other people' (1032). If he has lied subsequently, it has never been through principle or a deliberate act of will—for 'never did a premeditated lie approach my thought and never did I lie for my interest'—but only because of shame and embarrassment. In other words, he has never acted in accordance with 'rules' and abstract 'principles' but in response to the natural impulse of temperament. This explains both his moral elevation and his lapses. Yet even when he has fallen far short of the high standard he set himself, his lies were always against his own interest—not against that of other people. It was particularly in social gatherings, where he was compelled to keep

[1] Op. cit., p. 94.

up a show of polite conversation about trivialities, that he was apt to 'utter fables in order not to remain speechless' (1033). On really important occasions he has, he insists, always had a high regard for truth, and he points out that, when he came to write his *Confessions*, he often lied *against* himself in order that he might not seem to be presenting himself in a too favourable light. 'Yes! I say and feel with proud high-mindedness that I have carried good faith, veracity, and frankness as far as and even further (so at least I believe) than any other man has ever done; as I felt that the good outweighed the evil, it was to my interest to say everything, and I *have* said everything' (1035). If he has sometimes affirmed more than the truth, it was simply because of *le délire de l'imagination*; these additions were not really lies. As he was quite old when he wrote his confessions, his memory was often at fault and so 'I filled in the gaps with details which I imagined as a supplement to these memories, but which were never contrary to them'. 'I liked to dwell on the happy moments of my life, and I sometimes embellished them with adornments which were provided by tender regrets.' Then there is this 'singularity' of his character that he often related the unsavoury aspects of his life 'in all their turpitude', while he often kept quiet about his good deeds because he did not want to appear to be making his own eulogy. He goes on to relate two incidents from his childhood which he deems to illustrate this point.[1] Then he returns once more to his fundamental thesis. 'No! when I have spoken contrary to the truth which was known to me, it has always been in indifferent matters and more from embarrassment at having to speak or for the pleasure of writing than for any motive of self-interest or of profit and loss to others' (iv. 1038).

All this merely illustrates his earlier affirmation that his concern for truth has always sprung from 'feelings of rectitude and equity' and from the 'moral directions of his conscience' rather than from any devotion to abstract principle. Since truth is a virtue only when it brings no advantage to oneself and no harm to other people, it is in every other respect 'only a metaphysical entity from which there results neither good nor ill'.

It is obvious, therefore, that the long abstract argument of the fourth *Promenade* is inspired by an intensely personal motive, for Rousseau seeks in general principles a means of preserving the idea of his own essential goodness and innocence: he has often given way to weakness, but he has never sinned. The whole argument constantly circles around

[1] Cf. iv. 1036–8.

his own feelings of guilt without ever really allowing him to face the full consequences. Some of his most tormenting thoughts are associated with his abandonment of his children, but he cannot bring himself to speak openly of this question in his present mood. At the same time he feels a compulsion to bring up the question and so he introduces it, indirectly as it were, into his discussion of the embarrassments of polite social conversation. In this way he partially alleviates his feeling of guilt without fully acknowledging the extent of his own unnatural behaviour. In a more general sense the confusion of the philosophical principles involved—the appeal to the idea of utility and to that of intention—also betrays his uneasiness. Suddenly, at the end of his long and perverse argument, he confesses with a somewhat pathetic in-genuousness: 'Yet I do not feel that my heart is sufficiently satisfied with all these distinctions for me to believe that I am completely free from blame' (1038). He at once limits the significance of this admission by saying that he has not perhaps examined with enough care 'what I owed to myself' and what was due 'to my own dignity'. Even to amuse others he ought not to 'degrade himself'; nor ought he to have allowed the pleasure of writing to induce him to add gratuitous decora-tion to the simple truth. One who, like Jean-Jacques, adopts the motto *Vitam impendere vero* should be able to overcome such weaknesses. 'Never did duplicity dictate my lies, for they all came from weakness, but that ill excuses me.' However, there is perhaps still time for him to profit by past errors, for 'it is never too late to learn, even from one's enemies, how to be wise, true, modest and less presumptuous' (1039).

Rousseau's moralizing is not free from the ambiguity and incon-sistency which mark his other efforts to attain inner peace. (It is indeed significant that the following *Promenade* is a typical escape from internal conflict since it deals with his idyllic stay on the Île de Saint-Pierre.) The desire to find the truth about himself and the fear of facing it are strangely intermingled. In general the pressure of anxiety is too great for him to be able to achieve full insight; truth can emerge only if he abandons the thought of himself as an 'innocent man'; but this is im-possible, for such a conception of himself is his last protection against a catastrophic disruption of his whole being. The partial integration and contentment he has so far been able to achieve are derived from this view of himself as a 'good' man. If, therefore, some painful memory or feeling enters his mind, it must be 'explained' in a way that is consistent with this overall view of himself. Such was his reaction to the memory of the lie against Marion. The ninth *Promenade* deals in a similar way with the question of his own children.[1] If he abandoned them, it was not because of any evil impulse in his own nature but because he feared 'a fate a thousand times worse for them and almost inevitable through any other way [than that of putting them in a Foundlings' Home]' (ix. 1087). He still 'shudders' at the thought of what would have happened to them if he had left their upbringing in the hands of Thérèse and her infamous mother who would certainly have turned them into 'monsters'. Once again—and his earlier attempts to explain and excuse his behaviour have a similar purpose though the actual form of the argument varies— Rousseau refuses to accept full responsibility for a guilty act. Yet he is unable to push these guilty thoughts from his mind and his honesty compels him to admit that his character still stands in need of moral improvement. The inevitable result is that though his philosophizing gives some relief to his feelings, it cannot provide a permanent escape from conflict and his reasoning is constantly distorted by the pressure of personal feeling.

Perhaps the medium of moral philosophy was particularly unsuited to the intimate purpose of Rousseau's last writings, for, as he is constantly asserting, he seeks 'happiness' in a state of mind that will protect him from all inner division and torment. But the anxious desire for *truth* about himself may be incompatible with such an aim since it brings to the surface of consciousness thoughts of guilt and remorse which militate against his search for contentment. A certain nagging desire for sincerity and honesty—in addition to more abnormal pressures —brings him back again and again to ideas which have a disturbing effect upon his mind. He is torn between the need to find the truth and the desire to escape from it with the result that he is divided against himself. Reflection and philosophical thinking would thus seem to be the medium least likely to bring him the 'happiness' for which he strives.

In the tenth and last *Promenade* we find him preoccupied neither with the question of truth nor with the metaphysical and psychological aspects of reverie, but with concrete memories of his own past life with Mme de Warens. The date—12 April 1778—is Palm Sunday and the fiftieth anniversary of his first encounter with Mme de Warens. As he looks nostalgically back through the long corridor of time, the past becomes bathed in a poetic radiance which seems to give those far-off events a blissful perfection and effulgence which are all the sadder for

[1] Cf. *supra*, p. 77.

having been of such short duration. In those days he was little more than an adolescent and his soul, as he puts it, had not yet assumed 'any definite shape' (x. 1098): it was a plastic, malleable substance that needed only the impress of strong yet loving hands to mould it into a definite form. It was Mme de Warens who was most suited to provide that happy companionship, made up of 'love' and 'innocence', which alone could give his young life the basic inspiration it so urgently needed. 'Ah!' he writes sadly, 'if I could have been sufficient for her heart as she was for mine! What delightful and peaceful days we should have spent together!' The more he ponders on this 'short and rapid period' of happiness, the more deeply is he convinced that it was then—and then alone—that 'he was himself, completely, without admixture or obstacle'. Then alone 'could he truly say that he had lived'. For the rest of his life he has been the victim of forces stronger than himself; he has been so 'agitated, tossed about and torn by other people's passions' that he has rarely had the feeling of being a free agent. 'But during those few years, loved by a woman full of gentleness and compassion, I did what I wanted to do, I was what I wanted to be . . .' (1099). Thanks to her influence he was filled with 'the taste for solitude and contemplation' which fed on 'the expansive and affectionate feelings that were meant to be its aliment'. 'I needed a woman-friend after my own heart and I possessed her. I had desired the countryside and I had obtained it. I could not bear subjection and I was perfectly free, and more than free, for I was tied by my attachments alone. I did only what I wanted to do.' The pressure of immediate emotions upon his memory is such that all unpleasant aspects of those days are completely forgotten. He no longer recalls that he was not always so happy with Mme de Warens, that the presence of Wintzenried had greatly upset him, that he had been unfaithful with Mme de Larnage. . . . But now he does not feel the pressure of erotic impulse, powerful ambition, or the restlessness of youth; nor is he a Saint-Preux striving to possess some ideal Julie; no longer is he even the lonely meditator anxious to experience the ecstatic contemplation of God and Nature; he yearns solely for that quiet security, for that sense of being completely at one with himself, which could come only from the thought of abandoning himself to the trusting, almost filial devotion that marked his past relations with *Maman*. Only at that time did he feel that he was truly himself.

Yet we should probably not be justified in treating this particular memory as Rousseau's final answer to the problem of his tormented existence. This tenth *Promenade* was begun on 12 April 1778; Rousseau left for Ermenonville on 20 May and died on 2 July. It looks as though he could have finished this *Promenade* had he so wished (even when due allowance is made for the possibility that he was revising some of the others during this period). Instead of writing, he spent the last weeks of his life botanizing and walking. Whether he considered that botany was a far more satisfactory means of expressing himself than writing we do not know. What he says in the *Rêveries* about this hobby certainly suggests that it has considerable advantages over writing. Whereas writing is inevitably connected with the need to express something of his most intimate self and so exposes him to anxiety—for although it brings temporary relief to his emotions, the effort has to be constantly renewed—botanizing has the psychological advantage of allowing him to escape from the machinations of his persecutors and avoid 'the memory of men and the attacks of the wicked'. Having banished all painful thoughts from his mind, he can enjoy an innocent pastime that is so well suited to a man who feels himself to be 'forgotten, free and at peace'. The great attraction of botanizing as he pursues it is that it is an activity enjoyed for its own sake, without any scientific or utilitarian purpose; it makes no demands on his imagination or intellect, while preserving him from the dangers of melancholy and boredom. No longer able to plunge into 'this vast ocean of nature' or soar up into the celestial regions of the imagination, he can nevertheless attain a certain expansive satisfaction by 'extending' his being on to his environment: instead of contemplating nature *en·masse et dans son ensemble*, he now studies it in detail, though he insists that 'he learns in order to forget'. In other words, if he cannot now enjoy *ces chères extases* of earlier days, he has at least found a very agreeable stimulus for his sensations: it is a circumscribed and yet very positive form of enjoyment which satisfies his great love of walking, stimulates observation and curiosity and brings him into invigorating contact with a reality greater than his own. As he wanders among his rural haunts, he also recaptures something of the former pleasure of identifying himself imaginatively with Crusoe and Columbus, for he is discovering and in a sense creating his own world with a freshness and innocence that owe nothing to 'the authority of men'. In this way he forgets not only the attacks of his persecutors, but the oppressive influence of his own stifled sense of guilt and unworthiness. He has the fascinating illusion of watching the rebirth of his own mental and emotional existence as he fashions a new world out of the pristine innocence and richness of unspoilt nature.[1] This rebirth of his own world is largely due to his fertilizing contact with a nature that is virginal and pure and at the same time has the power to reflect back to him the beauty and majesty of its Creator. Moreover, the result of his botanizing excursions is in one way similar to his literary activity: the herbarium he collects and builds up for himself is a kind of *journal*, as he himself says, the subsequent contemplation of which will enable him to revive memories of all the pleasures derived from his various expeditions; he will be able to 'read' his plants in the same way as he has hitherto read his words and so be once more in the presence of an objective embodiment of his own personality strengthened and protected against the ravages of time.

This interest in botany suggests that the great hopes with which Rousseau started his enterprise were unable to sustain him to the end. At the beginning of the seventh *Promenade* he confesses that 'the collection of my long dreams is scarcely begun, and I already feel that it is drawing to its end' (vii. 1060). Writing was being abandoned in favour of botany. No doubt declining health and his removal to a new home were partly responsible for the triumph of his new 'amusement', but it seems that there is also a deeper reason related to the contradiction inherent in the whole project as he conceived it: all his efforts cannot succeed in transforming the act of writing into a genuine means of self-fulfilment. Although it represents a movement towards self-knowledge, as well as allowing him some measure of self-expression and justification, there is an important sense in which the work remains a mere pastime. The desire to flee from his enemies and the determination to be happy 'in spite of them' also reflect a desire to escape from himself. He tries to do this by creating an idealized self-portrait and by exploring attitudes which are ultimately related to his inner life; but all this remains a mere substitute for a truly personal decision. In this way he hopes to find 'rest' and so mask or appease the anxiety and security which are part of his real self. Unfortunately for him the act of writing and the feelings expressed through it are not strong enough to overcome the deeper causes of conflict and so bring permanent integration to his personality. He has indeed confessed the facts, as he rightly says, but he has not clarified the whole complex of emotions associated with them. Paradoxically, therefore, his earnest efforts to remember certain moments of his life and to be aware of himself as a particular kind of

---

[1] As M. Munteano points out in the interesting article already quoted (p. 116), Rousseau was always attracted by 'the moment of birth' and 'the phenomenon of second birth'. Cf. *supra*, p. 286 n.

man are bound up with a profound need to forget some of the actual past and the type of man he *really* is. In a more general sense this communion with his *alter ego* which he hoped to enjoy through the re-reading of his *Rêveries* could not be a genuine substitute for personal relations or an individual act of will. In living contact with others he might have been able to find some solace and support—as indeed he still did at given moments of his life—but in his heart he was convinced that there was only one 'good' man—himself—and that it was useless for him to seek another. He thus remains enclosed within the circle of his own thoughts and emotions, occasionally breaking through to the external world, but never achieving a settled and contented attitude towards his environment.

Nevertheless, his increasing interest in botany during the last months of his life does suggest that he was able to bring some relief to his troubled soul by subordinating the problems of personal life to a definite physical activity which absorbed most of his energies while still allowing him opportunities for the enjoyment of various forms of inner experience. The predominance of his botanical interests means that he is freed from the necessity of identifying himself completely with any specific mood or attitude. His main efforts being directed upon an objective reality of a physical kind, he can now luxuriate in a kind of dispersal of existence, a loosening of personal centre, which relieves him of the necessity of bringing order and consistency to his thoughts and emotions, although he can still enjoy them if and when he so wishes. It cannot be said that Rousseau has thereby solved the problem of his inner life by taking any final or definite decision concerning its ultimate significance, for he has had recourse to a much simpler solution—that of leaving it indefinitely in suspense.

X

CONCLUSION

ALTHOUGH the unfinished state of the *Rêveries*, with their incomplete enumeration of personal attitudes, suggests that Rousseau could not bring his quest for self-knowledge to a definite conclusion, perhaps any final 'choice' he may have made must not be sought in the personal writings themselves, but in his everyday mode of existence; his preference for the pleasures of the simple rural life implies that he ultimately accorded priority to experience rather than thought, believing that questions which were apparently unanswerable by means of meditation and reflection became less insistent as soon as they were absorbed into the activities of daily life.

However, as it is plainly impossible to make a complete break between thinking and experience, he must have carried over into the practical concerns of ordinary life some of the values he had struggled to make explicit through his writings. Indeed, throughout his career we have observed the complex interplay of writing and personal experience, and, in particular, the influence of his literary activity upon the elusive process of self-evaluation. The final adoption of a 'simple life' and his acceptance of himself as a 'man of nature' may have been intended as a defiant response to the pressure of intimate personal impulses which could not be satisfied by thinking and writing alone. In this way his life during these last years represents a sort of compromise with his most urgent psychological problems, and especially with the need to counter the (for him) disturbing fact of universal persecution.

As has already been suggested, freedom need not be accepted as an immutable quality that an individual possesses in some absolute manner, for it may express itself as a self-relationship involving the whole personality in its efforts to realize itself through the concrete circumstances of its own particular situation; as such, freedom may thus attain different modes and degrees of fulfilment, the nature of its ultimate emphasis being sought in the general movement and direction of a man's existence—in his personal 'style of life'. Naturally such a movement is meaningless apart from the individual acts and choices which give it substance, but as this shifting, complex pattern of particular relations and responses seems to be governed by a more fundamental 'intention' than is often discernible in their immediate circumstances, it is permissible to look for some value or 'ideal' which helps to give them cohesion and purpose. But this ideal must be interpreted prospectively as a basic choice towards which the personality moves rather than retrospectively as the result of a simple 'quality' it may be deemed already to possess; and because this ideal is after all a part of living experience and a goal of personal endeavour, its true significance may not be at once apparent and the individual himself may attain only a gradual understanding of the ultimate meaning of his efforts.

It would be erroneous to try to explain the connexion between Rousseau's delusions of persecution and his struggle for self-realization as the mere consequence of some kind of abnormal psychological determinism, because, if his conscious striving for self-expression is affected by his delusions, the meaning of the delusions themselves cannot remain uninfluenced by the values which affect other aspects of his behaviour. The literary elaboration of his paranoid condition with its heavily charged emotional tensions and evident dependence on earlier states of mind has sometimes led critics to interpret it exclusively in terms of its 'abnormal' psychological antecedents. These factors ought certainly to be taken into account, but it is equally important to realize that the act of writing itself, however 'paranoid' its mode of expression, is an *existential* act aimed at eliciting a specific emotional response from others and (ultimately) a genuine transformation of Rousseau's own personality. No doubt the first manifestation of this condition made it seem a highly idiosyncratic and disturbing personal act which those against whom Rousseau's wild charges were directed mistakenly accepted as objectively intended, factual statements capable of verification or (as they thought) refutation by public argument; consequently, they were treated either as the wild ravings of a lunatic or the wicked machinations of a criminal. But they were neither, for, as we have suggested, Rousseau's terrible accusations were an indirect expression of his need for others; if he seemed to repel them, it was only to draw them more closely to him with (as he hoped) renewed devotion and fervour. He behaved in this way because he was incapable of expressing his need directly, his feelings for others being inseparable from a tormented form of self-evaluation in which other people were meant to contribute to his own need of assurance and esteem, and especially to his need to see himself as a 'good' and 'innocent' man. He was not immediately concerned with the impersonal 'truth' of what he said (although the indifference or hostility of others unfortunately forced him on to the defensive and made him try to prove the 'facts' of the case), but with establishing a satisfactory kind of personal relationship with other people and his own inner self. That this aspiration remained unfulfilled was, from one point of view, the great tragedy of his life— the cruel misfortune of a man overwhelmed by the 'need to love and be loved'.

It was the failure of this attempt to establish deeper personal contact with others which impelled Rousseau to seek refuge and consolation within himself. 'Reduced to himself as his sole resource', he strove to be happy 'in spite of them'. But the constant presence of this defiant 'in spite of them' reveals the compensatory nature of his striving, so that the most personal of his writings, the *Rêveries*, which he claimed to be composing for his own pleasure and nothing else, are still haunted by the ghost of the 'others'. With them is associated not merely the idea of animosity and hatred, but also an anguished awareness of their power to perpetuate the idea of an evil Jean-Jacques; the need to destroy this false image by the simple process of substituting for it a portrait of the 'good' man constitutes one of the principal motives behind the personal writings. But the attempt to portray the authentic Rousseau could not remain uninfluenced by a certain apologetic intention. Just as Rousseau's friends and enemies failed to understand the existential implications of his paranoid delusions, so did he himself fail to account for the element of subjective bias in his own attempted self-justification. The 'evil' portrait no doubt lacked objective reality in the sense that it did not properly resemble the original figure, but his error was to suppose that it actually existed in others' minds with all the attributes he ascribed to it; he did not realize that it was not (as he believed) merely the work of his enemies, but also the expression of a deep, if obscure, need of his own soul. To say that it was just a 'projection' of his own unconscious thoughts would perhaps be to over-simplify a complex psychological mechanism, but there is certainly an important sense in which Jean-Jacques needed to believe in the reality of his 'persecutors' since their presence provided him with an outlet for feelings he could not openly face: as a means of alleviating the intolerable anxiety associated with feelings of guilt and unworthiness, this image served to conceal from him the truth about his own state of mind: as long as he was aware of the hostility of his 'persecutors', he could believe that he was being attacked *because of* his innocence. Persecution thus acted as a kind of objective guarantee of Jean-Jacques's 'goodness'. That the theme of persecution has this subjective function is confirmed by his inability to accept the simple fact of his innocence, the very persistence of his perpetual reflection upon the whole question being an ironical commentary upon the attitude of a man who claimed to be averse to 'thought' and happy in his day-to-day existence as a 'good' and 'innocent' 'man of nature'.

It is, however, impossible to reduce the whole problem to such simple psychological terms, for in seeking to establish on a firm basis this image of himself as a good and innocent man, Rousseau is not engaged in a purely theoretical examination of his character since self-awareness is intended to lead to a more effective form of personal fulfilment. Far from exhausting the significance of his search for personal value, the dichotomy between the 'good' and 'evil' figure is meant as a mere prelude to the achievement of a consciousness in which conventional distinctions between good and bad will be largely transcended: he aspires to a mode of existence which allows him simply to *be himself* as he really is. *Il faut être soi*, he had told Bernardin de Saint-Pierre, and the thought is constantly with him. Sustaining all his efforts at self-portraiture is his desire not merely to destroy error but to achieve a positive form of self-expression characterized by a sense of *absolute personal unity*. To be fully *one*, that is his steadfast hope. Until he is one, he cannot be said properly to exist, and certainly any thought of complete happiness is inconceivable without true personal stability. He can only be himself in a happy plenitude when his whole being is as it were gathered up into a single intense mode of consciousness that is without conflict or contradiction.

He realized that this unity could never become a permanent feature of ordinary life. In its perfect form complete personal unity could be achieved only in the next world, and this conviction constituted one of his strongest motives for believing in immortality: it seemed incredible to him that God should have given man a glimpse of perfect bliss here below if He did not intend him to enjoy it more fully. Perhaps it was only in the unrestricted realm of purely spiritual experience that true happiness could really be found. 'I aspire to the moment', he had written in the *Profession de Foi*, 'when, freed from the body's shackles, I shall be *myself* without contradiction, without diversion, and shall need only myself in order to be happy.' If this aspiration could not find perfect fulfilment in this life, certain privileged experiences like those of reverie might momentarily put it within his reach. His last work is still haunted by thoughts of those rare, fleeting moments when he was 'fully himself' and 'himself without diversion or obstacle'. This ideal unity had already been adumbrated, though at a much less personal level, in his didactic writings where he had extolled the quasi-paradisaical existence of the primitive man and the child, the happiness of both being dependent upon a remarkable facility for an effortless identification with their own essential nature and for the enjoyment of a perfect coincidence of consciousness and being; they *were* what they appeared and felt themselves to be. Jean-Jacques himself too could recall certain moments of his life when he had enjoyed a completely spontaneous form of happiness which convinced him that he would not die 'without having lived'. However rare and fleeting, such experiences had been vivid enough to persuade him that the ideal of personal unity was not just an idle dream.

But what the savage and the child and Jean-Jacques himself at certain privileged moments of his existence had achieved without effort could not alas! remain the permanent ideal of the mature Rousseau since he—like other men—was forced to accept the reality of his existence as a *thinking* being. If he was to achieve this state of perfect unity, it could only be through a movement which—whatever its ultimate goal—had been initiated through reflection. The exceptional nature of Jean-Jacques's position as a man surrounded by evil persecutors also presupposed the need for a conscious and deliberate effort of separation from all that was not truly himself. This had meant quite early on in his life a withdrawal from the busy, everyday world with its false values and diversions, and a retreat into genuine solitude. He knew that the search for solitude was not without its difficulties and for a long time he had been compelled to struggle against inner doubts and the gross misunderstandings of others, knowing that the world he was leaving would accuse him of misanthropy and wickedness. Had not his erstwhile friend Diderot maintained that 'only the wicked man lives alone'? To which Rousseau had replied: 'The wicked man's hell is to be reduced to live alone with himself, but it is the good man's paradise' (1124). Solitude was beneficial to the man who knew how to deserve it because it gave him a genuine feeling of being truly himself. There he could listen to the secret 'judgement' uttered by the voice of conscience which, once it was heeded, allowed a man to discover 'all the rest' by giving him 'self-contentment' and the power to 'please himself'.

A particularly attractive feature of this kind of personal fulfilment was its link with an enjoyment noteworthy for its *immediacy*. In no sense was Rousseau concerned with an ascetic, otherworldly mode of existence remote from all earthly pleasures. He might indeed see the fulfilment of his hopes only in the next life, but the thought of immortality served mainly to reinforce his desire to savour a more complete and uninhibited enjoyment of the present moment. We have already noted his insistence on this point at the time of his 'reform', which was aimed at the achievement of greater personal freedom and an increased opportunity for being himself in his spontaneous authenticity. His temperament too, dominated as it was by the effects of a sensibility and emotivity which could brook no delayed response, impelled him in the same direction, leading him to think of happiness as the enjoyment of himself in the immediate present—not in some remote and uncertain future. His growing belief in his 'goodness' and 'innocence' seemed to lend still further justification to this attitude: in his old age (he believed) it only remained for him to recover something of that pristine purity which had been especially evident in 'the first forty years' of his life and which had been partially tarnished but never completely effaced during the unhappy period of his social existence when he had become temporarily estranged from himself—the victim of a false pride which had failed to understand the true meaning of 'self-love'. 'Self-love' expresses an intrinsic absolute quality dependent only on the individual himself, whilst 'pride' is a relative feeling based on a false external criterion, and especially on man's soul-destroying tendency to compare himself with others. The onset of persecution, which had at first appeared to be an unmitigated disaster likely to drive the unhappy Jean-Jacques into madness and despair, eventually proved a blessing since it taught him to rely upon himself and to look within his own nature for spiritual and moral solace. Because of the world's hostility, he could now rediscover and re-affirm that selfhood which had for long been seduced by the dangerous example of worldly values.

The final crystallization of this attitude is perhaps to be found in his description of himself in the *Dialogues* as a man of 'nature' and 'temperament', for, as the 'man of nature' who 'enjoys himself and his existence', he at last finds an absolute norm by which the authenticity of his character can be effectively tested. Through his temperament, he claims to have achieved the most unaffected and sincere expression of himself. There too he can find that stable, permanent self which protects him against the vagaries of existence and the contradictions of his own character. Inspiring his whole attitude is the desire for a personal self free from tension and anxiety, and in the spontaneous reaffirmation of his own 'innocent' and 'good' nature Jean-Jacques thinks he has at last found true fulfilment. Yet the mere fact that this elementary but fundamental truth had remained hidden from him for so long meant that his authentic 'nature' could not be recovered without an effort of will. In this respect his viewpoint is rather similar to that described in *La Nouvelle Héloïse*, for there too we find characters who have, as it were, 'recently come forth from nature's hands'. Rousseau—like Julie —also needed some kind of 'shock' or 'revolution' to jolt him into an awareness of his true destiny. The vicissitudes of life itself, with their melancholy evidence of friends' treachery and enemies' malevolence, were enough to set him on the path of self-discovery. As a man of temperament, therefore, he was not simply a being who had regressed to some primitive, archaic level of infantile existence, but a fully conscious person who, through anxious effort and deliberate reflection, pursued an ideal which at last enabled him to reconquer and re-create his 'original' character in all its pristine goodness and purity.

Perhaps the supreme expression of this drive towards self-fulfilment in the form of immediate, absolute 'natural' selfhood is to be found in his insistence on the ideal of *self-sufficiency*—the most striking leit-motif of his last years. Already in the second *Discours* the 'primitive' man had been defined as a being who could remain satisfied with the feeling of his own self-sufficient existence. The most noteworthy difference between primitive and civilized man is the tendency of the latter to live constantly outside himself, to base his search for happiness on principles that are really alien to his true nature, whilst the former is content to be himself in his immediate self-awareness. No doubt this represents a way of life that can never be followed by civilized beings because primitive man is mainly an isolated creature of sensations, who has not properly developed his human potentialities. But as a being who can 'carry himself completely in himself', this primitive type represents an ideal well calculated to attract the ageing Jean-Jacques whose declining intellect and imagination make him increasingly aware of his growing dependence on 'sensations'.

The attractiveness of this ideal was bound up with his conviction that it offered him unique opportunities for avoiding the tyranny of clock-time. The abandonment of his watch at the moment of his famous reform had been a symbolic expression of his determination to live henceforth freed from the tutelage of conventional time. In his imagina-tive writings this idea becomes identified with the theme of an 'eternal present'. Certain moments of *La Nouvelle Héloïse* already show how fascinated Rousseau was by this notion. In such experiences he could feel that he had achieved a mode of being that was absolutely immediate and yet timeless. The concrete, positive aspects of ordinary finite experience become imbued with the quality of an 'eternity' that has at last penetrated the activities of ordinary existence. Normal forms of happiness are fleeting and precarious: 'scarcely is there a moment, in our most vivid enjoyment, when the heart can truly say: I should like this moment to live for ever'. In the timeless present, on the other hand, Jean-Jacques finds 'a simple, permanent state' which is no longer composed of 'fleeting moments' but has the characteristics of absolute permanence and plenitude.

This aspiration towards a kind of self-sufficient immediacy culminates, as we have seen, in the ecstatic mood of reverie which transmutes the crude, contradictory components of everyday experience into the pure 'feeling of existence', thus enabling him to overcome all internal tension and escape from the anguishing sense of time's instability and evanescence: at last Jean-Jacques believes that he has touched the secret of a primordial, ultimate experience which, though still related to the world inasmuch as it 'fixes' the distracting activity of the mind and senses, carries him up into the highly rarefied atmosphere of personal being where the self is free to savour the intrinsic quality of its existence in a complete and unalloyed contentment. In this supreme experience he at last feels that he is 'self-sufficient like God'.

At first sight Jean-Jacques's language suggests that he is very close to delusions of grandeur as he usurps a privilege which he had previously accorded to God alone: the 'absolute happiness' of complete solitude. But unlike the true megalomaniac, Rousseau never believes that he *is* God; though perhaps thinking that he has in some way discovered the secret of God's nature, he still realizes that he is dealing with a possibility—albeit a dazzling possibility—of everyday existence. At such times he is abandoning himself—irresponsibly perhaps—to the fascination of an ideal which seems to promise the perfect fulfilment of his inner being. God's existence is invoked rather by way of analogy than as a real attribute of Rousseau's own personality: he is here using the strongest and most telling language possible to describe the intense fascination of the ideal by which he is momentarily absorbed: he is not putting forward an idea which he seriously suggests can be made part of his personal 'philosophy' of existence. Moreover, when it is set within the context of his outlook as a whole, this mood of reverie emerges as a very privileged experience which never becomes a completely integral and permanent feature of his ordinary life. Indeed, the very perfection of this condition owes much to the idealizing power of a creative genius operating on data supplied to it by memory and imagination: in its highest form Jean-Jacques may never have enjoyed reverie as a truly living experience, but only as a mood seen through the prism of nostalgic reminiscence. Attained at most on a few brief and rare occasions, it tends to remain a possibility rather than an actual constituent of daily life—an entrancing dream rather than a lived reality enjoyed in the fullness of the immediate present.

As Rousseau's description of his state of mind clearly shows, he had for the most part to remain content with less exalted forms of happiness. Abandoning the dream of a pure and permanent indulgence in the ultimate 'feeling of existence', he would return to the psychologically conditioned pleasures of finite time, and especially to the less intense but more readily accessible resources of memory and imagination; he would let his mind and his emotions range freely over a variety of personal moods, each of which gave him some satisfaction though none could bring absolute fulfilment. The ideal of self-sufficient enjoyment no doubt remained with him until the end, for he continued to seek a form of self-realization which would take him beyond the vagaries of his own divided personality and the temporal limitations of finite existence itself, but this ideal remained an unfulfilled aspiration rather than an actual achievement. Moreover, if he did occasionally succeed in losing himself in his dreams, he was soon brought back to earth by the nagging thought of his persecutors whose inescapable presence, haunting him like some infernal spirit, symbolized not only the unrelieved hostility of the outside world, but that element in his own personality which, though partly dissociated from the rest and ignored by him for what it truly was, still formed part of his personal existence, whether he was willing to acknowledge it or not.

When he began the *Rêveries* Rousseau no doubt hoped that the act of writing itself would enable him to give substance to his dream of self-sufficiency by enabling him to overcome the tension normally involved in the separation of subject and object. Through writing he strove to be both self and object in the sense that the Jean-Jacques who actively expressed himself through his personal writing would, by the attainment of authentic self-knowledge, *be* what in the written words he *appeared* to be. The personality elaborated through literary activity would constitute an objective, permanent, and authentic image—a faithful mirror into which he had only to gaze Narcissus-like in order to be confronted by an unclouded reflection of himself. The living man and this image would differ only in that the latter was purer and more stable than the fluctuating personality constantly threatened by the insidiously destructive influence of time. Henceforth he hoped to be himself and yet be aware of himself in a way that gave him an enhanced sense of his own reality; as he read his own words, he would abolish all temporal conflicts within himself through an activity which permitted him to enjoy an experience which was immediate and yet contained all that was best in his past life. In this way his existence would be doubled.

This dream never became any more real than the rest. Actual writing might afford escape from inner tension, but once composition was over and he was confronted by his own written words, the result seemed unsatisfactory and incomplete, for he was still perturbed by the thought that this, after all, was not the complete truth about himself and that the warm personality of the living Jean-Jacques signified more than the frozen immobility of the written word. Reluctantly too he also had to recognize that the act of writing did not overcome that anxious reflection which continually thrust him back into the very problem from which it was meant to be a partial escape—the problem of his relations with others. The others were involved not merely in the delusions of persecution, but in all the contradictions of a heart which, as he had stressed from the very beginning of his personal writings, was both 'self-sufficient' and 'loving'. The apparent satisfaction derived from lonely self-communion (even of a literary kind) was inseparable from the contrary need so often and so pathetically expressed until the very end—the need to love and be loved. The flight from his 'persecutors' was, as we have already seen, an indirect desire to secure their affectionate attention. If he was eventually frustrated at the level of living experience, this merely led him to seek the same satisfaction on another plane. Indeed, the whole body of personal writings seems to be addressed to an ideal 'other' capable of accepting and understanding his true character. No doubt this 'other' is idealized beyond the limits of everyday humanity, and the sympathetic hearing elicited from such a perfect audience may seem so utterly remote from all ordinary ideas of reciprocal affection that even the unhappy Jean-Jacques will despair of ever finding this ideal recipient of his confidences. But in spite of disappointments he continues his search until the very end. However deep the subjectivity of his last years, it has finally to be completed by the experience of the ideal 'other'. He may be constantly 'feeding on his own substance'—and a substance which he claims to be 'inexhaustible' —but he cannot permanently think of himself as being absolutely alone. The other must always be there, however remote and idealized his appearance. The precise qualities which Rousseau seeks in him may vary according to his changing moods, ranging from the sympathy and love typical of a normal human companion to the god-like qualities characteristic of truly exceptional beings. In the *Rêveries* his description of the pleasure he found in the company of children, young people and simple men like the old soldiers of the Invalides shows that the emotional comforts he sought from others were by no means exceptional. His tragedy was that, as soon as he was in a position to savour such experiences, his mental horizon became darkened by fear and suspicion. But even then he would find solace in the creation of a dream-world filled with beings whom he had created 'after his own heart'.

It is clear, therefore, that however strongly attracted Rousseau might be to the ideal of a self-sufficient life set apart from the world of men, he could not permanently dispense with the 'other', even though it was an 'other' fashioned in accordance with his own subjective needs. He came to recognize that true solitude—unlike mere loneliness—meant more than a complacent absorption in his own moods since it had to be implemented by the presence of a reality other than the individual self. What he seeks is not complete isolation but participation in a circumscribed group, the mutual self-sufficiency of whose members will be enough to protect them against the dangers of the outside world. In this respect we recall the point already made by Amiel—that Rousseau was always attracted by the ideal of an 'insular' existence: not only did he always have a great love of islands as such—he dreamed of spending his last years on some remote island like Corsica, Majorca, or Cyprus while, significantly enough, *Robinson Crusoe* was his favourite book —but he also had a strong predilection for human 'islands' whose inhabitants were content to live in the immediacy of one another's presence. This preoccupation probably lies at the root of his devotion to the *ménage à trois* and perhaps of the still more intimate relationship constituted by his idyllic life with Mme de Warens at Les Charmettes. One of his last regrets was that he had not been able to spend his whole life in this way. 'Ah! if I had been sufficient for her heart as she was for mine!' On the more imaginative plane the whole society of Clarens was another island of friends miraculously created and preserved amid all the turmoil and conflict of the world. Even in his political philosophy the ideal community as envisaged by Rousseau in the *Contrat Social* was itself a sort of compact island where each inhabitant could feel fulfilled and protected by his participation in a social life based on the ultimate truth and integrity of 'the law'. If we limit ourselves to Jean-Jacques's personal life, it is clear from a description like that of *la matinée à l'anglaise* in *La Nouvelle Héloïse* that he was always attracted by the security and happiness involved in the type of group-relationship which absorbed him into a reality greater than himself and yet permitted him to enjoy the feeling of his own individual existence.

Frustrated in his efforts to make such an ideal the basis of a day-to-day existence contained within these 'insular' limits, Rousseau turned to the more extensive and seemingly more stable domain of physical nature. Although he was at times prepared to enjoy the beauties of the world for their own sake, he normally tended to relate his experience of nature to his own complex inner needs. Although on occasion he could feel himself filled with a 'sacred enthusiasm' which, as it brought him face to face with 'the moral beauty and intellectual order of things', let him penetrate to the very centre of the 'universal system', he was usually content with less exalted moods which allowed him to enjoy the consoling presence of a physical reality attuned to the needs of his own tormented soul: at such moments nature became a 'common' or 'universal mother' who was ever ready to welcome her unhappy children into her arms.[1] It was not only the mountains, trees, and flowers which comforted him in this way, for he found great delight in contemplating the quiet waters of some translucent lake which could 'lull' and 'rock' him into a feeling of cradle-like security.

However, Rousseau's personality was too complex, and the circumstances of his life too unsettled, to leave him permanently satisfied with a mood of this kind. He was not content to become passively absorbed into some primordial unity, for he clung tenaciously to the uniqueness of his own individual existence: through nature he did not seek to lose, but to find himself. Even his use of the island-theme involves an imaginative identification with the figure of Robinson Crusoe—the man who created his own 'world' by making a desert island the objective extension of his own personality; on other occasions too he projected himself into the character of a Christopher Columbus, the triumphant explorer of unknown lands who created a world by the fact of discovering it. His own love of botany also owed something to the thought of observing and studying a world of flowers and plants which offered themselves to him in all their freshness and innocence.

[1] It is worth noting that Rousseau also applied this image of the 'common mother' to the state: 'la patrie se montre la mère commune des citoyens' (*Political Writings*, i. 278).

In such moods nature enabled him to affirm himself in a highly personal and active way.

That none of these attitudes could really provide his personal existence with that *assiette solide* it so desperately needed is proved by the intrusion into his happiest moments of a desire for an unattainable, nameless ideal which left him dissatisfied with everything he had experienced hitherto. However self-sufficient the feeling of existence might be, however 'eternal' the intensity of the moment, he always seemed to be overwhelmed by the 'nothingness of his chimeras' and filled with a bitter-sweet yearning for a form of happiness which, though unattainable and indescribable, was vivid enough to reveal the fragility and insufficiency of all finite pleasures. Already in *La Nouvelle Héloïse* he had insisted—through the person of Julie—that complete happiness can produce a satiety which results in an unbearable sense of *ennui*. A man may suddenly be conscious of a feeling of unutterable emptiness—*un vide inexplicable*—which shows that it is his destiny to yearn for 'what is not' rather than be satisfied with 'what is'. The whole function of imagination and desire is to carry him beyond the immediately given towards new, if inaccessible, realms of being. This tendency to reach out beyond the confines of the finite world may reveal itself in diverse circumstances—during the contemplation of nature, in reverie or amid the solitude of intimate musing.

In view of all this it is not surprising that Rousseau should often turn his gaze upwards towards the region of divine being and at times become lost in a feeling of indescribable ecstasy before the majesty of God's creation. But even these more explicitly religious moods did not bring a final answer to his anxious question: 'What am I?' even though they did inspire him with the hope that one day, in the next life, he would be truly *himself* 'without diversion and obstacle'. His moments of complete personal fulfilment being too fitful and transient to bring him absolute peace, he continues to be driven on by a relentless need to attain a radical form of self-knowledge which will enable him both to be aware of himself and be himself at the same time. His passion for truth and justice may have often been tainted by dubious personal motives, and his elaborate self-portrait often masked important factors which, if they had been acknowledged, would have changed much of its emphasis; but a certain honesty and sincerity subsisted in the face of many illusions and acts of self-deception. Jean-Jacques might try to hide from himself and others certain unpalatable aspects of his character, but in the long run he could not forget any genuinely integral part of his total self. More especially, he could not permanently overlook the reality of that profound *moral* consciousness which prevented him from sinking permanently into some form of facile emotional escapism. However attractive the contemplative ideal might appear to be in certain moods, it could never bring him complete peace because it failed to reckon with the promptings of a conscience that refused to be quietened by thoughts of 'innocence' and 'goodness'. For all his lapses, Rousseau could never completely cast off that sense of moral earnestness which always marked him off from so many contemporary *philosophes* and was perhaps not unrelated to his Protestant, Genevan background. Already in periods of emotional stress, he had professed a kind of 'heroic' ethical outlook and, in his maturity, he had insisted upon 'conscience' as the foundation of all true morality. In his personal life his moral consciousness expressed itself as an ineradicable sense of guilt, which no thought of 'innocence' and 'goodness' could completely overcome. He himself insists that the writing of the *Confessions* was partly prompted by the memory of wrongs done to others—the unwarranted inculpation of the servant-girl Marion, his desertion of the luckless music-master Lemaître, and the graver crime of having abandoned his own children.

Even the other person, whose psychological function has already been considered, is involved in this moral issue since he often represents in Rousseau's eyes the 'ideal' being who will help him to obtain the *absolution* he cannot win by his own efforts. If the personal writings are addressed to an ideal 'other'—ultimately envisaged perhaps as a remote posterity—it is partly because he feels that in this way later generations will grant the absolution refused him by tyrannical and hostile contemporaries who will not see him as he really is. If the *Confessions* seek to alleviate an oppressive burden of guilt by portraying him *intus et in cute*, it is ultimately because he wants to feel that his existence has been properly *justified*. Through confession he hopes to become *transparent* to the other. To be transparent is to be permeated by light, and so to be restored to an original purity and integrity which eliminate all idea of inner division and personal guilt. To be transparent is to have the unity and permanence which befit a man whose heart is, in his own oft-repeated words, 'as transparent as crystal'. To be exposed to the other's gaze in this way is to feel that he has at length discovered not only the purity and translucence of those lake-waters by which he once dreamed of happiness but also the stability and permanence of the rocks which lie concealed in their depths.

However, Rousseau's ultimate difficulty is that he can never see this ideal 'other' as a living person. Already his way of making an absolute division between his innocent self and his wicked persecutors suggests that he is condemned to a solitude which excludes the possibility of his ever finding a man with a heart capable of responding to his own. To satisfy all his needs such a person would have to possess almost divine qualities. Perhaps this explains his occasional, but extremely significant tendency to invest human beings, whether real or imaginary, with divine attributes. We are apt to find him prostrating himself before some finite being as though he were in the presence of God. It is not only in a state of self-sufficient reverie that he compares himself to the deity, for in a much earlier experience he had opened his heart to Mme de Warens as though she too were God. At the imaginative level M. de Wolmar, as we have seen, is also endowed with the qualities of a divine father and, at special moments, seems to be the incarnation of God on earth. In the same novel Rousseau had on one occasion compared the power wielded by the father of a family to that of God Himself, for 'he too [the father] among all mortals is master of his own felicity because he is happy like God Himself without desiring anything more than what he is enjoying'. Fascinated by God's power, Jean-Jacques extends this attribute to all who resemble Him. He considers, moreover, that man's loftiest aspiration is towards a mode of being which would make him 'free, good, and happy like God' and allow him to rest secure in a god-like 'self-contentment'. But God's omnipotence does not manifest itself as mere self-sufficiency since, at the human level, it involves a more positive attitude towards those whom He calls His children. As in the case of his other moods, Rousseau's conception of God is by no means uniform. At certain moments he is prepared to see God's power as a source of warmth and comfort, a genuinely *consoling* presence which often provides him with an opportunity for a self-absorbed quietist ecstasy. At such times God may tend to merge with a physical 'nature' which is not far removed from the idea of a 'common mother'. But if God's creation sometimes appears as a comforting presence capable of allowing him to feel at one with himself and external reality and so of discovering a primordial unity which brings security and personal happiness, it is clear that we ought not to forget the role of the 'moral' father—an all-wise, but on the whole less indulgent figure, as early medieval predecessors had already acknowledged with awe, and with fundamental repercussions on the development of their faith. No doubt Rousseau, for the psychological reasons already given, could not expose himself to the permanent presence of an all-seeing eye which 'sees the bottom of our hearts' for this would have meant the disruption of his self-portrait as an innocent man and the consequent destruction of that security upon which his whole life ultimately rested. But the sterner moral influence, to which he had been subjected from childhood, was too powerful to be completely ignored. 'I do not fear his all-seeing eye', says the rehabilitated Saint-Preux. The little boy afraid of his father? The timid Jean-Jacques quailing before his father? Something of that perhaps, but much more also: it is the remark of a man who wanted to lay before God—that just and perhaps frighteningly just Being (though not so frightening as he supposed for those who accepted the fact of the Incarnation)—the intolerable burden of his own guilt.

Rousseau's misfortune was that he could not bring himself to make a full and explicit acknowledgement of that guilt, and it is here that we can see the fundamental difference between him and Christian thinkers. His choice of himself as 'a man of nature' prevented him from assuming his guilt; indeed, in so far as it presupposed a view of himself as 'good', this choice was partly intended as a means of perpetuating the image of the 'innocent' Jean-Jacques. On this vital point his attitude separates him completely from the Christian who escapes from existential anxiety by undertaking a qualitative transformation or 'conversion' which lifts him on to a higher—and explicitly spiritual—plane of existence. Jean-Jacques prefers to move back into his own being and there discover an essential quality, a 'true' self, which acts as a defence against anxiety by revealing the true nature of the personality whose basic qualities have been obscured or stifled by the pressure of its milieu or a truly misguided conception of its true nature. Whereas great Christian thinkers like St. Paul, Augustine, Pascal, and Kierkegaard recognize the necessity of a spiritual 'rebirth' which can come only after a genuine act of repentance and the frank acknowledgement of 'sin' (so that regeneration ultimately depends on the inflowing of divine Grace), Rousseau, as a believer in 'nature', presupposes his ability to achieve his own salvation. Nature may indeed depend on God as its creator, but the initial impetus must come from a source of goodness within the individual himself. Between man and God no intermediary is needed since the former has all the necessary means of bringing him into a closer relationship with his Maker. In such a religion the division between the 'natural' and the 'supernatural' is less clear than in the case of Christianity where the individual can attain salvation only through the person of Christ.[1] Being unable to admit the possibility of a unique revelation of God through Christ, Rousseau, in spite of his boundless 'respect' for the Jesus of the Gospels—'if the life and death of Socrates are those of a sage, the life and death of Jesus are those of a god'—cannot accept any single person or object as the exclusive revelation of God on earth, even though he is inclined from time to time (as we have just seen) to associate this need for divine support with his feelings for particular persons.

If Rousseau is not prepared to accept Christianity as the solution to his own personal problem of achieving a final form of self-awareness (because, in his view, this religion would force him to abandon that fundamental principle of 'natural goodness' on which he deems his whole life and work to rest), he does not seek to integrate the different aspects of his inner life by adopting a kind of 'existentialist' position which would make him the creator of his own values. In spite of the extraordinary sense of solitude by which he was overwhelmed in his last years, and in spite too of occasional moments when he felt himself disorientated at the thought of being 'thrown and lost in this vast universe, and as it were drowned in this immensity of beings', his 'subjectivity' had very definite limits, for he did not believe that the existence of the individual had an absolute meaning independent of the universal 'order' of which he formed part. There is certainly a sense in which every man—like Jean-Jacques himself—has to win his way through doubt and anguish to an awareness of his own true being, but this being is itself linked indissolubly to a still more fundamental 'nature' that gives it value and meaning. In modern conditions, which replace 'reality' by 'appearance' and 'nature' by 'opinion', authentic personal existence is largely potential, but the main task of our time is more like one of rediscovery than genuine re-creation; it is largely a question of understanding more fully what was potentially there from the very first. Man, like the world, is God's handiwork—the creation of a higher power. Between man's deeper nature—and that includes Jean-Jacques, unique and unhappy though he is—and the universe around him there is a fundamental concordance which can be ignored or perhaps perverted by man's 'freedom', but never completely destroyed. To him who knows how to become aware of it, the 'divine image' or

[1] For Kierkegaard's reactions to Rousseau's *Rêveries* and his criticism of their religious viewpoint—'here', he says, 'is an example of what it means not to be well read in Christianity'—see his *Journals* (ed. A. Dru, Oxford, 1938), Entries Nos. 1204–5. I have discussed the question in an article 'Rousseau and Kierkegaard', in *The Cambridge Journal* (vii, No. 10, July 1954, 615–26).

'effigy' that each human being bears within himself can become a source of eternal bliss. The message of nature—and of God—is written in man's heart 'in indelible characters'. In this respect, as commentators have insisted, Rousseau looks back, in spite of certain doubts and hesitations, towards the metaphysical tradition of Platonism, while giving it an individual emphasis of his own. No doubt in his last years, as he experienced a growing tension between the needs of his own personality and the objective values of the universal order, he was more and more inclined to attribute to that order the characteristic features of his inner being, but he was never led to repudiate God's beneficence or to deny that one day Providence would justify Jean-Jacques by restoring him completely to himself. God, the immortality of the soul, the goodness of the universal order, these were unshakable principles upon which he never varied and in the perspective of which he was content ultimately to view his own existence. Hence the final emphasis of his life was not one of despair—but optimism.

Although Rousseau's last phase cannot be neatly explained in terms of some simple comprehensive principle, it does represent—in spite of many ambiguities and conflicts—a striving towards a definite personal end: the realization of himself as a single, unified individual who has been able to fulfil himself in accordance with his own true being. This aspiration towards the apparently simple unity of authentic selfhood is sustained by his belief in the goodness of 'nature', which impels him to look both outwards towards the universal order and inwards towards his own tormented personal self. But the mere fact that this choice thrusts him into a 'subjectivity' which is increasingly dependent on the obsessive image of himself as a good man confronted by the malevolence of a persecuting world suggests that he has not been able to resolve all the difficulties and complexities of his life.

If these principles ultimately helped to give a positive meaning to the aspirations of his last years—and especially to his desire to realize himself as a single unified individual who was fulfilled in accordance with his own true being—they could not completely overcome the difficulties and contradictions inherent in his earnest attempts to translate his personal ideal into the particular circumstances of everyday existence. Even though his belief in the goodness of a Creator who would never allow a true 'man of nature' like Jean-Jacques to plunge into the frightening chaos of despair set very definite limits to the influence of his growing 'subjectivity', the persistence of paranoid delusions and the instability of his personal attitude show that the quest for complete self-awareness and fulfilment had not been brought to a definite end. He certainly felt that at brief, privileged moments of his life he had attained the self-sufficient plenitude of a pure subject existing in his own right, or else the ecstatic happiness of a free individual enjoying intimate communion with an external reality attuned to the needs of his own soul; but even these experiences were not permanent or stable enough to save him from the torment of a ceaseless inner reflection which, almost in spite of himself, made him an object of ever anxious and ever dissatisfied attention. It was precisely this persistent need to be aware of himself as an object that tore him away from the blissful sense of complete personal fulfilment: he could not simply be and know himself to be at the same time, for his constantly renewed self-awareness exposed him to all the contradictions and divisions of his unfulfilled longings. Not inappropriately, therefore, the unfinished tenth *Promenade* symbolizes the inconclusiveness of all his efforts to give a decisive answer to the problem of his personal existence. At the very last he was like an explorer who, after being vouchsafed a dazzling vision of his journey's end, had eventually become lost in obscure, if fascinating, by-ways: it was left to later Romantic generations to follow the route which he had so painstakingly traced in his lonely and courageous efforts to be himself.

BIBLIOGRAPHY

A. *Primary Sources*

Œuvres complètes de Jean-Jacques Rousseau, I, Les Confessions, autres textes autobiographiques, edited by B. Gagnebin and Marcel Raymond, Bibliothèque de la Pléiade, Paris, 1959.

Œuvres complètes de J.-J. Rousseau, 13 vols., Hachette, Paris, 1865–70, &c.

Œuvres et correspondance inédites de J.-J. Rousseau, ed. G. Streckeisen-Moultou, Paris, 1861.

Correspondance générale de Jean-Jacques Rousseau, ed. T. Dufour and P. P. Plan, 20 vols., Paris, 1924–34.

Discours sur les sciences et les arts, ed. G. R. Havens, New York, 1946.

Lettre à M. d'Alembert sur les spectacles, ed. M. Fuchs, Geneva, 1948.

La Nouvelle Héloïse, ed. D. Mornet, Les Grands Écrivains de la France, 4 vols., Paris, 1925.

La Profession de foi du vicaire savoyard, ed. P. M. Masson, Paris, 1914.

Political Writings of Jean-Jacques Rousseau, ed. C. E. Vaughan, Cambridge, 1915.

Quatre lettres à M. de Malesherbes, ed. G. Rudler, Scholartis Press, London, 1928.

La Première Rédaction des Confessions, Livres I–IV, ed. T. Dufour, Geneva, 1909

Les Rêveries du promeneur solitaire, ed. J. S. Spink, Didier, Paris, 1948.

Les Rêveries du promeneur solitaire, ed. M. Raymond, Droz, Geneva, 1948.

The Letters of David Hume, ed. J. Y. T. Greig, 2 vols., Oxford, 1932.

New Letters of David Hume, ed. R. Klibansky and E. C. Mossner, Oxford, 1954.

B. *Secondary Sources*

[This list does not include general works already mentioned in the footnotes.]

AMIEL, H. F., in *Rousseau jugé par les Genevois d'aujourd'hui,* Geneva, 1879.

BELLENOT, J. L. 'Les Formes de l'amour dans "La Nouvelle Héloïse"', in *Annales Jean-Jacques Rousseau,* vol. xxxiii, 1953–5.

BERTHOUD, F. *J.-J. Rousseau au Val de Travers, 1762–65,* Paris, 1881.

BISSON, L. A. 'Rousseau and the Romantic Experience', in *The Modern Language Review,* vol. xxxvii, January 1942.

BOSWELL, J. *Boswell on the Grand Tour,* ed. F. A. Pottle, London, 1953.

BUFFENOIR, H. *Le Prestige de Jean-Jacques Rousseau,* Paris, 1909.

BURGELIN, P. *La Philosophie de l'existence de J.-J. Rousseau,* Paris, 1952.

CARLYLE, T. *On Heroes, Hero-worship, and the Heroic in History,* 1841.

CARRÉ, J. R. 'Le Secret de J.-J. Rousseau', in *Revue d'histoire littéraire de la France,* vol. xlvi, 1949.

DÉDÉYAN, C. *La Nouvelle Héloïse, étude d'ensemble,* Centre de documentation universitaire, Paris, 1955.

DEMOLE, V. 'Analyse psychiatrique des "Confessions" de J.-J. Rousseau', in *Schweizer Archiv für Neurologie und Psychiatrie,* vol. ii, 1918.

—— 'Rôle du tempérament et des idées délirantes de Rousseau dans la genèse de ses principales théories', in *Annales médico-psychologiques,* 1922.

332   BIBLIOGRAPHY

DUSAULX, J. *De mes rapports avec J.-J. Rousseau*, Paris, 1798.

ELLIS, M. B. *Julie or La Nouvelle Héloïse, A Synthesis of Rousseau's Thought*, *1749–59*, Toronto, 1949.

ELOSU, S. *La Maladie de J.-J. Rousseau*, Paris, 1929.

FRAENKEL, E. 'La Psychanalyse au service de la science de la littérature', in *Cahiers de l'association internationale des études françaises*, No. 7, 1955.

GAIFFE, F. *J.-J. Rousseau et les 'Rêveries du promeneur solitaire'*, Centre de documentation universitaire, Paris, 1936.

GAILLARD, E. 'J.-J. Rousseau à Turin', *Annales Jean-Jacques Rousseau*, vol. xxxii, 1950–2.

GILLIARD, E. *De Rousseau à Jean-Jacques*, Lausanne, 1950.

GILSON, E. *Les Idées et les lettres*, Paris, 1932.

GREEN, F. C. *Jean-Jacques Rousseau*, Cambridge, 1955.

GRIMSLEY, R. 'Subjective and Objective Elements in Rousseau's "Rêveries" ', in *French Studies*, vol. v, October 1951.

—— 'The Human Problem in "La Nouvelle Héloïse" ', in *The Modern Language Review*, vol. liii, April 1958.

—— 'Rousseau and Kierkegaard', in *The Cambridge Journal*, vol. vii, July 1954.

GROETHUYSEN, B. *Jean-Jacques Rousseau*, Paris, 1949.

GUÉHENNO, J. *Jean-Jacques*, 3 vols., Paris, 1948–52.

GUILLEMIN, H. *Cette affaire infernale*, Paris, 1942.

HEIDENHAIM, A. *J.-J. Rousseau, Persönlichkeit, Philosophie und Psychose*, Munich, 1924.

HENDEL, C. W. *Jean-Jacques Rousseau Moralist*, 2 vols., New York and Oxford, 1934.

HUBERT, R. *Rousseau et l'Encyclopédie*, Paris, 1928.

JOSEPHSON, M. *Jean-Jacques Rousseau*, London, 1932.

JURY, P. 'La Fessée de Jean-Jacques Rousseau', in *Psyché*, vol. ii, February 1947.

LAFORGUE, R. *La Psychopathologie de l'échec*, Paris, rev. ed., 1950.

LANSON, G. 'L'Unité de la pensée de Jean-Jacques Rousseau', in *Annales Jean-Jacques Rousseau*, vol. viii, 1912.

LOVEJOY, A. *Essays in the History of Ideas*, Baltimore, 1948.

MASSON, P. M. *La Religion de J.-J. Rousseau*, 3 vols., Paris, 1916.

MONGLOND, A. *Vies préromantiques*, Paris, 1925.

MORNET, D. *Rousseau: l'homme et l'œuvre*, Paris, 1950.

—— *Le Sentiment de la nature en France de J.-J. Rousseau à Bernardin de Saint-Pierre*, Paris, 1907.

—— *Le Romantisme en France au XVIIIᵉ siècle*, Paris, 1912.

MUNTEANO, B. 'La Solitude de Rousseau', in *Annales Jean-Jacques Rousseau*, vol. xxxi, 1946–9.

MUSSET-PATHAY, V. D. *Histoire de la vie et des ouvrages de Jean-Jacques Rousseau*, 2 vols., Paris, 1822.

OSMONT, R. 'Contribution à l'étude psychologique des "Rêveries du promeneur solitaire" ', in *Annales Jean-Jacques Rousseau*, vol. xxiii, 1934.

—— 'Remarques sur la genèse et la composition de la "Nouvelle Héloïse" ', in *Annales Jean-Jacques Rousseau*, vol. xxxiii, 1953–5.

POULET, G. *Études sur le temps humain*, Edinburgh University Press, 1949.

PROAL, L. *La Psychologie de J.-J. Rousseau*, Paris, 1930.

RAYMOND, M. 'J.-J. Rousseau: Deux aspects de sa vie intérieure', in *Annales Jean-Jacques Rousseau*, vol. xxix, 1941–2.

RITTER, E. 'Sur la famille et la jeunesse de J.-J. Rousseau', in *Annales Jean-Jacques Rousseau*, vol. xvi, 1924–5.

RODDIER, H. *J.-J. Rousseau en Angleterre au XVIIIᵉ siècle*, Paris, 1950.

RÖHRS, H. *Jean-Jacques Rousseau, Vision und Wirklichkeit*, Heidelberg, 1957.

ROTH, G. *Les Pseudo-mémoires de Mme d'Épinay. Histoire de Madame de Montbrillant*, Paris, 1951.

SAINT-PIERRE, B. DE. *La Vie et les ouvrages de J.-J. Rousseau*, ed. Souriau, Paris, 1907.

SAUSSURE, H. DE. *Rousseau et les manuscrits des Confessions*, Paris, 1958.

SCHINZ, A. *La Pensée de Jean-Jacques Rousseau*, Paris, 1929.

—— *État présent des travaux sur Jean-Jacques Rousseau*, Paris, 1941.

SEILLÈRE, E. *Jean-Jacques Rousseau*, Paris, 1921.

SELLS, A. L. *The Early Life and Adventures of Jean-Jacques Rousseau*, Cambridge, 1930.

SPINK, J. S. *Rousseau et Genève*, Paris, 1934.

STAROBINSKI, J. *Jean-Jacques Rousseau, La transparence et l'obstacle*, Paris, 1957.

TEMMER, M. J. *Time in Rousseau and Kant. An Essay in French Pre-Romanticism*, Paris, 1958.

TIEGHEM, P. VAN. *La Nouvelle Héloïse de Jean-Jacques Rousseau*, Paris, 1949.

VALLETTE, G. *Jean-Jacques Rousseau genevois*, Paris, 1908.

VOISINE, J. *J.-J. Rousseau en Angleterre à l'époque romantique, Les écrits autobiographiques et la légende*, Paris, 1956.

INDEX

PRINTED IN GREAT BRITAIN
AT THE UNIVERSITY PRESS, OXFORD
BY VIVIAN RIDLER
PRINTER TO THE UNIVERSITY